The Curtain and the Veil

AMERICAN CULTURAL HERITAGE SERIES 3
Jack Salzman, *General Editor*

A scene from the 1935 Lafayette Theatre production of Langston Hughes's *Haiti*, from which *Emperor of Haiti* was drawn (photo courtesy of The New York Public Library—Astor, Lenox and Tilden Foundations)

Helene Keyssar

THE CURTAIN AND THE VEIL

Strategies in Black Drama

Burt Franklin & Co.

Grateful acknowledgment is offered for permission to quote as follows:

To Harold Ober Associates, Inc., for "Montage of a Dream Deferred" by Langston Hughes, published in Harlem by Alfred A. Knopf, Inc., in 1951, copyright 1951, which appeared in the preface to *A Raisin in the Sun* by Lorraine Hansberry

To Kenneth Burke for material from *Philosophy of Literary Forms* by Kenneth Burke, 3rd edition, published by University of California Press, Berkeley, Calif, 1973, copyright 1941

To Theodore Ward for excerpts from *Big White Fog* by Theodore Ward (manuscript form)

To Stanley Cavell for material from *Must We Mean What We Say?* by Stanley Cavell, published by Charles Scribner's Sons in 1969, copyright 1969

To William Morrow and Co., Inc., for excerpt from *Crisis of the Negro Intellectual* by Harold Cruse, published by William Morrow and Co., Inc., New York, in 1967

To William Morrow and Co., Inc., for citations from *Dutchman* by LeRoi Jones (Imamu Amiri Baraka) published by William Morrow and Co., Inc., New York, in 1964

To Harold Ober Associates, Inc., for excerpt from *Emperor of Haiti* by Langston Hughes, published in *Black Drama in America: An Anthology* published by Fawcett Publications, Inc., in 1971, copyright Langston Hughes, 1963

To Random House, Inc., Alfred A. Knopf, Inc., for excerpts from *A Raisin in the Sun* by Lorraine Hansberry published by Random House, New York, in 1959

FOR MY FAMILY
and especially for
David and Anise

CONTENTS

PREFACE ix

ACKNOWLEDGMENTS xi

1. **Black Drama and Its Audience: Evolutions and Revolutions** 1

2. **Black Playwright for Two Worlds:** Willis Richardson's *The Broken Banjo* and *The Chip Woman's Fortune* 19

3. **The Inner Life Once Removed:** Langston Hughes's *Emperor of Haiti* 50

4. **Dialectics Toward a Theater of Black Experience:** Theodore Ward's *Big White Fog* 77

5. **Sounding the Rumble of Dreams Deferred:** Lorraine Hansberry's *A Raisin in the Sun* 113

6. **Lost Illusions, New Visions:** Imamu Amiri Baraka's *Dutchman* 147

7. **Night in August:** Ed Bullins's *In the Wine Time* 177

8. **Locating the Rainbow: Gestures of Drama and Political Acts** 207

APPENDIXES

A. **Drama and the Strategic Approach** 219
B. **A Survey of Criticism** 227

BIBLIOGRAPHY

Anthologies 231
General History and Criticism 235
Black Playwrights and Their Plays 256
Works Not Explicitly Related to Black Drama 297

INDEX 299

PREFACE

I CAME TO THIS study in a somewhat circular fashion. Initially, I was intrigued and impressed by a number of plays by black American playwrights that I discovered in a search for dramas that would be fruitful and "relevant" to black college students under my direction. (It goes almost without saying that university courses in American drama generally exclude black drama from their reading lists.) As I worked with plays by black dramatists, I was repeatedly struck by the richness of many of these works and the need this suggested for serious study of black drama.

Shortly after I became interested in black drama, I discovered that the writings of Darwin T. Turner were both helpful in providing a general perspective on the genre and illuminating in their specific comments on some of the plays. Eventually, I had the good fortune of studying with Darwin Turner; his guidance assisted me in focusing my own interests and in grappling with problems of criticism particular to black drama.

Concurrently I was becoming aware of the very limited helpfulness of most extant drama criticism. Literary criticism, criticism of plays based on thematic, textual, psychological, structural considerations existed; play reviews expressing fleeting impressions of performances could be readily found. For my work as a director or my pleasure as a reader, however, I found little commentary that was either useful or provocative, no criticism that would give me a model for an approach to black drama, until friends pointed me to the works of three very different writers: Kenneth Burke, J. L. Styan, and Stanley Cavell. These works, the significance of which is addressed most fully in the Appendix to this book, were crucial in helping me carry out my determination to undertake a study of black drama. Through the writings of Burke, Styan, and Cavell, I began to perceive a method of criticism that would allow me to investigate black drama in a way that would be personally rewarding, meaningful and useful to others, and possible within the limitations of my white racial heritage.

Among the most obvious questions that must be asked and that I must answer somewhat arbitrarily in order to proceed is just what plays are being referred to when one speaks of "black drama." In this study, the term refers to scripts written by men and women of African ancestry who can be identified with the United States by birth or prolonged residence. I exclude works by black playwrights who have lived in the United States temporarily but who were not born here or who remained culturally distinct from the United States. Thus, I have excluded black dramatists from Africa or Latin America. I do not include works by white authors even if a work focuses on black characters, race problems, or a black environment. I have used the adjective "black," rather than "Afro-American" or "Negro," because it is less limiting in its present connotations: "Afro-American" suggests to me a certain scholarly or scientific perspective; "Negro" connotes a time and attitude limiting to my subject and my own voice.

That I have chosen not to engage in detailed analyses of plays by white dramatists may be worth lamenting because there would be much profit in comparing treatments of similar themes, historical developments, influences, and so forth in black and white American drama. My decision here to focus on black drama was made simply because I can pay more adequate and emphatic attention to black drama by treating it separately.

That I am a white woman needs no apology but must be acknowledged by both myself and the reader. There are forms of criticism of black art that I would not attempt because my identity as a white person would be too limiting. There are also sure to be points at which a black critic will perceive nuances of which I am ignorant. The premise of my approach to the black dramas discussed in this study, a method that I call a strategic approach, is that the script itself, if paid attention to, tells its intentions toward an audience. If this holds true, as I believe it must in good drama, then the color of my skin and the consciousness that in some inevitable ways accompanies it should not invalidate my conclusions or responses to, and appreciation of, black drama.

ACKNOWLEDGMENTS

IN A BOOK whose concern is frequently with the authenticity and possibility of acts of acknowledgment, it is necessary to attempt with a few words to acknowledge those whose presence has made this work possible. There are many whom I have acknowledged privately who here require some public recognition for the guidance and affection they gave me as I moved toward and through this study. I confess to self-consciousness in this act of appreciation, and I ask those to whom these words are addressed to accept what I do here as a gesture toward acknowledgment, not a whole or perfect recognition.

My first gesture of thanks is a general one to all those at Morris Brown College in Atlanta who turned me toward black drama and helped me to discover both its importance and its context. Both students and colleagues at Morris Brown taught me more about drama in a black community than I could teach. Two colleagues from that time, Leslie Gerber and Cecil Tate, shared that time and were inseparable from the beginnings of this book.

Although the initial research for this study began during my time in Atlanta, I might never have proceeded further without the advice and consent of Darwin T. Turner. It was under his tutelage that my initial manuscript was written; it was he who guided me to see my own limitations with language and with a white woman's perspective on black worlds. Perhaps most important, his exhaustive knowledge of black drama was and remains an inspiration. Of all those whom I acknowledge on these pages, it is to him that I have had the most difficulty speaking my gratitude and for him especially that this public gesture is intended.

Many who inspired my thinking as I wrote early versions of this book were friends or teachers or both. Miriam Gilbert managed with wondrous kindness to remain both critic and friend throughout my original efforts. Thomas Whitaker also remained a friend while asking the right questions to lead me out of confusions in my theoretical gropings. Oscar Brownstein played an important role in my work by pointing me to Kenneth Burke and the concept of strategy.

In writing the final version of this manuscript, teachers who were not directly related to the work itself but who shaped my modes of thought have often come to mind. A. D. Van Nostrand taught me, quite simply, to read and write. George Morgan led me to understand how to be with others in the world authentically, and the importance of such activity. Ruth Miller not only supported my specific investigations of black drama but also encouraged me to continue writing and reading at a time when such assistance was truly vital. I had the extraordinary opportunity of working with Kenneth Burke at just the time when his writings were an essential inspiration for my own endeavors, and, at about the same time, I was given the gift of Stanley Cavell's *Must We Mean What We Say?*, a work that changed the way I look at the world.

For women who were drawn toward a professional life, particulary in the academic world, in the 1960s, there were few role models. I was especially fortunate at pivotal moments to encounter a few extraordinary women who inspired through their strength and individuality. I think here of Ruth Miller, Cleo Martin, and Virginia Elliot—all of whom marked my work through the examples of their professional lives. Even more specifically, I have had the good fortune in recent years to have before me the presence of Doris Abramson, whom I first came to know through her book on black drama, and whose friendship and colleagueship I now cherish.

It is an irony of the act of writing any manuscript that while the task itself is remarkably private, it is sustained most vividly through the quietness of friendship. In the early Iowa days of this work, Anthony Manna, Ruth Manna, Christine Roberts, L. William Franke, and Henry T. Webb all gave insight and support beyond measure. In my return to these pages, friends of more recent years have been inseparable from new perspectives on my work. To Marguerite Waller and Richard Pini I owe gratitude for friendship in which intelligence gives courage of one kind and affection gives courage of another. To Patricia Riggin I owe thanks for the gift of *For Colored Girls* . . . , as well as constant reminders that to play is not just an act of theater. Two friends cannot be thanked appropriately in these pages, but these acknowledgments would be incomplete without their names. One of these two, Catherine Portuges, remains a source of constant pleasure in the sharing of both lived work and lived moments; that she does so is a matter not of luck but of knowledge that she once risked the friendship to save the friend. The other, Barry O'Connell, has also been a companion in work with the special grace of helping me to understand what had to be done.

Over and over again, throughout my thirteen years of teaching, students have sharpened my wits and troubled my assumptions and understandings. To call attention to two or three students would do an injustice to what I hope the activity of a classroom is all about. Because she was a reminder of the joys of having a student when I most questioned such an enterprise, I ask Judi Pansullo to stand for all the rest.

Five people have assisted me significantly in moving this manuscript to a life in print. Caroline Thompson took on the often tedious chore of helping me to update the bibliography at a time when my own patience for such efforts was limited. Nancy Sunflower and Irene Rothberg typed away at endless pages with skill and smiles. Jack Salzman, my editor, not only remembered what he had previously read at the right moment but also encouraged me and helped shape fragments into wholes, blurs into form. Martin Dinitz accomplished all those editorial tasks that make pages into a book.

There must be one more gesture of gratitude. That is extended to my husband, Tracy Burr Strong, who began with me as this book began—both we and it tentative and tenacious—and who bears with me now, when this book and our child not coincidentally make their ways into the world.

The Curtain and the Veil

AFTER the Egyptian and Indian, the Greek and Roman, the Teuton and Mongolian, the Negro is a sort of seventh son, born with a veil, and gifted with second-sight in this American world,—a world which yields him no true self-consciousness, but only lets him see himself through the revelation of the other world. It is a peculiar sensation, this double-consciousness, this sense of always looking at one's self through the eyes of others, of measuring one's soul by the tape of a world that looks on in amused contempt and pity. One ever feels his twoness,—An American, a Negro; two souls, two thoughts, two unreconciled strivings; two warring ideals in one dark body, whose dogged strength alone keeps it from being torn asunder.

Even so is the hope that sang in the songs of my fathers well sung. If somewhere in this whirl and chaos of things there dwells Eternal Good, pitiful yet masterful, then anon in His good time America shall rend the Veil and the prisoned shall go free.

W. E. B. DuBois
from *The Souls of Black Folk*

1 | BLACK DRAMA AND ITS AUDIENCE: EVOLUTIONS AND REVOLUTIONS

> A book can speak in a murmur;
> drama and comedy have to shout.
>
> JEAN-PAUL SARTRE

AMERICAN DRAMA HAS few traditions and even fewer attempts to break with custom. We can trace the history of American drama from the eighteenth century to the present without ever discovering a mythos or form we could distinguish as distinctly American. Contrary to appearances, the realism to which American theater' has until recently tenaciously clung is not an assertion but an escape from a signifying identity. For two hundred years, the families and living rooms of American drama have prevented spectators from becoming genuine audiences and have allowed American theater to maintain a state of infancy that increasingly resembles senility. When we speak of even the "stars" of American playwrighting—O'Neill, Williams, Miller, Albee—we establish their maturity by reference to European parents. If we applaud the efforts of some American playwrights in the 1960s and 1970s to break from middle-class worlds and realistic modes, we do so with the relief that we have learned how to follow the footsteps of Brecht and Beckett and Pinter.

It is thus one of the peculiarities of American theater that for more than fifty years it has had in its midst a unique and vital body of drama that it has been unable to acknowledge as its own. That drama, black drama, has existed since the mid-nineteenth century and has thrived aesthetically if not commercially since the 1920s. While it is not startling to find that an art form engendered by black Americans has not been prominent in American culture, or that America has exhibited an adolescent blindness in ignoring some of its best work, it is revealing that a theater in constant need of new energy should neglect such an apparent and eager source.

1

Peculiar as it may be, the naming and examination of black drama are appropriate and necessary to any attempt to understand American culture. Both practical and substantive reasons exist for distinguishing black drama as a particular form. Throughout much of its existence, plays by black American dramatists have remained generally unknown to most theatergoers and unexamined by theater critics. In the twentieth century, black drama has repeatedly been excluded from "representative" publications (*Great Plays of . . .*) and until very recently has not been presented in the major centers of production of American drama; as Ted Shine, consultant for the first extensive anthology of black American drama,[1] has remarked, collections labeled "famous" or "best" American plays rarely include a single play by a black American playwright.

The pervasive racism of American society is, of course, the most obvious explanation of the neglect of black drama. The resistance of white Americans to legal, economic, and social acknowledgment of black Americans has impeded the public recognition of black artists in every field. That music created and performed by black men and women has in the twentieth century escaped some of the restrictions imposed on other black art forms may be less a disconcerting exception than a sign of the problem itself. While the blues and jazz that have vitalized American music are expressions of the particular joys and anguish of black Americans, the abstract nature of the language of music allows a dissociation of the social and the aesthetic to a degree that is foreign to poetry, fiction, or painting.

Such a dissociation is especially antithetical to theater. For theater is not only the most public of the arts, in that its existence is dependent on the presence of spectators; it also demands a recognition in public of the worlds it presents. We can read the narrative of a black sharecropper with pain or indifference, but both the activity of reading and the experience of a particular work can remain private. To encounter theater, however, we must not only venture into the world, to a public place, but as much as we may remain personally hidden as spectators, we also become identifiable as members of an audience. Once the world of the play unfolds before us, any recognition of that world we allow ourselves is made uniquely potent by its immediacy, by its coherence with our present. No matter what their verbal or visual grammars, fiction and poetry, painting and film exist in the past tense; theater, like music, lives only in a haunting present tense. And theater, unlike music, makes itself present not essentially through symbolic signification but through the activities of live human beings whose every gesture establishes our presence in a society.

The paradox of American theater is that it has persistently been

both excessively cognizant of its public role and stolidly timid about
accepting responsibility for that role. It has, ironically, established as
one of its few customs a tradition of ambivalent intentions toward the
audience. This ambivalence manifests itself most obviously in a conflict
between the desire to elevate and instruct and the desire to entertain
and palliate. The characteristic resolution of this tension has appeared
to be to subjugate instruction to entertainment, but the more stagnat-
ing effect has been that in a denial of that ambivalence itself, American
theater has conceived of entertainment as appeasement and has forsa-
ken the wonder implicit in the desire to elevate.

The tradition of ambivalent intentions toward audiences has roots
and resonances in both the culture and the commerce of American life.
Because theater has become an increasingly costly enterprise, unable
to support itself through ticket sales, it has repeatedly had to expend
energy on searches for financial support. The difficulties of finding
appropriate financial support are today a commonplace of discussions of
American theater. The problem, of course, is one not only of finding
sources of sufficient funding but also of determining and judging the
relationship of those who contribute money to the choice and integrity
of the plays produced. The issue is complicated in the United States by
a continuing conception of theater as a potential source of financial
gain. Although there is ample evidence that most theater does not
make a profit on its productions, there is still a prevalent expectation
that investment in theater might and perhaps should yield large financial gain. The situation is a bit like a lottery, but whereas most men
and women who purchase lottery tickets would not consider any attempt to manipulate their chances of winning, in theater those who
purchase a production asssume a right to control their potential gain to
whatever extent is possible.

Questions of commerce and culture thus become inextricable.
Those who attempt to control the financial results of theater obviously
try to predict the success of a play and arrive directly at a concern with
audience. The commonplace here has been that to make money, one
must "play it safe"; to take risks with material is to take unwelcome
risks with financial gain. Disguised within this adage, however, is a
much more complex issue than is immediately apparent. There is, initially, a whole series of questions of how one determines a play to be
risky, what risky material looks like, and why it is assumed that a play
whose concerns are "unsafe" is necessarily bad for the box office. Even
to propose these questions suggests a dismal context for any art, but
more dangerous territory still remains hidden. For, while American
theater does not appear to repress controversial issues or "shocking"
material, it has provided little space for stage worlds that truly question

the fabric of American society. The living-room settings and nuclear families of most American drama reflect back to spectators the familiar, harmonious world that affirms precisely the values and consciousness of those who perceive theater as a commercial enterprise. The very existence of these living rooms and the focus on familiar behavior and the psychological relationships of characters conceived as free individuals assert a middle-class consciousness that not only excludes other values and modes of living but also suggests that in fact there are no other possibilities. The characters who inhabit the worlds of American realistic drama may be more or less prosperous, knowledgeable, and satisfied with their personal lives, but the constraints upon them derive from their own internal limitations, not the constrictions of an unyielding social structure. To look upon American drama as a reflection of American society is to see a pervasive and open-ended middle-class world, coherent and harmonious in its values, offering the American dream of equal opportunity to all who are willing to struggle for the promise of security and comfort. Even in the most complex and interesting of American dramas, such as *Death of a Salesman,* or *Who's Afraid of Virginia Woolf?*, we are presented with no viable alternatives to the American dream. The faults lie, perhaps unavoidably but nevertheless solidly, in the protagonists themselves. For the middle-class white Americans who buy most of the theater tickets in the United States, the performance of drama is thus an act of reassurance: The worlds they see before them contain pain as well as pleasure, but the shape of those worlds does not disturb the world the spectator already knows.

That theater should identify and affirm the values of its audience is not in itself distressing or unique. The most vital periods of theater activity—those of Greece in the fifth century B.C. and of Elizabethan England—were in fact characterized by a coherence of its values and those of the societies in which it existed. But whereas the playwrights of ancient Greece and Elizabethan England could rightfully presume that their audiences also comprised a community, and that community extended into the larger society, no such judgment can be appropriately made in the United States. Not only are there in America class and ethnic divisions that refute the existence of a community that might coincide with an audience, but what genuine communities exist in the United States have been neither the subject nor the audience for the mainstream of American drama. Because American drama has behaved with such consistency and because that consistency confirms other aspects of American culture, the pretense and insufficiency of American drama have rarely been called into question.

Black drama is troublesome precisely because it does call into question the very foundations of American society. Nowhere in American theater is the tradition of ambivalent intentions felt more forcefully or fully than in black theather, but in contrast to playwrights in the "mainstream" of American drama, black playwrights have responded to the dilemma of relationship to the audience with explosive attempts to discover modes of drama that will address rather than repress the ambivalence. There have been instances when black dramatists have followed the direction of white dramatists and have mixed instruction with entertainment within the bounds of realism, in order to affect the audiences of middle America. But because the playwrights were unwilling or unable wholly to distort their material, their plays have succeeded sometimes despite themselves in defining the limits of dramatic realism in America.

The ambivalences of black dramatists are not only more severe but more complex than those of white dramatists. For the black playwright in America, sources of funding have been extremely limited and commercial success has meant recognition in a sometimes hostile and often indifferent white world. The special trap for the black playwright has been the temptation to make a choice of audience based on racial identity and then to construct a strategy and material to suit that audience. Conversely, if the black playwright chose to write authentically of the black experience he could only presume a genuine and unintimidated response from a black audience; if the black playwright chose to write of the relationships between black and white Americans so as not to alienate white spectators, he had to be prepared for the rejection of some black spectators for whom the world would seem inauthentic. Furthermore, if the black playwright desired, as many have, to instruct and elevate his audience, he had to recognize that what might be important questions for black spectators could be distorted by, and irrelevant to, white spectators; what might be educationally significant for white spectators could well be uninteresting to blacks.

These dilemmas for black dramatists have been recognized since black drama began to thrive in the 1920s. The potentials both for exceptionally powerful drama and for entrapment in the quicksand of these conflicts were foreseen more than fifty years ago by W. E. B. DuBois. Writing for the magazine *The Crisis* in 1924, DuBois predicted with astonishing precision the plights of, and possibilities for, both black playwrights and audiences:

> The most dramatic group of people in the history of the United States is the American Negro. It would be very easy for a great artist so to interpret the history of our country as to make the plot turn entirely upon the black man. Thus two classes of drama-

tic situations of tremendous import arise. The inner life of this black group and the contact of black and white. It is going to be difficult to get at these facts for the drama and treat them sincerely and artistically because they are covered by a shell; or shall I say a series of concentric shells?[2]

The task DuBois here puts to the black playwright—to uncover these concentric shells in order lucidly to reveal important acts—is also appropriate and difficult for the critic. The shells to which DuBois refers are constructed of racism and the disguised social structure of American society, but also embody aesthetic acts that can subtly disorient both the spectator and the reader. In his naming of two important "classes" of dramatic situations, DuBois gives us a tool that aids both in discerning ambivalent intentions and in tracing the evolution of black drama's own traditions. In the context of the plays of inner life or the plays of contact of black and white, we can begin to make judgments from the texts themselves about their relationships to audiences. Most plays of "inner life" are directed toward black audiences; most plays of "contact of black and white" are intended for audiences of both black and white spectators or white spectators. Two of the plays included in this study—Willis Richardson's *The Broken Banjo* and Ed Bullins's *In the Wine Time*—are vividly plays of inner life intended essentially for black spectators. Two other plays that I shall examine—Imamu Amiri Baraka's *Dutchman* and Lorraine Hansberry's *A Raisin in the Sun*—are plays of contact of black and white that assume both black and white spectators. One play—Willis Richardson's *The Chip Woman's Fortune*—is a play of inner life that fails in its attempt to work for a white audience. The remaining two plays I shall discuss—Langston Hughes's *Emperor of Haiti* and Theodore Ward's *Big White Fog*—combine the "classes" of inner life and contact of black and white and are ambiguous in their conception of audience, but in their very ambiguities and mixtures confront many aspects of the tradition of ambivalence.

These plays, which will become the center of my discussion, are not necessarily, by any mode of judgment, the "best" plays written by black Americans; that is to say, the plays I shall examine are not of a quality radically distinct from that of all other black drama. Nor are they unique in the clarity they bring to the relationship between black drama and audience. For the ambivalence I have stressed is indeed a pattern or tradition, one that began in the nineteenth century. As early as 1821, in New York, the African Company was supported and attended by black people; audiences for its performances were mostly middle-class and educated.[3] Later in the century, significant numbers of black people witnessed productions of *Uncle Tom's Cabin* and minstrel shows flourished, but these were clearly examples of black stage images intended not to establish a black audience but to satisfy the notions or fantasies of white audiences.

In the early years of the twentieth century, new and more successful attempts were made to establish theater for black audiences. Most promising among these efforts were those of the companies of the Lafayette and Lincoln theaters in Harlem. Although the plays performed in these theaters were written by white playwrights, the Lincoln and Lafayette did create a black theater audience, which steadily increased from 1910 until 1917 and the war years.[4]

There is no clear evidence of significant numbers of scripts written by black playwrights and intended for black audiences before the 1920s. Black men and women writing plays were, however, encouraged by the establishment of black community theaters like the Ethiopian Theater in Chicago, W. E. B. DuBois's Krigwa Little Negro Theater in New York, the Gilpin Players of Cleveland, and the Krigwa Players of Washington, D.C., which were eager to perform black drama. There was support for black playwrights, too, from *The Crisis* and *Opportunity*, magazines that in the 1920s began to award prizes in black drama.

With the establishment in the 1920s of black community theaters, one possibility that arose for the black playwright was to create some plays for a black audience and to write different plays for the white downtown audience. Willis Richardson, in the early 1920s, and Langston Hughes, later in the decade, are important examples of playwrights who wrote distinct plays for each audience. Scripts by such writers as Georgia Douglas Johnson, John Matheus, Jean Toomer, Garland Anderson, and Wallace Thurman also provide clear textual evidence of writing for *either* a white or a black audience.

During the 1930s, black theaters established by and for the black community continued to thrive in what Randolph Edmonds, a black playwright and teacher of drama in the 1930s, called the "little theater movement."[5] In addition to such grass-roots theater, a different kind of attempt to establish black theater for black audiences became part of the work of the Federal Theater Project. The FTP, like many of the projects of the Works Progress Administration (WPA), was oriented toward local communities; the FTP attempted to provide work opportunities to a special group of the unemployed, the theater people. An outgrowth of its initial attempt to create community theaters were the "Negro units," as they came to be called, theaters or companies of black men and women, usually from and in the ghettos of the large cities, especially Chicago and New York.

The Negro units of the Federal Theater continued their own ironic

patterns of relationship to spectators. Although many of the scripts of
the Federal Theater Project were first performed in the black communities, "success" for the general American public seemed still to be
essentially defined by the approval of the white critics and the removal
of the play from the community.[6] In addition, the most applauded
"black" plays from the Federal Theater were works like either the
Orson Welles *Macbeth*, called "black" drama only because it featured
black performers, or Hall Johnson's *Run, Little Chillun*, whose music
and voodoo created another kind of exotic appeal. In contrast, Theodore Ward's *Big White Fog*, first produced by a Negro unit of the
project in Chicago, and produced again in the early 1940s by the
Negro Playwrights Company, was acclaimed by black critics for its
passionate protest and forthrightness but, meeting mixed or few responses from white critics, never reached Broadway and was not published in its entirety until 1974. The black playwright of the 1930s did,
then, have some sources of financial support and some hope of an audience, but his difficulty lay in the implicit knowledge that while his
first audience might well be black, money and acclaim would come
only if he aimed for a white audience.

The dilemma for the black playwright in his relationship to audiences did not go unperceived by black theater artists. In the 1940s
they struggled consciously and purposefully with this problem by establishing two black theater companies: the Negro Playwrights Company and the American Negro Company. Although neither group articulated hostility toward white audiences and neither group attempted
totally to deny concern for a general, public audience, both companies
asserted their desire to become independent of the expectations, desires, and fantasies of white audiences concerning black people. An effect of, or at least an adjunct to, this was that their purpose caused
them to see the need to create black audiences.

Unfortunately, both attempts to form an all-black theater company
were of brief duration: The Negro Playwrights Company began and
ended in 1940 with its single production, *Big White Fog;* the American
Negro Company, which also began producing in 1940, was considerably more successful during World War II but, despite scattered attempts to keep it going, had ceased production by 1947. The causes of
the inability of these companies to endure are unclear. Doris Abramson
quotes Loften Mitchell's explanation that the failures of the Negro
Playwrights Company and other similar Harlem theater groups were
due to "lack of local support, Broadway's ever-present influence, and
the lack of good, native drama."[7] Abramson's own suggestion is that
"there will be no real support for ethnic theater so long as the people
of the community are striving to be successful, assimilated, middle-
class Americans."[8]

Abramson's admonitory tone may seem inappropriate coming from a white critic (I hear the voice of Baraka's Clay, from *Dutchman*, crying out, "If I'm a middle-class fake white man . . . let me be."), but her assertion points toward an important understanding of the conflicts within black drama. Abramson argues that the content and very existence of black ethnic drama are problematic for black Americans striving to become assimilated, middle-class Americans; to remind both black and white Americans of the distinctive settings, mores, and values of black Americans emphasized a barrier when many people were attempting to argue that there should be none and that none of importance existed.

Abramson is not inaccurate when she points to the possibility that the separate existence of black theater might call into question a fundamental principle of American society, that of the possibility of assimilation. But to leave the matter there, as she does, is to oversimplify the issue. The question of assimilation is only a portion of the conflict between black ethnic theater and middle-class America.[9] Black drama, which throughout the twentieth century has resisted the interior walls of realism, is a challenge to middle-class America both politically and aesthetically. It is not simply that black theater could discomfort white Americans and upward-striving black Americans: Black theater could reveal with dangerous clarity that America was not a classless society with one coherent dramatic vision.

Failure to confront the fundamental interrelationship of social, political, and aesthetic criteria is also characteristic of Harold Cruse's attempt to analyze the question of black drama in the 1940s. Cruse's main argument, similar in its thrust to Abramson's assertion, explains the problems of the black ethnic theater of that decade in terms of the then new import of both the term and notion of integration.[10] But whereas Abramson oversimplifies the social and political implications for black theater of American values and class structure, Cruse limits the power of his discussion by skimming the surface of the plays themselves. In addition, Cruse mentions the conflicts in black theater companies in the 1940s between, on the one hand, the need for the playwright to experiment and take risks with his material and, on the other, the actors' desires for shows that would have long and financially successful runs. While Cruse contends that it was the actors who dominated the thinking of the companies, he fails to show why, then, the companies did not succeed commercially. Cruse only makes the barest attempt to analyze the relation between these internal conflicts within black theater companies and the import of integration to the plays themselves; to indicate, as Cruse does, that playwrights were wary of integration while actors embraced it for commercial reasons, does not suffice.

The social, political, and aesthetic problems of black theater in the 1940s were further complicated by the historical circumstances of the period. There was, notably, a war that was simultaneously profoundly affecting and physically distant from the American public. It was a war in which approximately a million black men and women served in the armed forces. For these men and women there was some improvement over the racial situation that had existed for blacks during World War I—new branches of the service were opened to them, black men and women in substantial numbers were trained as officers, and toward the end of the war, a few black troops were actually integrated with white troops—but most black soldiers began and ended their service segregated from their white fellow soldiers. Only in word and sometimes in movies did black soldiers receive the equal treatment and integration called for by black and white voices at home. Yet, ironically, it was a war in which the essential moral questions were racial and ethnic, and the stance of the United States seemed clear: We were fighting against those forces and nations that believed in ethnic and racial superiority and dominance; we were fighting for the freedom and equality of all men.

If one juxtaposes this historical situation with the tradition of ambivalent intentions in American theater, the complexity of any black theater's stance toward an audience in the 1940s becomes apparent. The harsh but eloquent racial statement made by the segregation of troops and by injustices to blacks at home in industry brought forth a protest from black playwrights, but from those audiences, both black and white, that sought in the entertainment of the theater relief from the fears and tensions of war, there was little call for serious drama that sought to extend feelings of anxiety and oppression. Indeed, as Fannie Hicklin has noticed, there was so little serious drama of any merit during this period that neither the Pulitzer Prize Committee nor the Drama Critics' Circle made awards in 1941–42 or 1943–1944.[11]

For the white playwright who felt it impossible to ignore racial issues made eloquent by the war, sugarcoated treatments were one answer: *South Pacific* comes immediately to mind. No "*South Pacifics*" by black playwrights appeared during the 1940s, but it is notable that one of the best and most successful black plays of the period, Theodore Ward's *Our Lan'*, was concerned with the postwar frustrations of black people expecting a new freedom. *Our Lan'* evoked a sense of restraint and distance by setting its situation on an island off Georgia just after the Civil War—a time and place that seemed remote, yet laden with analogues to the late 1940s.

Once the war was over, the issue of integration was not as easily evaded as it had been in previous years. The United States now had to uphold its image as the defender of freedom. Black newspapers and magazines had increased in number and circulation during the war and had called a new attention to the achievements of blacks both at home and abroad.[12] Legal paths to confrontation with racial injustices were given public attention by international trials of war criminals. The financial prosperity in the United States during and after World War II increased the numbers and financial success of the black middle class, and the next step for these men and women was a call for full integration.[13]

Black playwrights had protested injustices since the 1920s; events in the 1950s and journalistic attention to the issues allowed not only protests but demands for integration to be more widely and clearly heard. The more pronounced integration of troops after World War II, the Supreme Court desegregation decisions of the early 1950s, and the Montgomery, Alabama, bus boycott of 1956 helped to create a new context and potentially different audiences for black drama. Black playwrights in the 1950s could begin to think of their audiences as integrated (although this was not wholly true in the North until the late 1950s and only gradually became true in the South during the 1960s); they could also imagine the possibility at least of increased support for, and recognition of, their work.

Integration not only meant that the black playwright could conceive of his audiences as being racially "mixed"; he could expect to confront them with some realities of racial injustice and segregation and be acknowledged. The black playwright's voice of protest was not new, but the challenges in the plays to the behavior of audiences and the frequency and specificity of those challenges increased sharply. The political strategy of the period was to urge the possibility of legal equality, the likeness of blacks and whites, and the hope for a harmonious society. In the dramatic strategies of black writers there were now apparent attempts to demonstrate the basic likenesses of all peoples while protesting the specific ways in which possibility had been limited and harmony prevented. The plays that formulated strategies with these inherent intentions constitute a distinct type of American drama. Lorraine Hansberry's *A Raisin in the Sun* will perhaps be remembered as the archetypal script for this era, but plays like Louis Peterson's *Take a Giant Step* (1953) and Alice Childress's *Trouble in Mind* (1954–55) worked out of similar aims and understandings in the early 1950s, well before *A Raisin in the Sun*. Many works of the 1960s, including Baraka's *The Toilet*, James Baldwin's *Blues for Mr. Charlie*, Charles Gordone's *No Place to Be Somebody*, and Ossie Davis's *Purlie Victorious*, though ostensibly and sometimes resoundingly different in tone, content, and strategy from each other and plays of the 1950s, nevertheless can be at least basically contained within a genre identifiable by its attempts to persuade audiences to accept, understand, or approve racial integration.

Even though the integrationist plays do not generally include a positive resolution of relationships between blacks and whites, through the evocation of anger and dismay at unjust behavior these dramas suggest the kinds of attitudes that could lead to mutual respect and acceptance. Such a strategy is clearly aimed at white audiences more than at black audiences; the playwright's conception of his audience as integrated or mostly white is at least implicit in integrationist drama.

The quantity of scripts during this period, as well as the box-office success of many of those scripts, can deceptively imply that the black playwright's problems with his audience had been eliminated by the early 1960s. This was not so; the black playwright, if he chose to write for Broadway, still had the problem of recognizing (or denying) the distinct needs and assumptions of both black and white people in his audience. And although the values of the black and white middle classes that essentially made up audiences were perhaps increasingly similar, their needs and the means of achieving those needs obviously diverged at crucial points, as did the traditions and histories of the two groups. If, for example, both black and white people in an audience desired racial integration, what that meant to each group had to be different.

Furthermore, for the black playwright, the problems of perception and interpretations of materials, including language, persisted. White audience members have usually had limited experience in and of a black community, and their perceptions of that community can therefore too readily be projections of stereotypes or fantasy. Thus, to present to a white audience a black person in a Cadillac risks the danger of affirming the white spectator's notions of the irresponsibility of blacks, including some latent envy of that perceived carelessness toward money. But to explain the symbolic and social function of the Cadillac for some blacks is to condescend to black spectators and possibly abuse the stage's potential for instruction. Similarly, but even more problematically, to employ black dialect in stage dialogue threatens the ability of white spectators truly to see the characters on stage; many white spectators will be alienated by their inability to understand certain usages and will automatically conclude that the stage characters are ignorant or stupid because they do not speak in "standard" English. To make all black characters speak in standard English, however, would not only be perplexing to black spectators but would exclude an essential element of the texture of black life from the drama. Given the singular importance of the spoken language to the stage, such a gesture toward verbal conformity would be self-destructive and absurd. Thus, in integrationist drama, as in other forms of black art, the black artist is frequently faced with the conflict between revealing the actuality and continuing the illusion desired by white audiences (and, certainly, some black audiences). Some black dramatists have directly confronted this problem in their scripts, as in Childress's *Trouble in Mind*, in which a black actress confronts the falsehoods in the part she is to play. Other black dramatists have retained authenticity while appealing to white audiences through humor or satire. But to ignore the continuing strain of this dilemma would be a serious self-deception.

The difficulties and continuing ambivalence of integrationist drama were not, in fact, ignored. A major confrontation with the problems of black theater came in the 1960s, calling itself the Black Arts Theatre. Included within the general framework of Black Arts Theatre are the more specific intentions and scripts of Black Revolutionary Theatre. Even before these related movements became recognizable or assertive as aesthetic and political forces, there were signals of changes in the relationships of some black playwrights to their audiences. The most apparent sign was an increasingly conscious tendency to move away from living-room middle-class realism. To accomplish this, black playwrights turned or returned to language, situations, and forms that are distinct from white American drama and are identifiably black.[14]

The search for new forms and depths in black drama since the mid-1960s has brought forth such varied strategies that there is no simple generalization beyond the one just made that can accurately describe the relationship of the black-drama script to its audience. In plays like Baraka's *Dutchman* and Gordone's *No Place to Be Somebody*, already mentioned as loosely included within integrationist drama, we see the black playwright still addressing himself to a black-and-white audience, but conveying his own conflict about that strategy. In Baldwin's *The Amen Corner* and Elder's *Ceremonies in Dark Old Men*, the playwright's vision is sharply focused on the black world, but the understandings sought are neither hidden from nor irrelevant to white spectators.

The contrast to plays like those by Baldwin and Elder that can be perceived in Black Arts Theatre, as in the early works of Ed Bullins, is not only that the situation and characters are drawn from black environments but also that there is an attempt to create a new black aesthetic, to assert values and use forms that are black and intended for black audiences. In Black Revolutionary Theatre, black playwrights like Baraka, Ron Milner, and Marvin X go a step farther in that their intentions are not merely focused on black audiences but consciously exclude white audiences. There is also in Black Revolutionary Theatre a clear moral and political strategy, an articulated aim to incite to action, demonstrate clear distinctions between good (blackness) and evil (whiteness), and assert power through black separatism.[15] There is thus an ironic similarity between black integrationist drama and black revolutionary drama in that both call for changes in behavior and both could be called propaganda, but the kinds of changes and the persons whose behavior is aimed at are distinctly different and, at times, opposites.

While it is possible to identify the tenets of Black Arts Theatre and Black Revolutionary Theatre, many plays and playwrights of the last fifteen years do not fit neatly into one category or another. Both of the major playwrights of the period, Baraka and Bullins, have written a considerable number of plays, and within the repertoire of each can be found dramas that fit readily into Black Arts Theatre but are not clearly revolutionary, plays that seem very much a contribution to Black Revolutionary Theatre, and plays that seem transitional or ambivalent. Caution is necessary in any examination of relationships between black-drama scripts and audiences; it is particularly crucial, however, with the plays of the 1960s and 1970s, not to be led away from the script by aesthetics or aims that the playwrights articulated elsewhere, even though such statements can increase understanding of both specific elements in scripts and the whole picture of contemporary black drama.

I have stressed the racial problems of the black playwright creating for black, white and black, and white audiences because the critic's goal must be to reveal not only the dramatic situation described but also the dramatic situation that occurs between the play and the audience. At the core of what a play means is not simply what it is about or what it says, but also what it does. J. L. Styan states this concern neatly in his introduction to *The Elements of Drama*: "We are not judging the text, but what the text makes the actor make the audience do."[16] In my own work, here and elsewhere, I call what the text does its *strategy*. The term "strategy," borrowed from the work of Kenneth Burke, is meant to suggest the set of intentions or gestures to an audience that we can discover within the text.[17] The discovery of dramatic strategies considers the audience not only in terms of those responses that might be different because a spectator is black or white but also in terms of reactions a script would evoke in any person. Thus, the portrayal of the death of a father, for example, must be considered not just in terms of its particularities in a black or white household, but in a context of other social and historical events, as well as emotional responses all people might experience.

When I speak of an audience for any of the plays I discuss, I am thinking not simply of people occupying seats in a theater, but of people who are genuinely an audience for that play—who put themselves, in Stanley Cavell's terms, in the "present" (but not the "presence") of the characters onstage. The genuine audience acknowledges the characters onstage as separate *and* in its presence as audience; it is not, however, symmetrically in their presence.[18] To "acknowledge" means not only to know something *about* the characters of their stage worlds (not only to be able to recognize their existence or certain of their characteristics) but also to respond to the play in such a way that we "must do or reveal something"[19] about ourselves in connection with the play. This does not mean that we must make some overt social gesture outside the theater. While one could imagine a group of theater spectators departing after the curtain of a black theater production and marching on city hall, or smashing a window in anger, or standing quietly weeping on a street corner, none of these acts is necessarily an act of acknowledgment, although any of them might include some acknowledgment of the play. What the plays before us demand is that the audience member be unable to remain the same after the experience of this piece of theater, at least not without a conscious act of rejection. The recognition of such a change, at least to oneself, is an act of acknowledgment. When it achieves this, black drama returns us to the oldest function of theater.[20] We, as potential audience members, share with the playwright and other theater artists the responsibility for a play's failure or success in accomplishing such an achievement.

This is not what I take to be meant by "forgetting ourselves" in the theater. Rather, it means remembering ourselves, and thereby knowing that we are separate from the people onstage, but also knowing that they are there. I am not a true member of an audience if, while the play is being performed, I am thinking about the chores I have to do after the performance. I am also not genuinely part of an audience if I only see the characters before me as extensions of myself and my world, and not as themselves in their world. To "identify" with a character is a misleading notion; it is not that we are "one with" the stage figure, but that we acknowledge this separate person as someone who can be known.

To be an audience in the manner I have described is not necessarily an easy task, particularly in a world where we are not accustomed to paying the kind of attention that task involves. We who watch television while we read a magazine, while we eat a meal, while we talk to another are not much in the habit of being audiences. But surely it is with a genuine audience in mind that a playwright creates a strategy, and while it is the artist's responsibility to make that strategy such that we will remain an audience, it is our responsibility to be an audience in the first place.

The most forceful way to bring a larger public genuinely to

acknowledge black drama and recognize itself as an audience might be to direct "perfectly" mounted productions of each of the seven plays to be discussed in these pages, and to bring such production to spectators in every town and city. But such an endeavor is not only unfeasible, it ignores the fact that spectators today must be led to the theater, must be assisted to be genuine audiences. Such an effort would also temporally limit the occasions when access to these plays could occur. Further, such an activity would only hide but not eliminate the critical act. For drama, unlike poetry or fiction, demands mediation: Fiction and poetry can accomplish their acts between the page and the reader alone; to move from the text to the performance of a play, without which gesture a play is not itself, necessitates the intervening work of actors, and sometimes of directors and designers as well. Essential to the work of these actors, directors, and designers toward any performance of a play are acts of criticism of the most vital sort. The moment an actor reads aloud a word of a script, he is commenting on and revealing that text. Unlike the theater reviewer who comments on a performance after many prior acts of criticism, the true critic approaching plays as texts must then assist other readers to imagine those leaps that move a script from text to performance.

It will help any reader or spectator to fulfill his responsibility to a work if he approaches the plays I shall discuss as distinct theatrical events rather than as pieces of a puzzle that will eventually reveal what black drama "is." These plays remind us that there is neither a single "black experience" nor any one set of responses black dramatists wish to evoke in an audience. Somewhat paradoxically, however, these plays can also confront us with the experience of a complex but shared community. Onstage or off, theater does not create communities; nor does it destroy the class divisions that can at once be an assault upon and a masquerade of community. But when the curtain of theater is lifted it does reveal a world that is peculiarly whole, and our shared recognition of that revelation can make of each of us spectators an audience. In black drama, the raising of the curtain can also be the lifting of the Veil, the diaphanous barrier that DuBois saw enshrouding the "souls of black folk." To appreciate these plays is to acknowledge both the curtain and the Veil; such an acknowledgment might then make possible the experience of genuinely being a member of an audience and might help us to imagine how we can be persons in a community.

NOTES

1. James Hatch, ed., *Black Theater, U.S.A.* (New York: Free Press, 1974), p. ix.
2. W. E. B. DuBois, *The Seventh Son: The Thought and Writings of W. E. B. DuBois,* ed. with an introduction by Julius Lester (New York: Random House, 1971), II, 311.
3. Carlton Molette, "The First Afro-American Theatre," *Black World* 19 (April 1970), 4–9; and Herbert Marshall and Mildred Stock, *Ira Aldridge, The Negro Tragedian* (Carbondale, Ill.: Southern Illinois University Press, 1968), pp. 28–47.
4. For further discussion of the early problems and later labor disputes besetting the Lincoln and Lafayette theaters, see Harold Cruse, *The Crisis of the Negro Intellectual* (New York: Morrow, 1967), pp. 73–83. John Hope Franklin also mentions plays and players in these theaters, in *From Slavery to Freedom* (New York: Knopf, 1947), p. 506.
5. Randolph Edmonds, "The Negro Little Theatre Movement," *The Negro History Bulletin* (January 1949); also see "Negro Drama in the South," *The Carolina Play Book* (June 1940), 73–78, and "Some Reflections on the Negro in American Drama," *Opportunity* 8 (October 1930), 303–35.
6. This remains a problem for all American theater. See Robert Brustein's editorial on the relationship of Broadway to community and college theaters, *New York Times,* August 4, 1974, II.
7. Doris Abramson, *Negro Playwrights in the American Theater, 1925–1959* (New York: Columbia University Press, 1969), p. 94.
8. *Ibid.*
9. See my article, "Black Drama: Reflections of Class and Class Consciousness," in *Prospects* 3 (1977).
10. Cruse, pp. 209–12. Abramson's explanation also seems to me to conflict with other examples of successful ethnic theater, such as the Irish theater here and in Ireland.
11. Fannie E. F. Hicklin, "The American Negro Playwright, 1920–1964," Ph.D. dissertation, University of Wisconsin, 1965, p. 296.
12. E. Franklin Frazier, *Black Bourgeoisie* (New York: Macmillan, 1957), pp. 148–49.
13. Frazier, especially Chapters 1–9.
14. Many of the "new" black forms are also apparent in, or similar to, those of white drama as it has moved away from realism. This does not, I think, demean the search of these black playwrights.
15. For articulations of aims of the Black Revolutionary Theatre, see LeRoi Jones (Baraka), "In Search of the Revolutionary Theatre," *Black World* 15

(April 1966), 15, 20, 24, or Marvin X, "Manifesto: The Black Educational Theatre of San Francisco," *Black Theatre* 6 (1972), 30–31.

16. J. L. Styan, *The Elements of Drama* (Cambridge, U.K.: University Press, 1960), p. 2. Styan elaborates in a later chapter: "It is more than a truism, then, to insist that a play stands or falls with its reception by the audience. The playwright's object at all times is to set the audience to work. . . . The play animates the audience by a goad placed in the hands of the actors. The interest in the drama creates and recreates impressions that move in a progression exactly determined by the progressions in the action" (pp. 67–68).

17. For a more detailed discussion of the sources and critical functions of the term "strategy," see Appendix A and my article "I Love You. Who Are You?: The Strategy of Drama in Recognition Scenes," *PMLA* (March 1977), 297–306.

18. Stanley Cavell, *Must We Mean What We Say?* (New York: Scribner's, 1969), pp. 332–40, but especially p. 337. Cavell's book *The World Viewed* (New York: Viking, 1971), though ostensibly concerned with film, also contains important understandings of what it means to be an audience and how one looks at a work of art.

19. Cavell, *Must We Mean What We Say?*, p. 263 in particular, but all of the three chapters "A Matter of Meaning It," "Knowing and Acknowledging," and "The Avoidance of Love: A Reading of *King Lear*," is helpful to an understanding of Cavell's fruitful use of the word "acknowledge."

20. I am thinking here of the foundations of community as discussed by Tracy B. Strong in *Friedrich Nietzsche and the Politics of Transfiguration* (Berkeley: University of California Press, 1975), especially Chapter 6, and my own discussion of anagnorisis in "I Love You. Who Are You?: The Strategy of Drama in Recognition Scenes."

2 | BLACK PLAYWRIGHT FOR TWO WORLDS: WILLIS RICHARDSON'S *THE BROKEN BANJO* AND *THE CHIP WOMAN'S FORTUNE*

WHEN W. E. B. DuBois WROTE in 1924 that the "inner life" of black Americans and the "contact of black and white" in America were potential sources of both great drama and great dilemma for black playwrights, he discerned the careers of a number of his contemporaries. Just seven years earlier, in 1917, a young man named Willis Richardson had begun writing plays of the "inner life" of black people. As DuBois recognized, Richardson's concern with the ordinary lives of black people proved both enormously fruitful and persistently problematic. Richardson's plays reveal with significant clarity the power of dramas of the "inner life," as well as the frustrations inherent in such work when the playwright attempts to write for spectators outside the black community.

Although Richardson was not the first black American playwright, he is of historical and aesthetic importance in black drama as the first black writer to make a serious commitment to drama for and about black life. Born on November 5, 1889, in Wilmington, North Carolina, Richardson "came of age" during the 1920s, the period known in black literary history as the Negro or Harlem Renaissance. Evidence of his commitment to black theater can be found in his more than twenty one-act plays, an indeterminate number of longer dramas, his articles concerning black drama that appeared in *Opportunity* and *The Crisis*,[1] and the two anthologies of "plays of Negro life"[2] that he edited in 1930 and 1935. The later anthology, entitled *Negro History in Thirteen Plays*, is notable as the first collection of drama devoted exclusively to works by black American playwrights.

Willis Richardson also holds the distinction of being the first black playwright to have a drama produced on Broadway. The play, *The Chip Woman's Fortune*, appeared in 1923 with a revival of Oscar Wilde's *Salomé*. *The Chip Woman's Fortune*, presented by the Chicago

19

Ethiopian Players, was first produced in Harlem at the Lafayette Theatre and then moved downtown. It ran for only two weeks, and received scant critical attention then or since.[3] That the critics did not herald this "first" for the New York theater may be partially explained by the fact that black musicals had been seen in New York in recent years.[4]

A number of Richardson's plays were also performed in community theaters: *The Deacon's Awakening* in St. Paul, in 1921; *Mortgaged*, by the Howard Players in Washington, D.C., in 1924; *The Broken Banjo*, by the Krigwa Players of Harlem, in 1925. *The Broken Banjo*, the other play to be discussed in this chapter, not only achieved production but was awarded both the first prize in the 1925 contest of the Krigwa Players, a group sponsored by W. E. B. DuBois, and the first of the Amy Spingarn prizes, presented by *The Crisis* magazine.

Richardson's career as a playwright set precedents for other black dramatists, but neither the forms nor the concerns of his plays were wholly or obviously unique for the 1920s. Many of them could reasonably be described as naturalistic, one-act dramas; while naturalism, as contrasted with realism, was never a successful or well-developed style in the United States, other playwrights of the period, both black and white, wrote comparably brief plays in what could be called a naturalistic mode.[5] Richardson's subject matter, "the drama of Negro life," was at least superficially similar to the topics portrayed in a long list of plays about black life. "Plays of Negro life" by white playwrights in this period included works that are still occasionally restaged: Ridgely Torrence's *The Rider of Dreams* (1917), Eugene O'Neill's *The Emperor Jones* (1920) and *All God's Chillun Got Wings* (1924); Paul Green's *In Abraham's Bosom* (1924), and Marc Connelly's *The Green Pastures* (1930).

Nor were Richardson's plays solitary achievements of the black artistic world. In 1925, the year *The Broken Banjo* was produced in Harlem, the first serious full-length drama by a black playwright, Garland Anderson's *Appearances*, was presented on Broadway. Four years later, Wallace Thurman's *Harlem* also appeared on Broadway. And these productions were only the tip of the iceberg. Black drama was developing in a variety of locations in the 1920s. Richardson himself lived and worked most frequently in Washington, D.C., and had contact with the Howard Players in his hometown, but he also worked with writers and theater companies in New York and Chicago.[6] Richardson was thus not a unique figure as a black dramatist, but he did reach out more extensively than other black artists in an attempt to create genuine, serious black drama. He loomed large in a growing tableau that included the establishment of black community theaters and black college theaters, written declarations for a new black theater by such notable black thinkers as W. E. B. DuBois and Alain Locke, and scattered scripts similar in form and material to his own by such writers as Jean Toomer, Georgia Douglas Johnson, and John Matheus.[7]

Historically, Richardson was not only an outstanding figure in an artistic community, he was also a black man living in an extremely difficult time for black Americans. The period after World War I was one of strong racial tensions. Despite hopes aroused during the war that the participation of black men in the overseas struggle would provide them and their fellows with a new equality, the returning black soldier was in no better social or occupational position than before the war. The decade after 1917 included race riots in the North, heightened activity by the Ku Klux Klan in the South and the North, and basic strains everywhere concerning work, housing, and education. Often, this tension was relieved or hidden by a hysteria of frivolity; it was the time, as Imamu Amiri Baraka (LeRoi Jones) points out in *Blues People*, of the boogie-woogie, of all-night and sometimes all-weekend parties during which black men and women, and occasionally some whites, danced to the boogie piano that combined the "rhythmic contrasts" of the blues with some of the sounds of Western country singers.[8] It was a time of movement for black Americans: from Europe back home to the States, from South to North, from one rent-party to another. But it was a movement that never yielded progress for the majority of black people.

From within this world of frenzy and frustration, Willis Richardson wrote his plays and urged upon others the importance of black folk drama. His work during this period remains important not only as historical documents of a critical period in black social and cultural history, but also as individual artifacts that initiate a challenge to the prevalence of realism and expressionism in American theater. That Richardson conceived of many of his plays as "folk dramas" was neither inaccurate nor belittling to his works, which often bear striking resemblances to medieval morality plays in their allegorical structures and their characters who represent good and evil; in *The Broken Banjo*, he uses material that seems to lead to moralistic allegory, only to twist the characters and situation to show that there are no simple representatives of right and wrong. His choices of language, characterization, setting, and plot are generally more remarkable for their ordinariness than their exoticism. There is also an unabashed educative strategy in many of his works. These general characteristics of Richardson's drama connect his art both to the allegorical strain in some contemporary Black Revolutionary Theatre and to the attention given the lives of the "lowly" found in the contemporary theater of "black experience."

Richardson also serves as a paradigmatic figure in articulating through the differing strategies of particular plays the dilemma of the black playwright who must confront the racial segregation of his spectators. For both financial and educative purposes, he desires to affect both blacks and whites, but he also wants to re-create truly how black men and women struggle, survive, and fail in their worlds. Richardson's difficulties in working out strategies that combine these intentions are reflected in the two plays I have chosen for study. One of these plays, *The Broken Banjo*, reveals an effective strategy; the other, *The Chip Woman's Fortune*, seems to me strategically muddled and weak. I have deliberately chosen such contrasting works to suggest just what I mean by good and bad strategy, but these plays are not just illustrations of the method behind my judgments. Both textual and historical evidence indicate that *The Broken Banjo* was intended for a black audience, whereas *The Chip Woman's Fortune* was intended for a white or racially mixed audience; the comparison should raise questions about the specific relationship of strategy in black drama to the racial composition of an audience.

II

The Broken Banjo: A Folk Tragedy was presented in 1925 by the Krigwa Players of Harlem, a theater company founded by W. E. B. DuBois to encourage authentic black drama. *The Broken Banjo* is a drama of family conflicts. The tensions become intense when one member of the family reveals that another family member has committed a murder. The principal characters—Matt and Emma, a married couple, and Sam and Adam, Emma's brother and cousin, respectively—quarrel about food, money, and mutual responsibilities. During a struggle, Sam and Adam break Matt's prized banjo. Matt is furious when he discovers the harm done to his banjo; Sam defends himself by threatening to inform the authorities of Matt's responsibility for a previously unsolved murder. Although Matt elicits a promise of silence from both Sam and Adam, they eventually inform the police, and Matt is arrested.

In the strategy of *The Broken Banjo* we can discover why it was produced and awarded prizes. The apparent simplicity of situation and characterization is deceiving. A plot outline does not reveal how the play is complicated by Richardson's attempt to evoke concern and understanding for each member of the family. In contrast to the structure of many "family dramas," *The Broken Banjo* does not set up clear antagonists or protagonists in the small family it presents. Each of the characters in this play is clearly troubled and flawed, and each is also able to arouse distinct sympathies in an audience. In contrast to many tragedies, the pattern of action is not one of a persistent pressure toward a single climax, but one of wavelike motions of incident and reaction, tension and relief. By focusing attention on people who are ordinary folk, who are not elevated by their class or social roles in society, and by employing a stark situation and admonitory tone, the play recalls qualities of some medieval morality drama. In its patterns of staccato revelation and its evocation in the spectator of an ambivalent attitude toward knowledge, *The Broken Banjo* is reminiscent of some of the strategies of Sophoclean drama.[9]

The essential activity of *The Broken Banjo* is to lead the audience through a series of moments of belief and disbelief in the credibility of the characters' assertions. Richardson moves our interest, as audience, from one concern to another; he moves our sympathies from one character to his or her apparent opponent. Richardson leaves the audience with a sense, acquired from the whole play rather than from one final moment or climax, that although there are particular evils and human weaknesses to be avoided and condemned, neither situations nor persons are perfectly good or perfectly bad. This strategy intends to make the audience ambivalent in its judgments of what it sees on stage, but it is not an ambivalence meant to raise questions about reality and illusion, as in some dramas contemporary to Richardson's, such as Luigi Pirandello's *Henry IV*. Richardson's interest is distinctly moral. (One could argue, of course, that the moral and aesthetic are not distinct realms. The point here is that Richardson does remain primarily concerned with good and bad behavior, not real and unreal, beautiful and ugly.)

The first indication of Richardson's strategy occurs in the stage directions. The tenement dining room where the play takes place is to be "dull and dark looking,"[10] and thus suggestive of the mood of gloom and irritability of the first scene. That there are only two chairs in the room suggests the financial difficulties of the family but also provides a hint that, in a psychological sense, only two can comfortably exist in this space.

Matt, the husband, is seated in one of the two chairs as the play begins; he is playing his banjo. He is "short and strongly built;" he has the bearing of a laborer, not an exotic musician. In stage directions, Richardson states that "he [Matt] is not by any means a good player, but his desire to play well is his religion" (p. 303). Matt's absorption in his music commands our interest and perhaps the kind of respect we would give anyone clearly engaged in an artistic endeavor, but the weak quality of his strumming, which should be heard for a few moments before the dialogue begins, may also become annoying or amusing for an audience.

Thus, when Matt's wife, Emma, enters and immediately tells Matt to stop making "that noise," we may laugh or feel relieved that our sense of the poor quality of the music is confirmed, but we should also feel some hostility toward Emma because of her apparent lack of sympathy for her husband's efforts. As Emma orders Matt to go out to the yard to split wood and berates him for his selfishness, we sense that this scene is enacted daily. The tensions in their relationship are quickly made clear: Matt is a "loner" who does not get along with Emma's family; until recently, he has not worked. The rapid exposition does not seem artificial because Richardson presents it in the tone and context of habitual marital hassle. Our sympathies are not clearly directed, however. Although Emma's recounting of her hardships seems genuine enough, at present it is Matt, not his wife, who is working. Her complaints do not arise from an immediate weariness but are dredged up from the past. The audience is in the position of a person who unavoidably hears a next-door neighbor's squabbles, but who has little sense of the truth of bits heard through walls. Consequently, when Emma mentions her family's friction with Matt, it is not clear who is at fault.

Within sixteen brief speeches, much of the tone and situation of the play is set: We see a couple, young in years but aging rapidly through hardships, dissatisfied with their world and with each other. Although poverty is a basic cause of their difficulties, Matt's antagonism toward Sam and Adam provokes additional conflict between himself and Emma. This hostility takes on new dimensions when Matt labels Emma's brother and cousin "black." A white audience might have overlooked the term as simply descriptive; but Emma, and many black members of Richardson's audience, would have found it pejorative. Immediately, Emma, "defending her family," says, "Now don't start to callin' nobody black, 'cause you ain't got no room to call nobody black. Sam and Adam is just as light as you," (p. 304). That both Emma and Matt presume lightness of skin to be connected to virtue is reinforced when Matt counters by accusing Emma's relatives of being jailbirds. Because Matt has rather easily agreed with Emma when she said, "Sam and Adam is just as light as you," Richardson's point here would seem to be that skin tones are not relevant to virtue. The mention of skin color seems not a device aimed at a white audience to suggest that black and white are equally virtuous, but an admonition to a black audience to stop making character judgments based on lightness of skin.

I have called attention to this brief exchange concerning degree of blackness because, for me and, I would guess, any white spectator in the 1970s, these lines evoke discomfort. It is a lesson of the play, but one on which Richardson does not elaborate.

As if to emphasize the relative unimportance of "lightness," the dialogue then turns to the central issues of the play: crime, family responsibilities, and jail. Matt, as Emma puts it, "brags" that he has never been in jail. In retrospect, Matt's assertion will echo with irony, because Matt *is* a murderer, but since neither Emma nor we know at this point of Matt's crime and future punishment, his boast simply foreshadows eventual knowledge.

Matt recalls the prison histories of Sam and Adam not as simple insult but to get to his actual concern. He is angry because Sam and Adam constantly request food from him and Emma. Here, too, Richardson has established an issue to which the audience can find no easy response. Emma may be correct that to refuse food to family is stingy and disruptive to family ties, but Matt and Emma are obviously in no position to indulge others continuously.

At this point in the play, we have not yet met Sam and Adam. We may imagine them to be individuals who do merit kindness. Matt's argument, however, makes intellectual and emotional sense: he is not utterly selfish; rather, he sees no reason to be generous to men who are not his friends, who speak maliciously of him behind his back. Emma's barbed query, "Is you got any friends at all?" (p. 305) is met with complete candor by Matt, "No, Ah ain't got no friends. Ain't nobody likes me but you, and you ain't crazy about me" (p. 305).

Our sympathies are made to vacillate during this exchange. This is not the hackneyed situation of a mean miser, maliciously hoarding his possessions. There is a danger that such an erroneous, facile, response could occur if the play were performed for a white middle-class audience, but there is no evidence in these opening scenes that Richardson was interested in what would be a complicated breaking of clichés and prejudices. For a black audience in a community theater, who could perceive Matt not as a stereotyped black role but as another human being like themselves, Matt's honesty about himself and his relationships to others should be appealing. The tension between basic needs for survival and charity for blood relations would be real and important to a black audience or to any audience of folk for whom that plight was neither mundane nor remote.

The meaningfulness of Richardson's subtitle, *A Folk Tragedy*, begins to become apparent. This is not a pathetic situation in which flawless people are poor and unhappy; we are witnessing the struggle of likeable, imperfect folk to survive. Matt and Emma want to survive *and* retain some sense of dignity. What is apparent in the opening scenes is that both Matt and Emma struggle continually to sustain their self-respect. Since their quarrel begins in the opening speeches, and we have only their perceptions from which to make judgments, we are forced to believe and sympathize with first one, then the other; our sense of their desire for dignity is only disturbed by the quarrel itself. In a crucial strategic move, Richardson relieves this tension for a moment. Emma, in another bit of foreshadowing, asserts her devotion to Matt, concluding that he will never know the depth of her concern for him until he gets "in a big pinch" (p. 306). Matt responds by suddenly shifting attitude and suggesting to Emma that they quarrel too much. Emma concurs, and there are a few moments of respite, during which time the room is filled with a sense of their mutual underlying affection—and the resumed sound of Matt's banjo. These moments are vital to the rest of the play, because they make clear the basic bond between Matt and Emma and allow for their later gestures of love for one another.

Emma is only able to hold her tongue for a short time, but because of the revival of affection, her renewed queries about money seem less sharp; now she and Matt seem genuinely to listen to each other's needs. Out of the emotional reconciliation comes a practical resolution: Matt will buy Emma a pair of secondhand shoes that she needs very much. In return, Emma will tell Sam and Adam that they must stop mooching food.

This portion of the play concludes with a brief tableau; after Matt's departure, Emma silently regards the banjo, which Matt has left on the table. During this moment of quiet, Sam and Adam enter, disturbing the peace on stage and the moments of tranquility for the audience. For us and for Emma, the entrance of the surly, "mean tempered" brother Sam and the "lively and playful" cousin Adam should be met with mixed reactions: Emma might want the moment of repose sustained, but she can now attend to the undesired task of chastising Sam and Adam; we, too, might enjoy the respite from quarreling but are curious to know what Sam and Adam are like.

Richardson's strategy in removing Matt from the scene before the entrance of Sam and Adam is clear: to see Emma's relationship with her brother and cousin, we must see her alone with them. It becomes apparent, however, that we will not see Emma as she usually is with Sam and Adam, because she must now dismiss them. Sam and Adam immediately confirm Matt's description of them; they have been in the house for only a moment when Sam asks for food. But Emma does not fulfill her brother's expectations—she turns down his request. Sam interprets the refusal as a sign that Emma and Matt have been "fussin' "; but Adam, more jovially, suggests, "Matt's been spoonin' with huh and turned huh against us" (p. 308). Both of these interpretations are, as we know, in a sense true, so that Sam and Adam appear here to be clever but vulnerable because of their lack of necessary information.

A brief squabble ensues between Sam and Adam as Emma angrily goes to the kitchen in response to the taunts of the men. This serves two functions: it establishes an atmosphere and potential for violence and differentiates between Sam and Adam. Adam is clearly the milder of the two men, wary of violence and open in his responses to the world around him. Sam is gruff and volatile; his potential for trouble is symbolized by his knife, which he wields threateningly in this scene. Adam attempts to take Sam's knife away from him and almost naïvely at one point asks Sam, "What's the use of bein' so mean?" (p. 309). Sam's ardent desire to get his knife back is frightening, as is his response to Adam's memory of how Matt once beat them up: "He won't never beat us up again. Ah got him in the palm o' ma hand" (p. 310). This seems like idle boasting, but it is the important first hint that Sam may have a weapon to counter Matt's rejection—a weapon other than fists or his knife.

As Sam's hints continue, the audience is led into the central psychic "trap" of the play; that is, Richardson has engaged the audience in the play in such a way that our attitudes and emotions have no clear resolution independent from the play. Sam's grudges against Matt and his present sense of unwelcomeness are motivation enough for him to brag or lie, but, thus far, we have no evidence that Sam is deceitful. When he mentions, for the first time in the play, the unsolved murder of an old man, we, like Adam, have our interest aroused. But we do not want to believe any malicious hints from a person for whom we have no sympathy. Therefore, when Adam pries for more information and Sam says he'll "talk at the right time," we at least hope that such a time is only present in Sam's imagination.

The time arrives more quickly than we have expected. Provoked by Emma's revelation that Matt no longer wants Sam and Adam to come around and "eat all the grub," Sam attests that he has actually seen Matt kill old man Shelton. Sam's accusation is so stark, so unembellished, that initially our only response, like that of Emma, can be, "That's a lie." We have been shown Matt's volatile temper, but little in his demeanor has suggested that he has been carrying the memory of murder.

From this point, the moments of belief and disbelief alternate rapidly for both characters and spectators. Emma's first refutation of Sam's accusation is more damning than relieving: "Don't everybody know the one killed old man Shelton got away and ain't never been caught?" (p. 311). Sam answers bluntly that Matt's the one who was never caught. Emma, recovering her reason, weakens Sam's position: "If you had a'knowed that about Matt you'd 'a' told it long ago much as you hate him" (p. 311). This supports the audience's judgment about Sam, but he regains control of the debate and renews the ambiguity of the situation when he asserts that previously he had protected his sister's husband, but now that Emma has sided with Matt on the food issue, Sam no longer cares to protect her. Sam's motivation seems genuine; by announcing her husband's decision, Emma has seemed to ally herself with him. She has, if hesitantly, set up the lines of loyalty; since Sam did not witness her earlier quarrel with Matt, her one weak statement (p. 311) that she has not turned against Sam does not persuade him, and is only partially credible for the audience.

The strategic problem here is not only one of belief or disbelief in the reality of Matt's murder of the old man; it is also a matter of trust in each of the characters, Sam in particular. Thus the scene is more complicated than the traditional revelation scene of Greek drama, where the announcer of "the truth" clearly commands the audience's trust. The complexity here is typical of much modern drama, from Ibsen on, in which no voice is wholly credible. We might believe Sam's revelation, while wishing that he had remained silent. We then must also respect him for having held his knowledge so long, and we must understand why he speaks now. Sam's show of power is a natural response at a time when he feels threatened himself.

By this time, the audience will be anxious for some clarification of the uncertainty concerning the murder, and Richardson satisfies that anxiety. The detailed description of the murder that Sam now presents dispels almost all doubts as to the veracity of his tale, and we, like Emma, can only disbelieve out of faith in Matt. Doubt is again raised, however, when Adam asks why Sam did not tell him. Adam's question suggests at least two answers: Perhaps Sam is more discreet than either we or Adam had presumed; on the other hand, the fact that Sam has not shared his knowledge with Adam may mean that Sam is now inventing the story of the murder. The concreteness of Sam's report challenges an impression of deceit on his part. Yet, if he is telling the truth, not only is Matt guilty of murder, but we are guilty of too-facile judgment of Sam. He cannot be as selfish and corrupt as the audience might have assumed if he has remained quiet until this point in order to protect Matt.

Through a series of brief and increasingly intense moments, Richardson is building for the audience a trap that will eventually force us to admit that all the characters onstage share both virtue and weakness, that ready judgments of good and bad, right or wrong, are often unjust and dangerous. The scene in which Sam describes the murder is the first of a series demonstrating that in moments of even seemingly minor crises, individuals act their worst and their best. The ensuing scene, in which the banjo is broken, is another step in this strategy. Annoyed that Sam has not shared his knowledge of the murder, Adam attempts to show his own superiority on Matt's banjo; Sam tries to withhold the banjo from Adam, and in the struggle the banjo is broken. The scene itself is not heavily violent or intense, but, for both those onstage and those in the audience, the sense of presentiment is strong. The tension during the silent moments while Sam, Adam, Emma, and the audience await Matt's return is great: We can only dread Matt's response to the broken banjo and Sam's use of his knowledge—true or false—of the murder.

When Matt does return, bearing the shoes for Emma, he immediately notices the absence of the banjo. The scene that follows is puzzling and must be carefully prepared for if it is to work clearly. Emma initially seems to focus on the shoes in order to draw attention away from the banjo. When Matt discovers the broken banjo and threatens to return Emma's shoes if she does not reveal the culprit who broke it, Emma's fear of losing the shoes must seem to be a credible motive for her disclosure that Sam and Adam broke the banjo. If Emma's temper and occasional expressions of selfishness and irrationality have not been previously emphasized, it will seem absurd that she reveals the guilt of Sam and Adam, thus consciously causing conflict, simply to keep a pair of shoes. Her accusation of Sam and Adam must seem spontaneous, a rash action in response to something importantly threatening to her. The scene should parallel Sam's earlier description of the murder of old man Shelton, a scene brought on by Sam's desire not to lose something he wants.

Matt responds with uncontrolled rage to the knowledge that Sam and Adam have indeed broken the banjo. He calls Sam a "black dog," an insult that recalls his earlier jab at the color of Emma's kin, and lifts a chair to throw at Sam. But Sam, as we know, has a weapon other than physical violence; if Sam defends himself by presenting his knowledge of the murder, and if that information is accurate, Matt will be defeated in a much more permanent way than any physical battle could effect. Sam does use this weapon, and it indeed threatens Matt, but Matt's specific response is somewhat surprising in its demonstration of his immediate command of the situation. Matt shows his guilt not in a renewed or intensified outburst of anger but in sudden quiet, careful moves: He locks the outside door and, with the threat of serious bodily harm, forces Sam and Adam to swear their secrecy.

Matt clearly knows that this new battle is not petty, but, like each of the characters in crucial moments, he is only apparently in control.

Perhaps out of naïveté, certainly out of necessity, Matt accepts oaths of secrecy from Sam and Adam. Although Adam's wink of deceit as those oaths are given is meant for Sam and the audience, this scene can well be played as another in which it is difficult to discern where belief and disbelief are appropriate. Do Sam and Adam merely take the oath to escape a difficult situation, knowing that they will betray their words as soon as they are free? The revealed truth of Sam's version of the murder suggests that, despite his other faults, Sam is not mendacious, yet he is certainly not someone whom we trust. This is clearly an unpredictable situation, which is left tensely hanging as Sam and Adam depart.

The ensuing encounter between Matt and Emma is equally unpredictable. Once she is alone with Matt, Emma shows neither surprise nor anger nor hysteria. Her reaction suggests that crime, even murder, is an ordinary part of her world; it also recalls earlier indications that Emma has been psychologically prepared for the effects of Matt's bad temper and has also known her own inner strength for such a situation. Suddenly, Emma is at her best. She asserts firmly that Matt must make his escape; she has alertly perceived the sign of deceit in Adam's wink; she reasonably argues that when her brother is angry or drunk or both he will not hold to his oath. She also brings forth the cache of money she has carefully been saving for just such a moment of trouble. This secret fund may seen contrived and trite to an audience, but it neither greatly affects subsequent events nor is inconsistent with Emma's self-protectiveness. Her aura of control is so great that we and Matt believe she will get him out of his plight; she moves with a careful and determined sense that this is the only course to take, that any question about the moral or legal justice of the escape she plans for herself and Matt is irrelevant. She and we simply want them to be free, and we believe they will be.

Richardson has set his last trap; he leads us for the final time through belief to disillusion. As Matt pauses before his departure to acknowledge his own weaknesses as a husband and to affirm Emma's goodness, as Matt predicts a better world for the two of them, he hesitates a moment too long. Sam and Adam enter hurriedly with an officer, clearly come to arrest Matt. There is an ambivalent moment for both Matt and the audience in which, having anticipated his escape, we wish it to occur no matter what that entails. But Emma's voice brings Matt and the audience back to some kind of reason: if he harms the officer and escapes now, he will be hanged if ever caught; if Matt yields, his life will be spared and he will only have to serve ten or fifteen years, because the murder of old man Shelton was accidental. Matt departs with the officer, leaving Emma struggling to restrain her tears at the curtain.

The intended impact of these last scenes is clearly moral, but the views of justice and virtue are neither trite nor simple. The strategy of the play is meant to lead the audience to witness and admire love in a relationship where devotion is not immediately apparent or fixed. We should come to accept that drunkenness and bad tempers are evil, not in themselves, but because of the rash actions they provoke. Serious crimes such as murders, brought on by drunkenness and bad temper, are not to be condoned and must be paid for if disclosed, but these should seem of less danger or significance than disloyalty or denial of family bonds. What we are led to wish for this family is simple: survival. But we should understand that in the impoverished world of Emma, Matt, Sam, and Adam, achieving survival is not simple.

To acknowledge the events and lessons of *The Broken Banjo*, an audience must be able to accept the reality of its world. Matt's crime, Emma's serene control of both herself and the situation once she knows of Matt's guilt, and Sam and Adam's treachery must not simply be praised or condemned but must be understood in the context of the complexity of their world. Richardson's creation of consistently believable and interesting characters and his control of events so that they continually surprise aid any spectator to acknowledge this world, to be affected by it.

If, however, the questions the play raises about the ways in which we judge one another, and the lessons it urges about the nature of human virtue, are to be fully confronted, the audience must do more than accept the play's world as real. We should see the world of these people as relevant to our own world. Simply to pity Matt, Emma, Sam, and Adam does not suffice as a reaction to the play's strategy; we are compelled to discover something in them that is like something in ourselves. Such a discovery will involve much more extension of self and imagination for a white middle-class spectator than for a black working-class spectator. Richardson's strategy is not intended to create identification between the white middle-class spectator and the "folk" onstage; he makes no effort to show how the latter are like the former. Thus, the white middle-class spectator, and the black middle-class spectator to a lesser degree, because the racial barrier is eliminated while the economic barrier remains, may be unable clearly to perceive and acknowledge Richardson's characters, despite evidence that he has drawn them vividly. It is possible, for example, that a spectator coming to *The Broken Banjo* with no knowledge of the black working class other than newspaper reports of riots and stereotyped images of these people as drunken or drugged "outlaws" may only find confirmation of his preconceptions in the violence present in the play. This is surely not Richardson's intention, but because he makes no attempt to prevent such a reaction, I conclude that his concern is not primarily with people who might respond in this fashion. Had Richardson wanted to alter the images an "outsider" might have of black folk, he might have presented Matt initially as a notably admirable man and then revealed that he had committed a murder. That no such attempt is made suggests that Richardson was writing for an audience that could easily become engaged in the stage world before them and thus find the problems and behavior of that world to be personally important.

The Broken Banjo, then, is not hostile to black or white middle-class spectators, but it is not basically intended for such traditional theatergoers. *The Broken Banjo* not only exists outside a white world and a middle-class world, it subtly presents alternatives to the values and modes of behavior of a middle-class world. The script makes no attempts to explain Matt's drunkenness, but it does reveal that the drunken man can commit murder, and that "murder will out." Drunkenness is not bad because it is unseemly; it is dangerous because it allows one to act irrationally and to disrupt a community. The play makes no attempt to argue its attitude toward drunkenness or toward the policemen at the end of the script; Richardson assumes that his audience will know that the moral codes of the "inner world" are different from those of the world of courts and policemen. This would indicate an effort on Richardson's part to create a new audience for theater. By writing a script in which the characters are accessible to working-class black people and in which the questions provoked are important to black folk, Richardson has presented the possibility of making serious drama a valuable experience for those for whom the Broadway theater was not only often irrelevant or false in its expressions, but was also socially and financially out of reach. Such an attempt is strikingly similar to that of the Black Arts Theatre of the 1960s. Indeed, the notes and tones heard in *The Broken Banjo* will echo in my subsequent discussion of Ed Bullins's *In the Wine Time*.

III

Few of the tones found in *The Broken Banjo* are to be heard in Richardson's *The Chip Woman's Fortune*. As noted earlier, *The Chip Woman's Fortune* was the first nonmusical drama written by a black person to be presented on Broadway. Like *The Broken Banjo*, *The Chip Woman's Fortune* attempts to involve the audience in a sudden crisis that befalls an ordinary family of black folk; unlike *The Broken Banjo*, however, neither the crisis nor the characters it concerns ever become substantially interesting, disturbing, or amusing.

The plot of *The Chip Woman's Fortune*, though sometimes confused by digressions, is basically simple. Aunt Nancy, an aging woman whose only source of income is the sale of fuel chips—bits and pieces of wood and coal debris she scavenges from the street—has over a long period of time secreted money in a backyard hiding place. She has been carefully saving for the time when her adult son would be released from jail. That time has arrived, but it coincides with a financial crisis for the family Aunt Nancy has lived with during the years of her son's imprisonment. The family, who know nothing of either Aunt Nancy's son or her secret hoard, needs money to make a payment on a Victrola they have purchased on the installment plan. The need is serious because the father of the family, Silas, has been threatened with the loss of his job if he does not meet the payment. The situation forces an obvious conflict for Aunt Nancy, who feels both a debt to this family and a commitment to her son. The situation is resolved by the arrival of Aunt Nancy's son, who, when given his mother's savings, immediately gives Silas more than is needed to meet the overdue payment.

The difference between the two Richardson plays is not simply a matter of the "happy" resolution of the crisis in *The Chip Woman's Fortune* as opposed to the distressing disruption of the family at the conclusion of *The Broken Banjo;* it is not the relative weights of comedy and tragedy that distinguish the force of these two plays. The difference is that in *The Broken Banjo* the audience is held and twisted at every moment by the sense that something is really happening, that "anything can happen next," whereas in *The Chip Woman's Fortune*, although the situation provokes *activity*, neither events nor characters evoke the kinds of questions that suggest movement or possibility in any direction but one. *The Broken Banjo* is made of the stuff of both dreams and nightmares; *The Chip Woman's Fortune* tells a fairy tale but provokes neither the fears nor the wishes so central to both dream material and drama.

My harsh judgments on *The Chip Woman's Fortune* do not, in fact, seem justified in the opening moments of the play. The tone and content of Richardson's directions for setting and the initial lines of dialogue are natural and appealing in their simplicity and sense of character. Darwin T. Turner has noted that, "Although it evidences some of the supposedly exotic quality of black life which appealed to Broadway audiences during the twenties, *The Chip Woman's Fortune* seems realistic in characterization and language."[11] A 1923 review of the play by John Corbin asserts that it: "is an unaffected and wholly convincing transcript of everyday character. No one is glorified or otherwise tricked out to please; no one is blackened to serve as a 'dramatic' contrast. I am referring, of course, to points of essential character, not to that matter of walnut stain."[12] Whether "walnut stain" or "essential" character is Corbin's concern is ironically irrelevant; what is pertinent in comments like those of Turner and Corbin is that although they ignore the crucial strategic problems of the play, they accurately describe the first impressions made on us by *The Chip Woman's Fortune*.

The script of *The Chip Woman's Fortune* begins with a setting described by Richardson as "the very plain dining room of a poor colored family."[13] The room contains little furniture or decoration; its centers of attention are the fireplace, a Victrola, a clock, and a woman sitting huddled near the fire. For a long moment of silence, we are allowed to feel the quiet of this place and wonder about the woman gazing into the fire. The play's first sound is of the seated woman calling for her daugher Emma. An old, bent woman enters and quickly reveals that she is not Emma. The woman is Aunt Nancy. Richardson's directions suggest that, properly costumed and mannered, Aunt Nancy should be an immediately recognizable type. If "everyone of us has seen her kind" (p. 29), Aunt Nancy's appearance will assist the sense of authenticity Richardson is attempting to establish.

For a few lines, Aunt Nancy and Liza, the woman seated by the fire, inquire about each other's health. The dialogue reveals that Liza, a relatively young woman, has been ill, and that Aunt Nancy has been tending to her. Liza's health seems to be improving, but a somewhat despairing sense of irony is expressed about this situation in which the older woman is significantly stronger and hardier then the younger. In the midst of a pedestrian conversation, Aunt Nancy reveals that she is "'spectin' something." What that something is she will not tell, but she does say that Liza will know before the day is out.

One intent of Aunt Nancy's announcement is only too clear as a device of both the character and the playwright. It makes Liza curious; it is meant to make the audience eager for the play to continue. But it is so obvious a stratagem that rather than engaging the audience in the play itself, it may distract us to an awareness of the playwright's craft. It is as if Richardson were proclaiming that something is going to happen in this room, in this play, and such a loud assertion may seem inappropriate to the quiet, naturalistic setting. Perhaps foreseeing this possibility, the script briefly returns its attention to Liza, who now takes a self-pitying stance, grumbling that nothing good ever happens to *her*. Aunt Nancy attempts to relieve this moment by complimenting Liza's physical appearance and, in a gesture of intimacy, whispers to Liza something that makes the latter blush. Exactly what Aunt Nancy whispers is left to the imagination, but the context suggests something teasingly sexual and allows the members of the audience to smile while Aunt Nancy laughs.

The scene turns again to Aunt Nancy's secret, and both Liza and the audience should be satisfied by Aunt Nancy's explanation of her coyness: "Everythin' ud be upside down with other people knowin' what you was thinkin' about" (p. 31). The line is provocative, in terms of both ordinary life and this play, but we are not allowed a pause in which the notion might resonate. Too blatantly and abruptly, Richardson changes the scene. Liza suddenly remembers that she had wanted to see her daughter Emma, and just as Liza reminds Aunt Nancy of this, Emma appears.

The scene that follows between Emma and Liza again mixes easy everyday conversation with lines too overtly meant to forward the action or foreshadow events to come. Most of the conversation suggests an ordinary and believable relationship between mother and daughter. Liza notices that Emma has been combing her hair and putting on powder, and Liza asserts that this behavior is not only new but, in the instance of the makeup, improper. Emma's defense is to respond as little and as tersely as possible. In itself, this suggests a recognizable, if not very interesting, mother-daughter relationship, one that an audience might accept but that evokes no strong emotional responses. Superimposed on the presentation of the tension between Liza and Emma is Liza's attempt to connect her daughter's behavior, which is not, in fact, perceived by the mother as ordinary, with Aunt Nancy's secret. Then, at the end of the scene, Liza suddenly turns her attention to the Victrola. Neither of these concerns is well-motivated, nor is the general structural pattern of the opening scenes subtle or inherently necessary. The spectator can easily perceive that these scenes are composed of mundane conversation altered momentarily by the injection of a "clue" to future events. It will also be apparent to the audience that the plot is furthered by the exit of one character and the entrance of another. Because of their obviousness, these techniques for exposition may trouble some spectators, but most will probably accept such apparent exposition as a familiar mechanism of drama.

The scene between Liza and Emma may be more seriously irritating because it blurs rather than reveals character. Our natural instinct when we are at first presented with Liza is to pity her because of her illness and frailty, but her own self-pity and her persistent and shrill nagging of her daughter diminish our sympathy. Does she mean it when she says that she is "glad somethin' good's happenin' to somebody" (p. 30) in response to Aunt Nancy's excitement, or is that a begrudging statement meant to point out Liza's own condition? Certainly her later assertion of appreciation of Aunt Nancy, "Ain't no way in the world to help lovin' somebody that's good to you" (p. 32), would make claims for Liza's sincere goodwill, but that statement follows many lines of complaint and scolding of Emma. Is Liza's irascibility to be taken as the effect of the frustration of a confining illness or is it the natural, over-protective behavior of the mother of a teen-aged daughter? The matter is never clarified; our response may be different in each instance, and there is no additional evidence offered as to how we should respond. Liza is not, as are the characters in *The Broken Banjo*, a credible and meaningful mixture of human frailties and weaknesses. The problem is that we cannot achieve a sense of knowledge of the particular virtues and faults of this character, because her behavior is erratic throughout. Liza is not a character who undermines our presumptions; she is a conglomerate of features like the Potato Head toys that children construct arbitrarily from a collection of pieces. We are thus forced either to ignore her behavior and some of her comments in order to like or at least pity her, or to deny other indications of character and find her annoying if not unkind. As the play proceeds, we are given no further reason for either response, in terms of necessities either of plot or character. Our response to Liza is not complicated, it is confused.

Emma's character is puzzling in a less ambiguous way. She is clearly a stereotype: a pretty teenager, overdoing her makeup and spending excessive time on her appearance because of a romantic boy-girl fantasy. Her curtness with her mother, her inability to remember Aunt Nancy's instructions concerning the digging of medicinal roots, and her impractical desire for new phonograph records can all be attributed to the immaturity of adolescence. But Emma is eighteen years old. She seems well past the age when she would need to be told to comb her hair, and well into the time when she would be thinking about boys. Yet Emma at eighteen seems to be stumbling in the excitement of her first crush. How is the audience expected to respond to such naïveté? She is clearly a good girl, someone we should like: It is Emma who first articulates an appreciation of Aunt Nancy, pointing the way for her mother. One can only assume that the audience is to admire Emma's virginal innocence, to perceive her mother's protectiveness as proper and virtuous. An audience that would respond in this way must accept the appropriateness of such characterizations. The scene is clearly not meant to be comic. I thus can only understand them in the context of Richardson's conception of his audience as white; his intention would then be to suggest to white people the innocence of black women and to imply the similarity between the parental concerns of a white family and a black family.

Certainly, these signs of Richardson's intentions toward his audience are flimsy in these opening scenes; they, as well as the plot, become firmer in the long scene that follows the entrance of Silas, the husband. Silas appears in his store porter's uniform, which suggests that he has been steadily employed but also indicates the subservient nature of his job: In his work he is not his own man. He immediately and directly tells his wife that he has been "furloughed" for a few days—without pay—because he is overdue on payments for the Victrola. The man who owns the music store where the Victrola was purchased is a friend of Silas's boss. Silas is not only being punished for his bad behavior as a debtor, he is also being trapped. In her naïve way, Liza points to the ludicrousness of the situation: "So that's why you got furloughed, is it? 'Cause they goin' to take the Victrola away?" (p. 34). The large jump in the cause-effect relationship here may seem funny to an audience, but what is bizarre is the way in which society has behaved, not the connection made by Liza. Liza accepts the fact that this is the way people behave; the audience may recognize the truth in such actions but may find it a more perplexing truth than it seems to be for Liza. Nor is the situation as simple as Liza's words would indicate. Silas believes, and we are given no reason to question his judgment, that if he does not make his payments, he will be fired. Silas has been placed in an absurd position: The only way in which he can end his punishment and prevent worse financial disaster is by meeting his payments, but, since his only source of income is his job, the very nature of his punishment prohibits his redemption. He is thus in the dire situation of losing his daily pay when he most needs money to ensure a future income.

Although Silas's position may be absurd, it is not unbelievable. White employers have expected black employees to demonstrate moral virtue in order to retain jobs. It is known that white employers have consistently ignored the reasons for the black person's indebtedness or the effects on him of being fired. Thus, particularly in Richardson's time, Silas's situation might trouble both black and white spectators because of the difficulty in finding a solution, but it would not surprise the spectator or disturb his or her sense of reality.

Nor is the emphasis that the family places on the Victrola incredible. The Victrola can be seen here as a symbol of luxury that becomes a necessity; it serves a function similar to that of the car in the 1950s. The Victrola, like the car, can be bought by a working-class black family that does not have access to other luxuries. Because most people need some luxury to sustain their self-respect, to maintain a sense that life is worth living, they will obtain whatever luxury they can. What is prolematic in the importance placed on the Victrola is not that spectators will doubt the family's concern over the object, but that Richardson makes no attempt to clarify the symbolic necessity of the Victrola. Such an explanation may not have been necessary for black spectators of Richardson's time, but white spectators may too easily ignore the symbolic possibility of the Victrola and perceive it only as an indication of misplaced values.

Uncertainty about the white spectator's response to the Victrola points to a larger problem in Richardson's strategy. It is insufficient to say that the audience, black or white, will accept the authenticity of Silas's situation. Drama, or any art, must not only lead us to recognize the world it presents, but to see that world in a new way or respond to it in a particular and special fashion. But when we look at the details of the scene between Silas and Liza in which they discuss Silas's plight, no pattern emerges to suggest how a spectator, black or white, should react. How are we to feel about Silas's failure to meet the payments for the Victrola? When he says that he has "been doin' a lot o' promisin' and no payin' " (p. 33), are we to condemn his lack of thrift and sense of responsibility, condemn his deceit, or pity his inability to pay despite his hard work and good intentions? Are we to be worried by Silas's assertion that he will "do anything to save [his] job," (p. 34) or, with the puritan ethic assumed in us, do we admire his commitment to work? What good will it do to start charging Aunt Nancy room and board now, when what Silas needs is an immediate fifty dollars? Silas says he won't be able to keep things going if Aunt Nancy doesn't pay some room and board, but this suggests that he has either forgotten or does not accept the threat that he may well lose his job and not be able to keep things going anyway. Aunt Nancy's contribution certainly won't support the entire family.

In this situation, many of Silas's lines are nonsensical; they only make a kind of sense as clues to the revelation that Aunt Nancy has been hiding money in the yard and that Silas is aware of her hidden treasure. A strategy cannot work effectively unless the necessities of plot coincide with or purposefully oppose the necessities of character and situation, and neither occurs in *The Chip Woman's Fortune*. Why must this scene include pages of argument between Liza and Silas about the propriety of charging Aunt Nancy room and board, when the real solution, if indeed Aunt Nancy does have hidden money, is the suppressed hope that Silas blurts out at the end of the scene: "The old woman might get open-hearted and let us have fifty dollars or so" (p. 36)?

The only explanation for such unmotivated circumlocution is that it enables Richardson to maintain the basic virtue of all of his characters. Had Silas immediately thought of asking or demanding money from Aunt Nancy he might have appeared weak, dependent, or unfair. Requesting, instead, room-and-board money, seems only a fair business arrangement. Liza's objection that Aunt Nancy has contributed to the family through her nursing care and the chips and pieces of coal she gathers only partially refutes the justice of Silas's stance but does serve to reveal Liza's own sense of gratitude, loyalty, and fairness. As the following lines suggest, both Silas and Liza appear to be virtuous, but on closer inspection the purity of their motivation seems too great to be accepted comfortably:

> LIZA: Ah hope you ain't mean enough to try to take her money. Ah mean if she's got any.
> SILAS: No, Ah ain't been tryin' to take it. Ah just wanted to see what she had there. [p. 35]

Liza's statement is rhetorical; there is no evidence anyplace in the scene that Silas is mean or thieving. And Silas's response is childlike in its naïveté.

The audience must have difficulty in accepting the image of innocence we are given in Silas's behavior. Here is a grown man, in severe financial trouble, sneaking around his own yard. He surreptitiously watches his tenant guard her treasure, and we are told that his only motive is curiosity. The audience is asked to take this explanation seriously, but to do so demands that we deny common sense.

By the end of the scene, Richardson's intentions toward his audience are even more muddled. Silas departs saying, "Ah reckon Ah better change these clothes so they'll be clean when Ah do go back" (p. 36). The line is a clumsy way of getting Silas offstage. It diminishes any sense of real threat by suggesting that Silas assumes everything will be all right. Richardson's script makes it difficult for either a black or a white spectator to sustain serious concern for Silas's plight. The harsh and thoughtless treatment of Silas by his employer might ring true to a black audience, but there is little that would allow white spectators to be convinced of the seriousness of Silas's plight with his job and money. Richardson's intent is obviously not to confuse. Most likely he assumed that the inconsistencies in the scene would be overcome by the audience's interest in Silas's plight and the revelation of Aunt Nancy's treasure, and that these events would hold enough surprise to carry this part of the drama.

The scene, in fact, presents us with both the main source of tension in the play, Silas's need for money, and its potential solution, Aunt Nancy's hidden treasure. Neither the problem nor its answer in itself suffices to engage an audience. Perhaps Richardson hoped that any spectator would recognize the anxiety of financial pressure, would then be seduced by the exoticism of Aunt Nancy, and thus be led to pay attention. Given this attention, Richardson could then convince the audience of the virtue of his characters. Once the characters have gained the respect of the audience, the various epigrams they spout could also be respected. A line like Liza's "A lot o' people get by doin' the wrong thing" (p. 36) is not a conclusion to the action of the scene, but it is a truism no matter who speaks it. Were it to be acknowledged, it would be because the speaker is a virtuous woman who has captured the attention of the audience.

This strategy is repeated in the next scene, in which Emma returns to contribute her knowledge about Aunt Nancy. Pressured by the news of her father's "furlough," Emma repeats Liza's argument with Silas about the injustice of demanding money from Aunt Nancy. As with Liza in the previous scene, Emma appears generous, fair, kind, and appreciative. In order to defend Aunt Nancy from any further charges of selfishness, Emma reveals the remainder of Aunt Nancy's secret: that Aunt Nancy has been hoarding money for her son who has been in the penitentiary. This news is interesting, but it reeks of melodrama and sentimentality. It also seems inappropriate to Emma's fidelity to Aunt Nancy that the girl should confess her friend's secret so effortlessly; some signs of hesitation, of inner conflict between the desire to defend Aunt Nancy's virtue and the commitment to keep the secret certainly seem called for. In turn, this casual revelation of the last key to the plot diminishes the importance of the event for the audience. Richardson's strategy is again unclear.

After Emma informs her parents about Aunt Nancy's "jailbird" son, the play fragments, with one thrust toward the movement of the plot and another toward the moral instruction of the audience. Emma mentions that the son's crime was "somethin' about a woman" (p. 38); Liza and Silas suggest anxiety and distaste for the situation. If the audience is expected to react to the anticipated arrival of the ex-convict with fear, antagonism, or even aroused curiosity, such responses are quickly undermined. Silas and Liza see the advent of Aunt Nancy's son as just another addition to their many troubles. Liza sees the prospect as threatening to her health if it means Aunt Nancy's departure; Silas is willing to overlook the son if the latter's presence does not interfere with obtaining money from Aunt Nancy. Neither response allows the spectator any specific position from which he can await the play's conclusion.

The combination of the reactions of Silas and Liza to the news of Aunt Nancy's son creates an ambiguity without conflict, a disturbing vagueness that leads nowhere. Nor is any clarity achieved by the series of platitudes that follow, which seem only superficially to be an expression of the immediate experience:

> SILAS: . . . And even if she will agree to help us, Ah'm tired o' this kind o' life. Ah'm sick o' livin' from hand to mouth.
> LIZA: Ah reckon we ought to be thankful to be livin' any kind o' way with all the trouble we had. Some people get along

better'n we do, but a whole lot o' others don't get along as good. Ah only got one consolation besides believin' in the Lord.

SILAS: What's that?

LIZA: That things ain't always been like this, and they might not always be like this. [p. 39]

Such statements must seem trite to a black audience. They can only be seen as meant to educate and evoke sympathy from a white audience, to challenge white people to recognize the frustrations and also the fortitude of black people, and to help fulfill the wish that things will not always be like this. These intentions are socially important and potentially meaningful, even if many might question the political stance or sense of reality that supports them. But it is difficult to imagine that these words, expressed as rhetorical statements, generalized summaries of feeling rather than concrete, specific response to action, do anything except fall flat on unwelcoming ears.

The next scene, the most intriguing and problematic of the play, briefly revives a sense of drama onstage and should engage the audience. Aunt Nancy seats herself like a defendant before a jury to present her testimony to the family. Silas immediately plunges to the point: He tells Aunt Nancy of their troubles with the payments on the Victrola, and asks her for money; either payment for room and board or a loan will suffice. Aunt Nancy at first denies having any money, but challenged with Silas's knowledge, she quickly affirms that she does have some funds that she has been saving for her "child." That single word "child" provokes a lengthy digression from the subject of money. Silas attacks the son as a criminal; Aunt Nancy defends him with a variety of approaches. Most central, Aunt Nancy argues, is the simple bond of a mother and son, a bond no crime can weaken or destroy. Aunt Nancy then suggests that society is now structured in such a way that old people have to take care of the young; although the point needs elaboration, Silas's plight may be a subtle bit of evidence for this truth. Aunt Nancy then argues that going to jail is in itself neither significant nor disgraceful; it is the nature of the crime that matters. Aunt Nancy explains that her son had been going with a woman he thought was "clean," and after finding another man treating his woman roughly, had "beat the man up bad" (p. 41). Her son then realized that this woman had deceived him and beat her too. Aunt Nancy's intention is to clear her son's name by suggesting that, if his action was not good, it was nevertheless understandable and forgivable in terms of the initial harm done to him. One can assume that the audience would respond much as does Silas, who is dubious that such a minor crime would lead to long internment. Silas's doubt is quickly dissolved; Jim, the son, was in fact not imprisoned for his real crime but framed on a larger count by the man he had beaten up. The target of Jim's assault was a man who went to church and wore expensive clothes during the day but "trailed in the gutter" (p. 41) at night; unfortunately, this man had influence in the appropriate places.

The details of the crime, the frame, and Aunt Nancy's defense together complicate the problem, so that it becomes increasingly difficult to discern the real issues and the intentions toward the audience. One element of the scene recalls *The Broken Banjo:* There are minimizing of the importance in itself of a prison sentence and a suggestion of a call for sympathy for crimes arising out of anger and frustration. Disgust is expressed with the manipulative malice involved in framing a man. Implicitly, the audience is urged to refrain from condemning black men simply because they have prison records and to withhold condemnation of black society because it contains ex-convicts.

Throughout the discussion of Jim's past, Aunt Nancy pursues a number of arguments in her son's defense, but none of these are wholly convincing. The implicit analogy that Aunt Nancy makes between Jim and Christ, that "the Lord was locked up" (p. 41) too, is self-defeating. Her mention of the Lord reminds her audiences on stage and off that it is not being imprisoned but what one is imprisoned for that is important. But immediately after that reference, Liza, Silas, *and* Aunt Nancy agree that Jim's crime, beating up a woman, is a bad thing no matter what the cause. Realizing the weakness of her argument, Aunt Nancy is forced to return to the claims of maternal love; she elaborates on this position by urging that forgiveness by a mother is not nearly as great as that by God.

Richardson has avoided or rejected potentially efficacious elements of his own strategy. He could have evoked in a white audience an important, unsentimental response to black crime; he could have planted at least a seed of understanding or a sense of not fully understanding the complexities of meaning of a prison sentence for either a black or a white person. Instead, we are asked not to understand or probe but to forgive and to appreciate maternal love. Again, the overt intention of Richardson's play appears to be to establish the virtue of his characters, all of whom are admirable in this scene because they are able both to perceive and condemn wrongdoing and to forgive and love faithfully. If Jim seems the exception to this establishment of pervasive virtue, his failure to conform to the pattern is only momentary; the concluding scenes of the play attempt to deny the suggestion of human complexity that might be accomplished by contrasting Jim's behavior with that of other characters.

The strategy of the remainder of *The Chip Woman's Fortune* is relatively simple: We are led to a position where Jim appears as the re-

deemed hero, the figure of rescue, who defeats the forces of wickedness personified by the men from the Victrola dealer. This strategy is
initiated with a simple device. As the family awaits the arrival of
Jim—Aunt Nancy anxious to see her son, Silas hopeful that Jim will
share his treasure—a loud knocking is heard at the door. But the new
arrivals are not Jim; they are the men from the music company. This
should elicit the recognition of impending trouble and a sense of fear in
the audience. Such fear can exist, however, only if the connection between Silas's job and the Victrola has remained clear and emphatic;
this connection is brought out again when Silas approaches Aunt Nancy
for money, but its importance has been lost in a mesh of other details.

The impression Jim makes when he does arrive is consistent with
earlier attempts to establish worth and respectability through superficial appearance. He is large and imposing but dressed conservatively in
a blue suit and blue shirt. He is overly polite and immediately expresses his appreciation for the family's kindness to his mother. He is also
instantly revealed as both perceptive and generous; with only a glimpse
of the men outside and an uninformative remark from Silas, Jim
quickly grasps the family's need for money and offers all that he has,
his last fifteen dollars. As Silas starts to accept the money, the men
from the store barge in, roughly demanding the Victrola. Because fifteen dollars will not save the day (or the Victrola), Silas calls attention
to Aunt Nancy's savings, which Jim sends his mother to fetch. Jim then
demonstrates his strength by guarding the door, physically preventing
the men from removing the Victrola. Once Aunt Nancy turns the
money over to Jim, he in turn gives half to Silas. The men from the
store are paid off, and everyone expresses his or her gratitude and
appreciation of everyone else. In the concluding aura of contentment,
Silas announces he will get his work clothes and go back to his job.

Whatever doubts the audience may have had earlier in the play
concerning the credibility of characters and events, no prior action or
attitude was as incredible as Jim's nobility in this final scene. We are
asked to believe that a man who has just been released from prison,
and who has only the suit on his back and fifteen dollars, will empty
his pockets to a man he does not even know. Why should Jim, who
had no job and no known source of income, render himself penniless
for a stranger? Even after Jim is given his mother's savings, there is no
adequate reason why he should give away half his resources, more than
Silas needs. Nothing we have been told about Jim, and nothing we
know about other ordinary men and women, allows us to accept such
extraordinary generosity easily. Jim's role here is that of the fairy
godmother (or godfather), but to accept his role we must perceive the
world in which he functions as one of fantasy, not reality.

The conclusion of *The Chip Woman's Fortune* is, however, ironically coherent with the limits previously established by the script. There is no question but that both Jim and the men from the store will arrive, and Silas has already told us that he hopes Jim will let them have some of Aunt Nancy's money. It has been firmly established that the real evil lies outside the family, and that Jim must be considered as much within the family as his mother. Were Jim to deny money to Silas, he would disrupt even the minimal certainty Richardson has managed to create. No other ending seems probable; yet, as Fannie Hicklin states, the conclusion of *The Chip Woman's Fortune* is "contrived, melodramatic."[14] Although it is possible to imagine other, more believable resolutions to Silas's plight and Aunt Nancy's conflict, the context and strategy Richardson has provided allow for no other ending than one that is facile and sentimental.

Even given these apparent necessities of plot and Richardson's already clear intent to impress the audience with the virtues of his characters, the final portrait of Jim suggests a character so good he is almost laughable. Jim will protect the family not only with his appearance of physical strength but with his intelligence and knowledge of the wicked ways of the world. He asserts that he will immediately find a new dwelling for himself and his mother and that he will get a job; he thus fulfills still another American ideal. If the audience persists in remembering Jim as a man who beat up another man and a woman, that is clearly not the intention of the playwright. Jim is meant to join the ranks of the other good and true characters in the play, whose tarnish, if any should appear, can be quickly and smoothly wiped clean.

The Chip Woman's Fortune is about good people who are rewarded for their virtue. The intent of the play is to make the audience admire them and feel pleased with a happy resolution to their problems. A further intent may be to suggest to a white audience that because black people are worthy of admiration and respect, people in the audience should attempt to prevent plights such as the one presented and aid those in distress through the wickedness of others. But such an intent can only be fulfilled if the audience is persuaded that the characters and the situation are plausible and worth taking seriously. Richardson's confused strategy leads, instead, to disbelief and a sense of trivia.

It is important to stress that my incredulity in reference to *The Chip Woman's Fortune* functions in an entirely different manner than the disbelief felt by the audience watching *The Broken Banjo*. In the latter drama, the audience is repeatedly led to question the honesty and predictability of the people being portrayed; in *The Chip Woman's Fortune* we question the playwright's characterizations; we wonder not if the characters are lying but if the playwright can possibly be telling any truth about people.

The counterpoint of action Richardson employs in *The Broken Banjo* manipulates the audience toward an increasingly lucid sense of the internal necessity and sadness of the world of the play. Each event is tied to another; we perceive these ties, and feel genuine tension and frustration because we, as audience, cannot change the action. In sharp contrast, in *The Chip Woman's Fortune* numerous lines and events distract the audience's attention and are felt as distractions from the search for a solution to Silas's financial problems. Many of the most interesting elements of *The Chip Woman's Fortune*—Liza's illness, the injustice of Silas's punishment, Emma's fantasy about Jim, the false charges that led to Jim's conviction, the hypocrisy of the middle-class man who framed Jim—become superfluous, while the syrupy story of the secret fortune placed in the hands of the frog-turned-prince becomes central.

Another way of looking at the strategic weaknesses of *The Chip Woman's Fortune* can be found by employing Thomas Scheff's notion of "balance of attention" in drama.[15] Scheff argues that for a drama to fulfill its intentions toward an audience it must achieve a balance between the spectator's awareness of himself as a spectator and his identification with characters onstage. In Scheff's analysis, "identification" is not a straightforward activity or an obvious attribute of good drama; three factors are relevant to the degree to which a spectator identifies with a character: the extent to which he shares emotional experiences with characters onstage; the intensity of distress of these characters; and the kind and extent of "discrepant awareness" between characters and spectator. Drawing from the work of Bertrand Evans, Scheff describes "discrepant awareness" as the relationship between what a character knows, pretends to know, or suspects, and what the audience knows. According to Scheff's argument, our identification with characters onstage will be most complete where emotional experiences are fully shared, the distress of the character is intense, and there is no discrepancy between our awareness of the world onstage and that of the character. But such total indentification, Scheff contends, prevents catharsis, or the discharge of emotion crucial to both comedy and tragedy; thus, a balance between identification and self-consciousness must be arranged by the playwright in order for drama to do its work.

In the context of Scheff's propositions, the confusions I have suggested for the spectator of *The Chip Woman's Fortune* become more specific. The black spectator would identify too fully with Silas, because he would presumably share many emotional experiences (although there are some he would probably reject with ridicule), empathize with his distress, and be only slightly more aware than Silas of Aunt Nancy's fortune. Importantly, the spectator and Silas would be equally unaware of the possibility for Aunt Nancy's son's generosity.

Nor is there balance of attention for the black spectator toward any other character: Aunt Nancy is neither in distress nor consistently close enough to the spectator's awareness to evoke identification; Liza is in too much distress and too close to the spectator's awareness to allow sufficient distance for balance of attention. And it is difficult to imagine any black spectator sharing the emotional experiences of Jim or Emma to the extent that identification becomes possible.

For the white spectator, the balance of attention is thrown even further askew. There remains the problem of the degree of distress being too closely coupled with the degree of shared awareness for a modified identification to occur, but, in addition, few of the emotional experiences of the play's world can be presumed to be shared with the white middle-class spectator. This suggests a further discrepancy unexplored by Scheff. The white middle-class spectator might be aware of the emotions experienced by the characters in the play but remote from those emotions, whereas the characters within the play are wholly consumed by their feelings and unreflective. This creates a discrepancy that readily and dangerously leads to condescension.

IV

Any attempt to account for the failure of *The Chip Woman's Fortune* in contrast to the success of *The Broken Banjo* must admit to a degree of conjecture. Even biographical information rarely satisfies our curiosity as to the inconsistencies of quality frequently found within the work of one artist. Because these two plays do, however, begin from a common location—the inner life of poor black families—they provoke pressing questions about their relative degrees of effectiveness. *The Broken Banjo* does affirm DuBois's belief that the inner life of black people is a vital source for American drama; what considerations prevented Richardson from sustaining this energy in *The Chip Woman's Fortune?*

The answer suggested by both internal evidence from the two scripts and production histories is that plays of the inner life of black people in America contain special difficulties in their relationships to audiences. Richardson's two plays remind us that a script must not only contain inner conflict but must set up a conflict for the audience. The audience must be engaged in deciding, choosing—between characters, values, behaviors—in order for it to feel at all and certainly for it to feel the weight of instruction. *The Chip Woman's Fortune* reveals a wariness of allowing the audience such choices. This wariness in turn suggests Richardson's protectiveness here of the world from which he draws his material. In contrast, *The Broken Banjo* is uncompromising in its commitment to the revelation of the inner life of black people. This commitment may well be an indication of concern not only with black people as subjects but as spectators. The hesitations of *The Chip Woman's Fortune* may then be a matter of a confused or ambivalent sense of the racial composition of the potential audience. Richardson may have felt that the inner life of black people could only be exposed to a white audience in the guise of a fairy tale.

Such conjecture does not seem to be paranoid on either Richardson's part or my own. For the white spectator to confront a world that is mysterious outside the theater and suddenly present when the curtain rises is a difficult, if not dangerous, event. Richardson was thus confronted with an unyielding paradox: The truth of the "inner life" was that it contained little contact between black and white; the drama itself had to initiate such contact. To do so meant making the inner life accessible. The deep irony may be that when that world is presented with integrity and without deliberate maneuvers for contact with white spectators, its own poignancy and strength cannot help but move any spectator; when that world is distorted in an attempt to make contact, it becomes impossible to acknowledge.

Nor were Richardson's difficulties limited to the degree of fidelity with which he presented his world. They were further complicated by his conception of theater as a mode of education for his audience. Here, as in other aspects of his work, he seems to concur with DuBois's contention that "all art is propaganda."[16] Evidence for this attitude is apparent in both plays: at its most obvious, *The Broken Banjo* warns against drunkenness and urges loyalty among kin; *The Chip Woman's Fortune* admonishes the debtor and praises charity that begins at home. Importantly, Richardson does not attempt to hide his intention to instruct. Such forthrightness gives credence to his claim that these are folk plays; it is central to the tradition of the folk drama that the work present the audience with one or more morals. Most folk dramas, however, not only can presume a coherent community from which their audience is drawn but can make reasonably certain assumptions about the values of that audience. This kind of community might well be assumed as the audience for whom *The Broken Banjo* was performed, but once Richardson attempted to write for an audience of white spectators or black and white spectators, no such community could possibly be taken for granted. The dilemma then becomes apparent. Simply to unveil the inner life of black people would provide a limited experience for a black audience, but the kind of education relevant to the black spectator, and perhaps necessary to his acknowledgment of a play, would certainly not be appropriate for the white spectator.

Were these obstacles peculiar to Richardson's work, they might be conceptually interesting but of little general importance to an understanding of black drama. However, precisely because Richardson's problems become central to every black dramatist in the twentieth century, his work takes on added significance. From Richardson's time to the present, one black dramatist after another has had to contend with criticism politically and aesthetically hostile to the desire to instruct. And each black dramatist has had to consider just whom he is educating or ignoring and what he is willing to risk in order to make his theater viable.

NOTES

1. Willis Richardson, "Poetry and Drama," *The Crisis* 34 (July 1927), and "The Hope of a Negro Drama," *The Crisis* (November 1919), cited in Fannie E. F. Hicklin, "The American Negro Playwright, 1920–1964," Ph.D. dissertation, University of Wisconsin, 1965.

2. Willis Richardson, ed., *Plays and Pageants from the Life of the Negro* (Washington, D.C.: Associated, 1930), and *Negro History in Thirteen Plays*, compiled by Willis Richardson and May Miller (Washington, D.C.: Associated, 1935).

3. *The Chip Woman's Fortune* was reviewed in the *New York Times* (May 20, 1923) by John Corbin. In recent times, the only published book-length study of black drama, Doris Abramson's *Negro Playwrights in the American Theatre 1925–1959* (New York: Columbia University Press, 1969) fails to mention Richardson at all.

4. Fannie Hicklin's dissertation, cited above, and scattered comments by Darwin T. Turner are the only attempts I know to turn a critical eye to Richardson's drama.

5. I use "naturalism" here to refer to the mode of drama that focuses on the most elemental yearnings and instincts of groups of people, generally from a working-class background; naturalism explores communities and environment as contrasted with realism's concern with the manners and attitudes of individuals in middle-class settings. Gorky's *The Lower Depths* and the relatively unknown plays of Theodore Dreiser are prime examples of theatrical naturalism. While some of Eugene O'Neill's plays like *The Hairy Ape*, have been labeled naturalistic, they combine elements of expressionism and realism with naturalism. All such labels, of course, dangerously limit any full exploration of a drama.

6. Darwin T. Turner, *Black Drama in America* (Greenwich, Conn.: Fawcett, 1971), pp. 25–26, and Fannie Hicklin, "The American Negro Playwright . . . ," pp. 149–50.

7. For a complete listing of plays from this period and citation of particular works by Toomer, Johnson, and Matheus, see the "bibliography of Black

Drama," included in this book. Also published in *Library Bulletin* (Winter 1974–75).

8. LeRoi Jones, *Blues People* (New York: Morrow, 1963), pp. 114–16.

9. I am thinking here particularly of the wavelike pattern of relief and tension of Sophocles' *Oedipus Rex*. In *Oedipus*, there are repeated moments when it appears that Oedipus is about to discover the nature of his identity, but, for many sequences, information can be interpreted contrary to what is true. *Oedipus Rex* moves up and down, in and out through moments of fear and moments of satisfaction for both the audience and the king. I am, of course, greatly oversimplifying the strategy of Sophocles' drama. It is important to note, too, that the strategies of *The Broken Banjo* and of *Oedipus Rex* differ considerably, in that in the former the audience does not know anything about Matt's past, whereas in *Oedipus Rex*, it is expected to be familiar with the myth. This difference, which points at the presence of dramatic irony in *Oedipus Rex* and the absence of that sort of irony in *The Broken Banjo*, charges the kind of tension felt by the audience.

10. Willis Richardson, *The Broken Banjo*, manuscript copy from The Schomberg Center (New York, 1925), p. 303, reprinted from *The Crisis* (1925). All subsequent citations are from this source.

11. Turner, *Black Drama in America*, p. 26.

12. Corbin, *New York Times*, May 20, 1923, cited in Hicklin, pp. 151–52.

13. Willis Richardson, *The Chip Woman's Fortune*, in Turner, *Black Drama in America*, p. 29. All subsequent citations from *The Chip Woman's Fortune* are from this source.

14. Hicklin, p. 152.

15. Thomas J. Scheff, "Audience Awareness and Catharsis in Drama," *The Psychoanalytic Review*, 63, No. 4 (1976), 529–54. Scheff's article is helpful both as a persuasive understanding of the elusive and often mistaken notion of identification and as a tool for evaluating drama in terms of its relationship to audience. My thanks to him for sharing his work with me at an exceptionally opportune time in my own writing.

16. W. E. B. DuBois, *The Seventh Son: The Thought and Writings of W. E. B. DuBois*, ed. with an introduction by Julius Lester (New York: Random House, 1971), II, 319.

3 | THE INNER LIFE ONCE REMOVED: LANGSTON HUGHES'S *EMPEROR OF HAITI*

ONLY TEN YEARS AFTER DuBois's prophecy of two major genres for black drama, a black American playwright wrote an important play that appeared to be about neither the "inner life" of black folk nor "contact" of black and white. This is not to DuBois's discredit, for not even a person of his foresight could have been expected to predict the ingenuity with which *Emperor of Haiti* escaped these categories. Nor could anyone have foreseen the astonishing career of the author of *Emperor of Haiti*, Langston Hughes.

Langston Hughes was only eighteen years old in 1920, at the beginning of the efflorescence of black American art known as the Harlem Renaissance. Yet he became, and has remained, the paradigmatic figure of that period. John Hope Franklin refers to Hughes as the Renaissance's "most cosmopolitan as well as its most prolific writer," as a man who merited being called "Shakespeare in Harlem."[1] Such descriptions of Hughes as a true "Renaissance man" are not exaggerated; though best known as a poet, Hughes also made significant contributions to American letters as a writer of fiction, an author of articles on history and black culture, an editor of anthologies, and a playwright and producer for the theater. The achievement of Langston Hughes is characterized not only by abundance and variety of work but also by a continuity of effort that was not exhausted until his death in 1967.

In the context of such diverse artistic interests, Hughes's prolificacy as a playwright is remarkable. His first published drama, a play for children entitled *The Gold Piece*, appeared in 1921; from that time, until his death, he wrote eight full-length plays, three one-act plays, and more than twenty other scripts for opera, radio, and film. Moreover, in the 1930s and 1940s Hughes was involved in establishing three Afro-American theater companies: the Suitcase Theatre in Harlem, the Negro Art Theatre in Los Angeles, and the Skyloft Players in Chicago.[2]

Of Hughes's eight full-length plays, five were written in the 1930s. All of these were produced. The Gilpin players in Cleveland presented performances of *Emperor of Haiti, Front Porch, Joy to My Soul,* and *Little Ham. Mulatto,* written in 1935, was produced on Broadway and ran for an entire year, thus having the longest Broadway run of any play by a black American dramatist before the 1958 production of Lorraine Hansberry's *A Raisin in the Sun.* Another of Hughes's plays written in the 1930s, a one-act drama entitled *Don't You Want to be Free?,* ran at the Harlem Suitcase Theatre every weekend for two years, beginning in 1938.

In terms of artistic productivity and audience appeal, Langston Hughes could certainly have made claims to success as a playwright; but, as was true of Willis Richardson's, Hughes's importance in American theater has dissolved because of neglect by critics and producers of repertory theater in the United States.[3] Doris Abramson presents detailed descriptions and thematic analyses of *Mulatto* and *Don't You Want to Be Free?,* and Fannie Hicklin pays considerable attention to a survey of the plots of Hughes's plays while offering brief critical comments, but only Darwin T. Turner, in his 1968 article "Langston Hughes as Playwright," has made a careful and conscious critical attempt to reveal the strengths and weaknesses of Hughes's dramas.[4]

Despite the lack of thorough criticism of Hughes's plays, commentators have been aware of the enormous variety of form and situation in Hughes's scripts. Hughes's vision ranges from the comic to the tragic to the historical, and the environments he depicts include Haiti and the Deep South as well as Harlem. Among Hughes's plays are such differently structured works as *Don't You Want to Be Free?,* a collage of historical scenes written in 1936, and *Tambourines to Glory,* a comedy with music written in 1963.

Because of such diversity in Hughes's dramatic works, no single play of his stands out clearly as representative of the whole of his dramaturgy. I have chosen to examine *Emperor of Haiti* for two reasons: It captures, sustains, and synthesizes moments of emotional intensity and intellectual complexity with a cogent sense of theatrical effect; and, in its use of historical event as both context and metaphor, it suggests a type of black drama not otherwise discussed in my work. Because of its particular historical location and its concern with the internal strife of conflicting groups of black people in Haiti, the play appears to draw its energy from sources distinct from the inner life of black Americans or the contact of black and white Americans. While I will argue that *Emperor of Haiti* combines rather than escapes both of DuBois's categories, the apparent distinctness of this play merits careful analysis. *Emperor of Haiti* is also a play to which Langston Hughes felt a deep commitment. It was first produced as *Drums of Haiti* in 1935, revised and given the title *Emperor of Haiti* in 1938, recreated as an opera, *Troubled Island*, in 1949, and revised for the final time as a drama in 1963.[5] My discussion is based on the final script, but it seems appropriate to view it as a play of the 1930s, because those were the years of its initial conception.

II

Emperor of Haiti begins in the midst of the Haitians' struggle for freedom from the French. The date Hughes gives for its setting is 1791, but the kinds of historical events presented indicate that a later date, around 1803, would be more accurate.[6] The play is framed by real and important historical events: The overthrow of Napoleon's soldiers by black Haitians in 1803 and the assassination in 1806 of the self-proclaimed emperor of Haiti, Jean Jacques Dessalines. Act I occurs on the eve of what is presented as the crucial battle of victory for the slave-leader Dessalines and his fellow Haitian rebels.

There is little exposition of the preceding years of struggle in Haiti, although there is a clear sense of expectancy and preparation among the enslaved blacks who are about to battle for their freedom. The focus is immediately on Dessalines, and the first climactic moment of the play comes with the announcement that Dessalines has been elected leader of the Haitian forces.

In a mood of excitement and confusion, the first act of *Emperor of Haiti* reveals the commitment of the Haitian slaves to securing their liberty and presents Dessalines's rise to power. He stalks the forest rendezvous like the tiger that becomes his symbol. He is surrounded by supporters: Azelia, the woman who loves him; Martel, the wise old man who counsels him; enslaved cohorts who admire and respect him; mulattoes who tolerate him. The vision of victory, for both nation and individual, is present at the beginning of the play; by the end of Act I, Dessalines's speeches and the proximity of battle have created a sense that triumph over the French is an urgent necessity.

Act II occurs several years after the momentous victory prophesied in Act I. It portrays Dessalines, now emperor, at both the peak of his power and the moment before his downfall. This central portion of the play continually contrasts surface and interior. Dessalines's personal success has been astonishing: He has achieved liberty for his country; he is now married to a beautiful, cultured mulatto woman; he abides in extreme luxury; he has the power of an emperor. Beneath this surface comfort, however, lies a tangled web of deceit, distrust, and discontent. The country is barely surviving under the weight of severe economic and educational problems. The peasant workers permeate the land with complaints of excessive labor, and they have little real reward for their efforts. The mulattoes are envious of Dessalines's power and are plotting his overthrow. Dessalines's wife despises him. We witness Dessalines's struggles to find paths to stability and growth for his country, and his dismay at his own lack of education, but we also see that the fruit of his ignorance is a lack of awareness of the depth of fraud and dissatisfaction surrounding him. While Dessalines is preparing and later enjoying an elaborate but purposeless banquet, many of his supposed followers are readying themselves to kill their leader and take over Haiti that very night. Act II, like Act I, concludes with Dessalines about to go into battle, but in this instance, Dessalines alone expects victory.

Act III takes place the day after Dessalines's last venture into battle. The setting is a marketplace in a small fishing village on the coast of Haiti. What has only been reported or envisioned in Dessalines's palace in Act II is now revealed: The women in the marketplace articulate their discontent with the inequities and difficulties of their present lives in contrast to their earlier illusions of the meaning of freedom. The mulattoes, including Dessalines's wife, enter the marketplace; having defeated Dessalines, they are now about to sail for France. Dessalines confronts the enemy leaders with his sword and is shot to death. Azelia, the woman who first supported and still loves Dessalines, discovers a small group of ragamuffins scavenging the lifeless body of the fallen hero. In death, Dessalines is not only destroyed but demeaned.

The brief plot outline initially suggests a conventional dramatic strategy. The audience is immediately brought to admire and sympathize with Dessalines, then to feel fear and anxiety as we perceive his danger before he does, and, finally, to feel pity and sorrow but also a sense of inevitability at his death. This strategy is both modern and classical, in that Dessalines is an oppressed man and a king. In his double role, Dessalines elicits empathy while simultaneously commanding respect.

In at least one sense, Hughes employs a classical strategy only eventually to demonstrate its flaws for a modern audience. In classical tragedy, our admiration for the hero, and thus our final sense of loss, is often demanded initially because of the political position of the character. In *Emperor of Haiti*, Dessalines evokes the most admiration and sympathy when he is a slave, the least when he is emperor. In this play, Hughes seems to anticipate Arthur Miller's theory that "Insistence upon the rank of the tragic hero, or the so-called nobility of his character, is really but a clinging to the outward forms of tragedy."[7]

Hughes employs the outward forms; he does not cling to them. The foundation of the strategy of *Emperor of Haiti* seems to me very close to another of Miller's beliefs: Hughes evokes from the audience a tragic feeling by placing us "in the presence of a character who is ready to lay down his life if need be, to secure one thing—his personal dignity. From Orestes to Hamlet, Medea to Macbeth, the underlying struggle is that of the individual to gain his 'rightful' position in his society."[8] Hughes places us in the presence of Dessalines and vivifies Dessalines's struggle for human dignity, but this is neither the playwright's sole intent nor his central strategic device. Once having involved his audience in that struggle, in Act II he tosses us out to a place where we have to find our own bearings. Having gained his " 'rightful' position in society," Dessalines is stripped of his personal dignity. The audience has been led to faith in a man who now appears pathetic and deplorable. In Acts II and III, we are brought to feel fear and sorrow, not for the "Emperor" but for the man, the ordinary person, who has no place to be.

The revelation at the beginning of Act II of the changes in Dessalines and the only superficial success of Dessalines's empire is the essential surprise of the play, the trap that catches the audience unaware. By leading the audience to recognize how unpredictable the world before them is, Hughes draws the audience's attention closer to that world. Because we cannot find satisfaction in Dessalines himself, we are forced to turn to the world surrounding him, and here we find ourselves trapped again. From the opening moments of the play, Hughes has set up two interlocking movements; Dessalines appears to move toward his rightful place by leading himself and his people out of bondage; the slaves seem to move from their enslavement to their freedom by their struggle against and eventual defeat of their white, foreign rulers. But just as our initial perception of Dessalines and his achievement is incorrect, so are our early understandings of the difficulties of the community revealed to be facile and finally wrong.

An important element of Hughes's strategy is to make the original opposition that of whites against blacks, slaveholders against the enslaved. In this conflict, the details of the sufferings of the slaves evoke our sympathy for the black Haitians and our anger toward the white profiteers. Therefore, even a white spectator might share the characters' anticipation of satisfaction from defeat of the whites. Hughes, however, brings his audience to a second and parallel experience of pity and anger when he presents us in Act II with black men who are liberated in name but are now enslaved to arduous manual labor or imprisoned in roles they do not know how to play. We are here shown distinctions made on the difference not between white and black but between black and black, mulatto and black. The new oppressions are less overt but equally rampant and insidious. If we sorrow for the peasants at the end of Act III, it is not because of the defeat of noble strivings, or for the losses suffered in achieving order or justice, but from an emphatic sense of futility, a realization that past hopes were merely illusions, destructive in their final effects.

To surprise an audience while sustaining their concern about the turns in events and changes in behavior witnessed in Acts II and III of *Emperor of Haiti*, Hughes in Act I must fully engage the spectator in his characters and their plight. To accomplish this, he begins his play in a setting that impresses the audience with both its tranquillity and its potential for danger. The opening curtain reveals an abandoned sugar mill on a night brightened by stars and a full moon. Our attention is initially focused on the still figure of Josef, a young black man who stands before the mill inspecting his curved cane knife. As sounds are heard in the underbrush, Josef's body tenses. This visual impression of Josef, as well as the opening passwords exchanged with Azelia, Dessalines's woman, immediately evoke anxiety in the audience. Clearly, we are observing some important, covert event; the audience is separated from those onstage by curiosity about the events at hand, but united with them through the tension the characters and setting create and express. This opening moment is one of the few units of the play in which the audience knows and understands less than the central characters of the drama. Hughes has begun his drama by immediately establishing the "balance of attention" described in the preceding chapter. The intense distress of Josef and Azelia leads us to empathize with them instantly, but we are kept from excessive loss of self-consciousness by the "discrepancy of awareness" between us and them.[9]

The ensuing conversation between Josef and Azelia satisfies our curiosity, indirectly introduces Dessalines, and arouses our sympathy for the plight of the slaves. Azelia arrives bearing weapons, suggestive of her own active part in the slave rebellion that we quickly discover, is to erupt that night. She suggests motivation for that rebellion by narrating how that very day Dessalines had been whipped for leaving the plantation without permission. The grotesqueness of this whipping is emphasized by Azelia's revelation that the slaveholders mocked Dessalines for having "too much name" for a slave. The account of the beating makes concrete the suffering of the slaves and should elicit from the audience sympathy for the victim and anger at the master.

Martel, an aging slave-philosopher, is then introduced. Martel's language is distinctive; it is lofty, metaphoric, quaint, and archaic: "Even now yon moon looks out across the silver ocean, watching the slave ships sail toward the western world with their woeful burdens. The cries of black men and women, and the clank of chains in the night, rise up against the face of the moon."[10] Because Martel's language is so different in syntax and diction from the language of Azelia and Josef, who initially speak an ordinary twentieth-century American English undistinguished by dialect, Martel's speech may call attention to itself and distract the audience from the tension in the situation. But Martel's peculiar use of words elevates the scene from the potential bog of melodramatic sentimentality toward a reflective distance. Martel's references to Nature, to the woes of all black men and slaves, and to Africa suggest that this moment in history has implications for all men who have been physically or psychologically enslaved. By leading us to contemplate the resonances of this moment, Martel reminds us that we are in a theater and momentarily removes us from the distress of the drama's present. His language also distinguishes him from the other slaves; Martel's overt use of poetic figures suggests that he is a figure for both slaves and spectators to respect.

Martel's entrance also allows for further exposition of the situation and the introduction of central motifs of the play. We are told that the beating of drums will herald the rebellion and that Dessalines has been elected leader. Martel warns that the rebels must be wary of traitors in their own midst. Not much attention is given to the warning about traitors; however, the anticipation of the sound of drums and the satisfaction at Dessalines's election serve to prepare the audience for the next entrance—that of Dessalines himself.

In his presentation of Dessalines, Hughes employs a major device of Act I: He tosses out a seed that will sprout in the reversals of Act II and Act III, but quickly shifts loose soil around that seed so that it is barely visible. Dessalines's second line is, "I'm your leader, Josef" (p. 58). The audience might be dismayed by the hint of arrogance in that line were it not for Dessalines's immediate absorption in the plans for the night. The new leader quickly demonstrates by his questions about the battle strategy and his articulate, impassioned condemnation of the white slaveholders that he is in control of his role and committed to his task. At this point, past horrors are described, and Dessalines speaks of his commitment to alter radically the world in which these atrocities have existed. This serves both to encourage the audience's desire for a slave victory and to create admiration for Dessalines. No white person is seen in this act or elsewhere in the play. White people remain, particularly early in the play, the enemy outside. To the slaves, the whites are not human personalities but the hands that hold the whips; to the audience, the whites are presented only as the persecutors of the folk on stage who want their freedom. This creates an alliance of

audience with slave characters in an easy detestation of an abstract opponent. Such an abstraction also allows white members of an audience
to desire the downfall of the white masters without the simultaneous
confusion of self-loathing. The contact of blacks and whites, then, appears not to be a focal subject of this play but an assumption that the
world of this drama attempts to reject.

One element of Hughes's strategy in this first act is to alternate
between revelations of the ideals and social contexts of the rebellion
and exposition of the ways these events specifically touch particular
characters. Proclamations of commitment to the cause evoke the fears
and hopes of individual characters. Their concerns are then diminished
by reminders of ideology. The essential tool in this movement is Dessalines, who as friend, lover, or leader attempts to minimize the particular anxieties of his followers. Yet he cannot help being periodically
involved in their concerns.

When Azelia attempts to call Dessalines's attention to their love
and to her fears about their lives and personal commitment, Dessalines
clearly wishes to avoid such conversation but is forced to respond. In a
brief but crucial scene, Azelia reminisces about the past pleasures of
their love. Dessalines reminds her of the limitations of that love without freedom; he has no desire to indulge in sensual memories; his
thoughts are for the future and his people's cause. But Azelia's repeated avowal in this scene of love and fidelity to Dessalines seems
finally to gain the response she desires: He will marry her "like white
folks" after the slaves have triumphed. Seconds after their kiss, however, he is distracted by the anticipation of the approaching crowd of
warriors.

Like his presentation of Dessalines, this almost romantic interlude
is another of Hughes's uncultivated seeds. An audience cannot help but
feel an ambivalent reaction to the contrast between Azelia's affirmations
of personal affection and Dessalines's absorption in the grand changes
he is about to effect. We can empathize with Azelia's love for her man
and the anxiety that love produces; we can also admire Dessalines for
putting aside personal needs and feelings at a moment when the love
of an idea and of an entire people is crucial. These two responses can
further provoke an audience to impatience with Azelia for pushing her
own concerns upon Dessalines. The audience may also become annoyed with Dessalines for his lack of genuine tenderness. Hughes employs Dessalines's promise of marriage to diminish these tensions; we
are meant to miss this scenes's importance, only to have it revealed at
a later point.

The next scene introduces the slave Congo, who has been hiding in
a box of weapons in order to guard the precious guns. The scene serves

both as comic interlude to relieve the tension created by Azelia and Dessalines and as reinforcement of our admiration for Dessalines. Congo is a clown; his appearance from within the box of weapons can easily be played for humor as a jack-in-the-box routine. Congo's wit and laughter should serve as a pleasing relief from Dessalines's implacable earnestness, but Congo is not meant to appear too much the clown. He mocks the stupidity of the whites, noting that the slavemasters presumed the blacks were doing voodoo dances when, in fact, the slaves were plotting rebellion. In response to Dessalines's mention of his own beating that day, Congo quips, "That's nothing. My master uses a tree limb on my head" (p. 63). Within the repartee of this exchange, however, Congo makes clear the respect for Dessalines among the slaves, and, in response, Dessalines proudly asserts his new authority as leader. Congo also remarks his own African birth, and the note of pride in that heritage is clear. The scene can be important in further establishing black attitudes toward the white oppressors and the pride of both Dessalines and his followers. The audience should not confuse Congo with a stereotyped black fool, butting his own jokes at himself. He is a cousin not only of the Elizabethan court jester, or of Lear's fool, but also of Hughes's character Jesse B. Semple, whose tales of his daily life in Harlem are those of a man who is "laughing to keep from crying."[11]

Congo's exchanges with Dessalines are interrupted by the sound of others approaching. The expectation of new arrivals forces the expression of another area of tension for Dessalines, Azelia, and Congo. The sound heard is that of horses' hooves. Congo's inference, "It must be a mulatto. . . . No Negro's got a horse to ride on" (p. 64), leads the audience to make an assumption about the identity of the newcomer and indicates the resentment felt by the black slaves toward the mulattoes. As the characters on stage await the person on horseback, Congo expresses his distrust of the mulattoes. Azelia agrees that they look down on the slaves because the latter are darker complexioned (p. 64). Dessalines attempts to counter this distrust with two arguments: The mulattoes hate the whites, too, and the black rebels need the intelligence and education that the mulattoes bring to the rebellion.

No agreement is reached about the mulattoes' trustworthiness, but the dispute is ironically altered by the arrival of the rider. The man who appears is, in fact, not a mulatto but a black slave. Since Congo's prediction has been wrong, we can now become skeptical about his judgment of the mulattoes. But this skepticism about the merit of Congo's attitude is immediately deflated by the message the rider brings. The rider, a slave named Xavier, has come to announce that a mulatto has turned traitor to the rebels' cause and has warned the whites. Dessalines, outraged, immediately orders that both whites and "false mulattoes" (p. 65) be shot down on the road. For a moment, Dessalines's defense of the mulattoes seems negated; but when Congo says, in effect, "I told you so," Dessalines's response is a restrained, "They're not all alike, Congo. Some we can trust. Vuval is one. Stenio's another" (p. 65). We have no reason to distrust Dessalines's judgment. Indeed, he presents himself here as the ideal leader, a man who can act swiftly and clearly when necessary, but whose essential understandings are not swayed by the events or passions of the moment. Hughes's strategy is to instigate distrust in the audience toward the mulattoes while simultaneously setting up Dessalines as a rational man whose perceptions we can readily accept. By increasingly manipulating the audience to admire Dessalines and accept his perceptions of the world around him, Hughes intensifies the surprise and disappointment we shall experience in Act II when the errors of Dessalines's perceptions are revealed.

The remainder of Act I moves the audience to ever increasing regard for Dessalines and avowal of his cause. Women, children, slaves, and free mulattoes gather in an atmosphere of tense excitement and eagerness for victory. Yet, despite the sense of a shared concern, the black slaves and the mulattoes stand apart from one another; mutual suspicion permeates the jungle enclave. The blacks question the depth of commitment of the mulattoes; the mulattoes are wary of what they take to be the ignorance of the slaves. Although both mulattoes and blacks remain onstage throughout this scene, Hughes shifts our attention from one group to the other by varying the amount and kind of activity and the volume of sound projected from each cluster of people. At one moment our interest is led to a group of black slaves who are performing a voodoo ceremony. The elaborate costumes of the *papaloi* and *mamaloi*, the high priest and priestess of voodoo, and the loud and distinctive sounds of rattles, drums, and chants engage the audience thoroughly for a few moments. Our attention is held by the vivid movement, colors, and cadences of the voodoo ceremony, and by its difference from previous stage actions.

After a brief period, Dessalines moves the focus away from the voodoo ritual by asking the participants to be more quiet so that he can confer with other leaders of the rebellion. As the noise from the priests and their followers subsides, we hear the mulattoes' intellectual, analytical comments about the choice of Dessalines as leader and about the goals of the rebellion. The juxtaposition of the two groups and their activities reveals a sharp contrast between spontaneity and control, impassioned fervor and cool contemplation. Hughes clearly sets the two groups apart for the audience, but it is not clear whether he wishes to urge the audience's sympathies toward one group or the other. The display of voodoo practices might well affirm a white spectator's notions of the exotic qualities of black life.

No attempt is made to explain the significance of the voodoo ritual; thus responses will vary considerably, depending on a combination of ethnic and cultural backgrounds. White spectators might find the ceremony entertaining but foolish; this would allow them to feel a condescension toward the black slaves. Black spectators might enjoy the presentation of the voodoo ritual as an expression of a culture of which they feel proud.[12] If they are pleased by the voodoo presentation, they might then be annoyed when Dessalines and the mulattoes draw attention away from the ceremony. Some black Christian Americans might, of course, be embarrassed by the presentation of other black men and women practicing what they may see as a religion more primitive than their own; such a spectator might see the voodoo as a disturbing appeal to the fantasies of white spectators. The mention of voodoo practices may also simply be meant to sharpen for the audience the recognition of cultural differences between black and white worlds.

The portrayal of the mulattoes is equally ambiguous. The value the mulattoes place on education, expressed just after the mention of voodoo practices, could raise doubts concerning the blacks' ability to make intelligent decision, but because Dessalines is included in those labeled as "ignorant," the mulattoes' stress on education may seem elitist and pedantic.

These ambiguities of material and effect are not resolved. An emotional rather than logical resolution of tensions onstage is created by recalling what is common to both blacks and mulattoes—hatred of whites. Dessalines seizes the moment and brings his followers together through an impassioned speech that uses a variety of rhetorical devices to ignite their emotions. Dessalines's speech is a masterpiece of persuasive rhetoric. He employs identification with the audience, nostalgia, and abrupt switches from calm restraint to intense anger to gain control of both his onstage and offstage audiences. Dessalines vividly recalls the suffering of the past and of the day of battle. He proclaims the French to be "monsters of terror" and describes specific instances of French cruelty to the blacks. Dessalines cries "freedom," "blood," "kill" to his onstage audience, and they, in turn, cry back to him "Free, free, kill to be free" (p. 75).

The crowd before Dessalines has lost all hesitation by the end of his exhortation; they know only hatred and the need for freedom. Because the theater audience has been led through Act I to justify that hatred and embrace the reality of the need for freedom, we now feel a strong empathy for those on stage. The line between play and audience remains, but we are meant to desire the success, the victory, of those on stage.

I imagine the audience of *Emperor of Haiti* breathing a sigh of release at the curtain of Act I. A few moments are needed to draw away from the intensity of the emotion. The echoes of the drumbeats that have filled the theater a few moments before heralding the ensuing battle have died out, and our senses turn to the opening curtain of Act II, where we hope to discover the sought-after victory.

The first images of Act II satisfy our desires. Dessalines is onstage, seated in an "empire style" chair "of plush and gilt with a high back." Behind him are red velvet curtains and a coat of arms. The scene is striking in its contrast to the setting and appearance of Dessalines in Act I, but the surprise it may evoke in the audience is amended by the pleasure in the recognition that Dessalines and his forces clearly have succeeded in their mission. Dessalines is occupied with affairs of state: he is engaged in discussion with Vuval, a mulatto poet who briefly appeared in Act I and now seems to be counselor to Dessalines.

Our initial sense of satisfaction is quickly disturbed as the actual situation in the state is revealed through Dessalines's conversation with Vuval. The mulatto is in the process of taking care of correspondence for Dessalines, who can neither read nor write. The dialogue reveals that the class and economic structures of the new Haiti are creating enormous problems. Money is needed for roads, education, the operation of the government and the military. There are only two sources of funds: the ex-slave peasants and the landowners, who are mostly mulattoes. The peasants have barely enough to survive and are resisting increased work; the "nobles," who seem concerned only with increasing their own riches, expect favors and patronage from the Emperor. A huge gulf exists between a large, poor peasant class and a small, elite upperclass. There are no educated, concerned middle-class men and women to train and teach the peasants and to present the possibility of a gradual change in class structure.

The extravagant life-style enjoyed by Emperor Dessalines exacerbates the political and economic difficulties in Haiti. The contrast between the luxury surrounding Dessalines and the poverty of many of his followers is rhetorically and dramatically presented. Dessalines blandly states, "Everybody in Haiti wants to dress like me—and I'm the Emperor" (p. 76). But the contrast is more effectively conveyed by the obvious juxtaposition of the discussion of economic problems with references to an approaching royal banquet. The contrast almost reaches the point of parody. Just after Dessalines has cried out in anger, "Does no one, loving Haiti, find his pay in doing for her?" (p. 77), Popo, a former slave, enters to announce that he has laid out the robes of state for that evening's banquet. Popo continues, "I put the ruby crown out, too, and polished up the scepter" (pp. 77–78). The spectator now knows that although the blacks of Haiti won their victory and enthroned Dessalines, he is failing as a leader and as a man.

The audience has experienced only a moment of joy and relief; disappointment and confusion quickly become the only appropriate responses to the new empire and Emperor of Haiti. Our expectations have been only superficially fulfilled. We are led to understand that neither victory in battle nor the destruction of one oppressive enemy suffices to relieve either the woes or the corruptions of men. A weakness in Hughes's dramaturgy is apparent here. He has presented the new Haiti too abruptly; the audience would be more troubled by the inequities and hypocrisies of Dessalines and his government if the corruption were gradually revealed in such a way that we could *discover* it. Hughes has chosen the strategy of surprise, which is theatrically impressive but will not sustain the concern of an audience. Once the surprise is effected, we are left to witness at a distance rather than puzzle out the denouement; any new information we receive about the empire of Haiti will simply be an affirmation of what we already know. We may even retreat to an immediate examination of our own gullibility and susceptibility to the emotional pleas of Act I. This self-examination could better occur after the play.

Hughes takes the risk of losing his audience after the initial revelation of Act II. There is a profit to be gained by his strategy, however. If the audience recognizes at this point that it has erroneously cast aside reason under the power of emotional appeal, it may actually pay closer attention to the complexity of character and situation that becomes apparent in the remainder of Act II. The struggles of a man torn between the desire for personal power and political ideals, and the struggles of a nation torn by racial conflict and economic strife, have only begun to be exposed.

This exposure continues with the entrance of Martel. He and Dessalines discuss their dreams for Haiti. These dreams are not alike, and neither vision seems immediately "right" for the country. Gonzalo-like, Martel urges a country in which all men are free, in which hatred for white men is cast aside, in which "free men can dream a bigger dream than mere revenge" (p. 79). Dessalines, however, still recalls the blows on his back. He pragmatically argues that Martel has too big a dream, that they should be satisfied with creating a Haiti where black men can live in peace (p. 79).

Hughes's dramatic strategy in presenting these contrasting dreams is not clear. The playwright sets up the argument in such a way that Martel's views should have the greater impact. Martel has previously been presented as wise, eloquent, and humane; Dessalines has not only just demonstrated his hypocrisy and illiteracy, but in this dialogue he flaunts his success and distorts his role when he emphasizes to Martel, "I'm their Liberator. The peasants know that. They know 'twas Dessalines alone that drove the whites away." Despite the signs of Martel's wisdom and Dessalines's hubris, we do not know either character well enough at this point to wholly trust one or the other. The substance of the arguments does not convince us that Dessalines is ignorant or wrong. Dessalines perceives the concrete need for dams, factories, education; hard work seems the only path to these goals. He states convincingly that he has worked harder than anyone, and his practical sense that hard work by black men should first yield fruits for black men seems just.

The strategic problem here is that neither argument and neither speaker has been presented with sufficient cogency or subtly to convince a spectator of views other than those held before seeing the play. The white or black spectator who has previously believed in assimilation is able to ignore Dessalines's arguments because Dessalines has been shown to be naïve and arrogant; the spectator, most probably a black person, who has been committed before the play to the securing of separate black power could readily affirm Dessalines's arguments and remain deaf to Martel's point of view because Martel has not acted in any way that would clearly engage the spectator's sympathy. Since the play has not yet provided any distinct indications of the audience for which it was intended, we only presume that Hughes hoped with this scene to challenge both sorts of preconceptions, but that the playwright failed to make such challenges inevitable.

We are not allowed to linger with this problem. If the audience is not yet impressed with the changes in the style and values of Dessalines, we should become so in the next scene, which introduces the Emperor's wife. Dessalines's consort is not Azelia, the woman whom we would have assumed from Act I to be his mate. His consort is a beautiful mulatto woman named Claire Heureuse. Claire's first speech and her initial gestures tell all we need to know about her. She chides Dessalines for working too much, speaks of the servants as "stupid," and pats her husband on the cheek "as if he were a child" (p. 80). Although Dessalines clearly sees the beauty and breeding of his wife as a reflection of his own good taste and lofty position, for the audience, the replacement of the faithful, courageous Azelia with callous and condescending Claire Heureuse only further demeans Dessalines. To make the impression more profound and to satisfy the audience's curiosity about Azelia's plight, Hughes uses the brief appearance of Claire to remind Martel that he has news of Azelia. Azelia, Martel reports, has refused a proferred pension and is said to "look much older than she really is" (p. 80). Dessalines quickly changes the subject; it is one he wishes to avoid. He remembers that he once loved Azelia, but he has no sense of the woman's human dignity. He even puzzles that Azelia would not accept a position as a servant in his court. Dessalines's downfall, like that of Lear, has clearly much to do with his inability fully and genuinely to acknowledge other people.

Like the first shock of Act II, the second surprise—Dessalines's marriage to Claire Heureuse and his rejection of Azelia—seems to me excessively emphatic, if we are to retain any respect for Dessalines. But Hughes's strategy here is clearly to command our disappointment rather than our respect. As Scene i of Act II approaches its close, Dessalines, ignoring Martel's soft warnings of moderation, declares, "I'm a king! I'm on top! I'm the glory of Haiti!" (p. 81). At best, we can feel pity for the man who makes this boastful outburst, but because he is a man, an adult, his proclamation of supremacy may well assault the audience as odious arrogance.

To lead us so rapidly from admiration for a hero in Act I to disapprobation for a self-glorifying dictator in Act II creates the effect of a bizarre dream for the audience. The seeds of excessive pride, or irrationality, of indifference to love, and of racial conflict now become the material of the grotesque and destructive vision of Act II. Hughes's task then is to sustain the quality of nightmare while making the subsequent events of the play believable and meaningful. His strategy is to shift our attention from the internal disintegration of the hero, Dessalines, to the conflict between parties and the disintegration of the state. The final section of Scene i, Act II makes this shift firmly. We witness two mulatto leaders—Vuval, the poet, and Stenio—in a brief discussion that reveals more of the explosive conditions of Haiti than we might have expected. Vuval and Stenio begin the scene by mocking their "Emperor" for his ignorance and gullibility, but their condescending hostility has gone beyond words; they are on the eve of fulfilling a plot to overthrow the Emperor, to end the rule of the blacks, and to remove themselves and Claire Heureuse from the island. Whether the mulatto leaders plan to leave only temporarily, for self-protection, or permanently is not clear. If they plan to remain abroad, their plot to overthrow Dessalines is best comprehended as a gesture of revenge.

The revelation of the mulattoes' plot must create a confused sense of loyalties and desires in the audience. Another of our expectations from Act I has been destroyed; victory over the whites has not led to racial harmony in Haiti. If we look back, we can see that the motivation for this second rebellion is present early in the play. We "might have" known this would happen, just as we "might have" predicted the rejection of Azelia or Dessalines's lust for glory. The mulattoes' rebellion is not the only possible consequence of events and motives displayed earlier, but it clearly becomes one possibility, and a possibility that Dessalines has chosen to ignore. Forced to confront the fruition of those "bad seeds," the audience is now placed in a new attitude vis-à-vis the events onstage. For the first time in the drama, Hughes applies the technique of dramatic irony: We know more about the situation in Haiti than do Dessalines or his followers. The "balance of attention" established, then relinquished, at the beginning of the play is now resumed but reversed. Whereas previously the intense distress onstage was balanced by the characters' greater awareness of the circumstances, now our greater awareness creates the discrepancy necessary to counterweight distress. (In this play, we usually share knowledge equally with the characters only when there is little distress in the stage world.) Dessalines's exclamation, just before the Vuval-Stenio conversation, that he is the freedom of Haiti and the court's glory has a very different meaning for him than for us. For Dessalines, this is a declaration of the power of self and state. For us, those words suggest the weakness and imminent downfall of the state and the man.

The communication to the audience of significant and dangerous information that is not conveyed to Dessalines complicates our attitude toward Dessalines and the blacks. Dessalines's errors in judgment and behavior and his failure to recognize the dangers in his excesses merit punishment and have provided the context for the present mulatto threat, but the source of punishment is at least as corrupt and self-seeking as Dessalines himself. Unlike the situation in Act I of *Emperor of Haiti* or in the denouement of *Oedipus Rex, Hamlet,* or *Macbeth,* [13] establishment of order and prosperity for the state or, more precisely, for the blacks of Haiti, cannot be assumed to be linked to the conquest of either Dessalines or the mulattoes. In the traditional use of dramatic irony, the audience would like to cry out to the central figure or figures, "Watch out! Understand? Look around you!" The spectator feels a sense of his own limitations in being unable to alter the events onstage. Here, our sense of futility is even greater, because even if we were able to interrupt the stage world and tell Dessalines of the plot against him, there is no evidence that the Emperor would use this knowledge wisely. The present condition of this world is bad, what seems to be coming is equally abhorrent, and there is no vision of a practicable alternative that seems hopeful or pleasing. Martel's fantasies of a free, racially harmonious, peaceful Haiti may be pleasing, but they are too distant from the actual Haiti of the play to be taken seriously.

The response of those onstage to Haiti's political chaos is to turn to

champagne and feasting. For the mulattoes, the banquet of Act II
serves as a distraction, a cover for their treacherous plans and their
gradual withdrawals from the court. For Dessalines and the black
court, the banquet is an escape from the real problems of Haiti into
the fantasy world they have created. For the audience, the banquet of
Scene ii is neither distraction nor escape. The feast may be momentarily pleasing in its sensuous detail of sumptuous foods, jewels, music,
and elegant costumes, but the extravagance of what we see only accentuates the horror of what we know. The banquet is a nightmare that
calls into contrast the ugly gap between the dream and its actualiza-
tion, the rulers and the ruled, the hedonistic pleasure of the moment
and lack of insight into the future. This is no longer *our* dream; the
empathy of the audience in Act I is lost. Rather, we are like spectators
to someone else's subconscious visions. We can no more alter or arrest
those dreams that we can change a life by waking a friend from troubled sleep.

The pattern of effect of the second scene of Act II is much like that
of the first scene and serves to reinforce our horror and frustration.
Since we know that the mannerisms of royalty are about to become
irrelevant to the play's Haiti, we will be concerned for, as well as
amused by, such behavior. Similarly, when Claire Heureuse reenters
and immediately badgers "Lady" Celeste, treating the latter like the
lowest slave, our dislike for the Empress and her air of superiority is
renewed, but now our antipathy is inseparable from a foreboding sense
of menace. We recognize that Claire is not only a self-centered,
haughty woman but a grossly hypocritical manipulator whose entire
time as Empress has been spent plotting the overthrow of her husband
and the extension of her own power and position. Our feelings are no
longer limited to discomfort and a sentimental anger that she has replaced the loyal and virtuous Azelia; Claire Heureuse incites hatred in
the audience. Her behavior makes us desire her destruction.

From the opening presentations of the comical servant women and
the venomous Claire, Scene ii is a collage of brief moments in which
many of the characters in Dessalines's court are juxtaposed in their
various attitudes. Martel despairs that the drumbeats are "mournful
and heartbreaking" (p. 89), and that Haiti is not a happy land. Popo
swears his undying loyalty to his Emperor. Ex-slave nobles preen in
their new vestments; the old women servants gossip. The banquet itself begins with a ritualized parade of entrances that sets the gently
satiric tone of the entire feast. Clearly none of the guests are comfortable in their costumes or this elegant setting; the banquet is meant to
make the theater audience uncomfortable as well. We can see and feel
what the characters onstage are not ready to acknowledge: The vague,

fairy-tale fantasies we shared with the ex-slaves in Act I were not only thoughtless but foolish. Through the painful embarrassment of this scene, Hughes wishes the audience to understand that we should consider our fantasies more carefully before attempting to fulfill them.

Hughes does not force us to endure this particular embarrassment for long. The mode of the banquet abruptly shifts when a dance, initially meant to be light entertainment for the court, becomes increasingly strange and powerful. The dance begins with "a syncopated melody" to which a dozen dancing girls, adorned in gold and jewels, "whirl across the lower terrace." As the dance continues, a "weird drum beat" is heard and gradually overwhelms the other music from the orchestra. With only the drum playing, "a male dancer enters, feathered and painted like a voodoo god. The girls sink to the floor as the tall, godlike one does his dance of the jungle, fierce, provocative, and horrible" (p. 95).

Strategically, the dance is crucial; it creates a focus for the emotional chaos we have been experiencing. It is a vivid spectacle that at the least, creates a visual diversion for the spectator. In the midst of so much artificiality, the dance can appear vitally authentic; it is a reminder to those onstage and to the theater audience of an African heritage that differs sharply from the European culture being imitated by Dessalines's court. In contrast to our anticipation of the impotence of Dessalines's role as Emperor, the godlike presence of the male dancer suggests a black power that can control. The dance also reminds the audience that although we may think we know what is happening and about to happen in the world onstage, there still remains much in that world that is unpredictable and mysterious. The music of this dance, the rhythm of the drum, accentuates the impression of inexorable power and recalls the drums of battle heard in Act I.

Claire Heureuse breaks through the mesmerizing effect of the dance. She turns her head, covers her ears, and calls out, "Jean Jacques! Jean Jacques!" Her behavior suggests fear, and although she does not articulate the sources of that fear, we may guess that she is frightened by the power of black men suggested by the dance, and by the reminder of her heritage and history that have preceded her present position. Dessalines complies with his wife's implicit demand to stop the dance, but the drums of entertainment are immediately replaced with the sound of other drums from afar. The frenetic movement and timbre of the dance combine past and present and move us swiftly to the future. We are reminded of the plotted rebellion. Whatever ambivalent sympathies we have had during the dance are not resolved but are replaced by fear and anxiety for the unknown turmoil that is beginning.

Dessalines, too, is frightened by the drums heard outside the palace. Our fear is based on some ability to predict events that we do not like but cannot stop or alter. Dessalines's fear is rooted in ignorance of both himself and the world surrounding him. Our fear produces tension and attention to events onstage; Dessalines's fear produces hysteria. As the sound of the distant drums increases, Dessalines loses his control. He screams at this guests that he will make them work, that he was a tiger in the past and will be a tiger again. Raising his own glass, Dessalines "bellows" at this guests, "Drink to your Emperor! Drink!" (p. 97). Dessalines's guests are frightened and comply with trembling hands; we pity this man who has finally cracked before us while ironically boasting that he is a tiger of strength.

The end of Act II serves to increase our pity for Dessalines and re-establish some of our admiration for the man. There are some signs of humility in Dessalines as he tells his wife after his outburst at the banquet that though perhaps he is not wise, he is still a great fighter. As if his scream to his guests has cleared his head of false notions or made him see himself in the reflection of his guests' frightened faces, Dessalines is now able to say, "Oh, I know I'm nothing much but a fighter, Claire. But if fighting's the only way to get things done—then I'll get 'em done!" (pp. 97–98). Dessalines's newly revealed self-knowledge is not the striking awakening of an Oedipus to an identity previously denied; it more closely resembles the limited self-awareness of Willy Loman in Arthur Miller's *Death of a Salesman*. Dessalines, like Miller's fantasy-ridden salesman, must admit that his image of himself has been illusion, yet he does not allow that acknowledgment to admit defeat. Willy clings to his memories of his salesmanship; Dessalines firmly grips his sword in his hand as he goes off to fight again. Neither Willy Loman nor Dessalines ever really understands the world around him: As Dessalines exits to battle, he remains deceived by Claire and deaf to Martel's warnings that the peasants will not always need a commander to rule their lives. Dessalines's perseverance, his commitment to struggle in the only way he knows for his own life and the life of his country, must call forth renewed admiration from the audience.

With the audience incited by this rekindled energy, Hughes takes us in Act III to a small fishing village, the marketplace of peasant vendors and the site of the headquarters for the royal Haitian army. The contrast in setting and tone to the grandeur of the Emperor's court is as great as the earlier contrast between jungle and palace. There is a sense in the opening market scene of returning home, of coming out of the discomforting fairyland to a place where real people live genuine if difficult lives.

Hughes begins Act III slowly, with ordinary lives proceeding as usual. Market vendors and fishermen complain about their weariness, about their constant struggles for money; women complain and boast about their menfolk. The complaints are generally lighthearted and the tone is witty, playful, gently teasing. The scene provides relief from the nightmare atmosphere of Act II, but also serves to remind us that the individuals to whom we have paid attention are responsible to and for a larger community.

The entrance of a woman we recognize as Azelia begins to shift the tone of Act III. Time and Dessalines's rejection have clearly taken their toll on Azelia: She is not only physically weary but psychologically strained. Her fellows in the marketplace deem her crazy because she imagines she is carrying weapons rather than bananas in her basket and she says she was once Dessalines's wife. The market vendors pity Azelia or laugh at her. Her appeal to the audience is sentimental; we are called upon to pity her, too.

Ragamuffins enter the marketplace. Their presence provokes more serious conversation and raises questions for the vendors that become genuine questions for the audience. Should these "bad boys" be pitied because they are hungry, or spurned because they are lazy? Is there such a thing as too much freedom, which produces crime and indolence? Should these boys be scorned because of their backwoods dialect? These questions are not answered; rather, they are put aside by the appearance of a strange ship on the horizon. The ship is a signal that renews anxiety in the audience, since we know of the mulattoes' plans for exodus. The ship also provokes the peasant vendors to talk about the army, the mulattoes, Dessalines. The attitudes of the vendors toward Dessalines are mixed and suggest our own ambivalence toward him. One man states that "All the Emperor knows is fight!" Another responds, "He's a brave man though! You can't say he ain't. And 'cause of him, I'm free." We can affirm both views.

The talk of soldiers and Dessalines is preparation for the entrance of Stenio, Vuval, and a squad of soldiers. The villagers are alarmed, and so should we be. We are quickly informed by Vuval and Stenio that there is indeed cause for alarm: They are awaiting the arrival of Dessalines in order to "put an end to the presumptuous Negro who dares call himself 'His Majesty' " (p. 109). Although the audience may agree with this description of Dessalines, we have no reason to wish his death, particularly in such ignoble hands. Thus, we await Dessalines with fear and repugnance for the anticipated scene of violence, yet we also likely retain some hope for the unpredictable, since Hughes has not hesitated previously to thwart our expectations.

We are only given a brief moment to worry and wait. Dessalines arrives and is seized by Stenio's soldiers. The Emperor will not accept defeat easily; he breaks free, draws his sword, and tries to attack Stenio. Behind Dessalines's back, Vuval fires a pistol and kills the Emperor. While Vuval remains in a daze, Stenio laughs and kicks the body of the murdered king. Death for Dessalines is neither noble nor tragic; it is ugly, demeaning, and pathetic. Dessalines has become a victim of the greed and envy of the mulattoes; we can pity the man *as a victim*, but his previous behavior prevents us from feeling an intimate or intense sense of loss.

In death, Dessalines is reduced to food for the worms and refuse for the ragamuffins, who reappear to scavenge his body. As Dessalines lies on his face, his clothes torn off by the human vultures, Azelia re-enters. She chases off the boys, in pity for the "sick" man. Her concern for the unknown victim confirms that despite the gossip about her "madness," she remains a kind and humane woman. Only after the boys have left and she has knelt to help the fallen man does Azelia recognize the body as Dessalines's. Dissolving in tears and memories, she asserts that her love for Dessalines remains.

Azelia's discovery of Dessalines's body and her intense emotional response to the recognition of that body qualify a traditional recognition scene with another of Hughes's carefully conceived twists. In one form of the recognition scene, two people, at least one of whom has previously been disguised in some fashion, recognize each other's true identities. Out of that knowledge they come to know their own identities better. For the audience viewing a recognition scene, the experience is either one of surprise at the true identity of the characters onstage or, more frequently, relief that those characters now know themselves as well as we know them. A recognition scene can lead an audience member to understand the reciprocity necessary to an act of self-revelation. When one person reveals himself to another, whether that be in the same world or from the world of the stage to the audience, he commands the acknowledgment of that other person. Such an acknowledgment includes not only recognition of the person who has revealed himself but also recognition of one's own identity at that moment. To be present to the revelation of another is thus necessarily to be changed oneself, for even if the witness rejects the other, an act of recognition and of self-revelation has occurred.

Discreetly or overtly, the essence of drama is to provide an audience with a scene of recognition. In our ordinary lives, the weight of our disguises and the fear of recognition are so great as to make moments of mutual revelation rare and difficult. Even rarer are the moments in which one person will risk revealing himself to another while that other stands unknown. Through the creation of a separate stage world and the fiction of characters, the drama allows the characters onstage to reveal themselves to the audience without confronting the possible rejection by that audience of a character. (The audience's rejection of an actor poses a different problem.) Drama then allows the spectator to acknowledge the revelation while maintaining his privacy.[14]

The recognition scene Hughes provides at the end of *Emperor of Haiti* is purposefully incomplete. Azelia recognizes Dessalines, but Dessalines is dead. He can neither witness nor respond to the presence of Azelia or her identification of him.

Futility and incompleteness of recognition are evoked by the reappearance of Azelia and her discovery of Dessalines's body. The scene can be viewed as a sentimental appeal to the audience's pity for Azelia; indeed, Azelia's cradling of Dessalines and her laments over his body verge on the maudlin and can end the drama in pathos. Such an effect, however, is not the necessary or intended conclusion of the play, for it does not, after all, end with Azelia's tears. In a moment more affecting than that of Azelia's expressions of anguish, Claire Heureuse passes her husband's body on the way to her own departing ship. She glances down at Dessalines, shudders, and whispers, "Those scars!" A returning fisherman makes permanent the moment in our memories when he, too, passes Dessalines's body and remarks, "He musta been a slave once—from the looks of his back" (p. 114).

Claire Heureuse can identify Dessalines, but her perception remains superficial. Claire sees, but there is nothing in her vision comparable to the understanding Azelia expresses in the final line of the play: "He was a slave once . . . then king." These words are not merely a description of events; they are a warning about man's false illusions. Hughes's strategy throughout his play has been to show us that to be a king or to wish to be a king may be the same as to be a slave. It is appropriate that Azelia articulates this recognition, because only she has remained outside the enslavement of Dessalines's court.

At the end of his play, Hughes forces his audience to make a choice in vision. We can, with Claire Heureuse, shudder at the ugliness of slavery and death and feel revulsion at the sight of someone trampled upon, but still walk off to our own dreams of power and riches. We can also simply shudder in the presence of a world that offers only frustation and destruction. Or we can, with Azelia, reject the slavery of both bondage and elitism and begin to look at the world in a new way.

Finally, the choice that Hughes forces is one of accepting or denying the experience of *Emperor of Haiti*. If we find the two Haitian worlds of Acts I and II equally abhorrent, we can no longer find answers in personal dreams of power and glory. Nor can we deny the destructiveness of human conflicts aroused by differences in skin color. The fall of Dessalines occurs not only because, overblown with pride, he fails to acknowledge his excesses and weaknesses but also because the community around him is ridden with strife, first between whites and blacks and then between mulattoes and blacks. In *Emperor of Haiti*, Hughes urges that strivings for personal power and glory are specifically destructive to Dessalines and the black Haitians, but he does not suggest that nonblacks are secure from this self-destruction.

Hughes has thus created a strategy that unlike the conceptions of Willis Richardson's plays of the 1920s or some black plays of the 1960s and 1970s, is intended simultaneously for both black and white spectators. Certain elements of those concurrent intentions suggest potential problems. Hughes never clarifies, for example, whether the mulattoes' disdain for the black Haitians is a matter of social, economic, and educational disparities or whether it is a more complicated reaction to differences in skin color combined with differences in culture and economic status. Hughes may have assumed that black audiences would know the truth of the conflict and would not question the motivation, but this understanding would not necessarily be present for white audiences. The play suggests but never confronts the problem of the *nature* of racial strife. Hughes intimates by the parallel structures of Acts I and II that the tensions between blacks and whites resemble those between blacks and mulattoes, but it is never clear whether it is only the results or the motivations as well that are similar.

Other questions concerning the problems of being black in a Western world are also blurred. In Act II's crucial scene of the African dance, Hughes seems to be urging the acceptance, at least, by blacks of a valuable and authentic cultural heritage, but if we perceive the dance as a constructive force, how are we to respond to Dessalines's subsequent emotional outburst, which may not have occurred without the intense provocation of the dance? Hughes simultaneously commends education and rationality, which in the context of the play would be associated with Western civilization, and a dance that could be symbolic of African tribal culture. Certainly these two forces are not necessarily antithetical. To value an African dance does not mean one must refuse to learn to read, but Hughes does not make clear how one culture and set of values is to supersede or combine with the other, and the juxtaposition of cultures in these scenes does raise the question.

Furthermore, the language of the play is uneven and inconsistent, suggesting another ambivalence of direction. The same character will speak eloquent and "proper" English at one point, a halting dialect at another, and in still other moments that character will sound like one of Hughes's Harlem creations. Azelia, for example, will stray from "standard" verb forms, saying, "And Jean Jacques [has] took his last beating" (p. 56), instead of "Jean Jacques has taken his last beating," but she will in other instances speak with simple and "correct" eloquence: "They said Jean Jacques Dessalines was too much name for a slave to have. Let slaves have just one name, that's what they said" (p. 56). And, as indicated earlier, Martel's abundant use of metaphor and unusual choices of words never fit with the ordinary language of other characters. All this may disturb the audience's ability to imagine itself in one foreign place, to accept the world of Haiti. We may be forced to think about how Haitians speak, and this does not seem intended by Hughes's script except in the one question raised about the dialect of the ragamuffins.

Both the unevenness of language and the ambiguity of certain intentions toward audience in *Emperor of Haiti* can be understood simply as Hughes's failure to come fully to grips with the complexities of his material. One might conclude that Hughes's skills of characterization, dramatic structure, and visual theatricality inject this play with remarkable power, but that the brilliance of *Emperor of Haiti* is tarnished by its limitations of language and its inclusion of some scenes that do not obviously cohere with the play's basic strategies. To arrive at such a conclusion would imply that this playwright was good but not quite good enough, and it is not necessarily the function of criticism to attempt to explain such a shortcoming.

With Hughes, as with Richardson, however, the material itself suggests that what may appear to be weaknesses may be at least as much an insurmountable problem of the form as they are indications of the playwright's limitations. While Hughes's reasons for writing a play about Dessalines and revolution in Haiti were likely many and varied, a result, if not a cause, of this decision was that in so doing he seemed to escape the boundaries of writing about either the inner life of black Americans or the contact of black and white. By presenting both black and mulatto characters, ethnically and historically removed from all twentieth-century Americans, he avoided a number of sociological traps. He neither had to distort the inner life of black Americans to make it accessible to whites, nor did he have to relinquish the possibility of a white audience by adhering to an authenticity of black American life that might appeal to blacks but alienate white spectators. Nor did he have to narrow his material to that limited space in which white Americans and black Americans encounter one another. This latter space not only circumscribes the possibilities for characters and episodes but also makes any attitude other than that of overt protest difficult to achieve.

Yet the *Emperor of Haiti* makes undeniably clear that Hughes's choice of setting was neither an escape to the safety of uncontroversial territory nor, in fact, a rejection of concern with either the inner life of black Americans or the contact of black and white. Instead, I want to argue, Hughes's risk lay in endeavoring to confront both the inner life and the "outer" contact of black and white. By employing one of the oldest tricks of drama, that of historical distance, Hughes was able in *Emperor of Haiti* to confront a complex of issues that no contemporary American location could contain; he was also able to seduce both black and white spectators to a recognition of persons who might otherwise have been dismissed as abhorrent, unbelievable, or both.

Understood in this context, inconsistencies of language and the ambiguous functions of some scenes can be perceived not as a generalized ineptitude but as the specific confusion of a playwright struggling to combine often opposing strategic gestures. Little in the dramaturgy of *Emperor of Haiti* is innovative; Hughes borrowed the most traditional devices from the most obvious works, especially Shakespeare's plays. But the use of these devices, combined with the Haitian setting, enabled Hughes to create for the audience a genuinely original and significant experience. No one who is genuinely present to *Emperor of Haiti* can avoid some recognition of the corrosive corruption of extreme wealth, the necessity of rage and envy between grossly divided classes of people, the tenacity and absurdity of racial bigotry, and the depth of our vulnerability to self-delusion. Whether it is Dessalines himself or the erotic qualities of the voodoo dance that we acknowledge in *Emperor of Haiti*, it is *our* failure if we have not been changed in some fashion by the experience of this play.

NOTES

1. John Hope Franklin, *From Slavery to Freedom*, 2d ed. (New York: Knopf, 1956), pp. 504–5.
2. Darwin T. Turner, *Black Drama in America* (Greenwich, Conn.: Fawcett, 1971), p. 48.
3. T. J. Spencer and Clarence J. Rivers, "Langston Hughes: His Style and Optimism," *Drama Critique*, 7 (Spring 1964): 99–102. Although this piece does not present close criticism of any plays, it does deserve mention in a discussion of criticism on Hughes's drama because it attempts to explain reasons for Hughes's obscurity as a playwright in terms of "segregated thought patterns" and Hughes's failure to invent an innovative dramaturgy.
4. Doris Abramson, *Negro Playwrights in the American Theatre, 1925–1959*, (New York: Columbia University Press, 1969), p. 83. Abramson remarks that "Langston Hughes stands out as the only Negro playwright of [the

1930s] who managed to write literate plays that satisfied both Broadway and Harlem audiences." She does not adequately explain why these scripts were uniquely satisfying or why other black playwrights of the period were not as successful.

Fannie E. F. Hicklin, "The American Negro Playwright, 1920–1964," Ph.D. dissertation (University of Wisconsin, 1965), pp. 244–59. Hicklin's work remains unpublished and is limited in its evaluation of any one playwright by its generally large scope.

Darwin T. Turner, "Langston Hughes as Playwright," *College Language Association Journal*, 11 (June 1968): 197–309. This article, which focuses on five of Hughes's plays, cites the unevenness of language, frequent use of sentimental and melodramatic situations, and stereotyped characterization as significant detriments to their effectiveness. Turner also remarks the strength of plot, character, and thematic conceptions in at least two of Hughes's dramas, *Emperor of Haiti* and *Tambourines to Glory*. Turner's judgments seem to me both accurate and important but, again, only initiate the kind of study necessary for a just assessment of Hughes's work. This article is part of a longer study.

5. Turner, *Black Drama in America*, p. 48.

6. *Emperor of Haiti* does distort historical time and incidents, particularly in its limited acknowledgment of the role of Toussaint L'Ouverture, and Hughes gives no indication that such distortion has occurred. He clearly alters the material for the sake of dramatic effect and characterization; by condensing events and focusing on one hero, he heightens the intensity of historical events. It is not my purpose in this study to examine historical accuracy, but some facts about Haiti at the time of the play may be helpful. Where page numbers are indicated in parentheses in the following summary account, the source is John Hope Franklin, *From Slavery to Freedom*, unless otherwise noted.

In the eighteenth century, the island later known as Haiti, then called St. Dominique, was a French possession, inhabited by 452,000 slaves, 24,000 free black people and mulattoes, and 30,000 whites (p. 344, statistics for 1789). The French Revolution inspired in the free blacks a desire for economic and civil rights equal to those of their white neighbors and Frenchmen; in 1789, they requested such rights from the French National Assembly. This move spurred the island's enslaved blacks to demand their liberty. In 1794, as a response to turmoil in both St. Dominique and Europe, the French National Convention granted liberty to every man living under French dominion; St. Dominique thus became the first land in the New World to exist without slavery.

In the years following this declaration of emancipation, a former slave, Toussaint L'Ouverture, became the ruling power in St. Dominique. His primary concern seems to have been to sustain the power of the military forces, particularly as the threat of renewed subjugation, this time by Napoleon's troops, became real. Napoleon saw St. Dominique as part of an empire in North America; when Spain, which in 1795 had given the eastern portion of the Louisiana territory to the United States, ceded the rest of this territory to France in 1800, Napoleon saw his chance to make his empire and began his attack on Toussaint's forces. John Hope Franklin urges that Toussaint L'Ouverture's obsession with military power was so consuming that freedom was only a notion, not a reality (p. 345). Indeed, August Meier and Elliot M. Rudwick, in *From Plantation to Ghetto* (New York: Hill & Wang, 1966), mention that many refugees from the Haitian revolution, presumably white, migrated to the Louisiana territory after Toussaint's initial victories (p. 49, Meier). In 1802, the Haitians were defeated by troops from Napoleon's army, and Toussaint L'Ouverture was captured and brought to France, where he died in 1803.

Despite their victory, Napoleon's troops were greatly weakened by losses in battle and an epidemic of yellow fever. Two new Haitian leaders, Jean Jacques Dessalines, also a former slave, and Alexandre Petion, a mulatto, accurately perceived the weakness of the enemy and the strong support of their countrymen for renewed battle. By November 1803, Dessalines and Petion had led their men to victory over Napoleon's forces. In 1804, Dessalines declared St. Dominique a free and independent nation, renamed it Haiti, and subsequently proclaimed himself Jacques I, Emperor of Haiti.

7. Arthur Miller, "Tragedy and the Common Man," in *Aspects of the Drama*, Sylvan Barnet, Morton Berman, and William Burto, eds. (Boston: Little, Brown, 1962), p. 65.

8. *Ibid.*, p. 63.

9. Thomas J. Scheff, "Audience Awareness and Catharsis in Drama," *The Psychoanalytic Review*, 63, no. 4 (1976).

10. Langston Hughes, *Emperor of Haiti*, in Turner, *Black Drama in America*, p. 57. All subsequent citations are from this source.

11. Langston Hughes, "Foreword," and "Who Is Simple?" in *Black Voices*, Abraham Chapman, ed. (New York: New American Library, 1968), p. 99. Some works by Hughes that tell of Simple are *The Best of Simple* (New York: Hill & Wang, 1961), *Simple Speaks His Mind* (New York: Hill & Wang, 1950), and *Simple's Uncle Sam* (New York: Hill & Wang, 1965). For a complete listing of works related to Simple, see the bibliography.

12. See Zora Neale Hurston, *Mules and Men* (Philadelphia: Lippincott, 1935), for a positive presentation of black voodoo practices.

13. I am thinking of A. C. Bradley's notion that some Shakespeare plays move from chaos and upheaval in the state to some kind of re-establishment of order. Certainly Fortinbras's function at the end of *Hamlet* is to provide such a renewal of order, and Macduff asserts at the end of *Macbeth* that "the time is free," liberty is restored. In a pre-Shakespearean context, Creon could be said to take the state back to harmony at the end of Sophocles' *Oedipus Rex*.

14. I am informed but not prompted here by my reading of Stanley Cavell, *Must We Mean What We Say?* (New York: Scribner's, 1969), particularly pages 238–66 and 267–353. See also my article "I Love You, Who Are You?: The Strategy of Drama in Recognition Scenes," *PMLA* (March 1977).

4 DIALECTICS TOWARD A THEATER OF BLACK EXPERIENCE: THEODORE WARD'S BIG WHITE FOG

HISTORY, LIKE OTHER DISCIPLINES, has its truisms; some clichés of history stimulate an overabundance of picayune research; other commonplaces allow an avoidance of investigation that might otherwise reveal important understandings of ourselves. In American intellectual history, one such truism asserts a newfound intimacy in the United States in the 1930s between politics and the arts. For American theater in general, this particular cliché has remained a controversial source of both hope and alarm. For black American theater, the confluence of art and politics in the 1930s presented the possibility of both an economic and aesthetic salvation. The sixteen Negro units of the Federal Theatre Project of the Works Progress Administration provided hundreds of jobs for black men and women on relief, as well as financial and artistic support for theater productions in black communities; they also appeared to be interested in producing new scripts by black writers.[1] (A number of white playwrights, most notably Clifford Odets, also found Federal Theatre Project support for plays that were unquestionably political, frequently derived from a particular ethnic context, and liberal if not radical in their particular politics.) The hunger of the Depression seemed to offer a ready banquet table for the black playwright who wished to confront his community with the complexities of its world or who desired to raise his voice in protest against the conduct of contact between black and white Americans.

Were a fiction creating the archetypal black writer to arise in such a context, it could do no better than to take for its model Theodore Ward. Neither consciously prophetic nor deliberately innovative, Ward's work for the theater in the 1930s and 1940s was, nevertheless, novel in its time and now seems uncannily precedent to the theater of black experience of the 1960s. Like many participants in the 1960s Black Arts Theatre, Theodore Ward wrote out of the personal experi-

77

ence of poverty and chose to write for those who dwelled in the poverty of black ghettos. His major drama of the 1930s, *Big White Fog,* embraces the inner life of black people while strongly protesting the relationship of a black community to the white society that surrounds it. While Ward exploited historical incidents in his choice of settings and time, he seemed to trust his audience's ability to confront directly the political issues before them. He was thus akin to his colleague Langston Hughes, but at times even bolder in his strides than was his peer.

It is then one of the perplexities of American theater that Theodore Ward and his work have remained obscure. Despite Ward's own willingness to speak about his life and work, what little public information exists derives almost completely from an interview with the playwright conducted in the early 1960s by Doris Abramson.[2] From that interview, we know that Ward was born in 1908 in Thibodaux, Louisiana. He left home at thirteen and worked as a bootblack and at other odd jobs, making his way North through large cities, including St. Louis, and eventually arriving in Chicago. During the late 1920s, when Langston Hughes was already engaged in the Harlem Renaissance, Theodore Ward spent two years as a student at the University of Wisconsin, on a Zona Gale Fellowship in Creative Writing. Ward worked as a staff artist for Station WIBA in Madison,[3] then moved to Chicago, where he joined a leftist John Reed (Writers') Club[4] and became recreational director at the Abraham Lincoln Center. In 1937, Ward's one-act play *Sick and Tiahd* was produced at both Lincoln Center and DuSable High School in Chicago. At about the time of that production, Ward joined a unit of the Federal Theatre in Chicago as an instructor of dramatics. It was this Federal Theatre unit that in 1938 first produced *Big White Fog.*

Big White Fog met with opposition even before it was produced.[5] Many members of the Federal Theatre unit evidently objected to producing the play because of their discomfort with what they perceived to be the drama's advocation of revolution as the necessary response to the economic, political, and social oppression of black people in the United States. Despite this opposition and Ward's sense that the play was not "adequately publicized by the Federal Theatre,"[6] *Big White Fog* did achieve a financially successful Chicago production. The show ran for ten weeks and was highly praised by critics of the *Chicago Daily News* and the *Mid-West Daily* for its honesty, seriousness, and power,[7] although it was not until 1974 that the play was published in full.[8]

After the closing of the Federal Theatre in Chicago, Theodore Ward moved to New York City where, in 1940, he helped found the

Negro Playwrights Company. Here, Ward's career in the theater momentarily joined with the theatrical endeavors of Langston Hughes. Ward and Hughes, both authors by 1940 of scripts concerned with violence and revolution, economic distress, and inter- and intraracial strife, came together with George Norford, Powell Lindsay, Owen Dodson, and Theodore Browne to found a new theater dedicated to the presentation of authentic plays about black people written by black playwrights. The aim of the Negro Playwrights Company was presented in its "Perspective."[9] It sought to avoid the commercial exploitation and distortion of black life common to Broadway productions and, by so doing, to create a new and vital black audience for theater. The Negro Playwrights Company's concern for the encouragement of black audiences was not, however, an assertion of racial exclusiveness. The "Perspective" also stated a desire to "foster the spirit of unity between the races."[10] The creation of the Negro Playwrights Company was an important assertion of the distinctive needs and qualities of black theater. In the 1960s, similar concerns would give birth to the various companies of the Black Arts Theatre and Black Revolutionary Theatre. But the Negro Playwrights Company differed from later efforts in that the earlier company accepted racial integration as both a descriptive and prescriptive term.

With such goals in mind, the first, and only, production of the Negro Playwrights Company was a second attempt at Ward's *Big White Fog*. The New York production of *Big White Fog* ran for sixty-four performances to mixed critical reviews. Many of the negative comments about the play stressed again what was interpreted as its revolutionary stance, although weaknesses in dramaturgy and language were also mentioned by both black and white critics.[11] Perhaps more significant than the ambivalent comments of the critics was the apparent failure of the play to reach or create a substantial black audience: It is estimated that only 1,500 blacks, in contrast to 24,000 whites, saw the New York production of *Big White Fog*.[12]

Ward's own response to the partial failure of *Big White Fog* was to turn away from the overt depiction of immediate problems in the black community and to search in black history for the kind of dramatic moment he had been urging in *Big White Fog*. While he may not have been consciously following the example of his peer, the path Ward now chose was remarkably similar to that taken by Langston Hughes in *Emperor of Haiti*. Ward found his material in the events of the early post–Civil War period, when, particularly in the South, the question for both blacks and whites of what the newly freed black men and women would do with their freedom led to both heroic and tragic responses. In 1941, Ward composed a draft of a play, called *Our Lan'*, based on the struggles of a group of freed men on an island off the coast of Georgia. Ward, however, was unable to arrange a production of *Our Lan'* until 1946, when it achieved a brief and critically success-ful run off-Broadway and then was moved to Broadway, where it played for five weeks. Critics generally considered the Broadway ver-sion of *Our Lan'* to be less effective than its off-Broadway performances because of overproduction.

Our Lan' brought to Theodore Ward some of the recognition as a substantial and serious playwright that *Big White Fog* never achieved for him. In 1947, Ward was named "Negro of the Year" by the Com-mittee of Selection of the Schomberg Center of the New York Public Library. The drama critic Kenneth Thorpe Rowe found *Our Lan'* wor-thy of analysis in his 1960 book, *A Theater in Your Head*,[13] and Doris Abramson praises it highly: "To read *Our Lan'* is to realize that here is a nearly perfect play. It may be the finest play ever written by an American Negro."[14]

Our Lan' calls upon the audience to admire and pity black men and women for their courageous struggles to attain their own freedom; the play is intended to educate a white audience and arouse its emotional sympathies, and to show a black audience strengths and weaknesses possible in black characters. In terms of its intentions toward an audi-ence of both black and white spectators, the play is much like Hughes's *Emperor of Haiti*. *Our Lan'* is also similar in genre and thematics to *Emperor of Haiti:* Both plays use history to suggest analogies while maintaining a distance from immediate problems; both concern the as-piration among blacks for ownership of property, their need for educa-tion, their problems in relation to power, the interracial strife between mulattoes and blacks.

What distinguishes *Big White Fog* from both *Our Lan'* and *Em-peror of Haiti* as well as from many other black and white American dramas is neither its thematic concerns nor its form. The play could be said to be *about* many of the same issues—poverty, bigotry, power, education—that have persistently plagued black playwrights. It is also a play whose surface would melt rapidly in the unctuous flow of Ameri-can dramatic realism. *Big White Fog* could in fact be called a drama of family strife, though such a description would be far from sufficient. In its concerns with the tensions within a single family and the conflicts created for each member of that family by external society, *Big White Fog* resembles a long list of dramas in which the private world of a few people is invaded and displayed to suggest a microcosmic view of the ills and errors of many ordinary people. The extent to which this pri-vate world is exposed and the particular qualities and commitments that are revealed in *Big White Fog* are, however, distinctive. Perhaps even more significant, the apparent familiarity of Ward's approach eventually reveals its own confinement.

II

The setting for *Big White Fog* is the living room of a two-story brick house on Dearborn Street in Chicago. Ward indicates in his stage directions for Act I, Scene i, that this house is to be seen as one of many that had been vacated by "better class whites, following the invasion of the district by Negroes during the period of the great migration and the world war." Ward provides sufficient detail about the decor and furnishings of this living room to establish immediately a situation of modest comfort revealed as much through the use of light and color as by the tasteful but unassertive objects in the room. The noted presence of stained glass windows is a key to both the accuracy of detail and the mood Ward wishes to establish. Stained glass windows are characteristic of early-twentieth-century midwestern houses; they provide a device for changes of color and light and, therefore, of tone and mood as the drama proceeds. The stained glass windows also suggest that this room is a sanctuary, a chapel protected from the invading glances of the outside world.

Whether viewed on paper or onstage, Ward's careful attention to the details of the set firmly place *Big White Fog* in the tradition of realism, but in his attempt to make his stage world accurate and natural, he does not avoid a symbolic use of that same physical space. Each major step in the deterioration of the harmony and prosperity of the family in *Big White Fog* is reflected in the changing appearance of their living room. In Act II, a busy typewriter and a sick, blanketed child disturb the pleasant order and stability of that central room; by Act III, the furniture has the same frayed, dulled appearance of poverty that characterizes the persons in the room; by the last scene of the play, the room is displayed in total disorder in preparation for the family's imminent eviction.

Implications of symbolic meaning through realistic changes in detail are central to Ward's presentation of his characters as well as his setting. In our initial encounter, the family of *Big White Fog* is as ordinary and undisturbing as the room in which they dwell. The mother Ella, is a pleasant, loving housewife, concerned with the welfare of her family; the father, Vic, is a hardworking bricklayer; their four healthy, active children—Lester, Wanda, Caroline, and Phillip—suggest a wholesome household. The Dearborn Street house is the home of Mrs. Brooks, Ella's mother, and Uncle Percy, Vic's self-indulgent brother, in addition to the immediate family. Juanita, Ella's sister, and her ambitious husband, Dan, are frequent visitors to the house. The other characters who appear in *Big White Fog* are all tangential to the family and represent various aspects of the world outside.

Each of the central members of the Mason family can be further distinguished by his or her particular desires: Ella wants harmony and happiness for her family; Vic wants the freedom to make a worthwhile life for himself and his children; Les wants an education; Mrs. Brooks wants a clearly middle-class, socially esteemed position for herself and her offspring; Wanda wants the freedom to enjoy her youth; Juanita wants comfort and security; Dan hopes for financial success and the satisfaction of running his own business; Uncle Percy wants to enjoy the pleasures of wine and women. Although these varying needs will clearly create some conflict in a family that must function as an intimate whole, the discord thus created, while perhaps interesting for its sheer familiarity, is not necessarily the stuff of which a serious or important drama is made.

What I have thus far omitted in describing the characters and setting of *Big White Fog* is what distinguishes this family from others. The Masons are not just any family at any time; they are a black family, living out, struggling through, the decade from 1922 to 1932 in the fog of white America. It is precisely the ordinariness of the needs and desires of the Masons in the context of their being black in white America that creates the extraordinary sense of futility and frustration in the course of *Big White Fog*. Petty squabbles at the beginning of the play are apparent but not important; this is a family with a deep sense of integrity and mutual concern that seems to separate them from, and stand as a bulwark against, the outside world. But strong as the bulwark is, it cannot withstand the outside pressures. All of the difficulties of the family are initiated by problems they encounter because they must venture outside their living room in order to survive. The Masons are torn apart by their inability to satisfy their needs in ways that are not an affront to their basic values or mutual trust. And much of that inability is rooted in the racism of the surrounding society.

The toll of that racism exacted from each member of the family is apparent from the beginning of *Big White Fog*. Act I, Scene i, exposes the hobbyhorses of each character but also immediately draws the audience to know the Masons as a black family surrounded by a "big white fog." As the curtain rises, we discover Ella Mason retrieving a letter from the mailbox. She is in "deep thought" when her sister, Juanita, enters for a visit. Juanita questions Ella about the letter. Ella's response partially satisfies our curiosity as well as that of her sister. The letter is for Les, the oldest son, and probably concerns his application for a college scholarship. Although the women go on to other subjects, an aura of suspense is maintained for the audience throughout their conversation: We want to know the substance of the letter.

Many of the tensions of the family are revealed in this conversation, which would seem too abrupt and serious for the occasion if we were not clearly told by Ella that she and her sister have gone through similar discussions before. Ella calmly shells peas while she talks with Juanita; the steady rhythm of the domestic task tempers the abrasive quality of their conversation. We are thus introduced to the rituals of a family as well as the issues that concern this particular family, and these rituals, as well as at least some of the specific concerns, evoke an easy climate of familiarity. As in the opening scene of an Ibsen play, in less than fifty lines we are given an abundance of information: Ella is clearly both poorer than her sister and much less concerned about material success. Their mother, Mrs. Brooks, still intimidates her daughters but is a good grandmother; she is proud of her DuPree heritage and scorns Ella's "black crank" husband. Ella's husband, Vic, is passionately committed to the Back to Africa movement with some support from Ella; Juanita, her husband Dan, and Mrs. Brooks disapprove of the Back to Africa movement; Dan is starting a kitchenette (apartment house) business to make money. Juanita is contemptuous of Vic's title and of the Garvey movement, which is the source of that title, but she has not cast her sister and brother-in-law aside with scorn. Indeed, what Juanita wants is for the two brothers-in-law to work together. When Ella mentions Vic's interest in his race, Juanita answers with no hint of condescension, "Oh yeah. Then he ought to be trying to do something for it here—(Joining her [Ella] on couch enthusiastically) like going in with Dan and opening that kitchenette— Everywhere you turn our people are crying for some place to stay, and they're bound to make money" (I-i-4). In the end, Juanita is still thinking about money, but she is eager to share the envisioned financial success.

In this opening scene, Ward prevents the audience from stereotyping Juanita as a selfish, materialistic social climber. Ward shows us not only Juanita's pretensions but her affections as well. Similarly, while Mrs. Brooks quickly demonstrates a snobbery whose source is her DuPree name and light skin, the very first thing we discover when she enters is that she has been out playing ball in the park with the Mason children. Mrs. Brooks's prejudices are repugnant, but we notice, too, that while she complains about everything from her weariness to her "black crank" son-in-law, the children attest that "Grandma" not only does more than is necessary but enjoys her life in this household.

The tension among the three women makes us welcome the entrance of Les, whose scholarship letter, we now recall, lies waiting for its recipient. To the relief of those onstage and in the audience, Les's letter contains good news: The chairman of the scholarship fund is certain that favorable action will be taken on Les's application. The family is elated, as is Les, although it is he who gives us the cue that some anxiety is still appropriate when he tells his sister Wanda that "everything's not settled yet." Here is revealed one element of Ward's technique: A troubling situation appears to be resolved, but a hint is made that the solution may not be permanent. To what extent these clues are recognized as such is a matter of the prior attitudes and experiences of the audience. For example, Juanita imagines Vic's response to the news and self-righteously says, "It should make him see this country in a little better light." A white spectator who has never experienced or has ignored racial injustices may well share Juanita's attitude, but a black spectator may be skeptical of this optimism and worry about the certainty of Les's "award." Variations in response will depend, too, on the date of performance or reading, because a black student's receipt of a college scholarship would have been less surprising in 1970 than in 1940.

Up to this point in the play, elements of a dialectic have only been named, brought into tentative confrontation, or implied. With the entrance of Wanda, after Les's momentary triumph, a dialectical strategy becomes increasingly emphatic. Two or more opposing possibilities are repeatedly brought to confrontation, out of this confrontation some momentary resolution is achieved, and that resolution then becomes one attitude to be opposed in still another confrontation. Such a strategy has the advantage of an inherent fluidity. Thus, while Wanda seems pleased for Les, her announcement that she plans to end her own education immediately challenges the assumptions with which we have just been led to agree: that education is a valuable undertaking. Once Les has gone to deliver newspapers, Wanda expresses her cynicism about his award: "It's a fine break all right—marvelous—when he gets out of school, maybe they'll give him a job on the railroad figuring out how many calories there are in the average bowl of dining car soup!" (I-i-10). Ward perceives that the audience will be ambivalent toward Wanda's declamation and moves to confront the problem in our response. Both Ella and Juanita express dismay, which Wanda counters with, "You needn't pretend to be so astonished, Aunt. Nor you either, Mama." Ward intends to jar his audience with the truth of Wanda's prediction, but he recognizes the difficulty spectators may have at this point. The exchange between Wanda, Ella, and Juanita could call into question a black spectator's possible surprise at Wanda's words. The white spectator's response here is unpredictable, in that he may recognize the truth and be moved by it, or he may condemn Wanda's view as cynical or silly. The first response of any spectator could also be sympathetic laughter at the ironic truth in the absurd "job" Wanda describes.

Wanda's condemnation of education is not allowed to remain as a simple truth for any spectator. Her attack is not only an assault on the family's naïveté, it is a defense of her own decision to drop out of high school. Wanda's decision to leave school is partially based on a realistic sense of the futility of education for a black person, but it is also her vision of an immediate way to acquire the trappings and comforts of the material things for which she longs: "I've got as much right to nice things as anybody else. If I go to work, I can get them." Because the job Wanda has in mind is that of a soda jerk in a drugstore, the audience cannot help but question the wisdom of Wanda's choice. Is she behaving like a foolish teenager or like a bitter but clear-sighted adult?

In the course of the continuing argument about Wanda's schooling, Wanda brings up the name of Uncle Percy as an ally whom she emulates. Uncle Percy has clothes and goes places and does things, and Wanda urges, "At least he's not kidding himself like the rest of you. He knows there's nothing for us in this country and the white folks proved it, too, when they ripped his uniform off his back when he came home from France" (I-i-13). For some members of an audience this will be new and startling information, but for many black spectators it will be an unpleasant reminder of a sordid historical event, which would have been familiar to blacks in the 1930s or 1940s. The passage is almost too obviously a furthering of the expositional function of Scene i, but the mention of Uncle Percy also serves to complicate the issue rather than clarify it as Wanda intends. The sentimental appeal of Wanda's description of Uncle Percy's behavior is at least partially deflated by Juanita's counter: "You can't hold all the white people guilty for the act of a few drunken bums, and it's no excuse for his throwing himself away" (I-i-13). Ward is quickly establishing a pattern of dialogue that repeatedly tempts the spectator to affirm strongly the position of one character only to find that position immediately shaken by the words of another.

Wanda finally runs from the room, crying out bitterly her frustration with being a Negro girl in a country where she has nothing to look forward to. As she departs, she asserts her independence from the family. Her exit creates a sense that there is a tense space onstage that needs filling. The entrance of Vic, Wanda's father, fills this void but only momentarily relieves our discomfort. Vic is immediately confronted with the new problem of Wanda. He surprises his wife, and probably the audience, by defending Wanda's position. Since we know little of Vic at this point except that he is a father and a Garveyite, we expect him to be horrified as a father that his daughter is about to quit school. But Vic's bitterness about "white folks' lies" is as sharp as that of his oldest daughter, and he adds, "There isn't a word of truth about a black man in all her books put together" (I-i-15).

Scene i rushes to its conclusion with a series of speeches overburdened with metaphor and rhetoric. With no pause or preparation, Ella erupts from her calm control and previous support of her husband's positions to an attack on Vic in which she screams that she is sick of his explanations, his promises, and his unfulfilled visions for himself and his family. We are meant to see her as motivated by her concern for the welfare of her child, but it is not clear that her fury is appropriate to the occasion. Vic is injured by Ella's tirade, but rather than yield to the pain, he responds by affirming his hope for the future in a visionary sermon in which Africa is compared to a weeping mother crying out for her long lost children:

> But I'm still trying—What do you think I'm carrying a hod by day and wrestling in the movement all night for?—Wanda's just reached the point where she sees what a girl her color is up against in this country! Be patient a little longer. (He turns and goes towards stairs) We'll soon be out of this rut and on our way to Africa. (The word recalls his hope, so that he halts on the stairs, as a vision of it rises before his mind's eye) Africa! I can see her now, like a mother weeping for her long lost children, calling us to return into our own. Soon, and it won't be long now (his tone grows gradually exalted), you're going to see the black man come out of the darkness of failure into the light of achievement, wearing the cloak of human greatness about his shoulders. . . . Yes, Lord! And our enemies shall tremble when he stretches forth his mighty hand to gather in his share of the God-given stars of glory! (For a moment he remains clutched in his own spell, then awakens to ascend with dignity.)   [I-i-16]

Vic's words move from a personal plea for patience in the particular situation to an inspired call from the preacher in his pulpit. Both Vic's rhetoric in the second half of his speech and his stance on the stairs evoke the image of the clergyman before his congregation. We are given no reason outside the speech to doubt Vic's sincerity, or to find inappropriate Ward's description that the family is spellbound and Ella is rendered helpless by Vic's oration. The swift movement from language like "out of this rut" to "the cloak of human greatness" may, however, discomfort some spectators. Vic's speech, somewhat like Martel's language in *Emperor of Haiti*, is overtly metaphorical. Black spectators may feel comfortable with the imagery, but the diction here could make it difficult for white spectators to concur with the intended admiration in Ella's final line in this scene: "What can you do with a man like that?"[15]

The extreme intensity of emotions onstage at the end of Act I, Scene i thus comes perilously close to disrupting the delicate relationship Ward has thus far established between the world of the play and the audience. Ward's intentions in Scene i are apparent: He wishes the audience to perceive and respect the sanctity and insularity of the family, and he wants to establish in the audience a wariness of the threats from the outside world to the family's stability and aspirations. Scene i exposes the audience to most of the characters of the play and identifies these characters in two ways whose relationship to one another is not yet clear. We know the characters in terms of their attitudes toward being black in white America, and we know these people as participants in a family. The audience is also shown the connections between the seemingly mundane events of ordinary life and the visions as well as pervasive frustrations of many black people. Ward makes assumptions about the values of the audience—that, for example, we find the unity of a family important and desirable—and he plays to these values while setting snares to begin to disturb settled preconceptions. These elements of strategy work effectively until the last moments of the scene, which suddenly impose an inspirational oration on the spectator. We are asked simply to accept this ritualized gesture as potent, rather than being seduced to the desired response.

Despite these intrinsic problems, both the cacaphony at the end of Scene i and the Back to Africa plea of Vic's speech set the stage effectively for the first movement of Act I, Scene ii. In contrast to the high pitch of the end of Scene i, the initial conversations of Scene ii are low-keyed; in complement to Vic's speech, Scene ii expands greatly on the workings and concerns of Marcus Garvey's Back to Africa movement. In contrast to the pervasive presence of women in Scene i, Act I, Scene ii is dominated by male characters; that Scene ii is also less shrill and less nervous in tone than Scene i suggests a somewhat stereotypical attitude toward men and women.

Act I, Scene ii begins with a relaxed conversation between Les and Uncle Percy on a Saturday afternoon a week after Scene i. Les is reading *Looking Backward*, by Edward Bellamy; he describes the novel to Uncle Percy as a book about socialism.[16] The nature of the book and the fact that Vic has given it to his son are keys to both Les's intellectual rearing and Les's eventual commitment to socialism. Par-

ticularly in the 1938 production, when American socialism was a notable although limited political movement, the mention of this particular
book would catch the attention of at least some members of the audience. The spectator's attention is immediately distracted from this
political note, however, by Uncle Percy's offer to give Les some fash-
ionable clothes to "tog down" the young man for college. Les's joy
gives the audience reason to like Uncle Percy; the mention of clothes
for college also makes Les's college future seem more concrete and
close at hand for both him and the audience.

The light tone and release from tension for the audience continues
with the entrance of Claudine, Wanda's "very pretty mulatto" girl
friend. Claudine begins to flirt unabashedly with Uncle Percy; her attempted seduction of Percy appears comic rather than offensive because her obvious nervousness and assertions of worldly experience
suggest a girl posing as a woman rather than a genuine adult. While
laughing at Claudine's antics, however, the audience will feel some
wariness because Claudine, as Wanda's best friend, can be seen as
"setting a bad example." Claudine's impudence is also an inappropriate
invasion of the wholesome spirit of this family room.

Richardson continues a pattern of interruptions when Claudine's
flirtation scene is broken off by the entrances of Wanda and Vic.
Wanda and Claudine exit quickly; their departure is followed closely by
the entrance of Dan, Juanita's husband; thus we see alone for the first
time the four central males of the play: Vic, Dan, Les, and Uncle
Percy. The men begin to talk about their various jobs, but conversation
rapidly turns to the more basic notions each man has about his presence in America. Although discussion becomes debate, the dialogue
never seems posed or set apart from the situation. The language remains colloquial, vivid, and concrete; the movement of the verbal battle sustains a sense of spontaneity and uncertain outcome.

Dan initiates the dispute by deprecating a Garveyite he picked up
on a recent trip: "What didn't he say—the fool! (Quoting) 'Jerusalem
for the Jews,' he kept preaching, with the white folks egging him on:
'Ireland for the Irish, and Africa for the Africans'—It was disgusting.
But I doubt if it ever occurred to him he was playing right into the
white man's hands" (I-ii-7). Dan explains that his passenger was playing
into the white man's hands by advocating segregation. Vic counters
that Dan simply does not understand "the new spirit," which is "out to
wrest our heritage from the enemy." Dan responds, as would many
members of the audience, that his heritage is in America, but Vic
counters that what that heritage means for a black man is a lynch rope.
Percy approvingly assents, "You said a mouthful, Captain." As the debate proceeds, we are torn between insights and attitudes that ring

with equally forceful truth. Dan's pragmatic advice to "out-wit the white man. Get something in your pocket and stop expecting the millennium" must certainly be persuasive to many spectators, but the weight of that argument is lightened by Vic's somewhat indirect retort that Dan's education is like a pair of knee pads: "I mean it enables you to crawl through the travel and mud of white prejudice without the least sense of pain or dishonor, that's what!" (I-ii-8).

Ten years before the publication of Ralph Ellison's *Invisible Man,* Ward is dramatizing in the dispute of these men an argument that Ellison will display in his novel: Dan's position is much like that of Bledsoe, the college president, in *Invisible Man.* "You let the white folk worry about pride and dignity—you learn where you are and get yourself power, influence, contacts with powerful and influential people—then stay in the dark and use it."[17] But the message Vic reads in this, like the epigram of the invisible man's dream, is that it will only "keep this nigger boy running,"[18] with dishonor and no real possibility of attaining any worthwhile goal.

Vic's positions increasingly appeal to the dignity and pride of black spectators. Although he never convinces Dan, Vic appears to be substantially winning the battle when Dan throws in still another obstacle by bringing the dispute to their immediate situation. Dan argues that even if Vic persists in his desire to go to Africa, he is not about to leave yet, and, in the meantime, he would do well to join Dan in his newest business venture, the ownership of a kitchenette, a group of flats. Vic has no convincing argument either against the monetary benefits of the venture or against Dan's point, "If the race gave Negro business half a chance, we'd soon get somewhere" (I-ii-9). Vic's response to Dan's proposition is "Bunk." This answer is disappointing in its implicit refusal to consider the idea rationally, but it is also a satisfyingly terse assertion that Dan's notion is foolish. Dan's offer to Vic suggests, too, that the former is not as selfish as the latter has charged.

No verbal synthesis is reached as the argument draws to a close; the audience is likely to feel an uneasy ambivalence if each actor maintains the strength that his lines suggest. We long for a meaningful resolution, but Ward holds any conclusion in abeyance. The ambivalence of the audience is supported and emphasized, in fact, by the visible shifts in Uncle Percy, who has altered his own stance during the conversation. Initially, Percy supports Vic's contentions with illustrations or exclamations of his own about the hopelessness of winning in America against the white establishment. Like a choral figure, Percy responds to the central argument with a voice that speaks from a larger community. Percy also agrees with Dan that it is better to be bled by a black man than a white one, as long as someone is going to bleed you, and the penciled figures representing financial gain that Dan presents are convincing to Percy, as they well might be to the audience.

Allowed no solution, we are once again interrupted in our musings by the entrance of other characters. Ella and Mrs. Brooks have returned from shopping; they and their costly groceries make the question of money even more immediate. Les enters next, with news that shocks Vic and may be meant to sway the audience to Dan's position. The Black Star liner, a renovated ship purchased by the Garveyites to supply funds and eventually transportation for the move to Africa, has been stopped at port by the government as unseaworthy. The news report includes the supposition that the leaders of the Back to Africa movement have been easily misled and further relates that Marcus Garvey has fled to Canada.

The introduction of the newspaper story acts as a new voice in the dialectic and as another sign of the dangers lying in wait outside the Mason's house. The audience is not led now to dismiss all of Vic's judgments about America, but we are certainly made significantly more skeptical about the wisdom of the Garvey movement. Vic's reaction to the news, a response of outrage and disbelief, evokes the pity of the audience, but it also creates disappointment and distrust in Vic as a source of wisdom. Dan's gleeful response to the news of the Black Star Line's misfortunes is despicable, but any anger the audience feels toward Dan's gloating does not diminish the increasing sense of ambiguity as to the real source of truth in this world. Vic is quick to reply that the contents of the news are all a white frame-up, but we have no definite evidence within the play to support either interpretation.[19]

During Vic's assault on these latest tricks of the white man, he has been joined in his home by some of his fellow Garveyites, but before these new characters have time to assert their presence on stage, Ward manipulates another quick shift of attention for those both onstage and in the audience. At precisely the moment when the audience must feel a desire to weigh the various allegations about the Garvey movement, the mailman arrives with another letter for Les. After a few moments of joyful excitement, the mood and movement of Scene ii abruptly changes: Contrary to the expectations of some, but fulfilling Vic's and Wanda's general suspicions, Les's scholarship application has been rejected because he is black.

For the audience, the denial of a scholarship to Les is not wholly unexpected but is still disappointing. The wording of the earlier letter and the warnings of various characters about the attitudes of white people toward education for black people were meant to evoke in the audience a distrust, which has now been fulfilled. We remember with irony Les and Percy's overeager plans for Les's wardrobe. Yet there is still no way logically to understand or accept Les's rejection. The characters onstage now cry out the words that most black spectators must be feeling; the white spectator watching *Big White Fog* may not know quite how to feel here and might respond in humiliation or with anger at "those" white people. The responses of the characters are very much in keeping with each's previously established attitudes: Percy curses the "dirty bastards" and reaches for his bottle; Ella moans about injustice; Dan's anger is aimed at the informant who revealed that Les was "colored"; Mrs. Brooks seeks a culprit in their midst. Wanda only exclaims incoherently, but we remember her earlier cynicism, which now seems to merit more support. Only Vic remains relatively calm, but his response is controlled anger rather than indifference. He quietly asserts that only white people "could be guilty of such a cheap, petty piece of business," but he goes on to reassure Les that everything will be all right.

How can everything now be all right? Vic's line at first seems to express the kind of empty comfort so often offered in difficult situations. As such, it is annoying. But Vic's words are not hollow. Vic has quickly seized on his own gesture of rejection: In what he calls his answer to his son's letter, he uses his entire savings of fifteen hundred dollars to purchase fifteen hundred shares of stock in the Garveyites' Black Star Line. The mixed response of the family to Vic's action can only emphasize the ambivalence the audience must feel at this point. Vic's purchase of the stocks is a commitment, a refusal to accept the society that has hurt his son and his family; the assertiveness of this act creates a release for the audience from a sense of frustration. Vic transforms anger into action; he acts where we cannot because of our immobility as audience. Yet, though the audience empathizes with Vic's need for action, most spectators will be dismayed by the particular action Vic takes.

Dan's calls to reason repeatedly interrupt Vic's gesture and confirm the audience's anxiety about Vic's rashness. From Dan's point of view, Vic's purchase of the stock is not an answer but a foolhardy tossing of good money to the winds. If we had for a moment forgotten, Dan reminds us that the integrity and feasibility of the Black Star Line have just been brought into question. For the first time in the play, for both characters and audience, there is a clear opposition between logic and emotion. The logical response is to wait until the problems of the Black Star Line are clarified; the emotional response is to refuse the frustrations of deliberation by making (or applauding) some assertive action. After all the conversation, all the possibilities tossed at us, we the audience now need a bang, not a whimper; we need a synthesis, not a continuing contradiction of opposites.

Although Vic's gesture is forceful, it is not synthetic; Ward does not allow us any sustained sense of resolution. The dialectic is renewed almost as soon as its first step is concluded. At the end of Act I, Scene ii, only Vic's external family, his fellow Garveyites, seem satisfied by Vic's decision. As Ella sobs in her chair, the counterpoints of the renewed dialectic are each articulated, first by the son, then by the father:

> LES: Seems like the world ain't nothing but a big white fog and we can't see no light nowhere!
> VIC (fervidly): Look to the East, Son, and keep on looking! Beyond the darkness and mist that surrounds us here, Africa, the sun of our hope is rising! [I-ii-18,19]

Vic's curtain lines are doubly ironic. Ward has transfigured the white person's usual image of dark Africa into the source of light and hope through the metaphor of the rising sun; he has used the white man's mythical notions of black and white, lightness and darkness to create a reversal of perception. This image of hope rising is also dramatically ironic; it suggests that the remainder of the play will defeat or disperse the "big white fog," that the action will now rise to a noontime high of fulfillment, when, in fact, what we have seen is the beginning of the setting sun, the movement into gloom and defeat.

Unlike much traditional drama, *Big White Fog* has no single, distinct climax but, rather, a series of climactic moments. Nevertheless, in the customary terms of drama criticism, the end of Act I can be perceived as the turning point of the play. Looking back on *Big White Fog* from the perspective of having read or seen the entire play, we could say that Vic has committed his rash action at the end of Act I, and the remainder of *Big White Fog* depicts his downfall and the gradual downfall of his family. This is not a wholly accurate description of the play's structure, however, because *Big White Fog* is conceived not as the tragic drama of one man but as the tragedy of a society. Throughout Acts II and III of *Big White Fog* there is an aura of consuming defeat, which emanates from Vic, but our attention is continually dispersed, and our hopes and fears are repeatedly encouraged and discouraged on the spears of other characters. The dialectic continues, but we move through the levels of hell, not Vic's prophesied paradise.

Like some of Reginald Marsh's Depression etchings, Ward's strategy in Acts II and III is a scheme to defeat wishful fantasies in the audience by making us feel an increased loss each time the carousel turns and the magic ring is out of reach. Each time we think no worse suffering could be imagined, another appears before our eyes. It is difficult for the audience to know what to expect in Act II after the opposing visions of father and son at the end of Act I. The exposition at the beginning of Act II is surprising in its specifics but not shocking in the sense of being opposite to what the audience expected, because there was no clear path to anticipate. The first picture presented to us in Act II is a bit puzzling. A typewriter has been added to the living room furnishings, and, in the middle of the day, Vic is dictating to Wanda while Ella and Mrs. Brooks look on. But we are soon informed by expository dialogue similar to that in Act I, Scene i, that Vic is on strike, is about to leave for a convention of Garveyites in Harlem, and is preparing a paper for that convention. Les enters and provides us with the information that in the year that has passed between Act I and Act II, Dan has established his kitchenette and prospered, and has employed Les to enable him to earn tuition to attend a local college. Les also reveals that the Masons are beginning to suffer financially from the strike. Scene i of Act II serves to satisfy the audience's curiosity about events and to re-establish attitudes toward the characters, with particular focus on Vic and Dan; Scene i should also worry the audience, because it conveys a sense of nervous activity in the living room and instability in the family.

More sharply and definitively than at any time in Act I, Ward moves the sympathies of the audience to Vic and his family as opposed to Dan and his. We pity Vic and feel anxiety for the family because of their financial difficulties; we are carefully brought to a new admiration of Vic as we hear bits and pieces of the eloquent speech he is preparing. Vic is shown as a diligent and committed worker who commands the audience's respect for his industry, but that respect remains permanently tarnished because of his earlier foolishness with his savings. Les commands respect because he has not been defeated by the scholarship rejection but has gone to work to obtain his own education. In sharp contrast to this depiction of virtue and strength in the Mason family is the description the family gives us of Dan's ventures. When Les enters, he is disgusted with Dan because Dan has just evicted a young woman and baby for failure to pay rent after only three weeks' delinquency. To confirm that these descriptions of Dan's greed and ostentation are not just jealous rumors, Dan and Juanita suddenly appear with a new Cadillac and elegant clothes. The Masons' disdain for the means Dan has used to obtain his "fortune on wheels" is clear in their greetings to Dan and Juanita, but none of the family can hide some honest sense of awe for the beauty of the new possession.

Although the arrival of Dan and Juanita seems arbitrarily contrived to confirm visually what we have heard, their visit has internal purpose: They have come to take Vic and Les to the train to depart for

Harlem. Now the strategy of these scenes becomes clearer. Vic must admit that he cannot take Les to New York because the strike has severely limited their income. Not only is the poverty of one family severely juxtaposed to the prosperity of the other, but we are reminded by omission rather than overt suggestion that Vic was able to give money to his "other family," the Garveyites, and he therefore has none left in reserve for his own children. Once again, the intended impact of events and values on the audience is intentionally ambiguous. We cannot admire Dan's success because of the indications of his lack of compassion, but we cannot wholly pity Vic in his present plight, because we have seen him rashly bring this on himself and his family.

The situation and our responses to it are further complicated by the continuation of Vic's dictation of his speech. Even Dan is impressed by Vic's eloquence, but Dan adds that it is too bad that Vic "can't see anything but Garvey." As train time approaches, Vic and Dan are launched once more into their argument about the most effective way of winning against the white man. Again each man presents strong statements that appeal equally to our reason, so that neither seems incorrect. Dan insists that the white man's own method of individual achievement does work for blacks, and he is obviously a vivid example of that theory. But individual achievement suggests self-interest, whereas Vic's retorts express concern for the conditions of the group. The energy of the statements and the force of the positions are so engaging that we are almost unaware when the debate moves from reasoned counterstatement to insults. Before Vic departs, he accuses Dan of "cutting his own brother's throat to get somewhere," and Dan accuses Vic of being "weak and shiftless." When Vic asserts that he will call a taxi rather than go to the station with Dan, Ella's retort that they are acting like children seems an accurate perception as well as a welcome plea to change their behavior.

That the battle between Dan and Vic should be much more troublesome to the audience than a child's quarrel is clearly marked by Ward's focus on actual children. With a fine dramaturgical pen, he draws our attention to Vic's excessively harsh reprimand of his youngest son for some minor mischief. Ward has subtly brought any parent in the audience to identify with Vic's misplaced anger; how often have we yelled at a child when the scream was really meant for ourselves or another adult? The moment serves to diminish gradually the tension of the scene while emphasizing for us our ambivalent identification with both Dan and Vic. The focus on the children at the end of Act II, Scene i, also indicates that the argument is not only an intellectual debate between two adults but also an issue that will affect the lives of the young; more concretely than ever before in the play, the problems of dealing with the world "outside" are disturbing the tranquillity of the family inside.

Scene ii of Act II occurs six months after Scene i, but a sense of continuity of effect is created by calling our attention immediately to the children of the Mason family. Ward's strategy is to play on our aroused concern for them while contrasting the heat of the earlier August scene with the dreary winter gloom of a January afternoon. We are immediately drawn into another of the minor but meaningful conflicts that bombard the Mason family. The struggle this time is Ella's: She is torn between her desire to give moral comfort to her husband and his supporters and her need to care for her younger children, both of whom are ill with flu. Ella apparently has settled the problem when we see her; she is doing all she can to nurse her sick children, but she has also spent her few spare coins preparing an eggnog for refreshment for the Garveyites, who are coming out on a dismal, snowy night to honor her husband. Ella has determined how their meager resources should be spent, but she still feels conflict between pride in her husband, who is about to be commended as a leader of men, and anger at her husband and the external world, which has placed her family in such a position that their children are ill because the family cannot afford necessary shoe repairs.

Ella's tension is part of the continuing effort of the play to make clear that the choice between love and responsibility on the one hand and material possessions and appearances on the other is not as easily resolved as we might think. Love and material needs overlap in both Ella's concern for her children and her concern for her husband; in both instances, the question of human dignity is paramount. The spectator may be initially prone to condemn Ella's decision to provide eggnog for her guests when she cannot provide shoes for her children, but Ella's own protestations make clear that the eggnog is for her a symbol of unwillingness to yield to despair. Ella's first concern is her family, and her husband is central to that family; because part of his world exists outside the Mason's living room, she must acknowledge that world or retreat to a private cell of suffering. We are therefore led to admire her fortitude and to pity her in her struggle, even if we do not agree with her specific choice.

Ella's struggle raises the question for the audience of other sources of money, and that is the question to which the action of Scene ii, Act II now turns. With an adult man and two nearly adult children in the family, how can the Masons be so poor? Ella raises this question as she seeks money for new shoes for her younger children. Ella turns first to Wanda, who is now working regularly and has already been contributing most of her income to the family. Wanda at first responds angrily that all her mother speaks to her about now is money, but a few seconds later Wanda says that perhaps she will be able to get a few dollars from her boss that night. The spectator will be momentarily annoyed with Wanda for her harsh retort to her needy mother, but the sense of this young girl as the major support of an entire family should also evoke admiration for her.

When Vic enters after shoveling snow all afternoon, we wait expectantly with Ella for some helpful addition to the family funds, and we are as disappointed as both Ella and Vic that he has brought home only a few cents. We pity the eloquent man who can find no job better than one a child could hold. As each door to money closes, our sense of frustration and futility is increased. In a despair that complements the growing anxiety of the audience, Vic begs his son to quit school for a term and contribute to the family the money he now earns for his tuition. When Les agrees, we admire his decision but empathize with his bitterness. We are here led to react to the immediate misfortune of the interruption of Les's education, but we can also be alarmed that Les may not be able to resume his education the next quarter. The world we are being shown has little place for optimistic expectations.

Vic now turns to Percy in an attempt we know will be futile. Percy, of course, has no money to give, but he does provide information that presents a new problem. Percy suggests that the family turn to Wanda, because, having seen her in an expensive sealskin coat, he infers that she is "doing all right." This revelation is a surprise for both the family and the audience, and suspicions are immediately raised. All of the spectator's previous knowledge of Wanda floods back: Her desire for nice things does contradict her apparent self-sacrifice for her family; her friendship with the seductive Claudine seems not to have touched Wanda's innocence, but we cannot be sure this is true. In a united burst of outrage, the family confronts Wanda: Where has she obtained the expensive coat? The family obviously suspects some immoral behavior, and only reluctantly accepts Wanda's protests that she bought the coat herself on credit. For the audience, there is relief that Wanda's possession of the coat does not signal some further moral decay for the family, but we are likely to remain both suspicious about the true source of the coat and partially sympathetic to the desires of a young girl for something pretty and comforting amidst all this distress and responsibility. Our reactions to Wanda's coat are a good example of Ward's control in his attempt to persuade the audience away from simplistic or convenient judgments. Our first conclusion may be that Wanda is a prostitute, and as such we condemn her. If we hesitate with this understanding, we still feel distressed because it seems damnably selfish of her to buy an expensive coat when her family is hungry. We should have at least a third reaction that she is a young woman who understandably covets some luxuries. All of these reactions, and others, are certainly natural and provoked by the script, and none of them are wholly antithetical or inappropriate.

With so much suffering apparent onstage, the question of blame now arises for both family and audience. Into an abyss of confusion as to who is the accuser and who the accused, Dan enters to add his reproach. Dan's anger is aimed at Vic: Dan's assertion is that he is paying Les to go to school, not to support the family, and that Vic had no right to change those rules. Dan's appearance also suggests another hope, another door to knock on for money, and we are allowed to hope for a moment that Dan will, indeed, provide the monetary answers. If we expect resolution here, we are disappointed. Dan presents Vic with a business proposition that seems fair enough: He will purchase Vic's shares of stock even though those stocks are really worth very little. Vic cannot accept the business deal, for to him it means an acknowledgment of the worthlessness of his commitment to the Garvey movement. As Ella begs Vic to reconsider Dan's offer, we, the audience, feel our sympathies shifting from Vic to Dan, Ella, and the rest of the family. Ward impresses us with the integrity of Vic's position but opposes that integrity with the truths of the illness of the children, the bitterness of Les, the temptations for Wanda, and the growing sense of strain for the entire family. There is no appeal to the audience for a particular response to these dilemmas, but there is an increasing sense aroused that ideas are blurred and weak while the various hungers of human beings are clear and strong.

The audience is momentarily released from this confusion of response by the introduction of a new character, Nathan Piszer, Les's college friend, who is labeled a "young Jewish student." His entrance at this point in the play is an intrusion, despite the family's gestures of welcome. Piszer himself affirms this sense when he hears that he has arrived just before a celebration for Vic. Piszer is the first white character to appear onstage; unlike Claudine, Wanda's black friend, he is never addressed by his first name in this scene; he is always addressed as "Mr. Piszer" or "Piszer." Pressed by the family to stay for the festivities, Piszer remains throughout the scene during which the Garveyites arrive and present Vic with the title of "Lord of Agriculture." Structurally, Piszer's role is transparent: He introduces the family to the ideas of socialism as an alternative mode of achieving freedom and security, and he acts as a choral voice asking naïve questions about the Garvey movement that the spectator might want posed but that the Masons would presumably not need to ask.

Piszer's effect on the audience is more complicated than his function in the movement of episode. His sudden arrival will jar any spectator; his whiteness may create discomfort and a clear sense of intrusion for a black audience, as well as for a white audience because by now the white spectator should be accustomed to the black cast. Some whites may also be relieved at finding a more accessible presence onstage. The degree to which Piszer creates definite reactions because he is Jewish will vary according to how the role is cast and played. His name will identify him as a Jew for most audience members (and if read or pronounced as close to "pisser" will certainly evoke laughter or embarrassment), but despite Ward's willingness to allow Piszer to appear as the "Jewish intellectual," without much further character delineation, Piszer escapes the kind of stereotyping that automatically commands hostility or laughter. His astute perceptions of society, his favorable mention of socialism, his questions to the Garveyites all appear knowledgeable and thoughtful. The audience should also be struck that there is enough honest intimacy between Les and Piszer that when Piszer questions why the huge masses of poor in the world have not united, Les can answer that it is because of "the same thing that makes them call you Sheeny and me Nigger!" (II-ii-17).

Piszer's uneasiness in the presence of the Garveyites allows the audience greater freedom to experience its own embarrassment and hesitation in response to the Back to Africa ritual. Members of the audience who have been or who know actual Garveyites are allowed a nostalgic moment with the plumed and uniformed men and women who come into the Masons' living room to make Vic a Lord of Agriculture of the Provisional Republic of Africa, but others, like Piszer, who have not had this experience will be puzzled or amused by this strange ritual presentation. Piszer's presence allows diverse reactions in the audience. We may find the royal trappings of this visionary society pompous and foolish, but we may also respond with admiration to Vic's powerful acceptance speech. For black audience members, to whom this speech seems clearly directed, Vic's words can have an intense and deeply emotional effect. His speech is ostensibly intended for his fellow Garveyites onstage, but his repeated call to his "Brothers and Sisters" concludes, "Let us pledge our hearts and minds and the last ounce of our strength to carry on . . . to carry on without ceasing until our cause is won and the black man has achieved his place in the God given sun, a free man, honored and respected in the eyes of the Nations of the World" (II-ii-20). This is clearly meant to exhort the audience to unity and commitment. The conventions of the modern theater (and particularly of dramatic realism) may keep Big White Fog's spectators in their seats, and the previously raised questions about the wisdom of the Back to Africa movement may prevent them from espousing

Vic's particular cause, but the end of Act II, Scene ii, is meant to evoke a spirit of community in the audience. That this community is not fully accessible to white audience members is, I believe, an undeniable if not necessarily intentional effect of the play.

This insular respite from discord provides only the illusion of permanent synthesis in the dialectic process. The scene allows the audience a brief period of emotional harmony; it also serves as the point from which Ward can persuade the audience that moments of community drawn from a ritual sharing are transient and do not suffice. Although that communal sensation is vibrant enough to linger for much of the play, Act II, Scene iii, and all of Act III work increasingly to undermine any wishful notion that such a moment can endure indefinitely or provide an answer.

The calm at the end of Act II, Scene ii, is immediately disrupted in Scene iii by the sounds of discord between Caroline, the youngest child, and her grandmother Mrs. Brooks. The harsh exchange as this scene begins is ostensibly only a matter of impatience on both their parts over the dressing of a doll, but underneath Mrs. Brooks's annoyance, the audience will recognize her distaste for the black color of Caroline's doll. When Caroline comments that, "Poor lil black Judy, Grandma treats that honey child like a orphan, don't she?" (II-iii-1), we are sensitized to Mrs. Brooks's own prejudices. *214395*

The impatience of the oldest and youngest members of the family resonates first in Ella and Vic and then in Wanda. Ella and Vic are angry that neither has paid the paper boy; Wanda enters with a more serious complaint: Her coat has been repossessed by the sheriff for failure to meet payments. Ella and Vic are seeking some solution to Wanda's problem when Dan bursts in with an even more dismaying piece of news for Vic: Marcus Garvey's court appeal has been denied. Garvey has been arrested for what the dialogue vaguely suggests had something to do with money but was actually a charge of using the mails to defraud. The audience is here given Dan as a target for its own anger, because he has clearly come to say, "I told you so." But despite our pity for Vic, the news of Garvey's arrest cannot but further erode any spectator's belief that Garvey's Back to Africa movement remains the best answer to the problems of the Masons or black people in general.

Mrs. Brooks grasps at this occasion to do her own gloating and adds her ill-humor to an already fragile atmosphere. To her criticism of Vic she adds a petty attack on young Phillip; the source of both assaults takes us back to the beginning of the scene. Vic and Phillip are too black for Mrs. Brooks's social taste. Ella can no longer absorb this insult to her husband and child. As she defends them, she offends her mother in no uncertain terms by accusing her of racism and selfishness. Ward clearly intends here that the audience cheer for Ella and find no sympathy for Mrs. Brooks's intolerance; it is one of the rare instances in the play where a didactic message is unambiguously urged on the audience. This moment of instruction is quickly brought back into the dialectic, however, as it becomes apparent that Ella's attack on her mother, which is heightened and reinforced by Vic's furious retorts, is leading to a serious disruption of the family. Vic's anger is so intense that Ella is forced to retreat from her own attack to soothe her husband. Then she herself is horrified when Vic accuses her mother of speaking from shame because of her own illegitimate origin.

In presenting this bitter family argument, Ward forces spectators to endure a scene that many would prefer to escape or ignore. There is no obvious distribution of sympathies. Vic's points are sound, but if they succeed in arousing the shame of a spectator who, like Mrs. Brooks, takes pride "in the blood of [her] raping ancestors," they will also provoke the antagonism of the spectator who sees the unnecessary cruelty of Vic's barbs. Mrs. Brooks's notions are to be condemned, but we pity her defenselessness. Ella's pivotal position arouses our sympathy, until she is so frustrated by her impossible position that she scathingly labels her husband a "dirty, coppermouth snake," and asserts that she despises him. Ella's vituperation and her flight from the living room should leave the audience deeply troubled.

Mrs. Brooks also departs from this bedlam; before the scene is concluded, she has left for Juanita's. For most spectators it will be a relief to have her irritating presence removed, but some may see her departure as symbolic of the real destruction of the Mason family, and that perception would create tension in the spectator.

Even Vic's reflections on this event, which constitute a limited recognition scene, do not remove the despair the family wreckage evokes for the audience. Vic comes to a new understanding of himself and his world, but his particular recognition denies renewal or relief: "Prejudice . . . prejudice . . . everywhere you turn . . . nothing but . . . prejudice. (Bitterly) A black man can't even get away from it in his own house—Phumph! . . . And I was fool enough to think I could get away from it in Africa!" (II-iii-11). Vic's acknowledgment of his own blindness provides a complicated pleasure for the spectator. Consistent with the traditional effect of recognition scenes, as discussed earlier, Vic's self-knowledge inspires the audience to its own self-acknowledgment. The black spectator can admit that prejudice does not exist only in the white world "out there." Tangentially, the white spectator is drawn by Vic's admission to a new empathy, a sense of shared guilt, with black people.

Yet this remains a perverse recognition scene, because although the act of self-recognition itself suggests man's potential for growth and wisdom, what is here revealed about man is his pervasive and consuming self-hatred. The recognition scenes in such plays as *Oedipus Rex* and *Othello* inspire the audience with awe at what Arthur Miller calls "man's total compulsion to evaluate himself justly."[20] Such awe is elevating; it affirms man's potential for dignity. Vic's own compulsion to evaluate himself justly may evoke that awe, but it is simultaneously deflated by Vic's bitter, defeated assertion that it is man's limitations that he has now accepted, that it is man's compulsion to evaluate himself falsely that Vic has now acknowledged. Vic's recognition scene is limited because it is turned inward as ressentiment.

Ward then draws us into Act III with two opposing sensations again working on the audience. Vic's new self-awareness urges the possibility of a change in his behavior, which allows for some hope that the situation for the family may alter; but working against that hope is the blow to family unity felt in Mrs. Brooks's departure, Ella's assertion of hatred for Vic, and Vic's own belief that there is no hope. We enter Act III with the dim wish that a miracle will evolve from Vic's new stance, but with the expectation that all the real signs point to the absence of miracles and the further disintegration of the family.

Act III encourages that wish while finally fulfilling more than our expectations of doom. The act begins nine years after Act II; if the passage of so much time, indicated perhaps by program notes, arouses our hope that much could have changed for the better, the date, 1932, warns us that this was not a time for optimism in most families. (The nine-year gap may also disturb the audience's sense of continuity of action; it seems a weak and arbitrary device to emphasize personal and historical change.) The appearance of the living room confirms the threats of Act II and the warnings of the date: Although the furniture remains basically the same, everything, including Ella's mien, is frayed and suggests severe poverty. The first character to speak in Act III, Scene i, is a stereotypical, conniving Jewish used-furniture salesman named Marx. (The willfully confused reference to a variety of Marxes indicates Ward's independence from Communist Party dogma.) Ella is attempting to sell the merchant her furniture, but they cannot even approach agreement on a price that is acceptable to her. It is not clear whether the sympathies of white spectators would be wholly with Ella. Our natural tendency would be antagonism toward the manipulating merchant and pity for his victim. It is not certain, however, that his remarks about his own family's needs—"I'm a man vit a family. You vant me to ruin myself?"—are untrue, even if they are a blatant rhetorical device. Black spectators are likely to sympathize with Ella

and hear Marx's speech as a cliché, but some spectators, black or
white, may hesitate simply to dismiss Marx's plea. We also have no
information about Ella since the last act and thus have little sense of
how to feel about her, except to have some pity for her in what is
evidently a demeaning situation. We are curious about her, and that
curiosity is whetted when she drops the information during her bar-
tering that she is hoping to raise a few dollars to get herself another
place.

Wanda has been witness to this scene between her mother and
Marx, and our attention is drawn to Wanda's matured voice, which
rages furiously at Marx, then modulates to console her mother. During
Marx's departure, Claudine enters; the ensuing conversation between
Wanda and Claudine informs us that the Masons are about to be
evicted from their house, that Vic is at that moment in court concerning the eviction, and that, by inference, Vic is still a resident of the
household. Our worst expectations at the end of Act II have not been
fulfilled: The family remains basically together, but it is on the brink of
further disaster.

Knowing the present situation, we are provoked to ask if there is
any way the Mason home can be salvaged. There is the possibility that
Vic's appearance in court will effect some good, but Wanda's tone
suggests otherwise. Claudine satisfies our need to believe that there is
some way out, but the alternative she suggests to Wanda is calculated
to arouse still another set of ambivalent responses in the audience.
Claudine urges Wanda to get money from an old white man who would
gladly reward Wanda if she were "nice to him." Wanda is not appalled
by the suggestion; in fact, she has already approached the man for
money, as a gift, but her response to Claudine is that although she is
admittedly no virgin, she is also not a whore and can't go quite that
far. The ready reaction for the spectator would be to condemn
Claudine's scheme and applaud with some relief Wanda's rejection of
that plan. A black audience would be particularly antagonized by
Claudine's plan, since the man involved is white. But Ward again disturbs the responses of at least some spectators through Claudine's
counterargument, which is annoyingly persuasive. Claudine makes her
point seem simple: Wanda can save her mother from disgrace and all
that Wanda will be sacrificing in return is what Claudine labels a
"flimsy idea." Both Wanda and the audience are left to ponder a moral
choice. We have been led to want to see this family preserved in this
place, but the way now offered to accomplish this goal is as abhorrent
as the destruction of the family itself. We are forced to respond
thoughtfully, because Ward has carefully kept the tone of the scene
cool and refreshingly frank; this is not a question of a sentimental or

hysterical sacrifice but a harsh and difficult decision to be made in the gray areas of ordinary life.

Wanda goes offstage to dress for work without revealing a decision and thus sustains the curiosity of the audience. Les, returning home, reveals a not surprising commitment to the Communist movement. Dan commences another debate, this time with Les concerning Communism. We feel impatient because we have seen this all before; the gestures are the same, only the issues have changed. These similarities do not seem accidental to Ward's strategy. The restlessness evoked in the audience demands the kind of nonverbal action with which Ward concludes this play.

The conversation returns to the eviction notice and reveals that Dan and Juanita have been struck by the Depression, a historic cataclysm (which Ward has only vaguely established by the 1932 date and indirect remarks). Dan has now lost almost all of his money, but his attitudes remain the same. As another argument seems about to engulf the whole family, Ella explodes, "Oh, stop it!—I'm sick of listening to nothing but talk, talk!—For twenty years that's all we've had in this house, and ain't nobody done nothing yet!" (III-i-8). Ella's exclamation is a risky strategic advice. There is potential pleasure of recognition for the audience in having a character onstage articulating what spectators may be feeling, but Ella's comment may make us focus detrimentally on the talkiness of the play. Ward's central intention is to stimulate further our impatience for action, through Ella's frustration with talk. We are pushed to demand that someone do something, and we are prepared for some unpredictable event.

Ward keeps that action in abeyance through a series of further conversational episodes. The first of these is a dialogue between Wanda and Les that returns us to Wanda's decision. Les has seen Wanda leaving the white man's car the previous night. He now accuses his sister of being a "dirty little chippy." It is unclear whether Les is the righteous accuser or the protective brother who hopes to have his suspicions denied. Yet whatever Les's motives, he arouses the spectators' anger because they know that at the least, the situation is morally more complex than he allows. His abusive language also painfully recalls earlier altercations, such as the bitter scene that preceded Mrs. Brooks's departure from the family.

Les's insults drive Wanda to the edge of her control. As Ella enters, Wanda wildly begins to tell her mother Claudine's scheme as if it were fact, creating for the audience a concern that we are about to witness still another disruption of what little remains of the family community. Our anxiety is again relieved, this time by Les, who changes the subject to his own plan for a people's march to the governor to protest the starvation and evictions of the poor. This plan provides only a momentary respite, because Dan, reentering, reminds Les that only recently a similar "mob" had been brutalized by the police. Les's response to Dan is provocative: He urges that the sooner violence comes, the better; "The disinherited will never come to power without bloodshed!"

Les's cogent argument forces us to pay it genuine attention, but we are only allowed that attention for a moment. First, Dan distracts the spectator with his renewed accusations that Vic and Ella are to blame for rearing Les to be reckless. Such accusations can only arouse hostility toward Dan in the audience, even if they hold some truth. We are then further distracted and dismayed by the entrance of a very drunken Uncle Percy. By the time Vic returns from court, we have almost forgotten to be anxious about the verdict, and the information that the family has only been given twenty days to pay up or leave the house is not surprising. More disturbing as an addition to the play's dialectic than the actual verdict is Vic's description of the judge's reaction to Vic's old Garveyite uniform. Vic quotes the judge as commenting, " 'Oh, so you're one of the Niggers who think this country isn't good enough for you, eh?' " The effect of this statement is to close still another door that might have led to support from the outside world. What is impressed on the audience is that even the court, which many white spectators adjudge to be a bastion of dignity and justice, is only a man, as capable as any other of being callous and racist in his judgments. There is no hope here for the audience to clutch. If we attempt to turn our frustration on Vic for his stupidity in wearing his Garvey uniform to court, our anger is blunted there, too, as Vic bitterly tells Dan that he had nothing else to wear.

Act III, Scene i, is dismal and relentless. Each character is forced to present himself for a moment, carrying only the accessories of his former costume, emotionally ragged and unprotected. Even Mrs. Brooks returns by the end of the scene, disgusted with Juanita, who by now is renting out rooms to what Mrs. Brooks calls "those good-for-nothin tramps." We are deliberately drawn to perplexity by Mrs. Brooks's frantic assertion that she would "rather sleep in the street with you all than spot mah garment in the wallow they got over there." Her values are distorted, but we can pity her nonetheless for the paucity of her choices.

Only Les is able to laugh at the end of this scene. We still worry when he tells his grandmother not to fret, we are wary of his curtain line, "A lot of things can happen in twenty days," but we are left with our attention focused on him as the only possible source of salvation.

The second scene of Act III is a brief and ominous interlude that sets up for the audience a more vivid aura of tension for the play's conclusion. It is three o'clock in the morning. Mrs. Brooks is still awake, fretting to Les about Wanda's failure to return home that evening. Les is clearly troubled by this information but represses his anxiety until he catches sight on the street of Claudine, who is herself nervous and uncertain. The terse scene concludes with Claudine's assurances that Wanda really is all right, but Claudine's words do not reassure the audience. We can only conclude that either Wanda has yielded to desperation and sold herself to a white man, a conclusion that will evoke deeply ambivalent reactions because of the previous arguments for and against such a choice, or we can fear that Wanda is in some grave danger, since Les and Mrs. Brooks suggest that it is unique for Wanda to spend the entire night out.

After a moment's blackout, Scene iii begins with Ella's own early morning expressions of anxiety about Wanda. By now, Les is missing as well; because we last saw him worrying about Wanda and in the company of Claudine, we presume he has gone searching for Wanda, and his failure to return protends ill. The telephone has already been disconnected, and the anxiety in the living room is visible, when Wanda does return with Les and a poorly fabricated story. The family eagerly accepts Wanda's story of a broken-down car, but our clues from Claudine the previous night and from Wanda's earlier revelations prevent our feeling a sense of relief and provoke our curiosity further to know more about what really happened.

Indirectly, our curiosity is satisfied. Caroline, the younger daughter, triumphantly informs the family that they can now rent a new place, because Wanda has brought home money that she "borrowed from her boss." The spectator, of course, assumes this to be false, but reaction to that falsehood is confusing for the audience, because it does provide a practical resolution. Here, it is Les who opposes the apparent salvation of Wanda's money with his own plan to confront the eviction with the physical support of men connected with the Communist movement, in which he and Piszer are now involved. His argument is both directly and indirectly persuasive to the audience; his overt point that landlords must be stopped is convincing as a matter of principle; we also know that behind his stance is his knowledge of the corrupt source of Wanda's money. We are therefore disappointed and frustrated when Vic refuses his son's plan on the basis that the family now has enough money for a month, and in a month things can change again. The audience is torn between wishing that the truth were more apparent onstage, so that different gestures would be appropriate, and fearing the destruction that the revelation of that truth would bring. Even Dan's belated offer of his house, which should be a significant act, does not assuage this tension.

As in Act I, when news of Les's scholarship rejection created the context for vivid and incisive action, it is again the disclosure of the personal consequences of racism and poverty that brings about a decisive move. Phillip, the younger son, bursts into the living room tactlessly disclosing the news that Wanda is in jail. Wanda is, of course, no longer in jail, but despite Les's attempts to undercut Phillip's tale, Ella's aroused curiosity and Phillip's naïveté bring the entire story into the open. Wanda has been in jail, after being caught in a raid on a house where she was "laying up with a white man." She is home now because she has been released on bail put up by the madame of the house. The audience is relieved of its burden of special knowledge but must watch with new anxiety the despair that fills the faces of the family members as they recognize the nature of Wanda's sacrifice. Wanda herself returns to the living room and initially attempts to hide her disgrace, then slaps Les, whom she erroneously presumes to be the source of the disclosure. Although Wanda's initial deceit in this episode and her attack on Les suggest the further disintegration of the family, her exchange with her mother and her outcry as she hits Les make clear that there is still a vital family structure to be violated:

> ELLA (as Wanda reaches level): Where were you last night?
> WANDA (frightened): I . . . I just told you. Me and Claudine—
> ELLA: I want the truth!
> WANDA: I'm telling you, Mama.
> ELLA (emotionless): Didn't you just get out of jail?
> WANDA (struck): No, no—(Glancing searchingly around the eyes riveted upon her) Who said that? (As her eyes fall on Les) Les, did you—(Catches herself)
> ELLA (sensing the slip): Oh, so you were!
> WANDA (striding swiftly down and across to strike Les across the mouth with a resounding palm): Take that for your damn self-righteous pains!   [III-iii-7]

We can understand the anger and terror in her slap, we can perceive it as her futile claim of dignity, but we also recognize the gesture as a sign that even temporary resolutions are no longer to be found in verbal actions.

The slap, with the degradation of his family that it symbolizes, is enough to force Vic to change his mind and accept Les's offer of supporters to confront the eviction. Although the connection between Wanda's prostitution and the confrontation of the eviction is as irrational as the link between the denial of Les's scholarship and Vic's purchase of the Garvey stocks, both sequences can be perceived with admiration for one man's refusal to yield to injustice and dishonor. We thus move forward to the eviction scene fearing the consequences of a physical challenge between a mob and legal officers and with some exhilaration at the thought that man can fight the forces constricting him.

Ward sustains ambivalent emotional reactions in the audience, even at the conclusion of his play. Before the eviction scene itself has commenced, our exhilaration is tainted by Vic's bitter description of his daughter as "the little tramp." Vic's insult revives Ella's old fury with her husband to such intensity that she cries out her desire to see him dead. In retrospect, Ella's curse seems an excessively contrived bit of irony, but Ward may achieve his intention to intensify the audience's anxiety through Ella's hyperbolic wish. The play has prepared the audience to expect material disasters and spiritual defeats, but not death.

It is death, however, that concludes the action of *Big White Fog*, and it is only in actually witnessing that death that we can recognize it as the play's inevitable, though unexpected, last word. The movement from Ella's ominous damnation of her husband to his actual murder is rapid. It intensifies the confusion for the audience in the final seconds of the play. The bailiff arrives and, as Vic refuses to yield to the authority of the law, increasingly loud voices are heard approaching the house singing "The Battle Hymn of the Republic."[21] The sirens of police riot-squad cars are also heard approaching, and Caroline's warning that the police have guns reinforces our fear that serious danger is at hand. The cacaphony and visual chaos of various bodies pushing furniture in and out of the front doorway bewilders us. Then a barrage of gunshots, followed by a sudden silence, informs us, as well as those onstage, that someone has been shot.

Even this last, most spectacular event is calculated to arouse many responses in the audience. Not only is Vic the one who has been shot, he has been shot in the back; the audience is goaded to a fury that is augmented by the police lieutenant's arrogant attempts to retain control over the situation. Les's Communist friend Piszer persists in defying the police, and his success in sending them off may distract the audience for a moment from anxiety about Vic's condition, or may painfully remind it that in this struggle the defiant black man has been killed while the defiant white man survives. Whatever triumph we may feel in the retreat of the police is abruptly deflated by Vic's call for Ella, who remains aloof. The audience is faced not only with the sorrow of Vic's death but with an intensified pity and despair that Vic dies deprived of the comfort of his wife's love. In contrast to the consoling affirmation of family ties, which the death of kin often brings, Vic's death makes the dissolution of the Mason family unsparingly vivid.

Critics who admonish Ward for urging violent revolution as an answer for black people have not heard the concluding lines of *Big White Fog*. The police have been temporarily defeated, but a man is dead. The family may remain in their house this time, but it is a family without a father and one in which the mother is herself so nearly destroyed emotionally that she only crawls to her husband's side after he is dead and can no longer recognize her. Les optimistically remarks to his dying father that those who have come to their aid were both black and white, but, as Vic reaches out, he proclaims in his last line that his sight is gone. It is too late.

In the end, Ward has sustained the strategy of the entirety of *Big White Fog;* no audience who has participated in the experience of this play can leave the theater believing that there is a clear-cut program or easy answer to the dilemma of being a black person in white America. The dialectic strategy prevents despair; violence, too, will find its antithesis, but the absence of despair does not insure relief from pain. Ward forces his audience, black or white, to acknowledge complexity and reconsider previous assumptions. The experience of this play is an intense sensation of vacillation and disruption. The work calls not for inaction but for careful and continuously skeptical consideration and reconsideration of every action. It urges that no answer be perceived as whole or final, and it makes that urging tangible for the audience by moving it through a series of responses that feel temporarily satisfactory but are then unsettled. Reviewers who, when the play was produced in the late 1930s and 1940s, condemned it for its ideological stances, were, I believe, caught in a trap of their own rather than the play's making.

A more recent critic of American arts, Susan Sontag, plunges into a similar pitfall. She remarks that the "classics of Broadway liberalism" would be unacceptable now because "they were too optimistic. They thought problems could be solved."[22] Sontag then suggests that James Baldwin's *Blues for Mr. Charlie* and other black dramas are like the Broadway classics in that they are sermons but are sermons that have replaced liberalism with racism. She sees Broadway of the 1950s and 1960s as a stage on which moralism acquired new masks: The image of virtue was black; the image of evil was white.

Sontag's remarks suggest an encompassing view of black drama that not only excludes most of the plays approached in this study but is directly challenged by Theodore Ward's *Big White Fog*. *Big White Fog* presents a strategy for black drama in which the central experience is a negation of the notion that problems can be *solved*. The difficulties facing the Masons are not pieces of a puzzle that simply need to be arranged properly or logically for a satisfying coherence to appear. By leading the spectator to confront the frustration of a search for solutions, Ward raises the possibility that we must move in a radically different way than that of seeking cures for illnesses.

In *Big White Fog* there are analogies to the masks of Sontag's rhetoric, but their color is not morally connotative, for behind as well as on the surface of each mask is a black face, no one of which singly represents the author or good or evil. White society may be callous and corrupt, but the only white character of importance, Nathan Piszer, demonstrates more virtue than evil in his willingness to aid the Masons, and his sympathetic portrayal suggests Ward's desire to prevent the audience from stereotyping any one race or ideology. The black society is downtrodden and full of pain, but essential to the strategy of the play, as in Richardson's *The Broken Banjo*, is our understanding that not one of its characters is wholly virtuous; all of the black characters evoke both sympathy and hostility. *Big White Fog* is rich with sermons, but its preachers each speak from the pulpits of different churches. For the congregation, or audience, the experience is one of being moved by the power of each exhortation but repeatedly finding that neither emotional nor rational leaps suffice; no preacher can or does deliver the Kingdom of Heaven. If the strategy of *Big White Fog* urges a change in the spectators' behavior, it is to make them hesitate before offering their pennies to any church's collections.

If Ward failed in affecting the behavior of his audiences, it was not essentially because of weaknesses in his script. The dramaturgical lapses apparent in *Big White Fog* diminish the power of particular moments but do not destroy Ward's basic strategy. The sometimes too abrupt introduction of new events and information, the occasionally awkward dialogue, and the insufficiency of pauses to enable the audience to grapple with an event or position are rough edges in a script that needs smoothing but are not corners irredeemably turned. Langston Hughes's judgment in 1938—"If it isn't liked by people, it is because they are not ready for it, not because it isn't a great play"[23]— comes closer to the truth of *Big White Fog*'s public neglect than could any critical observations of dramaturgy.

Hughes's remark does raise the question, however, of just for whom *Big White Fog* is intended. The cumulative effect of my reading is to persuade me that despite Ward's concern with the authenticity of the inner life of black people, he does not work out his strategy in such a way that it prevents the white spectator from having a serious response to the play. Many moments of *Big White Fog* will be confusing, unimportant, or uncomfortable for the white spectator. But the drama can be perceived as a protest against the varied and profound sufferings of black people because of the racism and corrupt abuses of power of white people; as such it could even be viewed as intended essentially for a white audience, to persuade that audience to end its inhumane behavior. Such an understanding of the play would be a gross over-simplification, however, even if it might be the experience for some white spectators. The continuing dialectic described in this essay as the frame of Ward's strategy arouses pity for various characters, but it more consistently arouses doubt about the positions and actions they take. That doubt, and the concern that accompanies it about how a black person can best survive in white America, can be central to the lives of the black spectators; this response can also be felt, but perhaps with more difficulty, by white spectators.

A further difficulty for both black and white spectators of *Big White Fog* is that it simultaneously attempts the equally vulnerable tasks of assaulting the behavior of white Americans toward black Americans and the behavior of black Americans within their own communities. Although Langston Hughes attempted a similar move in *Emperor of Haiti,* he not only had the advantage of historical distance, but he also increasingly drew our focus away from the contact of black and white. Ward moves in just the opposite direction. The more enmeshed we become in the lives of the Masons, the more their destruction is associated with contact with white persons from the world outside. Ella appears most demeaned in the scene where she barters with the white used-furniture salesman, Wanda's debasement is pointedly at the hands of "an old white man" (we have previously been told that she is no virgin), and Vic's death occurs at the one moment when the stage is overwhelmed with white people. The big white fog not only obscures the ability of black people to see beyond a very limited point but is also poisonous when it enters their community.

That fog is also insidious in another, even more subtle manner. The play's realistic form and the values espoused by the characters act to affirm the pervasiveness of a middle-class consciousness.[24] And that consciousness is in itself a big white fog. Despite the appearance of the Communists at the close of the drama, there is no apparent class struggle in *Big White Fog,* nor is there an obvious conflict between the values of each of the Masons and those any middle-class spectator might hold. Yet, in terms of two major criteria for class—money and occupation—the Masons "fall" from what would be a middle-class status at the beginning of the play to a lower-class status by the play's conclusion. It is indicative, too, that the living room, traditionally the location for realistic drama, is the setting for the entire play, except for the final scene where the street seems to invade the house itself. The world that Ward has created tenaciously attempts to find its way within the American dream of a classless or harmoniously bourgeois society, but Ward's fidelity to the truth finally reveals more than he intended. That Ward's next play *(Our Lan')* escaped to an island society from the remote historical past was only a slightly different gesture from indications at the end of *Big White Fog* that our attention must now be drawn to the crowds and dialects of the streets and away from living-room mores.

In the end, the "big white fog" has penetrated those once seemingly protective stained-glass windows: We perceive the invading fog in the bailiff's men carrying out the Mason's furniture, and we hear the warning foghorn in the wail of the ambulance siren that is the final sound of the play. Ward recently said that the fog is meant to symbolize a barrier that can be penetrated,[25] but the play impresses us with the difficulty of that effort. What is frightening about fog is that it prevents us from finding our way in even the most familiar terrain; although the whiteness of the fog in Ward's play may be particularly threatening to black audiences, *Big White Fog* acts as a warning to any audience that in a moment we may not know where we are.

NOTES

1. John Houseman, *Run Through* (New York: Simon & Schuster, 1972), p. 186.
2. Doris Abramson, *Negro Playwrights in the American Theatre, 1925–1959* (New York: Columbia University Press, 1969), pp. 109–10. Many of my biographical data come from an interview with Ward conducted by Abramson in the early 1960s.
3. Fannie E. F. Hicklin, "The American Negro Playwright, 1920–1964," Ph.D. dissertation (University of Wisconsin, 1965), p. 285.
4. Harold Cruse, *The Crisis of the Negro Intellectual* (New York: Morrow, 1967), p. 50. The John Reed Club is best known as having spawned the *Partisan Review*.
5. Abramson, p. 110, and Theodore Ward in a 1970 letter to James Hatch, ed., *Black Theater, U.S.A.* (new York: Free Press, 1974), p. 279.
6. *Ibid.*
7. Hicklin, p. 287.
8. My own source for the text of *Big White Fog* has been a manuscript copy from the Schomberg Center of the New York Public Library. All citations are from this manuscript. The play is now published in James Hatch, ed., *Black Theater, U.S.A.* (New York: Free Press, 1974), pp. 281–319.
9. Negro Playwrights Company, *"Perspective": A Professional Theatre with an Idea*, New York Public Library, Schomberg Collection, George Norford Scrapbook (New York, 1940), unpaged.
10. *Ibid.*

11. Abramson, pp. 158–59.

12. Abramson, p. 116, citing Dennis Gobbins, "Story of Theo. Ward, Leading Negro Playwright," *Daily Worker*, March 9, 1950. Abramson notes (p. 296) that these figures cannot be validated and may be devised to "rationalize" lack of support for *Big White Fog*.

13. I mention this only because most books on drama by white critics omit any discussion of plays by black playwrights.

14. Abramson, p. 135.

15. Darwin T. Turner has pointed out to me that a black person would be accustomed to hearing similar metaphorical language in public places as ordinary as barbershops and beauty parlors, and that we find other black authors using similar language with ease.

16. Ward's choice of *Looking Backward* here as the example of a "socialist" book would suggest that Les is only beginning to read in the literature of socialism. By the time Ward writes, something by Debs would be a more likely choice as an indication of a serious commitment to American socialism.

17. Ralph Ellison, *Invisible Man* (New York: New American Library, 1952), p. 129.

18. Ellison, p. 35.

19. Vic's reference is unclear, but it may be that he has heard what historians now affirm, that there were at the time momentous rumors of a conspiracy of anti-Garvey black leaders and white government officials that leaked or contrived harmful information about Garvey and the Black Star liner to the appropriate authorities. I find no conclusive evidence on this matter. Because many spectators in 1938 would remember this event, as well as the subsequent charges against Garvey, it is likely that that audience, or a knowledgeable spectator today, would be swayed in this scene by his own presumptions concerning the incident. Ward seems to intend here that the ambiguities connected to the historical incident be accepted as much as possible as ambiguities.

20. Arthur Miller, "Tragedy and the Common Man," in *Aspects of the Drama*, Sylvan Barnet, Morton Berman, and William Burto, eds. (Boston: Little, Brown, 1962), p. 64.

21. The "Battle Hymn of the Republic" seems to me a strange song to be sung by Communist comrades, but I find no information to refute the possibility that it might have been sung on such occasions.

22. Susan Sontag, "Going to Theater, etc.," *Against Interpretation*, (New York: Dell, 1969).

23. Langston Hughes, cited in James Hatch, ed., *Black Theater, U.S.A.* p. 280.

24. For a further discussion of the relationships between realism in drama and middle-class consciousness see my article, "Black Drama: Reflections of Class and Class Consciousness," in *Prospects* 3 (1977).

25. Theodore Ward lecture, Richard Wright Memorial Lecture Series, University of Massachusetts (Amherst, Mass. 1974)

5 | SOUNDING THE RUMBLE OF DREAMS DEFERRED: LORRAINE HANSBERRY'S *A RAISIN IN THE SUN*

WHEN LORRAINE HANSBERRY died in 1965 at the age of thirty-five, she was not only the first black playwright to have achieved significant national recognition but also one of very few American women playwrights to have been noticed at all by the general public. Only Langston Hughes among black playwrights and Lillian Hellman among women playwrights had acquired comparable repute, and as noted earlier, Hughes's reputation was based more on his poetry than on his dramas. Lorraine Hansberry's fame has been due almost exclusively to the resounding success of her first completed script, *A Raisin in the Sun*, the subject of this chapter. Winner of the Drama Critics' Circle Award for best American play of the 1958–59 season, *A Raisin in the Sun* went on to play 530 performances in New York City and had countless other presentations on stage both in this country and abroad. For many Americans, the play may be best known in its film version, which won a special Cannes Film Festival award in 1961 and has since been shown repeatedly on television. In the 1970s, the play was applauded again in a reworked musical version, *Raisin*, which won the 1974 Tony Award for best musical. Hansberry's second play, *The Sign in Sidney Brustein's Window*, was produced in New York in 1964, and she has been given partial credit for two posthumous works adapted by her husband, Robert Nemeroff: *To Be Young, Gifted and Black* and *Les Blancs*. But none of these works drew either the acclaim or the critical attention associated with *A Raisin in the Sun*.

The success of *A Raisin in the Sun* is important to the history of black drama; it is also notable in a larger historical context. *A Raisin in the Sun* is the best known of the black dramas that transform into theatrical terms the political strategy of integration. The play includes only one white person in its cast, and this person, Mr. Lindner, appears in only two brief scenes; yet *A Raisin in the Sun* is vividly a

113

drama of "contact of black and white." Hansberry's strategy is an attempt to reveal to the white audience how much black and white people really are alike; she wants the audience to desire the fulfillment of the personal dreams of the characters of the play. If white spectators can acknowledge both this likeness and the aspirations of the characters, they can abolish their fears; black and white people might then live together harmoniously. Because white people are not ordinarily in situations through which they can see the daily lives of black people, the play will provide this experience. Black spectators will find nothing seductive in the presentation of black characters living out their lives, but the play can provide the pleasure and the terror of a rare instance of public acknowledgment that this place and these people are important.

Hansberry was not the first black playwright to present such a strategy to a Broadway audience. Most similar in approach, perhaps, was Louis Peterson's *Take a Giant Step*, produced in 1953, which dramatizes the problems of a black adolescent growing up in a white neighborhood. The play was generally well received but did not command the same attention given five years later to *A Raisin in the Sun*. Factors extrinsic to the relative merits or strategies of each drama, such as a growing public concern with the issues of segregation and integration, are certainly relevant to the different receptions given each production.

Hansberry's own biography is remarkably coherent with both the historical period in which she grew up and the conflicted world reflected in her drama. Born in Chicago in 1930, Hansberry as a child saw her father fight the Illinois Supreme Court so that his family could live in a house they had purchased in a middle-class white neighborhood.[1] Hansberry's father won the legal battle in the Supreme Court, but Doris Abramson quotes Hansberry as remembering the open hostility with which her family was met by their white neighbors.[2] Harold Cruse adds to that picture the ironic information that Hansberry's family were notorious slum landlords, but Cruse is so intent on displaying the limitations in Hansberry's work and background that it is uncertain how much credence should be given to the material he presents as facts.[3] It is documented that Lorraine Hansberry and her family owned property in the black ghettos of Chicago, but whether the family was corrupt or exploitive as landlords is unclear.[4]

Hansberry left Chicago to attend the University of Wisconsin for two years; she also took courses at Roosevelt College in Chicago and the University of Guadalajara in Mexico. In 1950, she moved to New York City, where she wrote for *Freedom* newspaper, lived in Greenwich Village, and came to know many of the black and white left-wing intellectuals of the period. During the 1950s, she began a number of playscripts, although *A Raisin in the Sun* was the first drama she actually completed.[5]

Aside from the facts and critical interpretations of Lorraine Hansberry's life as a girl and young woman, we also have the unusual document of a play about the playwright. The drama *To Be Young, Gifted and Black* is reputed to be structured from Hansberry's own words by Robert Nemeroff. The play concurs with what is known of Hansberry's Chicago childhood, her move to New York, her literary beginnings as a journalist, but it is less important as a factual resource than as a poignant presentation of Hansberry's struggles both to find the words that were to become *A Raisin in the Sun* and then to find the means to have the play produced. *To Be Young, Gifted and Black* is not very good drama; its moderate success off-Broadway probably had more to do with the extrinsic sentimental appeal created by Hansberry's death and the nostalgia of references to *A Raisin in the Sun* than with the play's dramaturgy, which is weakened by an ineffective episodic structure. Yet, whether as epitaph or sermon, *To Be Young, Gifted and Black* is still being reproduced and may at least help to maintain one black playwright in the mainstream of American culture.

Both admirers and censors of Hansberry's dramaturgy agree that mainstream American is the appropriate location for her work and reputation.[6] Although critical evaluations of *A Raisin in the Sun* vary considerably, there can be little dispute concerning what *A Raisin in the Sun* is about: The play dramatizes the efforts and frustrations of a family in pursuit of the American dream. The title of the play is itself an allusion to this theme. "A raisin in the sun" is an image drawn from a Langston Hughes poem that presents the basic rhetorical questions apparent in Hansberry's play. Hughes's poem, taken from the volume *Montage of a Dream Deferred*, is almost an outline of the events enacted in *A Raisin in the Sun:*

> What happens to a dream deferred?
> Does it dry up
> Like a raisin in the sun?
> And fester like a sore—
> And then run?
> Does it stink like rotten meat?
> Or crust and sugar over—
> Like a syrupy sweet?
>
> Maybe it just sags
> Like a heavy load.

Or does it explode?

Perceived as a poem about black people, Hughes's verse takes on particular concrete meanings, just as the black characters of Hansberry's play specify the elements of the plot because of their racial identities. There is little question, however, that the substantive center of both works is simply a description of what happens to a dream deferred.

In *A Raisin in the Sun* what happens to the deferred dream is just as Hughes imagines it. The Younger family of Hansberry's play are industrious, working-class Chicago black people. The sixty-year-old matriarch of the family, Mrs. Younger (Mama), came north with her husband years before the play begins in order to fulfill the American dream for her children. Although the family has survived except for Mr. Younger, who died of overwork, dreams of leisure and prosperity have almost dried up when the play begins. Walter Lee Younger, Mrs. Younger's thirty-five-year-old son, has been working for years as a chauffeur and is disgusted with his demeaning labor and his inability to go into business for himself; his wife, Ruth, is weary of her work as a domestic but is most deeply troubled by her sagging marriage, which she bears "like a heavy load." (Hansberry exploits Hughes's line: Early in the play we discover that Ruth is pregnant.) Walter Lee's twenty-year-old sister, Beneatha, is a medical student who has developed her own tough intellectual "crust." She is too immersed in her own plans and fantasies to understand or tend to the sore festering in her family. Even Travis, Ruth and Walter Lee's son, suffers: The ten-year-old's living-room bed is too public to allow him to get sufficient sleep for a growing boy.

In *A Raisin in the Sun*, the dream is not once but twice deferred. Indeed, as the play commences, the dream is not only being renewed but is tantalizingly close to becoming reality. A check for ten thousand dollars, the payment from Mr. Younger's life-insurance policy, is about to come into Mama's hands. Everyone in the family agrees that it is Mama's money to do with as she wishes, but each person, and Walter Lee especially, has his not-so-secret dreams of how to spend this sudden wealth. As we witness episodes during one month in the Younger household, we see the dreams revealed, suspended, destroyed, and renewed again. In the end, the Youngers will move into a new house that is the fulfillment of one fantasy and the beginning of others at the expense of many dreams deferred, and others blurred.

Doris Abramson has called attention to the similarities between the plots of *A Raisin in the Sun* and Richard Wright's *Native Son*, written initially as a novel and later made into a play.[7] Abramson notes that in both works, the central male character is employed as a chauffeur and

" 'explodes' because of a 'dream deferred.' "[8] Those similarities do
exist, but a more revealing comparison can be made between Theodore
Ward's *Big White Fog* and *A Raisin in the Sun*. Both works are concerned with the aspirations and frustrations of black Chicago families
and the individual members of each family play somewhat parallel roles
within the family itself and the larger society. Both plays also raise
questions about an African heritage, education, housing, marital relationships. These similarities suggest some congruence in at least the
dramatic image of the black family in America. What is more provocative, however, is that both *Big White Fog* and *A Raisin in the Sun*
reveal the potency of the American dream for black families while simultaneously showing that the dream evokes acute frustration and
confusion for many black people. While there are skeptics in each instance, members of both families have lived as if it were indeed true
that they had as good a chance for comfort and prosperity as any one
else in the United States. These people still hope that good, honest
labor will bear security as its fruit. In each play, the audience, at least,
is led to perceive the fallacies of such a belief. Part of the frustration
for each family occurs because the values and life-styles they embrace
or aspire to are distinctly middle-class, but racial barriers that are in
turn tied to financial and occupational limits not only prevent upward
mobility but tend to push each family increasingly into the lower class.
This descrepancy between class consciousness and actual participation
in a class is both less severe and more directly confronted in *Big White
Fog* than in *A Raisin in the Sun*. Neither play overtly employs the
language of class identity or class conflict, but spectators for each play
should be troubled by the distinction between what initially appears to
be a fluid world and what is eventually revealed as a rigid class structure. The important connection between *Big White Fog* and *A Raisin
in the Sun* is that not only over the course of two decades has little
changed in the explicit separations and injustices between black and
white Americans, but the structure of the society that determines the
nature of the contact of black and white has remained essentially the
same.

To achieve such an understanding is not, however, ostensibly the
main intent of either *Big White Fog* or *A Raisin in the Sun*. Indeed,
the strategy of *A Raisin in the Sun* is almost opposite to that of *Big
White Fog*. Whereas Ward attempted to show the flaws in any program
proposed as an "answer" to the difficulties of black Americans in a
white society, Hansberry writes to persuade a white audience to accept
racial integration. The strategy Hansberry uses to effect her intention is
exceptionally accessible to both reader and spectators. From the play's
first lines through its last, Hansberry leads the audience to feel at

home with the theatrical manner of *A Raisin in the Sun* and the world it presents. The realistic setting, characters, and dialogue of *A Raisin in the Sun*, bound to a linear plot that fixes the audience's attention by presenting a problem and withholding its solution until the last scene, are for a white audience comfortingly similar to the modes of American drama anthologized in paperbacks and seen yearly on Broadway. *A Raisin in the Sun* appears to be O'Neill without heavy symbols, Miller without allegory, Williams without flashbacks; from the moment the curtain rises on the customary box set, the audience feels reassured that this play will not assault its sensibilities or make disturbing demands on its relation to the stage.[9]

Equally central to Hansberry's strategy, the specific characteristics of the people on stage and the problems they confront are recognizable and familiar. There is, of course, for white spectators one essential difference in the characters before them: They are all black. But this is, simply, the point. No spectator can ignore the blackness of the people onstage, but the white spectator is also led to perceive how much these people are like him and his family. The audience is drawn into the family onstage by the presentation in Act I of incidents so like those we are accustomed to in our own families, be they black or white, that we come to feel kinship with the stage family. Hansberry impresses us so consistently with our similarities to the people on stage that when, in Act II, a strange white man who is in no way connected to the family enters the room, he is an intruder to white spectators as well as to black spectators and those onstage.

Nor does Hansberry rest with showing likenesses. The black characters onstage not only arouse empathy through the ordinariness of their problems and behaviors, they are often admirable and, more frequently, witty and funny. The Youngers relieve anxieties in white spectators and reaffirm self-respect in black spectators, but they also delight and interest their entire audience. *A Raisin in the Sun* resists classification as a comedy or farce because of its persistently somber undertone and the frequent proximity of events to tragic resolution, but Hansberry does skillfully and consistently use humor as a kind of insurance for the success of her intention: The laughter that the dialogue incites is more frequently with the Youngers than at them. That laughter insures that we will like these people, that we will find their presence before us pleasing. If the white audience can find the Youngers pleasing in the theater, they may then accept them in their neighborhoods and schools. Each moment of the play not only amuses us or holds us in suspense, it also provides a stone that when laid beside or above all the others, will seem to make a firm wall for a house we can imagine inhabiting.

II

The set on which the curtain of *A Raisin in the Sun* rises is of a realistically detailed living room. The furnishings here suggest many years of use; the dwelling is crowded and therefore initially chaotic and oppressive for the audience. The living room contains a bed for Travis, the young son, and a table used for family meals. The kitchen is suggested as a mere nook off the living room, and the two bedrooms, one for Mama and Beneatha, the other for Ruth and Walter Lee, press too closely on the walls of the main room. The play begins in the quiet of early morning sleep. The stillness is broken and the play commenced by the annoying ring of an alarm clock. Those onstage and off are being told that it is time to wake up.

The opening scene can hardly fail to elicit some sense of shared experience between audience and characters. Ruth, the young wife and mother of the household, is stumbling around the house attempting to rouse her family from sleep. She clearly plays this role every morning, and it is a chore that we can recognize while we also sympathize with the annoyance of those trying to catch a last three seconds of sleep. We discover immediately that the bathroom is outside the apartment, across the hall, and this, with the worn furniture, supports the impression that the Youngers are poor. There is a no-nonsense, assertive air about Ruth's reveille, but she also nags from her first words. Her nagging is softened because it is not self-pitying; it creates an honest identification in the spectator. The sound of Ruth's language, spoken in a consistent but always comprehensible dialect, augments the sense of verisimilitude created by the set and situation. The omission of verb parts and vowels, the frequent lack of subject-verb agreement, the persistent use of "ain't" may not be an entirely accurate representation of Chicago's black-ghetto dialect, but these variances from "standard" English usage create the illusion of a specific and appropriate language for this place:

> RUTH: Come on now, boy, it's seven thirty. . . . I say hurry up! You ain't the only person in the world got to use a bathroom. . . .
> (Ruth crosses to the bedroom door at Right and opens it and calls in to her husband.) Walter Lee! . . . It's after seven thirty! Lemme see you do some waking up in there now! (She waits.) You better get up from there, man! It's after seven thirty, I tell you. (She waits again.) All right, you just

go ahead and lay there and next thing you know Travis be
finished and Mr. Johnson'll be in there and you'll be fussing
and cussing round here like a mad man! And be late too![10]

The impression made by Ruth's speech may at first be somewhat disorienting for some white spectators, but its persistence and consistency
as the play continues gradually dissolve any special consciousness of the
language. The use of dialect, then, is part of Hansberry's strategy. The
white spectator should eventually be able to admit that he understands
what is being said, that if the differences between the language onstage
and the language of the spectator do not create an impossible barrier in
the theater, they need not create hostility in the world outside.

While the spectator is juggling all these immediate impressions of
the place, Walter Lee enters and, though not yet quite awake,
promptly informs the audience of the central object of conflict in the
play: After two brief questions about the availability of the bathroom,
Walter asks, "Check coming today?" Both the question and Ruth's answer that "they" said it wouldn't come until Saturday and that she
"hopes to God" Walter is not going to start talking about money first
thing in the morning provide important information about these characters' anxieties and the events of the play. The immediate mention of
the check and the indication from Ruth that it is a constant subject of
conversation make us curious about the check's source, and significance. We are made wary of Walter, to whom the check matters so
much. There may also be some sympathetic recognition of Ruth, who
seems weary of the subject of money. We, as audience, want to hear
about the money, but as a secondary response we might admit that at
eight o'clock in the morning we in our own homes might not want to
talk about money.

The audience is given another clue to tension between Ruth and
Walter when Ruth asks Walter what kind of eggs he wants. Walter
replies, "Not scrambled," and Ruth obviously proceeds to scramble
eggs. This may stimulate laughter in the audience, but it also creates a
slight antagonism toward Ruth and sympathy for Walter. Moments like
this, in which we laugh at a line or action but then catch ourselves in
an awareness that there is an underlying bitterness or sobriety, recur
frequently in the play and are central to creating an experience for the
audience that is felt as both troubling and pleasurable.

The next line locates the action in time for the audience and
suggests the kind of news that interests the Youngers. Reading the
newspaper, Walter says, "Set off another bomb, yesterday!" We know
that the play is occuring sometime after World War II, and we are
reminded that this is a time in history when many people vaguely

feared this new form of holocaust. The dialogue goes on to reveal more of the tension between Ruth and Walter—Walter's friends are keeping Travis up too late—but then Ruth's nagging is suddenly interrupted by Walter's unexpected observation, "You look young this morning, baby" (p. 350). This is not only a surprising comment for the audience to hear, but it also draws us to Walter. His tender and sexual acknowledgment of his wife extends our sympathy for him as the victim of Ruth's complaints. We are then dismayed when Ruth refuses the compliment and pleased again by Walter's light retort: "First thing a man ought to learn in life is not to make love to no colored woman first thing in the morning. You all some evil people at eight o'clock in the morning" (p. 350). These lines illustrate cogently one of Hansberry's strategic devices: Walter makes the comment specific to "colored" women, but it is as true (or untrue) for white women as well. In the act of laughing at Ruth and Walter—at others—both black and white spectators can recognize themselves. The black spectator can respond directly with a "yea" or an "okay" to the articulation of a common experience; the white spectator will take an extra step of applying the assertion to the women he or she knows. Even such minor moments of self-recognition contribute to the important and distinct experience that theater can give us.

The next episode furthers our empathy with the family. Travis comes in to breakfast, asks about the check, thus reminding us of its imminent arrival, then asks for fifty cents and gets into a minor row with his mother. Everyone will recognize here a familiar morning scene, including Ruth's scoldings about her son's uncombed hair and the child's sullen politeness. As Travis leaves for school, however, there is suddenly more fun and affection displayed on stage than may be apparent in most homes. Ruth speaks what she knows Travis is thinking to himself: "Oh, Mama makes me so mad sometimes, I don't know what to do . . . I wouldn't kiss that woman good-bye for nothing in this world" (p. 352). Ruth has changed the mood for both her son and the audience. She is both funny and tender; we laugh at her and we like her. We can also recognize the game being played between mother and son, and we can probably associate with both sides. We may well go farther and admire Ruth, knowing that often we are neither as clever or as understanding or as honest in similar situations. As Walter did a moment earlier, Ruth has now become a particular and interesting personality; she is no longer any mother or wife in any household, but she is not so unique that she disorients us.

Hansberry's sense of timing here is perfect, for we are not allowed to linger in this tenderness until it becomes maudlin. Travis breaks the mood by simply being a young boy. He exploits his mother's good humor by renewing his plea for money, which she again refuses to give, and it is now Walter's turn to gain his son's affection. In the first really troubling moment in the play, Walter hands his son fifty cents and then fifty cents more to "take a taxicab to school or something!" Both Ruth and the audience know that Walter is deliberately challenging Ruth's authority with her son and daring her to a confrontation. Walter has asserted his power to both his son and his wife, and although the audience may not feel the disgust that Ruth exhibits and may find Walter's gesture familiar, it also knows that what Walter has done is wrong for both his child and his marriage.

With Travis now departed, Walter gets the conversation back to the subject on his mind from the start of the scene: the check. Although our curiosity may have been diverted by the intervening dialogue, we are glad to find out more about this matter. Walter is quick to reveal his purpose: He wants Ruth to convince his mother to give him the money she is about to receive so that he, with two other men, can invest it in a liquor store. Ruth responds with some skepticism but mostly with disinterest. As she reminds Walter to eat his eggs, the eggs again become a source of humor and a more serious message. In a funny but bitter diatribe, Walter summarizes his frustration and his view of the condition of marital relationships: "That's it. There you are. Man say to his woman: I got me a dream. His woman say: Eat your eggs. Man say: I got to take hold of this here world, baby! And a woman will say: Eat your eggs and go to work. Man say: I got to change my life, I'm choking to death, baby! And his woman say—Your eggs is getting cold!" (p. 355). Verbal repetition and the juxtaposition of the sublime and the mundane lead us to laugh in response to Walter's scenario. Our laughter may be limited, however, by annoyance at his narrow vision of woman and by sympathy for the real pain breaking through his parody. We are meant to hear the plea for help in his words and feel disturbed for him. Hansberry makes it even more difficult to withhold pity from Walter when, as he continues describing his present sense of himself, Ruth does interrupt to tell him to eat his eggs. Ruth's defense is that Walter has said the same thing every day, and that it is nothing new that Walter would rather be his own boss than the white man's chauffeur. Her defense mellows our response to her, as does her final quip, "So—I would rather be living in Buckingham Palace." Our sympathetic laughter is cut off quickly, however, by Walter, who resumes his attack, this time specifying that he is talking about what is wrong with "the colored woman." What he argues is that black women do not make their men feel potent, that they are castrating through indifference.

The intentions of this series of speeches, and our reactions to them, are complicated and perhaps not clearly conceived by Hansberry. Walter's words can divide both men and women in the audience and black people from white people. One could perceive his attack as the somewhat didactic and well-known argument that, because of the conditions of slavery and its aftermath, the black man has been rendered impotent, and that the legendary endurance of the black woman, coupled with her easier access to jobs, have exacerbated rather than assuaged the black man's impotence. Those who disagree with this understanding of history may be distanced from the world of the play, and even those who concur with Walter may feel uncomfortable with this "reality." Walter's words may also draw our focus to the differences between white people and black. But it is equally possible that the white audience may see Walter's assertions as remarking another point in common with black people. It is, after all, as common to Archie and Edith Bunker as to Walter and Ruth Younger that the man perceives his lofty dreams as going unappreciated by his small-minded wife. At least some white men in the audience might, therefore, be driven to protest Walter's belief that it is the *unique* plight of black men to be cursed with "women with small minds." This would be a trap fully in keeping with Hansberry's intentions to persuade white people of their likenesses to black people. The device could be especially successful because it would suggest further that black people, as well as white people, erroneously think of their problems as racially distinct.

Hansberry's wish to draw our attention here to sex-based roles rather than racial identities is substantiated in the very next scene. Beneatha, Walter's twenty-year-old sister, enters and is immediately engaged in a sarcastic and increasingly sharp exchange with her brother. We pay close attention to Beneatha because her responses to Walter's jabs and queries are quick, witty, and often very funny. Their repartee reveals Walter's anxiety about the claims of others in the family to Mama's check and thus makes us uneasy about Walter because of the suggestion of his selfishness. Our curiosity about the fate of the money increases because we are now given two other possibilities: that Beneatha will get the money to finance her medical studies and that Mama will take the money and "buy a house or a rocket ship or just nail it up somewhere and look at it."

While we ponder the potential conflict over money, we are also being assaulted with an increasingly forceful impression of Walter's sexism. Walter's first remark to his sister is paternalistic; his second, "You a horrible-looking chick at this hour," will warn some spectators of his attitude toward women through his use of the word "chick." He proceeds from there to a more overt sexism, commenting—and the impression is that he has said this before—that it "Ain't many girls who decide to be a doctor." Finally, Walter is blatantly chauvinistic and demands to know why Beneatha couldn't just be a nurse "like other women—or just get married and be quiet." When Walter is finally pushed out the door to go to work, his parting assertion that these (he is looking at Ruth and Beneatha) are the "world's most backward race of people" amuses or annoys, but convinces us only that Walter's perception of women is parochial.

The blatancy of Walter's chauvinism suggests that Hansberry intends the audience to refuse both Walter's perception and his attitude. It is not clear, however, that some spectators, particularly in the late 1950s and still in the 1970s, might not cheer Walter on sympathetically. Hansberry's central intent that we recognize the characters as distinct but knowable people, with whom we share problems, will work whether we support or condemn Walter. Her attempt to "raise our consciousness" about sex roles is not skillfully controlled or clearly conceived but occurs as a repeated provocation throughout the play.

Just as in the previous scene with Travis, the heaviness of the confrontation of the man with the women is broken on the edge of a departure. Because Walter has given his son extra money, he now has no money of his own and must return to ask Ruth for carfare. Her teasing response, "Fifty cents?," when Walter asks for some money will elicit laughter and relieve anxiety about both characters.

Once Walter has left, it is time for Mama's entrance, and her imposing appearance makes clear that the stage needs to be somewhat emptied to allow the audience to receive Mama for the first time. Her first line and movement set up much of our response to her. The voice of authority and decorum sounds in her "Who that 'round here slamming doors at this hour?" We know this is a person who commands respect. But her immediate attention to a scraggly little plant trying to survive on the one windowsill in the apartment is a symbolic gesture that reveals the softness in Mama and leads us to expect, too, that her decisions will reflect concern for the vulnerable and the brave.

The following scene affirms our initial impressions of Mama. She is, foremost, a mother. As that role is overbearing, she arouses our impatience; as it is loving, she elicits our affection. She moves into the room and begins to put things and people into order, telling her daughter to get dressed, her daughter-in-law how to handle Travis. In her bickering with Ruth about the latter's rearing of the boy, it becomes clear that Mama behaves as the stereotypical interfering mother-in-law. This revelation arouses our antipathy for Mama and our sympathy for Ruth. The pattern of effect is continued when Ruth decides, somewhat to the audience's surprise, to plead to Mama Walter's case for his business venture. Mama's response to the request is more negative than was Ruth's initially, but Mama's grounds, although we may find them foolish, are not disputable; she feels drinking is wrong and a liquor business only adds a bad mark to her ledger in life. We don't dislike Mama for her refusal, but we may be disappointed by her obstinate refusal to consider Walter's dream. Our desire for Mama's assent is sharpened because Ruth explains her request in terms of the ambiguous but destructive "something" that is happening to her marriage.

As in most scenes of *A Raisin in the Sun,* the weight of gloom is not allowed to rest for long. After Mama's refusal, we are given further reason for anxiety in Mama's observation that Ruth looks ill and in Ruth's affirmation that she is tired. Then Mama comes to the audience's rescue with quick-witted remarks about white people. She tells Ruth that she will call Ruth's employer and say she has the flu, and when Ruth asks, "Why the flu?" Mama responds, "'Cause it sounds respectable to 'em. Something white people get, too. They know about the flu. Otherwise they think you been cut up or something when you tell 'em you sick" (p. 361). Amusement in response to these lines may be greater among black spectators than white ones, but it is difficult to imagine Mama's words offending anyone. The passage strikes at the absurdity of white people's assumptions about black people, but it does not suggest any unpardonable or unalterable sin. White spectators are urged to laugh at themselves in the way they might if a child reveals that she accurately understands something that adults have disguised because of the child's innocence. The passage also reminds white spectators of their responsibility to treat black people fairly. Mama's remarks here are capped by a statement that seems to deny identification but, in fact, urges it further. It arouses delight at Mama's proud and ironically comic sense of self: "Something always told me I wasn't no rich white woman," Mama says, and we share her glee in the assertion of the obvious as well as her pleasure with who she is.

If Mama is not going to take a cruise "like a rich white woman," then we can return to the problem of what she will do with her money. The remainder of Scene i provides us with hints that arouse our curiosity and set up the possibilities for the rest of the play. Mama's talk of her dream as a young woman of owning her own house suggests that this is her fantasy about spending the money. Mama's descriptions of her deceased husband's virtues, which seem at this point to be a sentimental gimmick to arouse sympathy for the widow, actually set up a sense of heritage that will become crucial in the final scene of the play. Mama's memory of the baby she lost with much grief brings the idea of pregnancy onto the stage, and may lead some spectators to guess at the end of Scene i that Ruth's collapse is caused by a condition as ordinary as the flu or fatigue, but different from them. These various hints sustain our interest in the events of the play, but also add to a sense of Mama as a good and easily recognizable woman who has suffered much and should be relieved of some burdens.

Before Scene i ends, we are also given the most overt example thus far of Hansberry's strategy. Beneatha returns to the stage from the bathroom. She becomes involved in a row with her mother so typical of the disputes that occur between a mother and an almost adult daughter that one can hear spectators saying, "That's exactly like *our* family." Beneatha initially annoys her mother by using the Lord's name in vain. The spectator's sympathies here will probably vary according to his or her attitude toward religion. Beneatha then mentions her latest hobbyhorse, guitar lessons, and is accused by Mama and Ruth of "flitting" from one interest to another. Beneatha's outrage at not being taken seriously is both so typical of her youth and so clichéd in its expression that we have to laugh at her, as do Ruth and Mama:

> BENEATHA: I don't flit! I— I experiment with different forms of expression—
> RUTH: Like riding a horse.
> BENEATHA: People have to express themselves one way or another.
> MAMA: What is it you want to express?
> BENEATHA: (angrily): Me!
>   (Mama and Ruth look at each other and burst into raucous laughter.) Don't worry—I don't expect you to understand.
>   [p. 364]

The passage is clearly a gentle jab at Beneatha's adolescent self-righteousness and the absurdity of her means of "finding herself." It may also be a more specific satire of the self-indulgence of middle-class white youths. The expense of Beneatha's "forms of expression" and their association with college life may indicate that these are ways of behaving that she has learned or imitated from white friends. As such, Mama and Ruth's laughter may be at Beneatha's unconscious imitation of white behavior as well as at the overly-serious manner in which she takes herself. Perceived as a satire of white adolescent behavior, the scene then allows the black spectator a laugh at white people and may find the white spectator suddenly realizing she is laughing at herself.

Sensing that Beneatha is not about to share in their laughter, Mama and Ruth then change the subject to Beneatha's latest boyfriend, a rich young man named George Murchison. This conversation returns us to the play's earlier concerns with stereotyped sex roles, and our sym-

pathies are switched now to Beneatha. Ruth and Mama are pushing for
George Murchison as a husband for Beneatha because he is rich, hand-
some, and comes from a "good" family, but Beneatha is not overwhelmed by these appeals. She makes clear that there is no marriage
in sight for her becuase she is emotionally uninvolved with George.
That she is able to reject such an eligible suitor because she neither
loves him nor feels a need to be married is both romantically and rationally attractive. We are thus led not only to commend her but also
to consider the possibility that marriage is not the only answer for
women. During this scene, the fact that the people onstage are black is
subordinate to the fact that they are female. If we miss the intended
blurring of racial distinctions, Beneatha finally proclaims it:

> BENEATHA: Oh Mama—the Murchisons are honest-to-God-real-
>   live-rich colored people and the only people in the world
>   more snobbish than rich white people are rich colored
>   people. I thought everybody knew that. I've met Mrs. Mur-
>   chison. She's a scene!
> MAMA: You must not dislike people 'cause they well off honey.
> BENEATHA: Why not? It makes just as much sense as disliking
>   people 'cause they are poor, and lots of people do that.
>   [p. 265]

Beneatha's lines appeal because of their honesty; she is not trying to
hide anything about black people or to set them up as better than
white people. The message is clear: We should not dislike people because they are rich or poor, black or white.

Beneatha is not allowed to go off triumphantly, however. She is
still childlike in both her behavior and her role in this household, and
she demonstrates that by attacking her mother on a subject about
which Mama is very vulnerable: God. Beneatha's cry—"There simply is
no blasted God—there is only man and it is he who makes
miracles!"—raises such fury in Mrs. Younger that she forcefully slaps
her daughter. The lightness of the previous scenes is broken; we are no
longer amused, but made anxious by the intensity of this confrontation.
We are made to know, probably with as much dismay as with respect,
that Mama is the authority in this household, as Mama forces Beneatha
to repeat, "In my mother's house there is still God."

The episode is too loaded for the audience's responses to be simple
or unified. No matter what we think intellectually of the two women's
beliefs, Beneatha arouses our impatience for not having learned when
to remain quiet, and Mama elicits our sympathy for her pain. Some
spectators may also feel dismay at Mrs. Younger's violent and au-

thoritarian display, while others may respect Mama for asserting her beliefs and rejecting the insubordination of a child. Part of Hansberry's intention here is certainly to make Mama's character more specific. Her reaction to Beneatha establishes Mama's intense commitment to her values and clarifies for the audience the individuality of each person onstage. Mama's actions bring another dimension into this stage world; she shows us the older generation, devoted to religion, demanding that the children respect God and the laws, and dismayed by the cynicism of the young. Spectators of different ages and backgrounds will react differently to Mama's behavior in this scene, but she does serve to provide some audience members with a focus of recognition onstage that they might not find as readily in Beneatha, Ruth, or Walter. Whatever the location of our empathy, the scene should resound with almost too much familiarity. The episode is not a gratuitous histrionic moment; it is fully within the bounds and intentions of Hansberry's strategy. Who in the audience could justly say, "Oh, *those* awful people?"

On these discomforting notes, the scene nears its conclusion. Ruth calms the tension briefly by mediating between Beneatha and Mama, but then Ruth herself collapses, arousing new anxiety in the audience as the curtain comes down on Scene i.

Scene ii of Act I confirms suspicions aroused in Scene i and draws our attention momentarily away from the Youngers by introducing us to Beneatha's African boyfriend. Scene ii also gradually enforces and extends the hints of desperation in the lives of Walter Lee and Ruth. It is the following Saturday morning, the house is a chaos of cleaning, and Ruth is mysteriously "out." There is an air of expectancy; it is the day for the check to arrive. Within thirty lines we are led to expect more than the check: In a phone call to his business partner, Walter reveals that papers are being prepared; Ruth, we are informed, is at the doctor's; Beneatha invites a visit from "Asagai," whom she labels "an intellectual." Within minutes, all of the events of the scene are set up, and the audience is made anxious to see what will occur.

In an obvious maneuver and somewhat didactic message, Beneatha informs her mother of the correct pronunciation of Asagai's name and of his Nigerian heritage, and warns not to ask silly questions of the man, because "All anyone seems to know about when it comes to Africa is Tarzan—" Beneatha's lesson is interrupted by Ruth's return. Ruth's demeanor and words tell more than we or the family want to know: She is pregnant, but that news has depressed her because it does not seem to her the time to bring a child into her world. There is an early hint that Ruth has actually not been to a physician, which, if heard, keeps the spectator uneasy for half the scene before Ruth admits that she has consulted with an abortionist.

As Mama takes a weeping Ruth offstage, and we are left puzzled and distraught, Asagai enters and shifts the mood and our attention. The scene between Beneatha and Asagai is meant to both amuse and inform the audience, although it may arouse some further annoyance with Beneatha, who, quickly forgetting her concern for Ruth, turns to the banter and gifts Asagai provides. Again, we are led to smile rue-fully at Beneatha's adolescent behavior as she revels in her new African robes and repeatedly is unable to laugh at herself as Asagai gently mocks her "mutilated" straightened hair and her overserious assertions of her search for identity. Our respect for Beneatha is renewed when, detecting Asagai's romantic intentions, she tells him that more than one kind of feeling can exist between a man and a woman. Beneatha goes on to make emphatic Hansberry's intention to disturb the audi-ence's assumptions about sex roles:

ASAGAI: For a woman it should be enough.
BENEATHA: I know—because that's what it says in all the novels
    that men write. Go ahead and laugh—but I'm not interested
    in being someone's little episode in America or— (with
    feminine vengeance) —one of them!   [p. 374]

Beneatha almost defeats her argument by her angry self-consciousness, but she is ironically saved and the audience is relieved by Mama's entrance. Mama now attempts to act properly and retell all the "right things" that Beneatha has suggested earlier. We are not allowed to see Mama's behavior simply as comic, however. Although she does not know much about Africa, Mrs. Younger does know how to be compas-sionate to a young man away from home: As Asagai prepares to leave, Mama invites him to dinner sometime soon. Both Beneatha and the audience are being shown that there is more to being a decent person than having intellectual knowledge. The message seems to pass by Be-neatha; as Asagai departs, Beneatha, dancing in front of a mirror, is imagining herself to be "queen of the Nile."

All this time, everyone has been waiting for the check, which fi-nally does arrive. New anxieties quickly replace the old. Mama forces Ruth's admission of her visit to the abortionist, but even that is inter-rupted by Walter's excited arrival. His entrance and the ensuing argu-ments about the way the check is to be spent provide no surprises for the audience. Despite Walter's pleas that he needs this money, that his needs should be heard, Mama remains adamantly opposed to the liquor store enterprise. Walter is stunned when Mama tells him Ruth is pregnant and considering an abortion, but even this news does not shift his focus from his own despair. We may agree or disagree with Walter's cynical assertions that life is money, that money is all that matters, but we are certainly drawn to pity him in his anguish, to know the emptiness felt at the loss of a dream. Even if we respect Mama's stance, we can wish she would give him the money so we could believe that a man's dreams can in fact come true.

Hansberry's strategy is the same at the end of Scene ii as in Scene i. Both Walter and Mama depart, making us eager for the curtain to rise on Act II in order to find out where they have gone and what is happening. We are left again with a recognition of these characters as people whom we care about, whose troubles we can acknowledge.

Act II confirms the appropriateness of our anxiety, affirms the attitudes and insights of Act I, and fulfills the unfortunate possibilities suggested earlier. Although Act II, like Act I, alternates between moments that delight and moments that trouble, both our awareness of Walter's frenzy and our knowledge that something will have to be done with the check create a presentiment of impending doom.

The act begins with a scene that will amuse and catch the audience's attention. Beneatha appears, dressed in her African costume, and begins to dance to the African music Asagai has also given her. As she dances, genuinely enraptured with the whole experience, a very drunken Walter enters and joins her. Walter proclaims that he is an African warrior and, as such, wields an imaginary spear, leaps and cavorts on the tables and furniture, and begins an oration to his "Black Brothers." As drunken antics, Walter's act is surely funny for an audience, but he appears so persistent and obsessed that the spectator is also made to wonder if this may not be some mystical and strange self-discovery that should be taken seriously. Had Hansberry extended this scene, the black audience in particular might have had a fuller sense of Walter's struggles with his identity. Hansberry may have cut the scene short because it risked alienating the sympathies of white spectators by emphasizing the distinctive African heritage of blacks, which in turn would call attention to a potential difference between whites and blacks.

Our bewilderment is arrested and our perspective changed when Beneatha's date for the evening, George Murchison, the rich man, arrives. Instinctively, we see the scene for a second from George's eyes because we, like George, have been intruding on a private family ritual. But the moment George rejects Walter's fraternal hand-clasp (and thus rejects an act of comradery from Walter) and retorts "Black Brother, hell!" our hostilities are turned on George and our association with the Youngers becomes effective. George's condescension toward Beneatha demands to be thwarted. We may find Beneatha's behavior immature or clichéd, but George is an outsider who has no right to interfere. His presence is as unwelcome and inappropriate in this world as would be the sudden entrance of the corporation—General Motors—that his initials signify.

Thus, when neither Beneatha nor Ruth is able or willing to squelch George, we are delighted that Walter tackles the invader. Hansberry's strategy here in bringing George into the scene is to provide a contrast between Walter and another black man. Hansberry leads us, black or white, to prefer Walter, whose African heritage has just been acknowledged, to George, who affects the worst aspects of white society. Walter mocks George from the younger man's "fairyish-looking white shoes" to his fraternity pins and his pretentious language. The attack on George is indeed inebriating for Walter and the audience, until Walter's drunken insights turn back on him, revealing the profound bitterness at the root of his antics and words. Once more, Hansberry has changed a light game into a potentially dangerous encounter. We are plunged into sobriety by the awareness of the depth of Walter's unhappiness.

As soon as George has left with Beneatha, now dressed "appropriately" in an evening gown, Walter begins to vent his anger on Ruth. We fear for another troubling scene. Ruth, however, calls forth all of her strength and love on this occasion. She surprises us by approaching her husband with tenderness rather than hostility. Ruth's attempt here to find some ground for understanding with Walter—"Oh, Walter. (softly) . . . Honey, why can't you stop fighting me?"—may seem inconsistent with her earlier expressions of hostility toward her husband and is not the behavior we immediately expect. This is a matter not of a confused portrayal of Ruth but of the revelation of a character who is genuinely feeling ambivalent. The Ruth who speaks here should remind us of the woman who earlier asked Mama to help Walter out. Ruth is troubled about her marriage, about her pregnancy, about the tension in her home; that her anxiety is expressed in both anger and love makes her more rather than less believable. Thus, we feel a pleasant surprise at Ruth's gentle words and offer of hot milk to Walter. We sit hopefully watching their attempts to talk to each other, to recapture some lost warmth, when Mama enters. All of the spectator's anxiety returns; Walter and Ruth have been allowed no time for resolution.

We now find out where Mama has been all day. Her previous hints are confirmed for the audience: She has spent the afternoon buying a house. Ruth cannot hide her delight. The spectator is caught in that pleasure until Ruth's probe for details pushes Mama to reveal that the house happens to be in a white neighborhood. This information allows Walter finally to vent his anger; his silence was ominous while Mama told Travis and Ruth her news. To Walter's, "So that's the peace and quiet you went out and bought for us today," Mama responds that it was the nicest house she could find for the money; houses put up for "colored" cost twice as much. The black spectator may be glad that white spectators are learning the truth; Hansberry intends that white spectators be at least troubled if not ashamed by this account, although it is not certain that such a reaction will occur, because we must accept Mama's words as truth if we are to be disturbed by them. Ruth is able to put aside the worry this added detail creates, but, for Walter, it is the final blow. Now the money is actually gone, and his dream appears to be not only deferred but destroyed. The audience is torn between pity for Walter and relief for Mama and Ruth. We are thus caught in the strife of this family. We may enjoy an affirmation of belief in one well-shared portion of the American dream—the desire for a decent home—that has actually been fulfilled for the Younger family, but we should be wary that the contentment Ruth and Mama are seeking in the ownership of a home may be threatened by the house's location in a white neighborhood and by Walter's frustration.

The ambivalence set up for the audience at the end of Act II, Scene i, seems irresolvable. We can wish that Walter were less self-pitying, but it is still distressing to see a man so destroyed. Because it is Mama's decision that has directly caused Walter's present suffering, we are tempted to turn our pity for Walter into anger at her, but simultaneously our concern for Ruth is relieved by Mama's action. Scene ii leads the audience to feel a temporary reconciliation of these contradictory sympathies. The scene begins with a brief episode between George and Beneatha that is intended to inflate our dislike for George, who announces that he is only interested in Beneatha because she is physically attractive and sophisticated, not because she has interesting thoughts. George's remarks are so callous and stupid that we applaud Beneatha's curt dismissal of him and achieve a greater respect for her stance as an independent woman. The scene also sets up the opportunity to demonstrate Mama's compassion and wisdom: Instead of condemning Beneatha's rejection of George, as we might expect, Mama accepts her daughter's word that George is a fool and urges Beneatha not to waste her time on him. Beneatha thanks her mother for understanding her this time. Our appreciation of Mama's sagacity relieves us of some of the annoyance we may have felt toward her as the source of Walter's pain.

The further elevation of Mama occurs just a few minutes later. Walter's employer calls. It is revealed that because of his depression, Walter has not been to work for three days. Instead, he has been driving and walking around, drinking, listening to the blues, and watching "the Negroes go by." These signs of the depth of Walter's own blues convince Mama that she has made a mistake. She informs her son that only about a third of the money has been spent on the down payment for the house. She will turn the remaining sixty-five hundred dollars over to Walter's care, with the stipulation that three thousand dollars are to be put in a savings account for Beneatha's schooling. The plan seems amazingly simple and satisfying, even if the sudden disclosure of remaining money is a bit contrived. Clearly, Hansberry's strategy is to build up our concern for Walter and to lead us to believe that there can be an answer for him in Mama's decisions. But we may wonder why Mama did not do something like this from the beginning. (The explanation that she was trying to prevent the liquor store venture does not really suffice.) Our relief that the tension in the household seems finally resolved is heightened by Walter's marked change of mood. When Travis enters and sees his father after Mama's new decision, the boy thinks Walter is drunk. But Walter denies this, saying, "(Sweetly, more sweetly than we have ever known him) No, Daddy ain't drunk, Daddy ain't going to never be drunk again."

If there has ever been any suspicion that Walter's dream is somehow unique or unique to black people rather than the archetypal American dream, such doubts are dispersed in Walter's vision of the future presented to his son. Daddy, Walter tells Travis, is going to make a business transaction. The results of that transaction will mean cars that are elegant but not flashy, a house complete with a gardener whom Walter will address as "Jefferson," and a choice for Travis of any of the great colleges in America. The white spectators are meant to see and respect the black man's dream and to recognize it as the same as the white man's. Walter doesn't really want a flashy car; black and white spectators will see that what Walter wants is what every man desires: to hand the world to his son. That Walter's thirty-five hundred dollars is not likely to fulfill such splendid fantasies is irrelevant at the moment. Hansberry's strategy is to lead the audience to believe that Mama's gift to Walter has solved all problems.

Scene iii of Act II introduces a new strategic element. It sets us up for a long, ironic fall through the display of Ruth's new contentment and her dreams for the future. Ruth is happily packing for the move; she shows Beneatha curtains she has bought for the new house; she tells her sister-in-law with beaming serenity of how Walter and she went to the movies the previous night for the first time in a long time, of how they even held hands. Walter enters. His mood, though more boisterous, matches his wife's obvious joy. We cannot help but feel pleasure in their happiness.

We do not wait long before a shadow appears to dim the good cheer. The introduction of the play's only white character is set up with humor and deliberately ironic juxtaposition. Only a moment before the doorbell rings, Walter is imitating Beneatha, suggesting that at some future time she will be leaning over a patient on the operating table, asking, "By the way, what are your views on civil rights down there?" They laugh and we laugh as Beneatha goes to the door to allow the surprising entrance of a middle-aged white man in business attire. Walter immediately moves forward to confront the situation with an air of authority that amuses the women. The white man introduces himself as Karl Lindner, chairman of a "sort of welcoming committee" from the neighborhood into which the Youngers are about to move. Lindner's verbal and physical awkwardness and the deliberate vagueness of his language warn the audience from the start that this man's intentions are suspect, but only Beneatha among the characters onstage seems immediately wary of this "friendly" white man. Lindner never faces the question of race directly, but piles one ambiguous and euphemistic statement onto the next, using one rhetorical device after another, in an attempt to gain the trust of his onstage audience; by the time he gets to his point, we know he carries a message of rejection, not welcome. Lindner has come to the Youngers to buy their new house from them at a profit for the family in order to keep black people out of the neighborhood. Hansberry makes Lindner's presentation of his mission dramatically ironic because everything we have seen of the Younger family defeats the "rational" core of Lindner's argument. His central point is that people are happier when they live in a community in which the residents share a "common background," and from his viewpoint, "Negroes" and whites obviously do not have that common background. But just before he articulates this conclusion, Hansberry has Lindner describe his community in a way that for the audience should clearly appear as a striking parallel to what it knows of the behavior and desires of the Youngers: "They're not rich and fancy people; just hardworking, honest people who don't really have much but those little homes and a dream of the kind of community they want to raise their children in" (p. 407). We might laugh at how well Lindner disproved his own point about "differences in background" were it not for the fact that his bigotry will harm others, will create pain and difficulty for people like the Youngers.

Walter and Beneatha are appropriately outraged. They firmly evict the man from the house. Even if the white spectator had privately shared Lindner's rationalized prejudices, Lindner's conniving dishonesty should provoke disgust at his behavior and applause for Walter's unhesitant refusal. Here, black spectators might feel fear for the Youngers, since black spectators would know what whites have done to the homes of blacks who have moved into white neighborhoods. Hansberry's purpose, however, seems less to arouse fear in black spectators than to provoke a recognition in white spectators. The white audience needs to *see* Lindner to know he is despicable; the black audience may have assumed that possibility.

The triumph of this scene is extended and relieved when Mama returns and is told of the event. Because the Youngers respond with humor rather than bitterness to Lindner's proposal, the audience can remain empathetic rather than pitying or ashamed. Through irony, parody, and exaggeration, Ruth, Walter, and Beneatha point out the absurdity of the segregationist position. They also note so openly and unthreateningly the fears of white people that such fears are reduced to foolishness. Even the white person's worst fear is articulated in the context of a joke:

BENEATHA: What do they think we are going to do—eat 'em?
RUTH: No, honey, marry 'em.
MAMA (shaking her head): Lord, Lord, Lord.
RUTH: Well—that's the way the crackers crumble. Joke.   [p. 409]

The jovial mood continues, both for characters and audience, as Mama is presented with gifts of gardening tools and, from Travis, an extraordinarily elaborate gardening hat. Even here Hansberry manages to reinforce congruence of values among black and white people with Beneatha's "Travis—we were trying to make Mama Mrs. Miniver—not Scarlett O'Hara."

The audience is almost brought to believe that the play can continue in this vein indefinitely, when the levity is broken once again by the sound of the door bell. Remembering what that sound brought the last time, the audience should react on cue. Walter reinforces our response with a display of sudden tension, the motivation for which is unclear, but which does serve to focus our attention on him. Our anxiety turns out to be appropriate, although its object in the stage world would not have been foreseen. The newest visitor is one of Walter's business associates, Bobo, whose frightened demeanor vividly warns the audience that this intruder brings even worse news than did the last. Bobo, like Lindner, cannot tell his story straightforwardly, but finally, in tears, he blurts that Willy, the third business partner, has vanished with all the money intended for the liquor store. Furthermore, Mama forces Walter to admit that this amount includes not only Walter's money but Beneatha's as well. As we might have vaguely suspected from Walter's earlier obsession with the liquor store venture, he never took the money to a bank but went directly to Bobo and Willy. The Youngers' first reaction is complete silence, creating discomfort for the audience. We are released from this oppressive paralysis when Mama turns to her son to beat him on the face, but Mama's final moans of memory, her recollections of how her husband killed himself with overwork to provide what has now been stolen away, can only evoke a mixture of uneasy pity and frustration in the audience.

The problem with this newest denial of a dream for the Youngers is that it provides no real enemy, no clear object of hatred on whom we can vent our anger and thus purge ourselves of anxiety and dismay. Walter has been foolish and deceitful, but since it is *he* who has been most directly exploited, our anger must be mingled with pity. Lindner is a kind of enemy, but he is not responsible for this misfortune. Willy, the third "partner," is an abstract, unknown figure, and therefore a difficult target for cathexis.

The audience turns to Act III with no sense of how all this can be resolved, but with the anticipation well established throughout the play that by the final curtain the problem of that money will have to be confronted in some fashion. That problem has, of course, now been partially eliminated, but like the conclusions of previous scenes, Act II, Scene iii, leaves the audience with the question of what will happen to the money that remains, invested, as it is, in the house. Hansberry repeats in Act III a strategic device she has used earlier in the play. She keeps the audience in suspense about the major question—what will happen to the new house?—while drawing our attention to a subordinate problem. In this instance, the distraction is what has come to be the second most important concern of the play, or what might be called the subplot of *A Raisin in the Sun:* Beneatha's concern with her "identity," as defined particularly in her relations to men. The man at the beginning of Act III is Asagai, who has ostensibly come to the Youngers' house to help with the moving, but who seizes the occasion to propose marriage and a life in Nigeria to Beneatha. Asagai is suggesting going "back to Africa" as an answer, at least for Beneatha. Since the suggestion is not well developed in the play, the effect on the audience is to let them know that such a possibility exists.

Beneatha's bitterness about Walter's loss of the money has brought her to a high degree of cynicism such that she now considers even a life of healing the sick to be a futile gesture. We can perceive these new hesitations about her career as consistent with her flirtation with various fads, but her poignant description of an incident from her childhood, when another child was badly hurt but returned from the hospital almost as good as new, suggests a serious and long-lasting motivation for a career as a doctor. Hansberry's strategy here is not carefully developed. The passage may serve once more to erase a sense of difference in values between black and white people, but the combination of Beneatha's provocative anecdote with her rejection of medicine as a career makes the strategy at this point ambiguous. At the end of the scene, after Asagai's proposal, Beneatha admits that she herself is "all mixed up," and perhaps Hansberry intends that the audience respond to Beneatha with the same tolerance and understanding that have been elicited for the ambivalence of other characters, with an added measure of patience because of Beneatha's youth.

During the entire scene between Asagai and Beneatha there is no clear indication of whether or not the family still intends to move, but, after Asagai's departure, Mama suggests with resignation that someone should tell the movers not to come. Our hopes that things might still work out begin to tumble, but they are momentarily renewed by Ruth's desperate cry that she will work twenty hours a day with her baby on her back if they will stick with their plans to move. Mama firmly denies such a possibility, however, saying, no, she has made up her mind and they can fix up their present apartment. Ruth's plea increases our admiration for her; her willingness to work so hard for what she wants fulfills the central ethic of American society. The intensity of her desire to move also should solidify the audience's wish that the Youngers still be able to acquire their house. Mama's limp suggestion that they instead fix up the apartment is in no way a satisfying solution; Mrs. Younger's resignation, while evoking some respect for her willingness to accept an alternative, should sharpen our disappointment and make acute our realization of the emptiness subsequent to the shriveling of the dream.

On this dismal note, Walter enters with his own resolution to the problem. His cynicism, like his sister's, has increased from his experience. To the horror of the entire family, Walter has called Mr. Lindner and asked the latter to come over so that they can now negotiate the sale of the house to the white man. Any hopes we may have had that the Youngers would have a new home are dashed. If the spectator is tempted to defend Walter's action on pragmatic grounds, Mama's voice intrudes to disallow such a response: "I came from five generations of people who was slaves and sharecroppers—but ain't nobody in my family never let nobody pay 'em no money that was a way of telling us we wasn't' fit to walk the earth. We ain't never been that poor. . . . We ain't never been that dead inside" (p. 426). Mama's pride and her horrified understanding of the nature of Walter's action call forth our admiration for her and our dismay and pity for Walter. Previously, Walter had made a mistake that destroyed our hopes and his for the fulfillment of the Youngers' dreams. Now we see that the result of that mistake also destroyed the man's spirit; as Mama implies, Walter's call to Lindner is a sign of death. Mama's words do not berate her son;

they are an expression of human dignity that tells us what dignity is—
and what it is not.

Mama's proclamation also focuses our attention on Walter.
Hansberry here has her strategy under remarkable control. Throughout
the play, the author has developed our concern for each of the characters as individuals and for each of their dreams and frustrations. We
have been shown three different women, not "the" black woman. Yet,
in subtle ways, Walter has stood particularly apart all along: He was a
man surrounded by women; his lows were nearer madness and his
highs nearer ecstasy than the depressions and joys of the other characters. The Younger women did not have identical dreams, but they
shared a desire for some greater sense of fulfillment, of comfort and
simple pleasure. None of them, however, was struggling with the loss
of self-respect that has been Walter's plight. What Mama's words lead
us to recognize is that Walter has been striving for dignity—just what
he lost with his call to Mr. Lindner.

What we want from Walter now is that he, too, recognize the challenge in Mama's words, and that he find in them the inspiration to
recapture the dignity he has lost. But Walter's defense moves him in
just the opposite direction: He falls to his knees in a hysterical imitation of the slave before the white "Father." Walter's behavior is painfully self-demeaning, but, if we feel a sense of disgust or condemnation, as Beneatha does, it is Mama who again leads us to the more
complicated, more appropriate response. After Beneatha has said that
Walter is no longer any brother of hers, that he is a "toothless rat,"
and that she despises any man who would behave this way, Mama tells
her, and us, how and why that rejection is wrong:

> There is always something left to love. And if you ain't learned
> that, you ain't learned nothing. (Looking at her) Have you cried
> for that boy today? I don't mean for yourself and for the family
> 'cause we lost the money. I mean for him; what he been through
> and what it done to him. Child, when do you think is the time to
> love somebody the most; when they done good and made things
> easy for everybody? Well, then, you ain't through learning—
> because that ain't the time at all. It's when he's at his lowest and
> can't believe in hisself 'cause the world done whipped him so.
> When you starts measuring somebody, measure him right, child,
> measure him right. Make sure you done taken into account what
> hills and valleys he come through before he got to wherever he
> is.   [pp. 427–28]

It is not difficult to find in Mama's words the "message" of the play:
When we measure someone, not just Walter, but any character on the

stage or any person in any world, we must measure him right. To ignore this lesson is not just to put aside Mama's somewhat didactic sermon; it is to refuse the experience of the entire play. Mama's speech should ring true to the audience, not just because we respect her or because we find a romantic appeal in this passage, but because Hansberry has so constructed her strategy that to acknowledge the world of this play necessitates a re-examination of each of our modes of "measurement." It also means that we must accept differences between characters and ambivalences within characters: to "measure right" is partially to avoid stereotyping. If, for example, we judge Ruth in her moments of hostility toward Walter, we must alter that judgment when we witness her gestures of love (the play prohibits us from labeling her the nagging wife); if we judge Mama when she is being tyrannical, we must also do so when she is generous and understanding. Furthermore, Mama reminds us that Walter is not on his knees now because he is essentially a weak and cowardly person. He is on his knees, as we have seen, because he has been through too much, because the world has "whipped him so." Because Hansberry's strategy has so persistently been an attempt to make us accept the Youngers as ordinary people like ourselves, it would be false now to expect of Walter a strength we would certainly not presume in ourselves. We cannot condemn Walter for falling after a beating. A black spectator can empathize with Walter, while a white spectator may feel shame at being part of the world that is responsible for the whipping; any spectator should recognize in Walter's experience, however, the defeat of having struggled and lost.

A Raisin in the Sun could end with Mama's speech. Such an ending would leave us with a message and a vague depression. We do not have sufficient reason to condemn Walter, but neither do we have the reasons his family has to love him and feel a deep anguish at his defeat. We have also only seen Walter rehearse his humiliation; although we have no reason to hope that he or other characters onstage will change his behavior, we would be left without a sense of completion were we not to see Walter's encounter with Lindner. Yet we feel a sense of futility when Lindner does arrive. There appears no way for the characters onstage to aid Walter or alter the situation.

There is also the important frustration in being an audience member who wishes to aid the characters on stage but cannot because one is in a world separate from theirs. When the playwright creates such an effect, the intent is that we transport the desire to change behavior, either our own or someone else's, into the world in which we do or can act. Drama presents to the audience the limits of a world and arouses the desire that someone break through those limits. In tragedy, the hero is most often thwarted in his attempts to deny or destroy the boundaries of his world, but our sorrow for him relieves us of our own impotence and allows us to act anew in our world. In *A Raisin in the Sun* we are led to the edge of tragedy, from where we can see the abyss into which Walter is falling, yet we are finally led away from that edge because Hansberry does not intend us to remove ourselves from her characters. In traditional tragedy, we are meant to see the central character or characters as other and greater than ourselves: Their falls thus create anguish; and their struggles provide hope. In *A Raisin in the Sun*, we are meant to see ourselves as like these characters in all important ways. Thus, neither pity nor awe is wholly appropriate, for the former would lead to self-pity and the latter to egotism.

More than in our experience of many plays, when we arrive at the end of *A Raisin in the Sun* we feel that everything else in the play has been set up precisely to accomplish the final scene. One reason for this sensation is that we know we are being told a story, and we expect a story to have a beginning, a middle, and an end. We have also been led to recognize that this is, in an important way, Walter's story, and his tale is not yet complete. Once engaged in the final episode, its surprising reversal and its emphatic assertion of survival tend to erase our memories of earlier troublings much as the baby that arrives after labor dissolves the memory of the pain that brought it forth.

Our attention is all on Walter as the final portion of the play begins. Walter has "set this scene," and the other Youngers, like the audience, are witnesses. Lindner, the white man from the neighborhood committee, returns to the Youngers' home expecting, as we do, that Walter is about to sell the house to the white community. Just as Hansberry has played with our curiosity in previously unpredictable scenes with Lindner and then Bobo, she now elongates Walter's response to Lindner. In words that approach a parody of Lindner's earlier speech, while sustaining an air of utter sincerity, Walter speaks slowly of his family, of his pride in his sister's studies, and with increasing emphasis, of his father. Our attention is held rapt because this is not the role Walter has rehearsed; we have no reason not to expect him eventually to come to his deal, but the words he speaks suggest a sentiment and pride we have not seen previously in Walter. We are thus only vaguely prepared for Walter's sudden reversal. Crying unashamedly in front of "the man" Walter finally says that the Youngers will move into their new house, "because my father—my father—he earned it."

With these words, Walter pays a debt both to his parents and to the audience. The time and trust they and we have invested in him are now rewarded. He is behaving with the dignity we have had only glimpses of since the beginning of the play. As he continues to speak, he affirms this trust for both black and white spectators: "We don't want to make no trouble for nobody or fight no causes—but we will try to be good neighbors." Hansberry thus reassures white spectators that the Youngers do not want to cause difficulties and reassures black spectators that the Youngers will *try* to be good neighbors but will not guarantee any particular kind of behavior.

If we contemplate Walter's sudden redemption, we will be puzzled by it. The only possible motivation we are given for Walter's change of mind is the brief appearance of Travis before Lindner's arrival. Perhaps we are to infer that the sight of his son jars Walter into understanding that it is not only he who will suffer humiliation and loss of a dream. But the script does not guide the audience to that conclusion. Rather, we are given no pause to search for an explanation of Walter's new behavior. The moment Lindner leaves, Ruth cries, "LET'S GET THE HELL OUR OF HERE!" The women become so hastily involved in other activities and conversations that they suggest that Walter's redemption is too fragile and too fortunate to be questioned. The bustle of activity at the end of the play prevents excessive sentimentality, but it also demands that the audience feel satisfaction without understanding.

If we look closer at that feeling of satisfaction, we will find in it the essence of Hansberry's strategy. We are pleased that Walter has behaved with dignity and relieved that the Youngers will go on, not in futile desperation but with a sense of a new world before them. They have not changed very much, nor did Hansberry lead the audience to demand or expect great changes. The conclusion of *A Raisin in the Sun* returns us to a world of buoyant wit, and our ability once again to share laughter with the Youngers reassures us of a shared vision of the world.

It is this very laughter, however, that prevents many spectators from perceiving the contradictions of the Youngers' world. Early in the play, our laughter relieves us from fully confronting the evidence that *A Raisin in the Sun* presents not simply the dreams of the characters but the complexities of "dreams deferred." Nor does the conclusion of the play make us ashamed of our good humor. The Youngers are back in high spirits. We can leave the theater happily persuaded that still another family has rightfully joined the infinitely extensive American middle class.

Such an experience of Hansberry's play is not a mistake; it may be what is essentially intended, but it is simply not whole. There is a confusion in the world of the Youngers, which Harold Cruse glimpses but finally misperceives: "The Younger family was carefully tidied up for its on-stage presentation. . . . There were no numbers runners in sight, no bumptious slick, young "cats" from downstairs sniffling after

Mama Younger's pretty daughter on the corner, no shyster preachers
hustling Mama into the fold, no fallen woman, etc."[11] Such omissions
may be glaring to some spectators, but can be understood as a decision
not to distract a middle-class audience from their recognition of the
Youngers as similar to themselves. To gain the aura of authenticity for
those who know the ghetto might mean to relinquish some contact
with a middle-class audience. To untidy the Youngers might be to di-
shevel as well the audience's social and aesthetic security that allows it
to recognize these people.

The difficulty with a genuine recognition of the world of *A Raisin in
the Sun* is not that Hansberry lies to maintain order; it is rather that
she is finally unable to lie. Her drama reveals more than the main
intention of her strategy would wish. The Youngers are not moving
into the middle-class when they move into their new house; they are
simply and only moving into a house. For many Americans, the act of
purchasing one's own house clearly signifies upward mobility and
membership in the middle class. This signification occurs for at least
two different reasons: In order to buy a house, the purchaser must
present some assurances of stable income and occupation, and the act
itself is one of choice. Since the dramatic structure of *A Raisin in the
Sun* can exist only because a choice does exist, we can allow ourselves
to believe that we are in the world of the middle class. But choice for
the Youngers is poignantly and emphatically a singular event. They are
only able to make a choice because the ten thousand dollar benefit
from Mr. Younger's life insurance policy has suddenly appeared in
their mailbox. Ironically, it is through death, not the nature of their
lives, that they are able to choose to buy a house.

It is made amply clear that Hansberry cannot lie about the limitations of this move for the Youngers. Ruth recognizes fully that she will
have to work herself to the bone to help keep up the mortgage payment, yet the early scenes of the play remind us that she cannot continue her pregnancy in health and harmony with her domestic work.
And what will happen when Ruth does have a baby? If the implied
assumption is that Mama will take over the rearing of another Younger
child, this must also be an assumption of further internal destruction in
the family, since the tensions caused by Mama's meddling in Travis's
upbringing have been poignantly demonstrated. Walter Lee's situation
is at least equally closed. Not only are there no new options for him to
change his occupation, for him to find work less servile than that of a
chauffeur, but the dream of going into business for himself has itself
been muddied. The theft of his share of the insurance policy concretely
removes his chance for starting a liquor business now, but it also

suggests that ventures into the world of private business necessitate a kind of cunning, distrust, and encounter with corruption that calls the entire operation into question.

To turn to Beneatha or Travis only further reveals the imprisonment of the family. Beneatha may be able at the end of the play to return to her fantasies of getting married and going off to practice medicine in Africa, but the audience, at least, should remember that such notions are now even more fantastic than before, because Walter Lee has lost not only the money for his business but Beneatha's money for school. Travis may now have a room of his own, at least until the arrival of the new baby, but how will the family find the fifty cents (if it is only fifty cents out in the white suburbs) for school activities when there is no new income and the pressures of taking care of the house will create even greater financial burdens? If Travis's own parents did not like the image of their son picking up extra money by carrying bags at the supermarket, how will the new white middle-class neighbors respond to the black boy who totes packages for a few pennies after school? The bustle of moving may allow all members of the family to repress momentarily their fears and despair, but Beneatha's earlier words to Asagai, her African friend, are the only authentic description of where the family really finds itself: "Don't you see there isn't any real progress, Asagai, there is only one large circle that we march in, around and around, each of us our own little picture—in front of us—our own little mirage which we think is the future" (p. 419).

Hansberry has succeeded in persuading the audience to the legitimacy of the Youngers' aspirations, but she has simultaneously shown the extreme difficulty, if not impossibility, for this family of fulfilling their dreams of change, stability, and comfort. Hansberry directly undercuts the central middle-class American notion of "equality of opportunity" by presenting the white man, Mr. Lindner, who finally believes that opportunities for blacks should not be identical with those for whites, that blacks should not move into a white neighborhood; this is only one direct instance, however, of the limitations of opportunity for the Youngers. Mr. Lindner slams a door on the Youngers that may have appeared to have been open; other doors for the Youngers simply remain closed.

Perhaps despite her intentions, Hansberry's play takes one additional step to undermine a belief in one great middle-class world for all Americans: At crucial moments her characterizations and plot structure call into question the very nature of the values and opportunities being presented as shared.

BENEATHA (hissingly): Yes—just look at what the New World
hath wrought! . . . There he is! *Monsieur le petit bourgeois
noir*—himself! There he is! Symbol of a Rising Class! En-
trepreneur! Titan of the system!
. . . I look at you and I see the final triumph of stupidity in
the world!   [p. 472]

Walter's subsequent courage in rejecting Mr. Lindner's bribe prevents
us from concluding that Walter is "the final triumph of stupidity in the
world." But while we may be forced away from this particular conclusion, the first lines of Beneatha's attack may resound with accuracy.
The world of *A Raisin in the Sun* is often affable, but the assaults on
class identity for black people suggest a paradoxically coherent confusion.[12]

That recognition may lead to at least small changes in the social and
political worlds from which the audience comes. Woodie King and Ron
Milner, strong contemporary proponents of a black theater, have urged
in the introduction to their anthology of black drama that "*A Raisin in
the Sun* reaffirmed in blacks the necessity for more involvement in
black theater."[13] Partially by the inclusion in its casts of such notable
black theater artists as Lonne Elder III, Robert Hooks, Douglas Turner
Ward, and Ossie Davis, the play "marked a turning point."[14] These
remarks emphasize the play as historical event rather than experience
for an audience. It may well be that this is how *A Raisin in the Sun*
will be best remembered, but the fact that it *is* remembered is inseparable from the play's ability to impress an audience. That impression may not have been as facile as it once appeared. *A Raisin in the
Sun*'s success raised the curtain for many subsequent productions of
black theater; it may also have lifted the veil for some spectators to
glimpse the complexity of black life in America. Even for black spectators who know that complexity in their daily lives, the act of witnessing its revelation, with all of the play's omissions and inconsistencies, can be important.

At the end of *A Raisin in the Sun*, Mama starts to leave, then
symbolically returns for her plant. The plant, like the family, is still
scraggly, but there is hope that it will flourish when cultivated in new
soil. Although Hansberry wanted us to see that plant as representing
the Younger family, some twenty years later it also suggests the place
A Raisin in the Sun has found in the evolution of black drama.

NOTES

1. Doris Abramson, *Negro Playwrights in the American Theatre, 1925–1959* (New York: Columbia University Press, 1969), p. 239.
2. *Ibid.*
3. Harold Cruse, *The Crisis of the Negro Intellectual* (New York: Morrow, 1967), pp. 267–84.

   Harold Cruse has, in fact, drawn considerable attention to Hansberry's background, citing her particular and limited experience of a black world as explanation for what he judges to be the failings of *A Raisin in the Sun*. In a lengthy assault on Hansberry and the left-wing middle-class intellectuals with whom she was associated, Cruse recalls the playwright's upper-middle-class background, her lack of familiarity with the black working class, and her family's notoriety as Chicago slum landlords. Cruse further declaims Hansberry's use of the old leftist jargon and her immerson in the "provincially sectarian, middle-class literary ethos," which gave rise to *A Raisin in the Sun*.

   These are not simply *ad mulierem* attacks: Cruse draws attention to Hansberry's background to support his accusations that she blurs class distinctions in her writing. I explore the inconsistencies in Hansberry's depictions of the Youngers' class identity at the end of this chapter; what is worth noting here is that Hansberry did come from a family that brought her comfort as a child and a college education without struggle, that she was apparently enamored of black and white left-wing intellectuals, and that after she had moved from Chicago to New York City, she lived in Greenwich Village, not Harlem. All this does point to striking differences between her background and that of the people she depicts, but one should judge the use Cruse makes of these distinctions in Hansberry's upbringing in the light of his disdain for those he sees as distracting attention from the problems of the real working class under the guise of a distorted socialism.
4. *New York Post*, July 1, 1959, p. 3.
5. Abramson, p. 240.
6. For a complete list of reviews and commentaries on *A Raisin in the Sun*, see the Bibliography under Hansberry.

   To suggest the range of remarks: Brooks Atkinson spoke of the play as a "Negro *The Cherry Orchard*," *New York Times*, March 28, 1959, II, 1:1; Gerald Weales condemned the outdated naturalism of the play in *Commentary* (June 1959), 527–30; Abramson sees it as "a summary, a proof, and an end of an era," in *Negro Playwrights in America*; Darwin T. Turner calls it "one of the most perceptive presentations of Afro-Americans in the history of the American professional theatre," in "Introduction," *Black Drama in America* (Greenwich, Conn.: Fawcett, 1971). Cruse's negative remarks are discussed in more detail in note 3 above.

7. Abramson, p. 242.

8. *Ibid.*

9. I am not saying that *A Raisin in the Sun* should be praised because it is like white drama, nor am I subtly condescending to Hansberry's play by suggesting that it imitates white American drama and is therefore not original. What I am urging is that the familiarity of *A Raisin in the Sun*'s form implements the play's strategy. It is neither a failure of invention nor a judgment on my part that only traditional white Western dramatic forms are good, but a direction appropriately taken for this play's intentions. The play only *appears to be* like a Miller or O'Neill drama; *A Raisin in the Sun* is not a "Negro" *Death of a Salesman,* not only for obvious reasons but because Hansberry's and Miller's intentions are wholly different.

My defensiveness here is inspired by the attack Clayton Riley makes on Abramson's "contempt" for black playwrights who do not live up to white standards. ("On Black Theater," Clayton Riley, in *The Black Aesthetic,* Addison Gayley ed. [New York: Doubleday, 1972], p. 310.)

10. Lorraine Hansberry, *A Raisin in the Sun,* in *Black Theatre,* Lindsay Patterson, ed. (New York: Dodd, Mead, 1971), p. 348. All other citations are from this source.

11. Cruse, p. 280.

12. The case I have been making here, both for and against Hansberry and *A Raisin in the Sun,* is not far removed from the case made by Georg Lukács in his discussion of Balzac. Lukács summarizes his argument at the beginning of the essay "Balzac: The Peasants," in *Studies in European Realism* (New York: Grosset & Dunlap, 1964), saying, "Yet, for all his painstaking preparation and careful planning, what Balzac really did in this novel was the exact opposite of what he had set out to do: what he depicted was not the tragedy of the aristocratic estate but of the peasant smallholding." But Hansberry is finally neither as historically accurate nor as deserving of the kind of praise that Lukács gives Balzac. Hers is not precisely the same case, because it is never clear that she knows what she is revealing. Like Balzac, she provides no solutions, but unlike Balzac, she tends to disguise the space within which she raises questions. This is not a matter of mendacity, but neither is it an instance of the insight of genius revealing itself despite itself.

13. Woodie King and Ron Milner, "Evolution of a People's Theater," in *Black Drama Anthology* (New York: Columbia University Press, 1971), p. vii.

14. *Ibid.*

6 LOST ILLUSIONS, NEW VISIONS: IMAMU AMIRI BARAKA'S *DUTCHMAN*

IN THE MID-1960s, a man who had previously been known as LeRoi Jones took on the name of Imamu Amiri Baraka. This act was a sign not only of a change in political and religious identity but also of the self-recognition of a leader of what had come to be known as the Black Arts Movement. In the new name, Baraka, meaning sanctity or holiness,[1] stands as the surname, and Amiri (sometimes spelled Ameer), is the African or "traditional" name; "*imamu*" is a Swahili word signifying the title "spiritual leader."[2] Coinciding with Baraka's change of name was his commitment to the orthodox Muslim Kawaida faith, and his return as a resident to Newark, New Jersey, the city of his birth in 1934. Baraka reclaimed his birthplace as both a political and cultural leader. In Newark, he established Spirit House, a community center for black drama, poetry, music, and politics, as well as the parent to the Spirit House African Free School.

That Baraka took upon himself the title "spiritual leader" may seem arrogant and presumptuous. There are ample evidences and statements from his peers and public, however, that the name is indeed appropriate. In the late 1950s and early 1960s, he was already establishing a reputation for himself as a beat poet, editor, and teacher. After his graduation from Howard University in 1953, and service in the U.S. Air Force from 1954 to 1957, he moved to New York City, where he lived in Greenwich Village while writing, teaching, and earning a master's degree in literature at Columbia University. In New York, he also edited the avant-garde magazine *Yugen*.[3] During this time, he was gaining national attention through poems published in a variety of journals.[4] He had also begun to write the plays that would firmly establish him as both a noteworthy writer and the "prime mover and chief designer" of the Black Arts Theatre.[5]

In March 1964, three plays by Baraka were produced in New York

City: *The Eighth Ditch*, *The Baptism*, and *Dutchman*. *Dutchman* was
the most successful of the three dramas; in May 1964, the play won an
Obie from the *Village Voice* as the best off-Broadway production of the
1963–64 season, as well as a $500 prize from Edward Albee. While
Dutchman was receiving its commendations (and its attacks) downtown,
Baraka was engaged uptown, in Harlem, in the establishment of the
Black Arts Repertoire Theatre School. Working with other black artists,[6] Baraka attempted to establish a center for the creation and performance of black drama, poetry, and music for the black community.
The project was short-lived, evidently owing to both internal dissension
and the termination of government funding because of the political
stance of the theater,[7] but it gave rise to numerous black community
theaters across the country, many of which remain vibrant and spawn
still other black theaters.[8] Baraka's own Spirit House in Newark was
one of these outgrowths of the Harlem venture.

From 1964 on, Baraka's work as a dramatist cannot be easily separated from his political activities, nor can either of these be extricated
from his efforts to establish a new and viable black theater. For Baraka,
black theater has meant a kind of black drama that would accurately
convey the life of the black American community while teaching that
community how to struggle for its identity and potency in white
America; it has also meant the creation of black community theaters
across the nation to be the working centers and stages for those plays
and other black arts. In an essay initially commissioned and then refused by the *New York Times*,[9] Baraka articulated his sense of the nature and intentions of a new black theater. The essay, eventually published in *Black Dialogue* and *The Liberator* in 1965, urges the creation
of a "Revolutionary Theatre:"

> The Revolutionary Theatre should force change, it should be
> change. (All their faces turned into the lights and you work on
> them black nigger magic, and cleanse them at having seen the
> ugliness and if the beautiful see themselves, they will love them-
> selves.) We are preaching virtue again, but by that to mean
> NOW, what seems the most constructive uses of the word. . . .
>
> The Revolutionary Theatre must EXPOSE! Show up the insides
> of these humans, look into black skulls. White men will cower
> before this theatre because it hates them. Because they have
> been trained to hate. The Revolutionary Theatre must hate them
> for hating. For presuming with their technology to deny the
> supremacy of the Spirit. They will all die because of this.[10]

Baraka's words here do not present an ideological line for black theater;

they do not say, "This is the *message* black theater must contain."[11] Rather, they tell what black theater must and will do. The meaning of black theater will be its actions, not a lesson that can be summarized. It is not didactic; it is a demonstration. It is a theater of action, not statement. Politically, it is revolutionary because, like every re-volutionist, it aims to "force change"; theatrically it is also revolutionary because, from Baraka's viewpoint, it will move opposite to the Broadway theater, which urges stagnation and repose.

What kind of script would fulfill Baraka's demand for a revolutionary theater? Literally dozens of black playwrights, including Baraka himself, have attempted to answer this call. Yet, despite the overt political concerns of this theater, no formulaic response has evolved. Baraka alone has written at least twenty plays, most of them since 1965. The one characteristic common to his plays and those of many of his contemporaries is that they emphasize a way of being in the world that is particularly black, and this emphasis is meant to affect a black audience. Baraka's own plays also persisently attack the class structure and values of white America and warn blacks of the dangers of seduction into the American middle class.

One of the best examples of Black Revolutionary Theatre from Baraka's work is *Great Goodness of Life (A Coon Show)*. First pro-duced in New York in 1969 as part of the *Black Quartet*, four new plays by four black playwrights, *Great Goodness of Life* evokes the impositional force of nightmare in its stark, symbolic presentations of characters and events, and has the effect of a nightmare in arousing terror in response to circumstances that might otherwise seem bizarre or irrational. Court Royal, the central figure of *Great Goodness of Life*, is a middle-aged black man who has spent his entire life working for the Post Office, a traditional cell of security and entrapment for the black man. The voice of a white judge and images from some unnamed but clearly authoritarian source suddenly appear to accuse Court Royal of "shielding a wanted criminal, a murderer."[12] Court insists on his innocence, despite the urgings of the "attorney" to plead guilty, but Court's general sense of guilt is finally so aroused by an assault of dreamlike sounds and pictures, that he confesses. Reduced in his con-fession to a trancelike existence, Court then follows the judge's orders to kill the criminal, who is revealed to be Court's own son. In the last lines of the play, Court's soul and behavior have become "white as snow."

Great Goodness of Life shows the black man demeaning himself in his command performance for the white man. The task is not to enter-tain whites, but to arouse the sensitivity of blacks to the ways in which the black man has been brought to demean and destroy himself by accepting and adopting the modes of the white middle class. Most painfully, this is viewed not only as self-destruction but as murder of younger generations. The play is intended to disturb a sense of false innocence and complacency in blacks and to make them question the white middle-class values that hypnotized men like Court Royal. White spectators may watch the play feeling increased guilt, sympathy for a degraded human being, or admiration for the drama's skillful theatricality, but there is no direct stimulus intended for them as whites (although ten years later the case of Peter Reilly might well have made Court Royal's manipulated confession less remote for a white audience).

Great Goodness of Life (*A Coon Show*) crystalizes one of the elements of the strategy already apparent in Baraka's earlier and best-known work, *Dutchman*. The later play clarifies within a script both the conceptions of black theater that Baraka presents in his 1965 essay, and one force of the difficult strategy of *Dutchman*. *Dutchman* is not fully conceived as a black revolutionary play, but, if the spectator is attuned, elements of its strategy can work in a revolutionary manner; *Great Goodness of Life* is meant to "tune in" the spectator, but the revolutionary tone is sounded specifically for the ears of black witnesses.

There is, as in most drama, an attempt in *Dutchman* to change the spectator's way of looking at the world. *Dutchman*, however, works in such a way that for spectators as well as stage characters, changes in perspective vary according to whether one is black or white. *Dutchman* makes manifest the ambivalent intentions that have been disguised or latent in earlier black dramas. While *Great Goodness of Life* and other black revolutionary dramas urge the need for separate dramatic strategies for black and white audiences by aiming their intentions only at black spectators, *Dutchman* acknowledges the encounter of two worlds and two modes of seeing within the one world it constructs onstage and within the space of the audience for which it is played. The play presumes our differences and confronts them; some elements of its strategy will work similarly on black and white spectators, but its essential strategic devices affect not what black and white spectators share as human beings, but what separates us as black and white Americans.

In *Dutchman*, the imprisoning paradoxes that black dramas had been revealing for forty-five years are boldly and baldly thrust at the audience; in the world of twentieth-century urban America that Baraka synthesizes and mythologizes, it becomes an insult to call a black man middle class. It is also possible in this world at once to perceive a black man as middle-class, a bastard, and the son of a "social-working mother." This is a play in which not to be a nigger is to be a "dirty white man," and in which, as *Dutchman* goes on to expose, not to dance with Lula, the drama's emissary from the white middle class, is to choose death as your partner.

For the many spectators who have witnessed productions of *Dutchman* since its first performance in 1964, it has remained singular, baffling, and troubling. For forty-five minutes we listen to a white woman, Lula, delineate what it means to have "made it" in modern America, to be middle-class. But Lula not only catalogs middle-class attributes—having an education, being able to make appropriate small-talk, wearing a three-button suit—she presents the other main character, the black man, Clay, to himself and to us as a model of these characteristics. While some, particularly those who are black among the audience, may be suspicious and angered from the beginning of the play by Lula's easy assumptions, it is not until Clay's long and explosive speech near the end of *Dutchman* that white spectators are fully forced to acknowledge their disorientation and black spectators are led to unmuted fear. At the end of Clay's speech, he warns Lula and the audience that the day may come when black Americans are indeed accepted into the fold of white middle-class society, and that will be a day when "all of those ex-coons will be stand-up Western men, with eyes for clean hard useful lives, sober, pious and sane, and they'll murder you."[13] This is not simply a threat that the rage of black people against racism will eventually and inevitably explode, it is a warning that the very central image of the good American life, the open door to the middle class, is not only a deceptive fantasy but a death wish if realized.

The inclusion of blacks and whites in the world of *Dutchman* is not, then, the "integrated" world of Lorraine Hansberry's *A Raisin in the Sun*. It is a world in which a black man and a white woman meet in the rushing anonymity of the subway, engage in conversation at once intimate and estranged, and come to a mutual recognition through violent action. Clay, the black man, and Lula, the white woman, are in the same physical place, but neither they nor we ever see them as alike. Lula attempts to seduce, taunt, bewilder Clay; Clay tries to ignore, rebuff, enjoy, and humor Lula. Finally, only rejection is possible. Clay's refusal is violently verbal; Lula's literally murderous: She kills him. In the end, we learn from this play that black people cannot rest peacefully in the same world with white people like Lula.

Although there may be a moral to *Dutchman*, the play is not a fable. Baraka has urged that we regard his *Dutchman* characters as human beings, not primarily as symbolic figures: Lula, Baraka has said, "does not represent anything—she is one."[14] Lula is not a fantasy or an emblem; she is not a character created by a synthesis of Baraka's understanding of important elements in the white American character (or even just the white American female character). Nor is she a figure like Edward Albee's young man in *The American Dream*—a creature who could never exist in the real world but who functions as a kind of flag to illustrate what that world is elementally like. Lula and Clay are real people, or, in theatrical terms, realistic characters, who can and do exist. We could not encounter Albee's young man on a subway train; we can and do, find people like Clay and Lula on a subway every day, even if we do not recognize them.

Creating the understanding that Lula is one of the people who ride the subway and is not *only* a representative of them, is central to Baraka's strategy. The playwright wishes to prohibit the audience from maintaining an intellectual distance from Lula and Clay. We are not to be allowed to say, "Well, yes, she does represent elements of American society, but there is no one around really like her." Literary symbols can trouble an audience, but they do not frighten us as would "real" people, because they cannot act like a real people.

Yet Baraka's intention is not limited to our recognition of Lula and Clay as a real white woman and a real black man. The subway on which we discover Lula and Clay is, according to Baraka's stage directions, "heaped in modern myth." From its title, *Dutchman*, through its use of apples and its allusions to places like "Juliet's tomb," Baraka's play is "heaped in myth." We are to perceive Lula and Clay, then, as real *and* mythical figures. This is not a contradiction. As anthropologists have shown us, myth is not a false or fictitious description of events in the world; rather, it is an expression of the particular, common, basic, and necessary ways in which men and women relate to each other and the world around them. The power and magic of myth are that it isolates and enables us to acknowledge those structures of human relationship that define who and how we are in the world. This power and magic are at the core of Baraka's strategy in *Dutchman*.

II

The first clue to the mythical nature of the world of this play is found in the title, *Dutchman*. Although the spectator may recall few details of the story, he will probably know that there exists a "legend of the Flying Dutchman," and may know that this legend has something to do with traveling forever, sailing on with no port or certain destination. Perhaps the spectator will think of being "in Dutch," meaning in difficulty; or "going Dutch," a situation in which each participant pays his own way; or the slang expression "beat the Dutch," which connotes being extraordinary. Or maybe one of the characters is a Dutchman, or a "new Dutchman," a New Yorker. However the spectator takes the word, it puzzles, suggests something not ordinary about the play. (What effect would it have if the play were called "The Subway?") Baraka has said in an interview with Larry Neal that "the most important function of art is to open you up." Baraka's title is intended to "open up" the spectator by stimulating associations that may or may not elucidate what occurs onstage, but which at least prepare us to make connections as the play proceeds.

If the title *Dutchman* serves to point to the world of myth and to unsettle the audience, the play's setting takes these intentions and elaborates their effect as a melody drawn from a musical phrase. By the very nature of its jerky movement and its underground location, the subway is unsettling and mythical. This is the same world that Ralph Ellison in *Invisible Man* and Richard Wright in "The Man Who Lived Underground" also found intriguingly effective. It is a subterranean world in which the natural and artificial, the ordinary and bizarre combine to disorient the audience, while allowing for the acceptance of events that might not be believed in the world above. That Ellison, Wright, and Baraka should all exploit the "underground" as setting suggests, too, its particular power as metaphor for the doubleness and duplicity of American society.

Baraka describes his setting as: "In the flying underbelly of the city. Steaming hot, and summer on top, outside. Underground. The subway heaped in modern myth" (p. 3). He goes on to suggest that there are to be flickering lights, indications of passing stations, perhaps the sound of the screaming train. The audience is to have a sense of speed, of movement; the lights and stations should suggest an ever changing world, but one with a persistent pattern. By indicating that the lights for this subway could be pasted on the subway windows, as admitted props, Baraka makes clear that this is not to be an authentic reproduction of a subway car. The set is not intended to put the audience at ease by showing us the familiar; it is meant to prohibit complacency by calling attention to those elements of the subway that are most threatening and disorienting. A subway may be a place we know and do not think much about, but this subway is meant to call forth discomforts and anxieties of subway-riding that we repress.

The audience's perception of the set as a subway, but one stripped of the naturalistic details that would make it comfortingly familiar (if still physically uncomfortable), is further achieved by Baraka's directions that as the play begins, only one seat is to be visible to the audience and we are to see only one man sitting alone on that seat. There are no crowds to make this man anonymous, no movement of bodies to distract our attention from the movement of the train. Although we are not allowed to deny that this is a subway, we are immediately led to a wariness that this subway ride will be different from others we may have known or imagined.

As if in opposition to the effect of the setting, the appearance of the man who sits on the subway is not initially disconcerting. What we see is a young, black man, dressed conservatively in suit and striped tie; like hundreds of other remembered subway riders, he is "holding a magazine but looking vacantly just above its wilting pages." In a brief but exceptionally provocative critique of *Dutchman*, Clayton Riley, a black drama critic and playwright, assesses Clay. He is "a character who possessed both the ability to be painfully recognizable to blacks who observed him, and one who was completely believable and welcome to the consciousness of all whites who watched his life unfold in perfectly understandable, pleasing blandness before them."[15] Although this description of Clay suggests how the audience responds to the character as the play evolves, Riley's comments are appropriate to our impression of Clay before he speaks.

It is only when the other major character of the play, Lula, appears that our uneasiness is extended beyond our responses to the set. Indeed, Baraka has Lula enter the play in such a way as to make the audience instantly curious and tense. We first see Lula as a face smiling in through the subway window at the seated, solitary man. The man, whom we eventually know as Clay, first smiles back casually, then glances away and back again with an expression of embarrassment. The woman's face disappears. The brief visual encounter is meant to puzzle the audience. The exchange of smiles suggests recognition, but the man's embarrassment is then not appropriate. The moment also unsettles because it is not common for a white woman to smile through a subway window at a black man. But the woman vanishes, and the man's return to his earlier posture of comfortable idleness seems meant to reassure the audience that nothing important has occurred.

To our surprise, and now Clay's puzzlement, the woman reappears. This time, she is more than a flashing image. Everything about her is meant to draw our attention to her, but her appeal and demeanor are particularly aimed to arouse our sexual interest. She is "a tall, slender, beautiful woman," dressed in skimpy clothes, adorned with sunglasses and loud lipstick, languid in her movements. Lula is thirty, ten years older than Clay. She is eating an apple, and apples in the hands of a beautiful woman are too obvious a part of our mythology not to be at least vaguely associated with temptation, seduction, sin, and war. Were this woman alone on the subway, we might simply question or admire her appearance; similarly, when Clay was alone initially, we looked at him, perhaps wondered about him, but were not particularly troubled by his presence. As soon as Lula stops by Clay's seat, however, all of our earlier uncertainties evoked by the play's title and setting recur and support an unavoidable anxiety. No matter what the qualities of a particular spectator's fantasies or fears about sexual encounters between black and white people, the simple visual impact of this white woman dangling with her apple over the quiet black man is enough to make most spectators uneasy. And this is not just any attractive woman but a woman who has already demonstrated strange behavior with her previous fleeting smile. We are warned that there is going to be some relationship between this white woman and this black man, and few spectators in America would be so accustomed to such a relationship that they would not find it at least intriguing, if not distressing or infuriating. Furthermore, Baraka forces us to pay attention to these two people because they are the only persons before us on the stage; neither they, nor we, are to be protected or distracted from what happens by the presence of others.

The opening dialogue increases our confusion and uneasiness. "Weren't you staring at me through the window" asks Lula, and we are given our first clue that something is amiss; that is not the way we perceived the opening scene. Clay, too, is taken aback, and suggests that it was Lula who was doing the staring. But Lula persists and startles us again, this time by the bluntness of her language as she asserts that Clay was staring in the vicinity of her "ass and legs." These certainly are words the audience would have heard, but not ones most spectators would expect of a woman on a subway. Clay, however, is more in control than we might be. He retorts that "staring through windows is weird business. Much weirder than staring at abstract asses." His remark rings true; we expect men to stare at women's bodies; we do not expect people to stare through windows at strangers. Clay's remarks also tell us something about him: He is not a bland "Tom" at the beginning of the play; he is cool and sharp.

As the dialogue proceeds, led by Lula, Baraka gives us increasing reason to be troubled by this white woman. We are also led to be sympathetic toward Clay for his persistent self-control in the face of Lula's strange comments and insults. Lula reveals that she has purposefully taken this train because of Clay; we and Clay are perplexed. Lula then accuses Clay of being dull. The insult does not distress him and probably seems basically accurate to the audience. His response that he was not prepared for "party talk" is a weak but acceptable defense. And defense is certainly the word here, for there is already the sense of a battle, although what kind of battle is not yet clear.

Clayton Riley's densely rich commentary on *Dutchman* again points the reader in the right direction for assessment of Lula and Clay's "conversation." The "word games," as Riley appropriately labels them,[16] develop in complexity and emphasize the sexual tensions in this encounter. Although Riley only drops the notion of word games and proceeds to other concerns, the term can usefully serve to indicate that while the dialogue between Clay and Lula can be heard as superficial sexual banter, these exchanges reveal both deeply imbedded rules and the breaking of such rules. "Word games" in this play can not be dismissed as "just words" or "just games" but are important actions between two people. And often these gestures are as violent as any physical thrust might be. The strategy here is to keep the spectator uneasy by making unavoidable the recognition that this black man and this white woman are talking about sex. Baraka further disorients his audience by seeming to reverse traditional male-female roles: Lula, the woman, is the aggressor. Many spectators will find her sexual candor and aggressiveness distressing, and even the spectator who finds these elements appealing cannot be expected to toss them off lightly. Yet, although sex is a persistent part of the game, it is not the only game being played. Lula starkly and rhetorically asks Clay, "You think I want to pick you up, get you to take me somewhere and screw me, huh?" (p. 8). Clay's ambiguous response, "Is that the way I look?" may be heard only as sexual banter, a question that would lead Lula to acknowledge Clay's sexuality, but it is intended as the first important clue in the play to Clay's self-containment and his recognition of Lula. Clay's question reveals that Lula is judging his desires on the basis of his appearance. The fact that Clay poses such a question is a device to make the white spectator wonder about the accuracy of such judgments while establishing a separate contact with black spectators. The black spectator is here led to a quick identification with Clay as part of a community that is repeatedly stereotyped. Clay's question is also a hint to the audience that Clay knows more about Lula, about the way in which she comes to conclusions, than is expressed in his "dull" conversation.

Lula, however, is blind to the implications of Clay's question. She proceeds precisely to attack the way Clay does look. Clay is embarrassed but intrigued by Lula's description of him as a boy from New Jersey trying to grow a beard, someone who reads Chinese poetry and drinks sugarless, lukewarm tea. This sounds perceptive on Lula's part; nothing that we see yet is intended to refute this impression. But if we have understood the intent of Clay's question, we will be nagged into doubting whether we can come to any accurate conclusions about Clay from his appearance. Lula's description of Clay may make him, as the earlier quotation from Riley suggested, "painfully recognizable to blacks," while relieving some of the white spectators' anxieties about this black man, but the fact that Clay appears to Lula as a "well-known type," is not meant to convince either a white or black spectator that Clay's behavior is predictable. Baraka does not dispel tensions or eliminate curiosity about the presence before us of a white woman sitting next to a black man.

From the beginning of *Dutchman* the spectator is shown that he cannot predict the next line or the next event of the play. We do not know what to expect of a relationship between a black man and a white woman. The white audience may feel they know what to expect of Clay, the black audience may have definite expectations of Lula, but Lula's overt behavior and Clay's subtle hints prevent any spectator from feeling at ease about either character. Lula's lines after her description of Clay are meant to confirm our sense, however previously indefinite, that we are right to be suspicious of any aura of predictability. Clay reformulates, thus emphasizing his earlier question, "Really? I look like all that?" to which Lula responds, "Not all of it. I lie a lot. It helps me to control the world." The strategy here is repeatedly to disconfirm facile or immediate responses. Baraka impresses the spectators with their lack of knowledge about Clay and Lula, while maintaining their curiosity and anxiety about the truth.

Lula's revelations to Clay about his identity work as an attempt at seduction of both Clay and the spectators. Although neither we nor Clay have much information about her, there is a sense onstage that the two characters have recognized one another and are about to move on to another phase of their relationship. To affirm this, Lula moves her hand along Clay's thigh. This highly erotic gesture should increase the nervousness of both black and white spectators. After all, this is not the kind of behavior one expects on a subway. Nor is it the kind of public behavior between a black man and a white woman to which many spectators have been witness. Lula's next remarks—that Clay is "Dull, dull, dull," that she bets he thinks she is exciting—are intended to disorient us even more than her gesture. Her remark is also annoyingly condescending for white spectators and emphatically so for black members of the audience. We are led to feel glad for Clay's moderate response that Lula is "O.K."

As the subway roars on its journey, the exchanges between Clay and Lula continue to oscillate between sexual maneuverings and Lula's assaults on Clay's identity. Most notable among these gestures is her offer to Clay of an apple, which he casually accepts. One can hardly witness this scene without remembering Eve and the apple she offered to Adam. The association not only reminds the audience of the world of myth but makes us wonder if the pain and self-awareness that resulted from the eating of that first apple will recur in some form here. A relationship is developing, and we watch warily to see what will happen next. In the midst of what appears to be an increasing affability between the characters onstage, Lula's assertion that Clay is a "well-known type" should annoy the spectators and remind them of Lula's presumptiveness. They are then led to applaud the deftness with which Clay handles this, subtly mocking Lula by inquiring if she knows him and his friend "anonymously." Clay needs to explain his question ("without knowing us specifically," he adds), and we are given a glimpse of his control of the situation.

Clay's refusal to be shattered by Lula's condescension actually provokes Lula to reveal, almost despite herself, a part of her personality we have not previously been shown. As if strangely distracted, Lula remarks that her hair is turning gray. She lyrically considers that aging is "always gentle when it starts." She thinks of herself "hugged against tenements, day or night." Her language here is different from before—both elusive and resonant. We catch a glimpse of a previously hidden portion of Lula, which is instinctively more recognizable than the surface character. Suddenly we see a tired, worn woman, no longer the tough, controlling aggressor. Her vulnerability will elicit sympathy from some spectators, but Baraka also intends the audience to feel disgust at Lula's self-pitying clichéd image. White spectators may long for her to remain like this, more like someone we can acknowledge without racial shame, but Baraka does not allow this comfort and swiftly returns Lula to her games.

Lula's next game is more playful and familiar in its calling forth of middle-class convention. She asks Clay to take her to the party to which he is apparently going. Agreeing, he adds that he should know her name if he is going to ask her to a party. (Lula insists that Clay invite her; she wants to play fully the etiquette of the female role.) Lula and Clay exchange names, Lula first asserting that she is "Lena the Hyena" then later telling her real name. Baraka employs this naming scene to reveal to the audience some of the previously hidden elements in the relationship between Clay and Lula. When Lula tries to guess Clay's name, her first attempts are Gerald, Walter, Lloyd, Norman, Leonard, Warren, and Everett,—all "hopeless colored names creeping out of New Jersey." There is an inside joke here, because Baraka's original name was actually Everett LeRoi Jones, but the more important point is that for the first time there is a clear indication that Lula does not understand who Clay is. "Clay" is *not* one of the names Lula guesses; it is not even similar to any of those names. Although this is a mere moment that can be missed in the rapid wit of the dialogue, Baraka plants another clue here, another warning to the audience—like Clay's question, "Do I look like that?"—that we, too, should not assume we know who Clay is. If we pick up the clue, we will feel warier of Clay. There is now evidence that we cannot fully judge who he is from his appearance. That Clay is clearly in control in this episode is substantiated when, after Clay has suggested that any of a number of last names will do, Lula attempts to label Clay again, and he responds, in a parody of her image, "Thass right."

The revelations of the names of the two characters also carry metaphoric warnings to the audience. Hyenas feed on carrion. Thus, when Lula first says that she is "Lena the Hyena," some spectators may take what sounds like a childish play on words as a much grosser threat than anything we have yet perceived. If this woman feeds on dead flesh, she may be a greater danger to Clay than he or we had imagined. The associations with Clay's name are more obvious. The apples have already led us to make connections between this relationship and that of Adam and Eve. Now we are informed that the young man's name is Clay, the material from which Adam, the first man, was made. Paradoxically, the word "clay" also signifies death.[17] Although many spectators may miss these signals, if we do understand them the wariness we have felt from the beginning of the play will move closer to fear. We are being forewarned of Clay's death and Lula's predatory relationship to Clay. The experience of *Dutchman* will be different for the spectator who is alert to Clay's death than for the one who is surprised, but Baraka leads the audience to understand that for those who can see, the signals are all there. The use of literary allusions provides knowledgeable white middle-class spectators with a set of clues from which they can draw the same conclusions the black spectators have drawn from the mere fact of Lula's whiteness and her overt behavior. For black spectators who recognize the literary allusions, there is a double sense of jeopardy.

An important element of the strategy of *Dutchman* is thus an attempt to persuade both black and white spectators that the omens of the murderous relationship between black people and white people are all there before us. If we do not perceive the signs it is the fault of our vision, not the absence of warning. Our failure to see may be a matter of will, not stupidity. It is not that we will learn something new but that we will come to know what we have always been.

Within the play, the warnings continue. After the name game, Lula attempts to regain control by telling Clay exactly how to invite her to the party. The suggestion here is that Lula cannot allow any initiative to Clay, nor can she allow him to use his own language. Lula acts by her own formula. She cannot let Clay speak in his own words; she wants him to imitate her. But Clay again rises above her assumptions and comments that her wording is "pretty corny." Now Lula asks the questions she seemed to have no need for previously: "What are you into anyway? What thing are you playing at, Mister? Mister Clay Williams? What are you thinking about?" Her questions make her less intimidating to the audience because she now seems less sure of herself, and they also extend our sense from the naming scene that we really do not know who Clay is. When Clay says to Lula, "I thought you knew everything about me?" it may be heard by some as a naïve and sincere question, but it is meant to impress the audience again with the sense that neither we nor Lula really know Clay.

Lula cannot handle Clay's challenge; offended, she idly turns her attention to a paperback book. The audience can be relieved at her withdrawal, even if Lula's motivation is unclear. Baraka instigates a hope here that she will soon get off the train, that we will not have to face any further encounter between these two people. Clay, however, has not relinquished the relationship.

It is now he who attempts to reestablish the erotic and playful mood of the earlier moment; he wants to fulfill the sexual promise of Lula's previous behavior. His next gestures prevent the spectator from viewing Clay as a man whose sexuality can be toyed with and then readily dismissed. Clay reminds Lula of the apples, then after a bitter yet still provocative response from her that she concludes with reference to "unbutton[ing] her dress and letting her skirt fall down," Clay asks straightforwardly if she is angry, if he has said anything wrong. Lula's response is another attack, but an attack made deliberately puzzling to the audience by her assertion that not only is everything Clay says wrong, but that is what makes him so attractive. We are meant here to see the perversity of her attraction to Clay. Mocking Clay's clothes, she challenges his right to wear an Ivy League outfit of three button suit and striped tie; she reminds Clay that his grandfather was a slave. Black spectators may be offended by Lula's presumption that she can question Clay's mode of dress in terms of his heritage, but they are also made to feel uneasy about their own possible participation in what Lula calls "a tradition you ought to be oppressed by." The white spectator may feel shame at Lula's condescending inquiry, or may simply agree with Lula, but might also ask for the first time why he feels more comfortable with black people whose appearance resembles that of middle-class whites. To pose such a question seriously is to refuse the badges of identity to which our society limits us.

Clay's response to Lula is another device to demonstrate the error of her assumptions. He answers that his grandfather was not a slave but

a night watchman. This does not stop Lula's assault, which is a renewed attempt to label Clay, to regain the control she seems to have
lost. But she does not win the new battle. Clay has a witty retort for,
or subtle alteration of, everything she says. He is only taken aback
when Lula pulls her various insults together into one thrust: "I bet you
never once thought you were a black nigger." Clay is described as
stunned, but he quickly tries to join in Lula's laughter and again responds simply, "That's right." Lula's remark suggests the kinds of assumptions she is repeatedly making about Clay. Her comment implies
that beneath his clothes, his educated manners and language, Clay remains "a black nigger," and that she knows this but Clay does not.
Although it is possible to hear Clay's response as simple agreement or
as an avoidance of confrontation, spectators can also perceive Clay as
consciously playing to Lula's assumptions and implicitly mocking such
stereotyping. About this, Baraka refuses the audience any final conclusion at this point. Indeed, it remains ambiguous whether Clay's "That's
right" refers to the fact that he is a "black nigger" or to the assertion
that he never thought he was one. What is clear now is that Clay wants
to make love with Lula, not to explain his identity to her. Lula's remark
is a challenge to Clay that he does not accept. For the audience, Lula's
remark is a threat; it is another sign of her aggression. It also prevents
even the most "liberal" spectator from imagining that the racial differences between Lula and Clay are not fraught with hostility.

Thinking, perhaps, that she is winning again, Lula pushes on, repeating her earlier conclusion that Clay is just corny. The white spectator may be relieved that Clay is obviously trying to avoid a real clash,
but Baraka's strategy here leads the black spectator especially to want
to see Clay defend himself better. Clay modulates anxiety, particularly
for the black spectator, in the next exchange when, after Lula mock-
ingly suggests that he should be on television, he retorts that she acts
like she's on television already. (Clay may appear to Lula as the perfect
image to present to the American public as the black middle-class man,
but she abolishes the distinction between a projected imitation and an
actual life.) As in an earlier episode, just a small challenge from Clay
cracks Lula's brittle façade. She repeats her revelation that she lies,
then simply states, "I'm nothing, honey, and don't you ever forget it."
Ignoring this simple statement of truth can be clear evidence of our
will to self-deception and the power that even self-acknowledged vacu-
ous images hold over us. Yet Lula's blunt expression of self-awareness
will surprise the audience, even allowing some pity for her as she continues that the only person in her family who "ever amounted to anything" was her mother, a Communist. Even for Lula, some sign of
separation from the white middle class is necessary for a sense of per-

sonal identity. As in her earlier expression of her fear of aging, Lula reveals the insecurity beneath her appearance of self-assurance. Little in her past is a source of pride or identity. The white spectator should be troubled by this revelation; the black spectator can say, "That's right."

Lula's introduction of personal information allows Clay to respond similarly. The new, if slight, intimacy is grasped by both characters as a means to move together toward some undefined triumph. Lula suddenly becomes a consciously histrionic cheerleader, urging Clay to mock with her the America where his father is "free to vote for the mediocrity of his choice," urging Clay to applaud her satirical description of his parents' noble values, which brought forth the "noble Clay Clay Williams." Once again, Lula is only partially obscuring an attack on Clay in one guise of a game. If she has no heritage of worth, she cannot allow him to have one. The moment is frantic enough to bewilder the audience, but it is so close to hysteria that we should feel a definite shadow of fear. As if she perceives this fear in the audience and revels in it, Lula suddenly switches tones and drops her voice to what Baraka calls "knifelike cynicism." Lula's cry, "My Christ, My Christ," is ambiguous and threatening. Is she disgusted with herself, with Clay, with what? Clay seems to ignore the change and simply continues the game with a "Thank you ma'am," which Lula does not appear to hear, but which reveals to the audience that Clay accepts the title of Christ, or martyr, or that he at least appreciates her perception of that role. But Lula does not let him go. She suddenly becomes a hardened Cassandra, and prophesies, "May the people accept you as a ghost of the future. And love you, that you might not kill them when you can" (p. 21). The audience may not know what to make of these lines, but the words trouble, whether perceived as clear or opaque, true or false. Clay asks, "What?" reflecting a bewilderment or shock similar to our own, and to ensure that he and we have understood clearly, Lula states more simply, "You're a murderer, Clay, and you know it. . . . You know goddamn well what I mean." The message here is to the audience, too: We also should know "goddamn well" that she means exactly what she says. There is no deeply hidden significance in Lula's assertion, except, perhaps, that she is now speaking of Clay not just as a specific individual but as any black man. According to Lula, if Clay is not "loved," and perhaps even if he is, he will fulfill the potential in him to kill when he can. The white audience might take this as a warning that love will prevent the black man from murder, but Baraka intends here to show the black spectator that Lula's potential "love" is irrelevant. Lula believes the black man needs love, but it is sex and sex as a source of power, not love, that Clay wants.

The warnings here are considerably more overt than previously, but they are not inconsistent with either Baraka's basic intentions or his portrayal of Lula. She, like the subway, is spasmatic; she jerks back and forth between an expression of self that appears truthful and one that is deceptive and distorting. Her weapon for defense is language: Her words seem most ordinary when she is playing her game of seduction, of manipulating Clay; her words become lyrical and metaphoric when she seems to be revealing the truth about herself and her knowledge of the world. Thus, when she speaks of her personal fears, she remembers, "Hugged against tenements, day or night," and when she articulates her recognition of Clay she calls him a "ghost of the future." Her problem is that when she is not playing, she can only bear the truth in the robes of metaphor; our problem, if we have one, is that we underestimate the power of metaphor to describe our worlds accurately. Metaphor, the play constantly reminds us, is the equipment of myth, and therefore, for Baraka, of racial and social reality in America.

Clay does not deny Lula's declaration that he knows what she means in calling him a murderer; he only asks, perhaps innocently, perhaps guardedly, "I do?" Lula presents her own kind of answer, with which Clay seems happy to agree. They, this woman and this man, will pretend that Clay is not a murderer, that the world is not as they and we know it to be. They will pretend that "the air is light and full of perfume," that the people cannot see Clay, that Clay and Lula are both free of their histories. Lula ends Scene i of *Dutchman* with a vision to seduce both Clay and the audience: "We'll pretend that we are both anonymous beauties smashing along through the city's entrails. (She yells as loud as she can) GROOVE!" (p. 21). Lula's "groove" is the shriek of an amusement-park rollercoaster-rider; it is the sound of a contrived thrill but one that nevertheless contains both fear and abandon.

The end of Scene i is exciting for spectators. The off-Broadway audience that may have looked to black theater for a glimpse at the exotic finds it here in *Dutchman*, but the bizarre, the wild and unknown is evoked not by Clay but by Lula. Yet underneath the frenzied high pitch of the end of Scene i lies a promise and a threat to the audience. Lula is suggesting that she and Clay will create a fantasy world in which they can "groove" together; that allows the audience to anticipate with dread and fascination that we will actually witness further sexual contact between this white woman and this black man. It also suggests an "answer" to the tensions between black and white people: Both can deny their history and create a new world from imagination. The threat to this new world is there in Lula's words, too, however. What Clay and Lula will be doing, Lula repeats three times, is *pre-*

tending. To pretend, one must know what "not pretending" in the same situation would be.[18] To pretend means to behave for a time not as oneself, while retaining the knowledge of how one would "normally" behave. In Lula's plan and Clay's acquiescence to that plan, the spectator, particularly the black middle-class spectator, is meant to recognize his or her own pretenses. The end of Scene i will evoke, at best, an uneasy anticipation.

At the end of Scene i, Lula and Clay have moved out of the world of history into the world of myth. Lula and Clay are attempting to deny the specific details of their characters and backgrounds; they will be "anonymous beauties," recognizing only their most basic sexual fantasies about each other. Yet the setting has been mythical from the start, and the process of Scene i has been to reveal Clay and Lula as real people with histories—a boy from New Jersey and a girl with a mother who was a Communist—so that their denial of these histories is important and their acceptance of the world as mythical seems appropriate. But myth is a revelation of truth, not an escape from it. Lula's mistake is that she believes she can create myth; she does not understand that myth is discovered, not made.

To show the audience Lula's error, Baraka reverses the apparent relationship of myth to reality in Scene ii. At the beginning of the scene, Lula and Clay are engaged in creating an imaginary world. Lula's language is more persistently complicated and metaphoric than in Scene i; it is the emotive language of sensuous imagery that she occasionally used to reveal a truth in Scene i. The setting, however, has now become significantly more naturalistic than in Scene i, although neither Clay nor Lula at first appears aware of the change. Other seats on the subway are now visible, and other riders enter the train as the scene proceeds.

The effect on the audience of the presence of other subway riders is to change our stance from that of the voyeur to a private and surrealistic scene to that of witnesses to a more public and ordinary situation. The presence of other riders also increases our self-consciousness in response to the escalating sexual interaction of Clay and Lula. The subway riders thus act somewhat as a chorus would, reminding the audience of the social context and values of the world in which Clay and Lulu live, though the riders say nothing. The riders do not function exactly as a chorus, however, because, having been omitted from Scene i, they do not know Clay and Lula as we do; nor, as subway riders, do they represent a community. They are thus intruders not only into the world onstage but into our world as well.

Clay and Lula have also apparently accomplished a transformation between the scenes. Clay's tie is open; Lula is hugging his arm. Clay's opening words are "The party!" and we do not immediately understand if he is announcing the nature of the scene before us or if he is anticipating the place to which they are about to go. The word does imply that Lula's command at the end of Scene i, "GROOVE!" is in some fashion being fulfilled. Lula quickly clarifies that "the party" is Clay's party to which they are both now planning to go. The dialogue that follows is an elaborate projection of how they and others will behave at the party afterward. There is a notable contrast between the way in which Lula and Clay are now relating to each other and their exchanges in Scene i. Until the very end of Scene i, each was an opponent to the other in his or her various games; now, creating a game together, they seem to be on one team. Lula provides the details of the game, of their lustful future together; Clay is too busy caressing Lula to do much more than agree and ask for more pleasant description from Lula. The mood of this episode is articulated by Lula's suggestion that the God they will honor is Lula and Clay, or, as Clay expresses it, "A Corporate Godhead." With its irreverent phallic connotations, the image suggests an unholy, erotic alliance as well as a perversion of the ultimate harmony of the American dream. The "Corporate Godhead" of Lula and Clay will titillate, bewilder, and distress its spectators.

The scene extends both the seduction of and the threat to the audience commenced in the early portions of the play. Baraka forces his audience to listen to what many of them will not want to hear: Lula's depiction of what she calls "the real fun in the dark house. . . . After the dancing and games, after the long drinks and long walks" (p. 24), we are now going to get some real sex. We, in fact, are not going to get an actual sex scene, but the descriptive words themselves will excite the sexual fantasies of some spectators and exacerbate the social fears of both black and white spectators.

What is importantly evident from the beginning of "The Party" episode is that these are Lula's fantasies, not Clay's. Clay is a willing participant in the sexual experience, but it is still Lula who is creating the scene. The details of Lula's fantasy should reveal much to us about her. Hers is a fantasy of conquest, of a superiority achieved through the defeat and humiliation of others. Thus, she imagines Clay defeating other men intellectually, and she sees both of them making "fun of the queers." She fantasizes that they might "meet a Jewish Buddhist and flatten his conceits over some very pretentious coffee." Most explicitly and most threateningly to Clay, she sees herself leading him, she conceives of him as her "tender big-eyed prey." If the audience has not been distressed simply by the fact of the increasingly open sexuality between Lula and Clay, Lula's depiction of Clay as her prey should warn us of what she is about. We might here recall that she labeled herself in Scene i, a "hyena."

Baraka intends that the totality of Lula's need to control become

increasingly clear as she continues on her verbal journey. When Clay
makes even the slightest attempt to add to Lula's fantasy, by suggesting that her hand that he will hold will be cold, Lula venomously
lashes out, "You Fascist!" Lula can respond only with facile labels to
any contribution from Clay; she also sees the world only in terms of
fascists and slaves. That this is not union, not even a momentary
mutual physical satisfaction, becomes transparent a moment later.
When Clay asks Lula what they will talk about in her apartment, Lula
answers, "About your manhood, what do you think? What do you think
we've been talking about all this time?" (p. 25). If this comes a surprise
and confuses the audience, it also appears to come as a surprise to
Clay. He responds, "Well, I didn't know it was that. That's for sure.
Every other thing in the world but that." While Clay's response may
be heard as an affirmation of his naïveté, it is not necessarily a revelation of innocence or ignorance. Walter Lee in *A Raisin in the Sun* and
Vic in *Big White Fog* could admit that what was at stake in their struggles with the white world was their manhood, but such admissions
were made only within the bounds of their black communities. Here,
on the subway, it is not that Clay misunderstands the issue, it is that
his manhood is not a matter to which he wants to allow Lula access.

For a moment it seems as if the introduction of Clay's manhood
into the conversation has jarred the entire mood. Clay is distracted
from Lula, notices other subway passengers, comments that the subway is slow. The audience is made to feel restless and uneasy. Are we
going to "get there" or not? We are purposefully not shown what Clay
is now thinking, and that will make white spectators uncomfortable,
black spectators hopeful that Clay is about to change his direction. Lula
verbally responds. She indicates that she will make a "map" for Clay of
his manhood while they talk, "And screw." Clay affirms, "We finally
got there." Lula attempts to resume the fantasy, but it no longer works
as before. She suggests that Clay will tell her that he loves her, but
that he will be lying. Clay says that "Maybe" he will tell her, but that
he would not lie about something like that. Lula persists in a deliberately challenging statement reminiscent of her closing lines in Scene i:
"Hah. It's the only kind of thing you will lie about. Especially if you
think it'll keep me alive." Clay will, Lula implies, pretend love to
avoid killing. Clay has, however, just said that he would not lie about
love, and we have no reason to doubt his words. Lula continues to
create her own image of Clay, but we are again led to question the
validity of her judgment.

Clay says that he does not understand, and Lula's response is a
shrill laugh and an opaque comment that she is simply doing what she
has to do:

LULA (bursting out laughing, but not too shrilly): Don't understand? Well, don't look at me. It's the path I take, that's all.
Where both feet take me when I set them down. One in
front of the other.   [p. 27]

The implication of inevitability, of necessity in Lula's behavior, should
remind the audience of the mythical figures with whom Lula has been
associated but also of her and Clay's attempt to remove themselves
from history. The essential compulsions we have glimpsed in Lula are,
like those of the mythical Eve, toward seduction, control, and destruction. These images can be seen as inseparable from American culture.
If there is an "American Adam," so, too, there is an "American Eve."
We are not able to understand fully what direction Lula is taking, but
to us, and to Clay, it sounds "Morbid, morbid." The subjects are becoming too serious again, and Clay makes a vain attempt to demand
what indeed the audience wants at this point. He asks, "There's no
funny parts?" Lula's response, that she thought "it was all funny," is
not the answer we or Clay want to hear.

Clay wants more of the fantasy, but perhaps to the relief of the
audience, Lula is through with that game. She has told the whole
story, she says, and then she summarizes much of what *Dutchman* is
about: "Except that I do go on as I do. Apples and long walks with
deathless intelligent lovers. But you mix it up. Look out the window all
the time. Turning pages. Change, change, change. Till, shit, I don't
know you. Wouldn't for that matter" (p. 28). Although Lula's words are
a response to events, her lines here prevent us more emphatically than
any previous speech from an attempt to avoid her danger. Suddenly,
there is no more game, no more pleasant fantasizing. Any illusions we
might have had that Lula did understand Clay, that they recognized
and acknowledged one another within the bounds of a transient moment, are destroyed. Whatever pretense of romance there was is over.
To make that clear, Clay again remarks how many people have entered
the train. We are back in the public world of ordinary events, where
dreams are private matters.

Lula now reveals what we have hardly had time to understand: The
crucial element of fear is missing in the world they had created with
words, but it remains potent in the public domain. She asks Clay if the
people in the subway car frighten him, and although his retort is a
question, "Why should they frighten me?" it is not a denial of fear. We
are increasingly aware that although the sexual encounter seems over,
there is something to beware, and Lula immediately tells us what it is.
She informs Clay that he should be frightened " 'Cause you're an escaped nigger." By saying so, she identifies him as a prisoner and be-

comes unavoidably threatening to both Clay and the audience. Her earlier barbs at Clay were insightful enough to amuse the white spectator occasionally, sexual enough to excite and trouble the entire audience. Now, however, she is simply a cruel, harsh, white female bigot. It is not that her character is portrayed inconsistently by Baraka; he has given us all the clues throughout the play, but her sexual games, her moments of vulnerability and her opaque language until now have allowed some white spectators to ignore those clues. Lula is not a simple woman; she "contains multitudes" and contradictions, but we may have mistakenly allowed that sense of complexity to block out her real viciousness.

Lula's assertion that Clay is "an escaped nigger" is only her beginning. She takes off from this point, accusing Clay of crawling over to "her side." Clay attempts to handle Lula lightly; he mocks her image of plantations with a parody of a romanticized version of black life on a plantation, but this sets Lula off on her own, new track. Lula becomes increasingly hysterical and mean. Baraka is showing us the same Lula who yelled, "GROOVE!" at the end of Scene i, but now she is dancing publicly down the aisles, taunting Clay with every word and move. Clay at first tries to make light of Lula's behavior and his own embarrassment. He suggests that maybe there was something in the apples, reminding the audience, of course, of what those apples symbolize, and he jokes with a sharp edge: "Mirror, mirror on the wall, who's the fairest one of all? Snow White baby, and don't you forget it" (p. 30). The pun ("It's no white, baby") does not stop Lula. She attacks Clay from every side: She mocks his sexuality, his Christianity, his appearance as a "dirty white man." She labels him a "middle-class black bastard" and makes certain that the remark is an insult. Attacking Clay's self-control, she challenges him to not "sit there dying the way they want you to die." This last comment arouses Clay's anger so much that he tells her to "sit the fuck down," but still Lula continues. She now begins to jig down the aisle, mocking Clay as an impotent "Uncle Thomas Wooly-Head" and telling the now attentive riders, "Let the white man hump his ol' mama, and he jes' shuffle off in the woods and hide his gentle gray head" (p. 32).

This entire action is a bombardment of the audience as well as an attack on Clay. Lula's behavior and her words arouse a variety of strong responses, some of them contradictory, in any audience member, but finally, with her performance, Baraka separates undeniably the black spectator from the white spectator. The entire audience can feel fear, loathing, anger as well as amusement at Lula's biggest act, and none of us may know quite how to handle these churning emotions. Both black and white spectators should feel angry and confused if they did not acknowledge the earlier signs of Lula's cruelty. Black spectators can, in addition, feel a frightening affirmation of the many instinctive suspicions they have about Lula simply because she is a white woman, and perhaps extend that to white women in general and to the culture of which Lula is a part. Black spectators may also take pleasure in seeing this woman apparently going mad.

The reaction Baraka most probably intends for the white spectator is one of humiliation, of horror at looking in the mirror, recognizing how ugly this Snow White really is. Yet white spectators may refuse (and have refused) this self-recognition, and instead feel angry at Lula and see her as other, as a mad whore who is not like one of them. This seems to me the most serious weakness of Baraka's strategy, that Lula's sharp wit, her unabashed seductiveness, her energetic imagination, may make her so particular that some whites will fail to recognize her as an ordinary person and will dismiss her as an aberration. Yet, as discussed earlier, had Baraka not intended the audience to perceive Lula as ordinary, the figure in the play could have been a much more abstract symbol of white America, more like the judge in *Great Goodness of Life*.

Whether or not black or white spectators fully recognize Lula, as enemy or kin, she has aroused enough anger in the audience and fear and embarrassment for Clay that any spectator should demand some response from him at this point. Clay provides that response, but it is a surprising one, despite our need for it or fear of it. We crave some reaction, some effort to puncture Lula's crazy balloon, but it is hard to imagine what that could be outside of direct murder. That Clay's response is verbal as well as physical is entirely consistenet with everything we have seen of him previously, but its unexpectedness further refutes whatever sense white spectators may have that they know something about Clay or about black men.

What Clay finally does is grab Lula, push her into a seat, and slap her as hard as he can. With this gesture, we expect further violence, but it comes in words, not physical action. Clay immediately satisfies our anticipation of murder by talking about the fact that he could murder her, easily, but his articulation of his ability to kill relieves our anxiety that he will actually do so. It is not Lula's body that Clay attacks but her arrogance, which has needed destruction throughout the play: "You telling me what I ought to do? (Sudden scream frightening the whole coach) Well, don't! Don't tell me anything! If I'm a middle-class fake white man . . . let me be. And let me be in the way I want" (p. 34). Clay's scream forbids either the audience or Lula to judge him or presume his transparency. Neither Lula, nor the audience, has the right to expect Clay to behave in accordance with a preconceived image—or in discord with such an image. We have little genuine evidence by which to judge the kind of man Clay is, nor, even if we could identify him, would we have the right to judge that identity.

Neither the remainder of Clay's speech nor his death makes clear or certain what he does want; instead, they make it vivid that when black people begin to articulate their desires and move toward effecting them, they are threatened with the loss of the dignity that the American dream dangles as the prize of social mobility. To some degree this is the dilemma to which Richard Sennett and Jonathan Cobb point in *The Hidden Injuries of Class:* In a class-structured society like that found in the United States in the twentieth century, to articulate and attempt certain goals, material and personal, and not achieve them is to be forced to admit to personal failure, despite the intellectual understanding that not everyone who is competent succeeds.[19] But to succeed is not necessarily to achieve dignity either, because it necessitates acceptance of external expressions of achievement and praise, often from sources whose sole grounds for respect are their positions of authority. The latter is a crucial element in Clay's fury; by sporting middle-class apparel he renders himself vulnerable to Lula's judgments, and it is a measure of her cruelty that she unyieldingly leads him to a place where he must admit the opposition between self-respect and identification with the middle class. Clay also perceives that for the black person the failure to make it into the middle class is even more complicated and frustrating than Sennett and Cobb suggest. The white worker who fails to move quickly and decisively up the social ladder concludes that he has no fully satisfactory explanation that does not include his own weakness; he thus feels guilt and humiliation. The black worker who similarly fails has the excuse or reason of his blackness, but to recognize in the source of one's dignity the cause of one's failure is to live by a paradox that the "Black Is Beautiful" slogan of the 1960s has failed to resolve.

Writing of Clay's speech, Clayton Riley asks rhetorically, "Now who understands all this, whom is this intended for?"[20] Riley talks about the black codes in Baraka's play, and Riley's not so cryptic question suggests that Clay's speech is a code message for blacks. Clay continues to mock white people for assuming they know black people just because they have "fucked one" or because they say they "love Bessie Smith" or "dig Charlie Parker"; he is affirming the distinct identities of black people. Clay affirms their strength, evokes their pride: "My people, they don't need me to claim them. They got legs and arms of their own" (p. 35). While not murdering Lula, Clay raises the specter of murder as the only answer his people may find if they get no other answers quickly. Riley's interpretation coheres with Baraka's strategy to present a variety of codes the audience can decipher, if it will.

Yet the rhetoric and diction of Clay's speech also strongly suggest a last attempt to protest to the white world—a last attempt to communicate. Black people do not need to be told, although they can revel in the telling, that Lula's version of the "belly rub" is "ol dipty-dip shit." It is white people who need to be told that, to be told that Bessie Smith used metaphors to keep her from killing some white people (while white people, like Lula, use metaphors to hide themselves). Clay says starkly that black people "don't need all those words," but because he does provide them, it seems appropriate to assume they are at least partially intended to break through the pretenses of the white audience. The "you" to whom Clay addresses himself is Lula; it is she who needs the final, generous warning:

And on that day, as sure as shit, when you really believe you can "accept" them into your fold, as half-white trustees late of the subject peoples. With no more blues, except the very old ones, and not a watermelon in sight, the great missionary heart will have triumphed, and all those ex-coons will be stand-up Western men, with eyes for clean hard useful lives, sober, pious, and sane, and they'll murder you. They'll murder you, and have very rational explanations.   [p. 36]

This is not a prophesy of the success of black people. It is a condemnation of Western white society, an admonition that if the white person persists in equating the black person's survival with prescribed middle-class behavior, the black person will indeed become a dutiful imitation. What he will imitate is a human being who is "useful, sober, pious, sane, and murderous." Clay's speech is meant to disturb not only the white spectator's prejudices but his whole mode of being. Clay warns the white person that if he continues his present behavior he will be faced with a nation of black Calibans who proclaim, as in *The Tempest*, "You taught me language, and my profit on't / Is I know how to curse." Clay's speech may well be, as Riley suggests, a code in the sense that the black person will understand and the white will not, that the white spectator will hear only Clay's profanity, not his prophetic curse. Yet all words here *can* be understood by both blacks and whites.

It is Lula who actually admits that Clay's words have been heard by a white person. Her shrillness gone, we are somewhat surprised to hear her businesslike voice suddenly saying, "I've heard enough." Clay agrees, and relieving any lingering fear or fantasy the audience might have that he might still pursue the sexual adventure, he affirms the obvious: "Looks like we won't be acting out that little pageant you outlined before" (p. 37). The audience feels released, eager to have

Clay get off that train, eager to get out of the oppressive theater and deal with or forget his words. Again our expectations are denied. As Clay reaches over to get his belongings, Lula stabs him twice in the chest and kills him. She then orders the other passengers to get his body off the train. They mechanically obey her, and she is left alone, recomposing herself. She has just finished writing something (her own history?) in her notebook when another young black man enters the subway car. She looks up and stares. We should recall with renewed anxiety and despair the smile she presented in the window to Clay at the beginning of *Dutchman*. As the play ends, an old black conductor enters, "doing a restrained soft shoe," and addresses the young black man, "Hey, brother!" The young man has the curtain line, "Hey."

Lula's murder of Clay is shocking, but, in retrospect, we have been prepared for it. If the white audience is surprised, it is because it has acknowledged only the overt signs of violence and murderous intent. The subtler indications have all pointed to Lula as the real killer. If we react with surprise, the horror for us lies in our recognition that we should have known. We have allowed our assumptions—about women, subways, white people's attitudes toward black people—to prevent us from seeing what is before us. We feel a loss of innocence, but what is more accurately the sensation is a recognition that we, black or white, never were innocent. It is a frightening experience for both the black and the white spectator: frightening or perhaps bitter for the black because it suggests that he or she can never feel safe; frightening for the white because it reveals his own unquestioned violence toward blacks and hints that armed with this knowledge, black people will prepare themselves for effective defense.

The very last moments of the play extend all these causes for fear. The presence of another young black man emphasizes, in case spectators are tempted to see Clay's murder as an isolated incident, that this pattern continues. The entrance of the black conductor is somewhat ambiguous. It may be intended to reassure black spectators and intimidate white spectators; the black man is not always or necessarily alone. There are "brothers" in this world to aid each other.

Dutchman remains with its spectator or reader. It lingers on, haunting one's memories like a dream whose central images cannot be forgotten. Baraka has written of his intentions, "We are preaching virtue and feeling, and a natural sense of the self in the world. All men live in the world, and the world ought to be a place for them to live."[21] *Dutchman* presents a world in which no man or woman should want to live. The purpose of the play is to reveal that world so the audience can acknowledge it as an unfit place for either black or whites. *Dutchman* also intends to impress the audience with the

knowledge that if we persist in ignoring the warnings around us, we
will destroy ourselves. The play warns black spectators to protect
themselves and white spectators to change if they can.

Although neither this intention nor Baraka's strategy is obscure, it
is difficult to realize *Dutchman* satisfactorily on a stage. Clayton Riley
attempts to deal with this troubling aspect of the play's history:

> So powerful is the work that no production of it seems able to
> completely capture and relate all the symbols within, not any
> production of it that I've seen or played in, that is. A difficult
> work, because it demands so much, because it speaks in shifting
> terminologies—codes, to be sure—some of which are more
> clarified by reading than by presentation.[22]

Riley's experience of productions of *Dutchman* resembles mine, as
both director and spectator, but his explanation does not suffice. The
"power" of *Dutchman*, as of any work, lies in its synthesized result, its
final effect on the reader or spectator, and is thus not an *ingredient* of
the text or performance. What Riley implies is that the text is more
effective for readers than for spectators because readers can linger
over, and return to, the intricate set of signs that the script presents.
Such a judgment is not unfamiliar in the world of drama criticism;
readers and critics of Shakespeare have made similar judgments about
his plays in almost every decade. Yet even with the most complex of
Shakespeare's plays, even, for example, with *King Lear,* productions do
occasionally capture the play with a sense of wholeness. It is precisely
those directors and actors who recognize that "power" as an abstract
concept cannot be acted or directed who achieve the fullest productions of Shakespeare's plays; that a play repeatedly resists a sense of
inclusiveness in performance may be a matter of the playwright's failure to make verbal language resonate in the theatrical terms, but it is
also often the failure of the theater artists' responsibility to discover
and expand each of the script's specific gestures to the stage world of
voice, body, color, line, and motion.

One problem, then, with *Dutchman*, as with many of Shakespeare's
plays, is that in an attempt to make the play accessible to an audience,
directors, actors, and designers have reduced the "meaning" of a script
to the explication of a single theme. The text also tempts actors and
directors to choose a strategy: to emphasize the qualities and moments
in the script that seem particularly accessible either to those already
vulnerable to the play's lessons or to those who enter protected but
whose defenses might just be weakened. This often, but not necessarily, suggests performing toward black *or* white spectators. But Baraka

is clearly, if ironically, making an attempt in *Dutchman* to address an audience of both black *and* white spectators.

This may be part of Riley's meaning when he addresses the problem of the play's power, but he approaches the performance problems of *Dutchman* more helpfully when he refers to the script's shifting terminologies. It is central to Baraka's strategy in *Dutchman* that we gradually perceive warnings of the dangers in the relationship between Clay and Lula, or that, if we have not understood the signs during the play, we recognize that we have missed something when Lula does kill Clay. But warnings in the world of the play, like symbols in our dreams, come in various disguises. Were Baraka's language not rich and complicated, it would not be true to the mythical nature of the experience he wishes to present. But the complexities of that language also make it difficult to grasp, particularly in a first hearing, especially if we are reluctant to acknowledge what we see and hear. *Dutchman*, in production, may leave an audience with the same puzzlement we have after awaking from a dream; we half wish we could re-experience the dream or the play so that we could contemplate more carefully the intentions of its signs, but we repress the dream and, perhaps, the play, too, because it presents understandings we do not really want. The black spectator is being reminded of the signs of danger he already knows; the white spectator may not want to acknowledge the signs of his own responsibility for creating that danger. Even when the fabric of a play reminds us of the texture of dreams, there remains the important difference (which we often forget in interpreting our dreams as well as our dramas) that it is each of us who constructs his dreams, while it is an "other" who weaves the structure and strategy of a play. With *Dutchman*, this is particularly important, because the play assaults the values and consciousness of the middle class, for which Baraka intended it. The attitudes the playwright can assume are shared by many members of the audience, both black and white, are the same values he calls into question. To allow the spectators to acknowledge the questions raised by the play, they must first be seduced into its world. The more successful that seduction—that is, the more we become engaged in the evolution of the relationship between Clay and Lula—the greater the risk that we will ignore many of the play's warnings and be shocked and bewildered, but not drawn to new understanding, by the play's last moments.

A final irony of *Dutchman* is that the difficulties it presents in performance may be a sign that its inherent optimism is already an error. *Dutchman* recognizes the different fears and desires of white and black spectators, but it also presumes that, dangerously constructed as it may be, there is, for a finite time in the theater, an audience of black and white middle-class people who form some semblance of a community. If, however, black and white spectators who come to the theater re-establish there only the world they have come from, they may be unable to be an audience; the spectators who might make up an audience may have already dismissed both the onstage and offstage contact of black and white.

In *Dutchman*, in the end, Baraka goes beyond the warnings of the dream; he shows us the deed that for different reasons, both black and white people might repress in a dream. Because *Dutchman* does still exist in the imagined world of the theater, the murder of Clay stands as one last signal. For the white audience, there may be no more warnings from Baraka.

NOTES

1. Ernest Gellner, *Saints of the Atlas* (Chicago: University of Chicago Press, 1969), p. xvii. The Berber word also suggests prosperity and magical powers.
2. David Llorens, "Ameer (LeRoi Jones) Baraka," *Ebony* XXIV (August 1969), p. 80, and Elsie Haley, "The Black Revolutionary Theater: LeRoi Jones, Ed Bullins and Minor Playwrights," unpublished doctoral dissertation (University of Denver, 1971), p. 108.
3. Haley, pp. 107–8.
4. Among the journals that published Baraka's poems during this period were the *Yale Literary Magazine*, *American Negro Poetry*, *Evergreen Review*, *Massachusetts Review*, *The Nation*, *Poetry*, and *The Village Voice*. Some of these are also cited in Haley, p. 47.
5. Larry Neal, "The Black Arts Movement," in *The Black Aesthetic*, Addison Gayle, Jr., ed. (New York: Doubleday, 1972), p. 263.
6. *Ibid.*, p. 261. Among these were Charles Patterson, William Patterson, Clarence Reed, and Johnny Moore.
7. *Ibid.* p. 262, and Clayton Riley, "On Black Theater," in *The Black Aesthetic*, p. 303.
8. The journal *Black Theater*, associated with the New Lafayette Theater in New York, is a good source for information about black community theaters and their origins in the late 1960s and early 1970s. Unfortunately, it is no longer published. Baraka's Harlem project stimulated similar endeavors both by example and support and because of participation in the Black Arts Repertoire School of men and women who then went on to begin their own groups in other parts of the country.
9. Imamu Amiri Baraka, "The Revolutionary Theater," *The Liberator* (July 1965), 4.
10. *Ibid.*
11. I am aware here that my language is similar to that of Stanley Fish in

Self-consuming Artifacts (Berkeley: University of California Press, 1972), but that is a matter of coincidence, not influence, because these pages were written before my happy discovery of Fish's work.

12. Imamu Amiri Baraka, *Great Goodness of Life*, in *A Black Quartet* (New York: New American Library, 1970), p. 140.
13. LeRoi Jones (Imamu Baraka), *Dutchman and The Slave* (New York: Morrow, 1964), p. 36. All other citations from this source.
14. Doris Abramson, *Negro Playwrights in the American Theatre, 1925–1959,* (New York: Columbia University Press, 1969), p. 276.
15. Riley, p. 298.
16. *Ibid.*
17. Readers may recall James Joyce's story "Clay" in *Dubliners.*
18. J. L. Austin, "Pretending," in *Philosophical Papers*, J. O. Urmson and G. J. Warnock, eds. (Oxford: Oxford University Press, 1961).
19. Richard Sennett and Jonathan Cobb, *The Hidden Injuries of Class* (New York: Vintage, 1973), pp. 250–51. These are central arguments made throughout the book.
20. Riley, p. 301.
21. Baraka et al., "The New Lafayette Reactions to *We Righteous Bombers*," in *Black Theater*, 4 (1969), 19. Recorded dialogue includes many voices; the quotation is from Baraka.
22. Riley, pp. 301–2.

7 | NIGHT IN AUGUST: ED BULLINS'S IN THE WINE TIME

FOR AT LEAST A decade, Ed Bullins has been the most important and productive playwright in the United States. He writes of himself, "To make an open secret more public: in the area of playwrighting, Ed Bullins, at this moment in time, is almost without peer in America—black, white or imported. I admit this, not merely from vanity, but because there is practically no one in America but myself who would dare."[1] I believe this self-definition to be as true as any comparison of this kind can be; more importantly, the statement reveals much that is central to Bullins's life as a playwright. In his plays and other public activities, Ed Bullins is a man who constantly takes risks. Through the risks he takes as an artist, he challenges others to look at worlds they have not previously known and to re-examine the values of the world in which they live.

Ed Bullins's stature in American theater derives mainly from his work as a playwright, but he has, in addition, made persistent and significant attempts to establish centers where black theater could thrive. Most notable among these ventures is his creation in 1967 with Robert Macbeth of the New Lafayette Theatre in Harlem. At the New Lafayette, Bullins wrote and sometimes produced his own plays and also edited *Black Theater*, a publication that was a key source of information and aesthetic commentary on the black theater of the late 1960s and early 1970s. In the introductory essay to a collection of his plays, *The Theme Is Blackness*, Bullins says of himself, "His work and The New Lafayette's cannot be exactly separated and identified. There is no other place, to his knowledge, where a collective entity of Black artistic knowledge, talent, craft, experience and commitment exists. In many ways, the New Lafayette is the true Black theater."[2] The belief and aspirations of that statement were not upheld by subsequent events. The New Lafayette Theater received a "final" grant in 1972 and was

177

unable to sustain itself without outside support. Since that time, Bullins has been the writer in residence with the American Place Theater and then with the New York Shakespeare Festival, where he has taught playwrighting and assisted Joseph Papp.

Bullins's position with the New York Shakespeare Festival suggests a recognition of the playwright by the "mainstream" of American theater, but it also indicates a change of direction for a man whose previous commitments had consistently been to black community theaters. Before moving to the New Lafayette, Bullins lived in California, where he was involved in community-theater projects and black cultural nationalism. In the mid-1960s, Bullins had been a cofounder of Black Arts/West, a community center for black theater and other arts. He was also a member of the Black Arts Alliance, and, in 1967, worked with Imamu Amiri Baraka in the Black Communications project and in filmmaking in San Francisco and Los Angeles.[3] In his essay from *The Theme Is Blackness*, Bullins also speaks of his involvement, just before coming to New York, in a San Francisco area project called Black House, which included among its participants Eldridge Cleaver, Marvin X, Baraka, and Sonia Sanchez.[4] Black House dissolved, Bullins attests, because of internal political friction, and Bullins's bitterness was such that he was preparing to leave the country when Robert Macbeth called him and convinced him to begin again in New York.[5]

In an interview with Marvin X, Bullins speaks of his time in black cultural projects in California as a time of purgation.[6] It was a period, he suggests, when he wasn't "at peace" with himself, "as an artist or a person." Working with other black artists to create black art for black people brought Bullins a new peace and a rejection of his sense of being a "misfit, a Western, Negro/artist misfit." During this time, he had begun writing plays, but his self-recognition as a playwright was not made firm, he says, until he saw productions of *The Toilet* and *Dutchman*. Bullins had already become an admirer of Baraka's work by reading the latter's plays. After seeing them, Bullins suddenly felt that he knew what he was doing, and that what he was doing was good.

What Bullins has been doing is writing, and writing with a productivity and variety that astonish. In the last ten years, he has written more than thirty plays, which range in form from brief, ritualized allegories resembling medieval morality plays to full-length works that escape ready genre labels but might be called "black poetic naturalism." Few of Bullins's plays repeat a structure or strategy, but all share an attempt to break the boundaries of realism and its reflection of the middle class and middle-class mores. This concern is apparent in the modes of dramaturgy Bullins explores and the kinds of characters and environments he presents. His characters are most frequently ordinary black street people, living on the ghetto fringes of American cities. Many of Bullins's plays bring forward the "outlaws" of American society, black men and women whom sociologists would call deviants.[7] Of the plays concerned with "the criminal element," two of the best known are *Clara's Ole Man* and *Goin' a Buffalo*. In *Clara's Ole Man*, a naïve young man attempts to pursue a romance in a household that he does not realize is a lesbian community; in *Goin' a Buffalo*, the world portrayed is one of pimps and prostitutes. When Bullins presents characters who are, or are striving to be, middle-class, he does so in a way that challenges their values and behavior. A recent play, *C'mon Back to Heavenly House*, makes vivid the dangers and duplicity in the lives of black hospital workers who emulate middle-class mores. The play is structured in a Brechtian mode and disturbs the security of the spectator by emphasizing the surrealistic quality of the characters' world. Bullins exploits the expectations of middle-class Americans in still another way in his collection, *The Theme Is Blackness*, which develops a theatrical form he calls "the black revolutionary commercial." Using techniques similar to those of television commercials, these compositions condense images or dramatic moments into theatrical epigrams.

While Bullins continues to explore new forms and subjects for his presentations, much of his energy is committed to a large project he calls the "20th Century Cycle." This, he says, "is the title given to a group of plays about the lives of some Afro-Americans. When completed, there will be twenty plays in number, each of them individually intended to be fully realized works of art."[8] Bullins has also indicated that although the tensions and situations in each of the plays constituting the "20th Century Cycle" will be distinct, the characters will form a group and be related by family ties.[9] *In the Wine Time, In New England Winter, The Duplex,* and *The Corner* were composed as part of his large project; either Cliff Dawson or his half-brother Steve Benson, or both, appears in each of these plays, and the plays' time periods, the 1950s to 1960s, are roughly similar.

In the Wine Time initiates the "20th Century Cycle"; it is characteristic of Bullins's concern with the "inner life" of black people and of his attempts to reject the confinements of traditional dramatic forms. The entire play occurs in one evening, a hot August night, on "a small side street of a large northern industrial city, in the early 1950s."[10] The central characters in the play are: Cliff Dawson, a man in his mid-twenties who is attending college on the GI bill; Lou Dawson, Cliff's wife, a woman in her early twenties who supports her family by working in a laundry and is pregnant when the play begins; and Ray, Lou's restless, teenage nephew, who has lived with Lou and Cliff since his mother's death some years before and now wants to join the navy, as

Cliff did when he was younger. Surrounding these people, and moving constantly in and out of their lives, are neighbors and friends. All of the characters are black, except for one neighboring family, the Krumps, and a white policeman.

The sultry summer evening is too stifling for anyone to remain indoors, so the characters gather on the front stoop of the Dawson's house. They talk, they laugh, they quarrel, they love; they drink the wine of the play's title. Occasionally, we are shown glimpses of "The Avenue," a commercial thoroughfare where the inhabitants of this neighborhood go to purchase their wine and liquor, to search out others, just to hang out. Until the very end of the play, nothing more momentous than this occurs. In the last moments of *In the Wine Time*, Red, an acquaintance of the Dawsons', instigates a fight with Ray. The fight is motivated by Red's efforts to capture Ray's girl, Bunny, and his attempt to trick Ray into drinking a bottle of urine. In the ensuing struggle, Red is killed. Cliff, taking the blame for the murder, is led off to jail by the policeman. Ray and Lou are left alone, to find their own strengths and directions.

The dissolution of the family and the loss of innocence for Ray at the end of *In the Wine Time* are thematic concerns common to other black dramas. In Theodore Ward's *Big White Fog*, the central male figure was also removed from the family by a violent final event. Strained marital relationships and the black male's manhood, dominant motifs in *Big White Fog*, *Emperor of Haiti*, and *A Raisin in the Sun*, recur in *In the Wine Time*. In Baraka's *Dutchman*, the loss of innocence is a central experience both for those onstage and for at least the white spectators in the audience. Yet *In the Wine Time* is not about the worlds found in *Big White Fog* or *Dutchman*. Although the family is disrupted in Bullins's drama, it is not destroyed, for the love that unites it endures. We come to understand Ray's loss of innocence in *In the Wine Time* as a result not only of the final murder but also of his mystical relationship with an ephemeral woman. In contrast to *Dutchman*, the world of *In the Wine Time* never was a world of innocence, nor is it a world in which characters *pretend* innocence, although the young, like Ray, must be initiated. *In the Wine Time* does not attempt to shock with that understanding but presumes the audience will simply recognize its truth. We are not assaulted by Bullins's stage world, nor are we carefully maneuvered into it. It is presented for us to be concerned about and recognize or deny. Bullins does not attempt to create empathy where there would be none without the play. In contrast to Hansberry's *A Raisin in the Sun*, there is nothing in the strategy of *In the Wine Time* that is intended to make the world of Bullins's play recognizable or acceptable to those for whom this world would be a foreign place. It is thus a world that white people and black middle-class people may find difficult to acknowledge, but that is not Bullins's concern. Instead, and again in contrast to Hansberry's intention, part of Bullins's effort in *In the Wine Time* is to make the world of the play authentic to the experience of those who would recognize inauthenticity.

It is more accurate, in fact, to say not that this is a world without innocence but that it is, rather, one in which innocence and virtue are redefined. Bullins engages the audience in a world in which behavior and values suggest an absence of many traditional American notions of virtue and strength. Almost everyone in the play drinks to a state of drunkenness and swears profusely. The drinking is a habitual and communal activity. As Lou says in Act I, "But their ignorant oil don't make them yell and hollar half the night like this wine makes us" (p. 600). Furthermore, Cliff, to his neighbor's displeasure, does not work but reveals no guilt because his pregnant wife remains employed in a laundry. Both men and women are sexually promiscuous. Brawls occur frequently; many characters carry a weapon of some sort; even the murder in the end does not seem astonishing. Given such behavior, it would be easy enough for *any* audience to turn away in disgust, whether its members live in a world similar to that of the play or come from a distinctly separate middle-class milieu. Bullins succeeds with a more difficult strategy, however, than one of moralizing against offensive habits. He leads us through the surface of this world into the more fundamental characteristics of these people. He shows us love that transcends and exists simultaneously with bitter quarrels; he presents trust and fidelity that have little to do with sexual monogamy; he demonstrates strength unconnected to the Puritan ethic of hard work; and he reveals a beauty in language through which obscenity becomes an element of poetry.

In its vision and strategy, then, Bullins's *In the Wine Time* is close to Willis Richardson's *The Broken Banjo*. Richardson's one-act folk play, as argued earlier, leads the audience away from facile judgments about the virtue or vice of each character by means of the situation's vicissitudes and ambiguities and the complexities of the characterizations. We are intended to perceive Richardson's characters as real, ordinary people who are capable of both good and evil; we are brought to care about what happens to them, because they are like us and are struggling valiantly within an impoverished environment that can too easily destroy them. In a manner similar to Richardson's, Bullins leads his audience through moments of tenderness to times of bitter denunciation, through revelations of both a character's generosity and his selfishness. By repeatedly showing the ambiguities of a situation and the complexities of relationships and characters, *In the Wine Time* does not let the audience sustain a conclusion that "he is right and she is wrong" (or vice versa). Neither does the play offer any hope that the characters might find solutions in a world other than the one in which they live. Bullins, however, finally moves his strategy toward both indictment and affirmation, whereas Richardson only urges acceptance of his characters and restraint from judgmental conclusions. *In the Wine Time* may leave its audience with sorrow because its characters are imprisoned in an environment from which their only immediate possibilities of escape are wine, prison, or the military, but it also exalts by affirming its characters' emotional strength, capacity for love, and vibrancy. It commands respect, too, for individuals who still share a sense of responsibility for one another. The play's intentions are those Imamu Amiri Baraka suggests are essential to all art: "Art should not tear down your values necessarily; but it should strengthen them so you can see what's wrong. So we can be stronger. So we can say, 'That wasn't the right way for them brothers to deal with that coward.' "[11] What is wrong with the world presented in *In the Wine Time* is that it stifles, suffocates, immobilizes the people who inhabit it. It is, as the drama critic John Lahr points out, a grimly death-filled world.[12] Bullins's strategy is to make the audience feel the morbidity and suffocation of that world by having the characters linger before us on their stoop, moving physically only to get more wine and return, moving in their relationships only in patterns we gradually realize are circular. Bullins leads the audience to crave some action, but when the moment finally arrives, it brings death and firmer entrenchment, not escape. The play intends to persuade the audience that the kinds of escapes possible in this world are never really liberating, that the activities imagined as escapes in fact bring home the reality of death and allow that reality to make itself present. The audience is shown that love alters the horror but does not prevent it, does not suffice. John Lahr remarks that the set itself is a "visual and symbolic cage,"[13] and the words with which Bullins describes that set make clear the "atmosphere of suffocation" the playwright wishes to impress upon the audience: "At left, the houses stand together on one side of the street in unbroken relief, except for a tunnel-like alley which opens between the Krumps' and the Garrisons' houses, forming a low, two-storied canyon, the smoke-stained chimneys the pinnacles of the ridges" (p. 593). Tattered posters from many years past, as well as old and new graffiti decorate a fence in this cage, while houses stand identically structured and identically assaulted by pollution. A designer of this set will have to be careful not to translate the vividness of Bullins's description into stage detail too pleasingly interesting rather than burdensome. With Bullins's set, as with other strategic elements in the play, the intention is to provide glimpses of dignity but also an overwhelming oppression.

Both affirmation and indictment of the lives of black folk begin with the prologue to *In the Wine Time*. The prologue is spoken by Ray, the Dawsons' teenage nephew. The story he tells occurs at the same time as the events of the play we are about to see, but he is clearly speaking the prologue from a point in his history years after this particular wine time. Ray's narrative re-creates his strange and wonderful romance in the summer he turned sixteen. Each evening during that summer, he waited on a street corner to "share a smile" and hear the "sad tune" of a woman he called a friend but with whom he had never exchanged more than that smile or unsounded melody. One evening, the woman did not appear. He returned home late and desolate. When she did reappear the following day, it was to tell him that she loved him, to tell him farewell, and to tell him that he would find her waiting out in the world when he was ready to search for her. The woman was evidently older than Ray; she was telling him gently that he had to mature before he could be with her. Ray's story ends: "I stood listening to the barber shop taunts follow her into the darkness, watching her until the wicked city night captured her; then I turned back to meet autumn and Cliff and Lou in our last wine time, meeting the years which had to hurry hurry so I could begin the search I have not completed" (p. 592). Even the bare outlines of the story and the fact of Ray's remembering it are enough to arouse the sympathies of the audience toward him and to create a vulnerability in response to the world it is about to be shown. Like Tom's speech at the beginning of Tennessee Williams's *The Glass Menagerie*, Ray's prologue sets up the play as a memory, asserting the fragility and importance of the events we are about to witness. Ray's tone is nostalgic; the person we see onstage is alone, slower and more careful than he would have been when the episode occurred. Ray's prologue functions as Tom's words did, in telling us of an important character who never clearly partakes of the world of the play (the mysterious woman in *In the Wine Time*, the father in *The Glass Menagerie*) but whose image remains with us; both Ray and Tom also introduce us to the people who will appear within each play. The particular way in which Ray speaks of Cliff and Lou in his prologue to *In the Wine Time* not only makes us curious and eager to meet these people but also provides a crucial key to our appreciation of them. For what Ray relates is that although Lou and Cliff had found his ephemeral romance strange and foolish, the night when Ray's mysterious friend failed to appear, he returned to a home where human sorrow was respected: "Cliff didn't laugh when learning of my loss; Lou stole a half glass more than I should have received." The audience can only wish to have such people in their own lives at such times.

Ray's prologue begins to implement Bullins's strategy by arousing our sympathies for the characters and initiating us into their world; it also sets up central tensions for the audience. By speaking in the prologue of the tight bonds between Lou, Cliff, and himself and of the anticipated birth of "Baby Man," Ray provides for a tension in the audience every time those bonds seem threatened in the play: "Summer and Cliff and Lou and me together—all poured from the same brew, all hating each other and loving, and consuming and never forgiving—but not letting go of the circle until the earth swung again into winter, bringing me closer to manhood and freedom to do all the things I had done for the past three summers" (p. 591). Ray's words caution the audience not to feel too threatened when they see hostility on stage, for hatred will be followed repeatedly by love. Ray's words do not warn us, however, that the circle will be broken during the course of this summer evening, so the audience is being guided into a trap, which will be sprung at the play's conclusion. We are forewarned, on the other hand, by the concluding words of the prologue, that the events of the play contain an ending to one time in the family's life and the beginning of another. This was, Ray tells us, their *last* wine time, and he is now engaged in a search that has no easy resolution.

All of these devices included in the prologue to *In the Wine Time* are important to the effectiveness of Bullins's strategy, but as most of the conventions and pieces of information could have been included in an opening expository scene, there remains a question as to the necessity of a prologue. The answer lies in the language of Ray's speech. It is strikingly precise, almost preaching in its rhythm and sensuality; it is self-conscious, chosen language that pleases as poetry but would discomfort the spectator were it part of dialogue. Such highly metaphorical speech is difficult to absorb in ordinary conversation, as was apparent with Martel in *Emperor of Haiti* and Vic in *Big White Fog*, but it can evoke a tone and define a speaker if distinctly set apart. We are in the presence of a perceiver who can see well and express what is before him and who enjoys telling stories. The first paragraph engages the audience in its speaker *and* his story:

> She passed the corner every evening during my last wine time, wearing a light summer dress with big pockets, in small ballerina slippers, swinging her head back and to the side all special-like, hearing a private melody singing in her head. I waited for her each dusk, and for this she granted me a smile, but on some days her selfish tune would drift out to me in a hum; we shared the smile and sad tune and met for a moment each day but one of that long-ago summer.   [p. 590]

The language enchants; it works magic on the audience. The alliterated "s" slides us along from one normally unnoticed detail to another; the rhythm of the words captures the rhythm of the woman moving along the street. The language sharpens our senses, but always through words we can readily understand; there is no condescension here, simply a man speaking beautifully of an event that matters to him and thus merits care in its description.

As the prologue moves on, it shifts form and diction to tell the audience of the variety of local qualities Ray perceives in this world. It begins with narrative, moves into dialogue, returns to narrative; yet always there is the progress of the story. The prologue introduces us to the sound of conversation but also prepares us for poetry and engages us in a story.

The prologue allows the audience access to Ray in a way the rest of the play cannot. He could not speak as he does here when he is sitting, later, on the stoop or meandering on The Avenue. This is not the language *of* the wine time, it is the language drawn from it, the language of more tranquil recollection. The Ray who speaks in the prologue is an older, sadder man than the boy we meet in this last wine time. But it is important that we know the private and matured Ray, for the sense we have of the man who speaks the prologue ensures that the handcuffed Cliff's parting words at the end of the play have not been spoken in vain: "It's your world Ray. . . . It's yours, boy. . . . Go on out there and claim it." The Ray we see in the prologue may not have yet claimed the world, but he has certainly held it in his hands.

The language of the prologue is gentle; it is sad but soothing. It is therefore in contrast to the rougher sounds of the rhythm and blues of the radio, radio commercials, gossip and street noise that are present as Act I begins. The first voice heard is that of the radio announcer. He jars us from the reverie Ray has just completed: "And here we are folks . . . on a black, juicy jammin' 'n' groovin' hot August night— . . . yeah one of them nights fo' bein' wit' that one ya loves" (p. 594). The words and the substance of the disc jockey's announcement are an ironic contrast to the tale we have just heard. As if to clarify to the audience that we are now in another world, Mrs. Krump, the white neighbor, stridently speaks next, calling to her husband, who is arriving home drunk, to "Get the hell on over here!" Cliff, who is sitting on the stoop with Lou, laughs at Krump, while Lou warns her husband to be quiet. At this point, Lou's sister, Doris, arrives with Ray's girl, Bunny. The sounds of the disc jockey and Mrs. Krump's raspy cries continue, bombarding the audience with cacophony.

The remarks exchanged while Mr. Krump is being watched "peein' aside the pole" reveal much about the characters onstage and their relationships. Of the group gathered on the stoop, Lou is the most concerned about Mr. Krump's feelings; she is upset by the comments of those around her and by Mrs. Krump's nagging. Lou thus elicits our empathy because of her kindness, but she also interferes somewhat with the fun of the scene. Cliff is aggravated by Lou's admonishments. When he tells his wife, "Goddammit . . . Lou. You always tellin' me to be quiet . . . I don't even make half the noise that some of our *good* neighbors do" (p. 595), he arouses our awareness of tension in their marriage and of his sense of superiority to others. We can wonder if the latter is an accurate estimate. Bunny, in the meantime, is impatient that Ray has not noticed her presence. If we hear her annoyance, we will be warned early in the play that she is a restless and not wholly trustworthy young woman.

As this cacaphony of conversation slows, Ray draws our attention and sympathy by offering to help Mr. Krump. Cliff tells Ray not to help, to stay where he belongs, but it is evident that Ray has aided Mr. Krump before. When Lou encourages Ray, he goes to guide Mr. Krump into his own house. During this disagreement, two other young men, Red and Bama, enter looking for Bunny and Doris. Red, Cliff, and Bama all taunt Ray for his kindness to the drunken white man; they suggest both that Ray is acting like a slave and that maybe he and Mr. Krump are related. This mockery is annoying to the audience, because Ray is clearly being simply decent. Yet it also suggests the hostility felt toward white people. A black audience may enjoy hearing this hostility openly expressed. Because none of the white characters is appealing, if we respond sympathetically to Ray's gesture it is because it is humane, not because we care about the Krumps. Mrs. Krump is a shrieking shrew who yells out the door at her husband, then turns and threatens to beat her twelve-year-old son. The son, Eddie, refused to help his father and barely responds to his mother. The father is known only as a drunkard. These are stereotyped vulgar white people, whose place in the play is to suggest that the ghetto neighborhood is not entirely black, to show that whites are no paragons of virtue, and to provide for a concrete source of antagonism toward whites.

This opening scene also initiates the spectator's distrust for Red. While Cliff's mockery of Ray's kindness is teasing and humorous, Red's is nasty. As Ray departs, Red kicks him. Red's action demonstrates where Cliff really stands, since Cliff scowls at Red and would probably hit him if Lou did not tug at her husband's leg to prevent a fight. While Ray is off, Bama and Red exit, leaving Cliff and Lou alone on the stoop. Cliff begins to complain about another neighbor, Miss Minnie. Lou again admonishes her husband to be quiet.

Lou's anxiety calls attention to Cliff's language as well as the substance of his complaints. Throughout the entire opening dialogue, Cliff and everyone except Lou have constantly used a variety of vulgar terms. "Sheet," "fucken," "goddam," "bitch," "ass," have all been spoken in the first episode of the play. This language may intentionally disturb the sensibilities of some audience members, but it is used so easily and lightly, and it is so clearly habitual in the characters' vocabularies, that it should become as easy to accept and ignore as the radio's constant noise. Occasionally, as when, in his private conversation with Lou, Cliff explodes, "Pussy! Cunt! Bitches!" the cursing serves to distinguish him from others and to emphasize his anger; but generally it becomes a natural part of the rhythm and texture of this world. There are moments when we should feel that were the language not violent, this place would be unbearably still; that may help us understand why obscenities are used so frequently.

As Lou and Cliff continue their exchange, the audience is made anxiously aware of Cliff's persistent anger. First, he attacks Lou for the way she is bringing up Ray. During that assault and Lou's defense, we are informed that Ray is the nephew of Lou's dead sister. Cliff has no immediate cause, excpet for Ray's kind gesture, to attack Lou's role as mother; he is just basically disgusted with the woman and the world around him. Cliff next talks of the suspicious gossip, which pervades the neighborhood, of how people do not like the fact that he is going to school while his wife works. As Cliff recalls his situation and frustration to Lou, we are shown that he not only is different from those around him but feels this difference with a disgust for those who can only cast disapproving glances. Lou reminds Cliff that some of the neighborhood disapproval has to do with his overt flirtatiousness. When Cliff denies any infidelity, Lou challenges him with the traditional evidence that she has found lipstick on his shirt. Cliff's silence in response to Lou's challenge suggests his guilt and unwillingness to confront the subject of infidelity. The moment makes the audience uneasy. Our experience is like watching a boxing match in which a fighter carefully and cautiously thrusts his punches for a number of rounds while being gradually smothered by his opponent's blows; we may want to see the full power of his punches released but fear the unknown outcome of a burst of force and passion.

This is not the moment for release. Cliff avoids Lou's charge and, apparently tiring of his harangue, returns to puzzling about why the Dawsons appear "strange" to others. Lou suggests that this is not because of their family's peculiar structure or work patterns but because they drink wine and sing and laugh and cuss like sailors. To our surprise, Cliff disputes the claim that he sings and laughs, then physically twists Lou's arm until she agrees she has lied. Cliff's action is puzzling. Doesn't he want to admit he is sometimes gay and happy? Perhaps he enjoys his complaints too much. The strategy prevents the audience from feeling that it knows Cliff, partly because he finds it difficult to acknowledge that anyone does know him.

Throughout this dispute between Lou and Cliff, their relationship appears erratic, full of such irritation and disagreement that the audience will wonder uneasily how and why they sustain a marriage. But our confusion may be dispelled when, once Lou has physically yielded to Cliff, he begins to caress her. She at first rejects his affection, but he continues to attempt to console her, toasting her as his Hottentot queen. The reference has a double intention: It suggests Lou's African heritage and, because the Hottentots were known particularly for their prominent buttocks, it asserts Cliff's sexual response to his wife. The compliment is not one that all audience members will necessarily understand; it suggests a way a black man can flatter a black woman without using white Western standards for beauty.

Lou protests this last compliment, too, arguing that she is more Ethiopian than Hottentot. When Cliff retorts that the features she is referring to come from "that Shanty Irishman who screwed [your] grandmammy down on the plantation," Lou, genuinely angered, asserts that, "Some things I just won't allow you to say." Although the substance of the argument has become of less consequence, the continued squabbling suggests that Lou is tough in her own way, that she, too, draws her limits and has insights. She holds her own with her husband, and we begin to see that although there is much hostility in this relationship, there also are matched resoluteness and candor on each part that keep the marriage honest. Thus, when Lou is brought to speak her mind defiantly in the following speech, her bluntness is not threatening to the audience; we understand that her words, coming out of genuine perceptions, are not idle blows, and we expect Cliff to be strong enough to receive them as important understandings: "Fuck you, Cliff! . . . Ohhh, just listen to that. You make me say bad things, man. You think you so smart and you know all them big words since you been goin' to school. You still ain't nothin' but a low-down bastard at heart as far as I'm concerned" (p. 602).

The spectator can take a just measure of these people from Lou's declaration and Cliff's response. Lou is not concerned with the kinds of surface impressions made by big words; she is not overwhelmed by the fact that her husband is going to school. She seeks virtue in a man in his self-respect and responsibility to others. Her words provoke spectators to consider where they find clues to human worth. Nor is Lou's stance condescending or self-righteous. When, to the audience's relief, Cliff breaks a momentary silence and agrees, "We do cuss too much, don't we?" Lou quickly smiles, too, adding, "And we drink too much." These are not people without faults, but they know themselves. By the time the lights dim on Cliff and Lou, with Lou concluding that they behave "Like niggers," Bullins has made his central characters unavoidably appealing. Although not even another black person might easily call Lou and Cliff "niggers," Lou's use of the defamatory term becomes a kind of intimacy.

From the edge of sentimentality, Bullins switches our attention to The Avenue, where Red, Bama, Doris, and Bunny are gathered. The Avenue appears as a raised platform upstage, which is lighted when necessary. It is the only physical place to which characters in the play can escape from the front stoop. By removing our focus from the tensions on the stoop, The Avenue scenes seem to provide respite for the audience as well as for those on stage. Red is trying to "mess with" Bunny, an attempt that angers Doris but pleases Bunny herself. The brief scene reminds us that Bunny is Ray's girl, that Red is callously ignoring that knowledge, and that Bunny is silly and frivolous. As Doris urges Bunny to "make it back to Ray," we are discreetly warned that this flirtation between Red and Bunny may cause trouble.

After the mention of Ray's name on The Avenue, the scene returns to Derby Street, where Ray is departing from the Krumps' house after cake and milk. We are given another sign of Ray's thoughtfulness as, in leaving, he invites Eddie to come down and join the people on the stoop. Clearly, although "little white Eddie" has no place in this world, Ray is attempting to make the younger boy feel more accepted. Ray's return stimulates Cliff to resume his earlier cursing of the neighborhood, to which Lou responds with irritation, just as she did before. If we have not noticed previously that such exchanges are enacted over and over, night after night on the Dawsons' stoop, we cannot avoid this understanding now. The renewed bickering between Lou and Cliff also serves to reveal more about Cliff and his past. Cliff has been in the navy, or as Lou qualifies it more precisely, he has been in the "guardhouse" in the navy. For Cliff, the memories of that time are important: Despite the acknowledged time he spent in the brig, he continues to think of himself as a sailor, an image that pleases him. Lou disparages Cliff's fond memories. In a brutal statement, she proclaims that the navy "failed . . . to make a man or sailor" of Cliff. It was she, alone, Lou attests, who made Cliff into a man.

It is difficult for the audience to discern where the truth lies in these memories; the spectator probably assumes that there is some accuracy in each account. The mention of Cliff's long periods in the navy brig may make the spectator wary of him and curious about the sort of behavior that caused his imprisonment. But we should also be painfully struck with the ironic sense that Cliff remembers his time in the navy as a period of freedom compared to his present situation. His assertion that he remains a sailor also suggests a wanderlust in the man; that knowledge can add to the audience's tension. Lou's boasts of what she did for Cliff are not pleasing either. She is taking all the credit for Cliff's manhood, which is certainly self-inflating, although it may be true that by marrying Cliff, as she narrates it, she abbreviated his time in the brig. Her claim that she only married him to free him is at best a partial truth, in terms of both Cliff's relative freedom and Lou's motivation. Lou may be thoughtful about other persons, but she has already shown herself to be too brash and tough to have married Cliff simply out of kindness. In this same exchange, she persists in irritating Cliff by calling the brig the "guardhouse," until Ray comes to Cliff's defense, reminding Lou each time she employs the word that the appropriate term is "brig." Bullins indicates that Lou is destructive to Cliff in her refusal to perceive what is important to him.

Cliff again wearies of the argument, but the audience's hopes for a respite are thwarted when Cliff stops the conversation by urging Ray, who has become his ally during the dispute, to pour himself a drink. This only sets Lou off again. She blames Cliff for making Ray into a young lush. Both Cliff and Ray deny this, recalling for Lou that Ray was already drinking with his mother before she died. Lou's nagging is becoming increasingly irritating, but the audience may well sympathize with her concern about the amount of alcohol consumed by her husband and nephew. Cliff's attempts to turn the focus to Ray are a relief, but not an answer to the problem. As Cliff and Ray go on drinking, Cliff begins to insist from the borders of drunkenness, "It's your world, Ray. It's really your world." The words, at this point in the play, seem somewhat sentimental, not very seriously intended; yet they do still strike a melancholic chord in the audience.

Lou does not like Cliff's latest proclamation. She tries to stop him, but he will not desist. Neither will yield to the other, so they ignore each other and turn to separate audiences; Lou addresses Ray and Cliff addresses an imagined God. This double monologue is presented simultaneously onstage. If the speeches are expressed with equal force, as the personalities of the characters and the visual presentation in the script would suggest, the spectator will therefore be unable to hear all of either speech. There is an impression of struggle onstage that the audience will reflect in its attempt to hear as much as possible of both monologues. Lou's speech is a worried apology for Cliff's bad ways and a defense of her own responsibility to Ray. She is anxious about the bad habits she and Cliff are instilling in Ray with their own overindulgence in liquor, but she wistfully admits that "it sho' do relax me." Cliff's monologue contrasts sharply with Lou's sad humility. In a mocking cynicism, he addresses God as a shyster, heretically attesting to the foolishness of people like the Krumps, "little red lobsters" who "still think they have to face You in the mornin'." The bits we hear of Cliff's speech will strike us as witty and funny, if troubling to some in their gross denial of God. Ironically, the double monologues end with Lou proclaiming the presence of the devil while Cliff sings, "Yes, Lord, yes, Lord, yes, Lord, yes, Lord." If the audience hears little else in these speeches, they should be intrigued by those concluding invocations, in which, from the sounds of sadness, humility, gloom, and apology, the word "devil" rings out, while from the roar of pride and laughter, scorn and insult, the name of the Lord is chimed.

The double monologue forces the audience to absolute attention. It also works with the subliminal effect of a television commercial to persuade through flashes of sound and image rather than coherent statement. The simultaneous speeches assault our senses; in doing so, they make us feel a suffocation like that felt by the characters onstage. We are bombarded by sounds of words and emotions, but the situation is structured in such a way that we are unable to sort out or clearly understand what is being expressed. Even if we strain to listen to either Lou or Cliff, we will not be able to hear well, and we will be choosing to listen to one but not the other. That choice will tell us something about our own sympathies. We may also feel a secret relief in our inability to understand fully, for we may hear enough of the bitterness and anxiety in Cliff and Lou to tell us that more would be painful. Although the double monologue is not a device of our own creating, it may function similarly to the way John Lahr describes the characters' relationship to some of the elements of their world: "The disc jockeys, the checker games, the fights coming out of windows become events, perhaps even devices, which hold back the oppressive blankness surrounding them."[14] The audience may recognize these speeches as a theatrical device, while accepting them as a relief from the oppression of the more naturalistic scenes. The only limitation to Bullins's strategy here is that the words spoken by both Cliff and Lou are worth hearing, but what we lose in the superimposition of sound may be more than made up for in the experience of struggle forced upon us.

Carried too long, however, this pressure boggles the mind, and the audience must feel released when Lou cries out, "Stop it, Cliff! You're drunk 'n' crazy 'n' drivin' me out of my head." Ray now becomes the pacifier, assuring both Lou and Cliff that "it's all right. It's all right." Once again, it is Lou who insists on maintaining the tension; she now admonishes Cliff to get "some fear of the Lord" into him. Although the audience may know that her concern merits respect, her badgering is again annoying for her family and the spectators. It is thus a pleasure to hear Cliff's apt and humorous retort to Lou's protest that she knows better than he does: "Is that why when I get you in bed every night you hollar (whining falsetto) 'Yes, Lord. Yes, Lord. Ohhh . . . Jesus . . . one more time' " (p. 607). Ray giggles, and we are delighted to giggle with him, delighted to be reminded and to have Lou reminded that she is not always so much holier than everyone else. Even Lou is disarmed by Cliff's reminder. Although she cannot admit to her defeat, she indicates it by asking Ray to pour her and Cliff another drink.

Lou's request seems like a signal to end the tension onstage, which is now becoming cumbersome to the audience, despite the relief of Cliff's jest. But the spectator is not yet released. In asking for the drinks, Lou has allowed herself one more jab at Cliff; she has called him Ray's "no-'count step-uncle," an insult Cliff cannot ignore. He feels "demoted," which is just what Lou affirms that she intended. It is now Ray's turn to grab the moment. As if to reassure Cliff of his importance to him, Ray asks Cliff if he thinks his nephew can get into the navy. Cliff responds casually that of course he'll sign the papers for Ray when Ray is old enough, but Lou triumphantly argues that Cliff can't do that because he is a "step" uncle.

This newest quarrel has the appearance of being just like others we have seen, but it is not, because there is now a concrete problem to be dealt with. The other disputes were obviously ones that would never be resolved, or would vanish in the morning to be renewed the next wine time. But, Ray informs Cliff, Lou, and the audience, he is about to turn sixteen, and he thinks himself ready to set sail. Although there is no decision reached in this episode, Ray's plan is an issue that can create a more lasting anxiety in the audience, because it suggests no easy compromise and yet necessitates an answer. Lou and Cliff sense the particular difficulty Ray's request about the navy has created, and it drives them into sensitive areas they have not dealt well with before. About to lose a child to the adult world, they resist this loss. Cliff is willing to let Ray go, but it seems "so soon" to him. Lou cruelly takes the occasion to remind Cliff that he could enlist when he desired because he came from the Virginia woods, where there were no birth certificates. She ridicules Cliff for considering himself Ray's guardian while having no job and drinking up the few dollars he gets from the government.

Lou's cutting condescension is more than Cliff can take. For the first time, the violence apparent in Cliff's language and his playful wrestling with Lou is made threateningly physical. He slaps her hard. Then, in a menacing voice, he tells her that she talks too much. The audience's sympathies are torn because Lou does talk too much and she should be quieted, but what she says may need saying. Cliff's blow frightens because of what it suggests about his own nature and their marriage. In addition, the audience must empathize with both characters because they are acting out of genuine concern for Ray and out of fear of losing this boy, whom they love. Cliff even evokes admiration, because he is willing to sacrifice his own need for Ray so that Ray can get out of Derby Street: "He's got to get out of here . . . don't you Ray? . . . offa Derby Street and away from here so he can grow up to be his own man." When Lou, in tears, suggests that getting away from Derby Street did not make a man out of Cliff, he goes on, "No, not like me . . . not tied down to a half-grown, scared, childish bitch" (p. 609). His words are as frightening as his slap in the resentment they express toward Lou. The hollow sensation Cliff's violence elicits in the spectator is suddenly and surprisingly removed when, to Lou's protest that Cliff does not have to be tied to her, he responds simply, "But I love you." The strategy of Act I of *In the Wine Time* has been to make us recognize and feel the frustration and suffocation of the characters, but with Cliff's stark avowal, we are also exposed to the underlying warmth that sustains them.

To remind the audience that the affection binding Cliff and Lou is special, Bullins immediately pulls the lights down on Derby Street and up on "The Avenue," where we are greeted with the rough sound of Doris's "Red . . . you mathafukker. . . . Stop that!" as we see Red slapping Bunny. Clearly, this is a parallel to Cliff's slapping Lou, but there is a nastiness in Red's action, an attempt to hurt and control without affection, that should be vividly different from the episode with Lou and Cliff. With Red and Bunny, the spectator feels disgust and then unrelieved fear as Doris threatens Red with her own little knife. Red uses violence to intimidate Bunny; Cliff's explosion was an expression of his own pain. The audience is led to distinguish between two actions that look the same but are importantly different in what they do and mean.

To clarify the difference in the relationships, Bullins now returns the attention to Derby Street, where Ray is apologizing for instigating the fight between Cliff and Lou. Lou tells Ray that it is all right, that this is not a unique episode in her marriage, but she is not as forgiving with Cliff, who also attempts to make peace. Lou reminds Cliff and the audience of what we knew only from the prologue—that she is pregnant and therefore particularly vulnerable. The spectator's automatic reaction to this reminder would be a renewed anger at Cliff, but Bullins again arrests the facile response through Cliff's reasonable defense that the baby is not, after all, due for another six months and would probably not be hurt by his slap. This does lead, however, to more sensitive subjects. Lou accuses Cliff of not really wanting the baby;

Cliff admits candidly that this is true because he cannot take care of a child at this point. When Lou suggests that Cliff could get a job to take care of the baby, Cliff argues that he does not want a demeaning, dollar-an-hour job, and that that is precisely why he is going to school. Lou then raises still another question: What good will it do Cliff to study business, since it will not be easy to get either a job in a business or the money to establish his own? Lou's reminders may ring true to the audience (Wanda's warnings in *Big White Fog* and Walter Lee's experience in *A Raisin in the Sun* may be recalled), but, more importantly, they increase our sense of Cliff's imprisonment in this world, of his inability to find a place where he can define his own space.

Cliff's immediate answer to these troubling questions is that he could ship out again or they could go on welfare, but these are clearly unhappy solutions. There is no "right" side to be taken in these issues. As in Richardson's *The Broken Banjo* and Ward's *Big White Fog*, the audience is tossed back and forth from one seemingly accurate insight to another of equal persuasive power, but here each of the accurate perceptions is of a futile path or obviously closed door. Bullins now employs the double monologue again to accentuate the spectator's ambivalence and frustration. The second set of monologues is more troubling than the first, because what we hear are angrier and more bitter tones. Lou's speech presents her disappointment in Cliff; she argues that he is not a man, that he is not like her father, who labored with his hands to bring up his children to fear God. Lou chastises herself for having mistaken Cliff's brawn, his fighting and drinking and loudness, for manliness. Yet Cliff's monologue asserts precisely that he is a man, that he has the self-respect to not be used as an animal "for the plows of the world." For Cliff, there is still "a world out there" that can be his and Ray's, but if forced to be a beast of burden he will turn that world into a "jungle or a desert."

It is Lou who once more ends the double monologue, screaming at Cliff, "You're nothing." Any portions of Cliff's speech heard by the audience persuade us that Lou is wrong, that Cliff *is* a man struggling for his dignity. Although the audience is therefore led to condemn Lou, the condemnation is tinged with anxiety that Cliff's assertions are merely dreams that will bring frustration and will not fill the new baby's stomach. Lou's frustration and Cliff's dreams bring them both back to the immediate, concrete issue of Ray's desire to enlist in the navy. Ray's evolving identity as a man is really the issue here. Lou states that she does not want Ray to be like Cliff. Having witnessed Cliff's misery and anger, the spectator may be tempted to agree with Lou, but Cliff's response, that the other choices for Ray—to be a "Derby Street Donkey," a "dirty bopper," and "avenue hype," or a "drug addict"—are not welcome alternatives.

Lou ends Act I asserting determinedly that she will not sign any papers for Ray, that he will not go into the navy; but the audience knows this is no permanent conclusion to the problem. We are left with a sense of frustration and anxiety, as well as pity for those onstage. Empathy for the characters may be somewhat blocked for middle-class people, however. The traditional high regard in the American white society for hard work and personal moderation would make it difficult for the white spectator or middle-class black spectator to accept without hostility the langorous evenings of drinking, swearing, music, and sex central to the identities of Lou, Cliff, and Ray. More probably, a white and perhaps a black middle-class audience would respond to the end of Act I of *In the Wine Time* by rejecting Cliff for his lack of industry and his coarse language. This spectator would pity Lou. Or the white spectator might feel guilt that his world has so limited the options for Cliff, Ray, and Lou. Yet Cliff's eloquence and the use of the double monologue are evidence that Bullins's main intention is not to stimulate disgust for Cliff or to protest injustice before a white audience. It is to arouse admiration for Cliff's commitment to his own dignity despite attacks on his behavior, and to elicit empathy but not unquestioning approval for Lou's impatience with Cliff's struggles. Such an intention can be fulfilled with any spectator, but it is likely to be more effective for the black spectator who does not bear the guilt of the white middle class and whose values are informed and complicated by experiences not available to white people.

II

Act II begins with a not so surprising but troubling scene up on The Avenue. As "mythic blues" play, Red is seen embracing and caressing Bunny. Bunny raises in the spectator's mind the question: "What will Ray say?" If we are tempted to take this infidelity casually, Doris warns us not to do so; this episode may provoke trouble because she would "cut that nigger's nut off if he had'a hit me like that, Bunny . . . and . . . that goes double for any jive nigger who lays a finger on me or mine" (p. 612). Because the spectator has already seen Red lay a foot on Ray, there is cause to worry that this seemingly inconsequential flirtation may increase the difficulties in the Dawson household.

When we return to the scene on Derby Street, the radio is repeating the high temperature of the evening, and a new character, Beatrice, is seen walking down the street. Beatrice, as Cliff describes her and Ray agrees, is "a snotty little stuck-up heifer," who politely addresses everyone on the street except Cliff and Ray, whom she ignores with her nose in the air. Beatrice's passage provokes a defensive unity between Cliff and Ray, intended to amuse the audience and extend the motif of sexual play initiated on The Avenue. In response to Cliff's lascivious inquiries, Ray admits that he is not "gettin' anything" from Beatrice or the other young girls on the street. Cliff, of course, proclaims that he would have had them, as Ray kiddingly puts it, "all sewed up." Ray's defense for his limited sexual activity is that he is in love with Bunny. As a reminder to the audience of Bunny's infidelity, this increases our fear that trouble is coming. Ray's protestation of love for Bunny also reminds Cliff of Lou, who has remained in the house, but when Lou does not respond to Cliff's call, he proceeds gently to tease Ray about the latter's relationship with Bunny. Cliff has been hiding from Lou the signs of Ray's sexual encounters with Bunny. The older man now tells the younger that he is "big enough" to "Clean up [his] own mess from now on."

The exchange between Cliff and Ray is striking in its intimacy and warmth. Although Bullins treats the episode lightly, it can be perceived as a rite of passage, the welcoming of the younger man into adulthood. As Ray and Cliff continue to talk "man to man," their obvious affection for each other produces agreement about the women on the block, about the wisdom of Ray's avoiding marriage, about Ray's departure for the navy. It is pleasing to watch the easy camaraderie and respect between the two men, a welcome relief from all the earlier squabbles on that same stoop. It therefore seems entirely appropriate that the comfortable intimacy induces Ray to confide in Cliff about the girl of whom Ray spoke in the prologue. Ray states the story simply, "I met a girl the other day . . . she's almost a woman . . . A pretty girl." At this point, the lights come up on The Avenue and the audience is shown "the Girl." Red, Bama, Doris, and Bunny are momentarily fixed in a tableau, then Red and Bama begin "a seduction dance" around the Girl. Doris and Bunny begin to dance, too, moving "against the attraction of the girl, in a symbolic castration of the boys." Like other scenes on The Avenue, this dance is initially pleasing to the audience as an escape from the repetitive tension of life on the stoop. It is particularly engaging because its silent movement is a welcome contrast to the noise and immobility of the Dawsons on Derby Street. Yet, similarly but more emphatically than in other scenes on The Avenue, the change in style is a deception. The release the characters seek on The Avenue and the audience expects from the nonrealistic style of presentation is not actually what we discover. The actions within the dance are threatening. Although we do not know whether the dance is a vision created by Ray or an "actual" event occurring on The Avenue, the

Girl now becomes at once a wistful fantasy and a symbolic threat to the lives of the community onstage. She is an intruder, a symbol of things desirable and mysterious outside the small world of Derby Street and The Avenue. She also disturbs an audience familiar with a basically naturalistic stage world.

Cliff warns Ray not to "get stuck" on the Girl, because Ray will be going away very soon, but Ray claims that the Girl will wait for him. When Cliff expresses his skepticism about the fidelity of women, Ray remarks that Lou once waited for Cliff. It is now Cliff's turn to reveal his most private knowledge:

> CLIFF: . . . Well, Lou Ellen is different because . . . well, she's
>   got character.
> RAY: My girl . . .
> CLIFF (cutting): And your aunt's got principle and conviction and
>   you have to be awfully special for that.   [p. 617]

It is difficult for Cliff to speak these words but immeasurably pleasing to the audience to hear them. They evoke hope in the audience and pacify anxieties about his and Lou's marriage. Love can persist even where there is anger, despair, and disappointment. The scene not only affirms the durability of love, it also affirms Cliff's complexity and worth. His admission urges the spectator to avoid judging human beings by fragments or initial indications of behavior; we are not to expect consistency or simplicity in any man.

The audience is eager for a more complete view of this side of Cliff, and the demand is met. Cliff goes on to say, "For someone to have all of them qualities in these times is close to bein' insane. She's either got to be hopelessly ignorant or have the faith of an angel . . . and she's neither (p. 618)." Lou is someone special. We accept that judgment from Cliff and, through that acceptance, know him to be special as well. We can't agree when Cliff adds, "I don't deserve her, I know," but we are not meant to agree; we are meant to admire Cliff's newly revealed humility.

As Cliff and Ray go on to share more of their private thoughts— about their women, about the navy, about the world "out there"— Cliff's memories and Ray's dreams for the future become entwined in a fantasy that is allowed and made vibrant by the concrete relationship between the man and the youth. Cliff's joyous descriptions of what it will be like for Ray to sail the seas to welcoming ports or watch the moon, "all silvery, slidin' across the rollin' ocean like a path of cold wet fire, straight into your eye," transcend the present and comment on it. The melting run of language and the precision of imagery, as well as

the mixing of memory and knowledge, past and future, can be likened
to passages from Tennessee Williams's dramas but, in fact, more immediately recall the sound of William Faulkner's prose. This scene, as
well as the prologue to *In the Wine Time*, indeed makes a special sense
of a passage from *Light in August:* "Memory believes before knowing
remembers. Believes longer than recollects, longer than knowing even
wonders."[15] There are tenacious freedom and joy in Cliff's memory
that transcend the knowledge of historical events and persists beyond
or despite the recognition of particular details of the past.

Cliff is brought out of his reverie by Ray's more pragmatic concern,
"Do you think I can get in, Cliff?" The audience is reminded of the
harsher realities of the world onstage when Cliff, answering Ray's
query if Cliff, too, will "ship out" responds: "Nawh . . . nawh . . . I
had my crack at the world . . . and I've made it worse, if anything . . . you youngbloods own the future . . . remember that . . . I
had my chance. All I can do now is sit back and raise fat babies. It's
your world now, boy" (p. 620). For the audience, the second hearing of
these words has a saddening and somber effect. It may be reassuring to
know that Cliff is not about to leave his wife and expected child, but it
is troubling to see a man in his twenties handing over his dreams so
soon, resigning himself to the memory of one unsuccessful "crack at
the world." The audience is provoked to feel shame for a world in
which dreams are squelched so easily, in which what would be called
irresponsibility is the only path to possibility.

It has now become literally as well as figuratively darker onstage.
While evening passes into night, a new character enters to change the
mood of the drama and introduce a new interest for the audience. The
new person is Tiny, "a small, attractive girl in her late teens." As she
walks down the street she is suddenly terrified by a loud "boo" from
the shadows on stage. The boo comes from Silly Willy Clark, another
new character. Cliff's "nearly hysterical" laughter in response to the
trick on Tiny releases the audience from the depression of the previous
scene. Returned to the crazy, chaotic, public world of Derby Street,
we find that it is a strange relief to be there. The neighbors stick their
heads out windows to discover what has caused the commotion; even
the local policeman appears to find out if everything is okay.

The appearance of the policeman "Murphy" is a double-edged device. It reminds the audience that white authority figures loom just
around the corner, and it bitterly suggests that whatever reassurance
the presence of the "law" creates should be countered with anger at
the condescension of these same figures. The policeman arouses Cliff's
ire by addressing him in a demeaning tone as Cliff, rather than as Mr.
Dawson. Cliff's direct response is to address the officer as Murphy,

which is not the man's name but a stereotyped label for any policeman. Cliff's remark, "Yeah, he said Cliff like he was sayin' boy," is appropriate to the pride and sensitivity that have already been established as essential to his character. A white spectator could learn from the episode, but its intention seems less a protest to whites than a model for blacks, because the scene focuses on Cliff's reaction rather than the policeman's behavior.

While Tiny has been venting her anger on Clark for his scare, the scene has returned to teasing conversation and barbed exchanges between Lou and Cliff about Ray and Cliff's lustful glances at Tiny. The effect on the audience is to suggest that nothing much has really changed since the beginning of the play; yet the conversation does move on to new territory. Tiny tells Ray that Bunny has sent him a message to keep his "ass" home, that she wants to ask him some questions about the girl he has been seeing on The Avenue. Because the audience knows what Bunny has been doing, this message evokes anxiety. When Cliff advises Ray to "knock her [Bunny] on her ass" if she "fucks with" him, Ray assures Cliff that he will do so. We may be amused by this bravado, but it does little to reassure us that trouble will be avoided. Lou and Tiny go into the house. Having challenged one another's drinking capacities, Cliff, Clark, and Ray go off to "The Avenue" to purchase more wine. Act II ends.

The final scene of Act II seems ordinary and mellow enough to allow the audience to relax. However, the addition of more liquor to an already volatile situation, the expectations of Bunny's arrival, and the unresolved question of Ray's enlistment in the navy should provoke at least curiosity if not anxiety in the audience. We want Act III to begin quickly, although we have no clear sense of what it will bring.

III

Act III at first seems to present just what an audience might have anticipated. Lou, Tiny, Doris, Bunny, Red, and Bama are gathered on the Dawsons' stoop, somewhat more drunk and more vulgar in their speech than when we last saw any of them. Lou immediately engages Red in an argument about his obscene language. Red responds, "Shit, woman, talk to your ole man, Cliff . . . I'm usin' Mr. Dawson's rule book." Red is, of course, correct, but our attitude must be uncertain because we have already come to dislike Red. The spectator can thus enjoy seeing Red criticized while being annoyed with Lou's prudish nagging about language she herself has used earlier.

It is Tiny who urges that they all stop arguing. The conversation then changes to the women's cynical comments about the men. Tiny summarizes these attitudes: "It's just that all men are messed up" (p. 626). The women in the audience might nod in agreement, but they are only allowed a moment to revel in their superiority. Tiny's query concerning Cliff's return is met with a dryly suspicious question from Lou, "You waitin' for Cliff now, Tiny?" The suggestion is that it is not just men who are sexually promiscuous. We are curious to find out more about Tiny and Cliff, but that subject is held in abeyance for a time as attention is now called to Doris's "bad" language.

The repeated mention by characters in the play of the "bad" language used in *In the Wine Time* suggests that Bullins is consciously making the use of vulgar language an issue for the audience; it is not a mistake in his strategy but a purposeful part of it. In speaking of the play's performance at the New Lafayette Theatre, Marvin X and Robert Macbeth admitted that the language was a problem for the audience:

MARVIN: The language divided everybody!

MACBETH: Yeah. You see the fact that one group of people didn't talk like another group of people, or didn't relate like another group of people, they got into trouble about who was connected to who, who was whose brother. So the language got in the way.[16]

Marvin X and Macbeth are probably speaking here not just of the play's use of obscene language but of the inclusion in one script of strikingly metaphorical language, lyrical passages, and indications of various dialects. Their perception is important, but their conclusion—that the language of black drama will continue to divide audiences until black artists and other black people "change the language" to the "language of our people"[17]—seems to me to miss Bullins's intention. Bullins's use of a variety of forms of language conveys a complicated, convincing impression of a world in which all people do not speak identically and individuals speak differently on different occasions. Words in *In the Wine Time* become actions appropriate to the situation. The particular quality of vulgar language as Bullins uses it is that it is a verbal expression of violence, which, during much of the play and for most of the play's characters, substitutes for more harmful physical violence.

Bullins prompts us to examine any remaining self-consciousness and indignation about the language to see if it is a wholly honest response to the world around us and to consider why we might be disturbed. After all, Lou, who most frequently voices the complaints the audience may have about the vulgar language onstage, herself swears vigorously when she desires or needs to. This implies either that Lou, and perhaps the spectator, is hypocritical or that she is actually distressed about other matters when she complains about language. Furthermore, Bullins includes enough disputes about language for them to become boring and repetitive; the comments about bad language thus become more annoying than the language itself. Conversations about language occur when other, tenser subjects are in the air; vulgar expressions are a signal of difficulty or intensity in the stage world.

The problematic subject being revealed at the beginning of Act III is Tiny's relationship to Cliff. After Lou's question, the subject is next referred to as a secret that Doris shelters. Once everyone knows that Doris "has somethin" on Tiny, others gather on the stoop straining to uncover the secret. "Scared and belligerent," Tiny eventually blurts, "You gonna tell her 'bout Cliff and me?" The question obviously affirms Lou's suspicions and those of the audience; the only ambiguity is whether or not Tiny is being "bad," as Doris suggests she is, and purposely revealing her affair to Lou. The audience should not be surprised or disappointed in Cliff as a result of this revelation, because both his emotional fidelity to Lou and his sexual promiscuity have already been evidenced. It may still be somewhat disturbing, but the audience has been urged throughout the play to accept that love and sexual monogamy are not necessary partners. The greater concern here for the audience is how this confirmation will affect Lou; given the admiration Cliff has expressed for her, the spectator probably will not want to see her hurt. In a stage direction, Bullins describes Lou's reaction as "disgust," yet we are given no further clue to her feelings because at that moment, Cliff, Clark, and Ray appear on Derby Street with the half-emptied gallon of wine they went off to purchase some time ago.

The addition of more drunken people to the stoop provokes further hostility on stage and greater tension in the audience. Now that everyone is gathered, the coupling of men and women is an immediate problem and quickly becomes a crisis as Bama pulls Doris down to his side. This arouses Tiny's wrath; she scratches at Bama's face, crying out that she thought Bama was coming to see her. During the encounter, Doris pulls out the little knife the audience saw up on The Avenue. Just as we become fearful that lasting hurt is about to be inflicted on someone, Cliff reaches the stoop; his presence allows Doris to put away her knife.

The relief we now are allowed lasts only a moment. Red and Bama continue to provoke everyone. As the noise increases, "bitchy ol' Miss Minnie," a neighbor, shouts from her window that she is calling the police about "all this disturbance." Whether to avoid the police or because he is genuinely feeling like a father of noisy offspring, Cliff announces, "Well, children, it's time that Daddy got to bed." He suggests that everyone else go home, too. Cliff and Doris both enter the house, leaving Lou outdoors long enough to defend Cliff's escape against Red's insinuation that Cliff is a coward. Asserting that "there's more than one way to be a coward," Lou then commands everyone to leave, after which she, too, enters the house.

Everyone begins to depart, and all seems quiet, except for Ray's snoring on the stoop and the sounds of Lou's "fussing" with Cliff inside the house. It appears to the audience that the play and the night are about to end in relative tranquillity. It is, therefore, somewhat surprising to hear Bunny's voice urging Ray awake so that she can tell him something. Both Bama and Tiny attempt to draw Bunny away, but she insists on telling him that she is now Red's girl. Asked repeatedly if he has heard her, Ray groggily tells Bunny, "Yeah . . . I heard you Bunny. You're Red's girl now." During this exchange, Red, turning to a building, urinates in a wine bottle. He then hands the bottle filled with urine to Ray, suggesting that they drink a toast to Bunny's new alliance. As Ray, still half asleep, lifts the bottle to his lips, Bunny, who has seen Red urinating into it, screams out to prevent Ray from drinking and knocks it to the pavement. Ray immediately wakes up; having only perceived the last action, he lashes out at Bunny. This gives Red just the chance for a physical attack he has been seeking throughout the play. Able to act in supposed defense of Bunny, Red "rushes" Ray. In a second, Ray, Clark, Bama, and Red are all engaged in furious combat. As the battle moves to a nearby alley, we see Red pulling a "bone-handled switch blade." While they disappear, Doris appears wielding her own knife, calling for Ray.

Despite the violent language, hostile barbs, and deliberate insults previously heard throughout the play, this final brawl and the attempted "trick" that precedes it can only be horrifying to an audience. What we may have thought was vulgar before now becomes modest in contrast to the notion of one man leading another to drink urine. What appeared to be brutal earlier now seems passive compared to this final violence. Yet exactly because of the persistent verbal violence in the play, there is a sense of inevitability in the physical fight, which, while allowing that fight to be terrifying, prevents it from being shocking. The audience may not even take the fight very seriously until they see the drawn knives.

After Doris, too, vanishes down the alley, the next sound we hear is at once disturbing and absurdly funny. It is the sound of "little Eddie's" voice urging, "Kill 'em. . . . Kill 'em" followed by Mrs. Krump's

cautioning, "Keep back, Edward . . . there may be stray bullets."
Bringing in the Krumps at this point suggests that such people relish
others' troubles and are irrationally anxious to protect themselves. The
two Krumps are such cartoon characters that the entire interjection
would seem absurd if it were not quickly interrupted. The new sound
is Red's voice groaning, "All right . . . all right." We then see Cliff run
into the alley, and we hear noise of a renewed struggle and another
groan. We know nothing more about precisely what is going on than
do the neighbors now hanging out windows. The strategic effect is to
make the moment more frightening, because we can only imagine what
actions accompany the groans; we do not have the relief of seeing
clearly who is safe and who is in danger. Ray's and Doris's appearance,
"splotched" with blood, informs us that some harm has been done, but
we still do not know what. A policeman enters asking, "What happened here?" The audience and the policeman are answered by Cliff,
who steps out of the alley, relinquishes Red's knife, and says, "I killed
him."

Lou is now back on the street and is incredulous as she repeats,
"You killed him . . ."; for a number of reasons, the audience must be
as disbelieving as she. First, we have seen no evidence that Cliff actually killed Red. Circumstantially, it is more likely that someone who
was in the alley longer, someone more involved in the anger of the
fight, someone like Ray, would have done the killing. More important,
Cliff's actions and words throughout the play suggested that at important moments he may have violent reactions but no intent to do permanent physical harm. The audience must therefore hope with Lou
that there is something more to tell, and Bullins has provided that
hope by keeping the actual murder offstage. When Lou urges,
"Cliff . . . Cliff . . . don't do it . . . don't leave me! Tell the truth," we
cannot know what she is thinking, but we must be provoked to wonder
what the truth really is: If Cliff has indeed killed Red, or if he is pro-
tecting someone else.

Cliff's answer to Lou and the audience does not resolve the ambiguity of the murder, but it does tell all we need to know about the
man. "It won't be long" he says, "I was protectin' my family . . . our
family." The audience is reminded that Cliff is a man who is sometimes
rough, sometimes gentle, often impetuous, but needfully controlled; he
is also a man who feels a deep responsibility to his family, and if that
responsibility, that love, has now taken the form of physical or verbal
protection, it is a commitment we can admire, even if its ambiguous
and necessary form is deeply troubling.

As the audience can begin to contemplate what Cliff is doing, Ray's
voice is heard, as if from another world, speaking of his "girl," repeat-

ing that she will "never be back." Ray's dreams have vanished, the world has changed actually and symbolically. But as the literal and the figurative are conjoined, Cliff, handcuffed to a policeman, challenges the despair expressed by Ray, by Lou's sobs, and potentially present in the audience. Cliff repeats his earlier proclamation: "It's your world, Ray. . . . It's yours, boy. . . . Go on out there and claim it." If, despite the ugliness and sorrow in this world, its most haplessly imprisoned victim can urge that there is something out there worth claiming, the audience, which is much freer, must feel challenged not to yield but to conquer.[18]

In the Wine Time, like Richardson's The Broken Banjo, is a tragedy of folk, not of a hero who falls from a great height because of hubris. It is the tragedy of people whose strength is revealed only in private places, whose world forces them to destructive actions, whose virtues are recognized only by those who cannot announce them. The play thus reverses many of classical tragedy's traditional structures and perspectives. Bullins's strategy is to use some of the devices of traditional tragedy to capture the audience and then to exploit our entrapment to make certain virtues recognizable to those in the audience who might otherwise ignore them. He impresses us with them by creating characters and events so distinctly credible, interesting, and ordinary that we cannot ignore or deny their existence. Once we have been brought to recognize these people as they are, we are led to judge them on the whole of their behavior, not on preconceptions of "type" or on momentary glimpses. The characters onstage set an example for the audience, not of the way the world should be but of how people, at their worst and at their best, can behave. If we can perceive their worst behavior, we must thereby also recognize their best, and, in so doing, we must regret their destruction.

Bullins further provides his audience with the experience of a gamut of complex and intense emotions. He offers laughter at people's foibles and wit, anger at their cruelty, impatience at their foolishness, joy at their ability to love, sorrow at their loss of one another. Yet despite the variety of responses an audience will have experienced during a performance of In the Wine Time, they will be left with one ineluctable recognition: The world they have witnessed is a prison that will not release even its strongest or most admirable captives. The physical appearance of the set; the relentless noise of the neighborhood, the radio and the language; the strain of human relationships persistently batter the audience and make them unable to avoid a sense of oppression. The patterns of the characters' lives make clear that there is no escape as long as this world remains essentially the same. Cliff has moved from the navy brig to the suffocation of Derby

Street to handcuffs that will be removed only in another jail; Ray's dream of escape is to imitate Cliff's attempts; Lou is left with the prospect of motherhood unrelieved by the sharing of dreams or responsibilities. This is a world similar to that portrayed by Richardson in *The Broken Banjo*, but one in which frustration and futility have become impossible to accept. Richardson's drama makes the audience respond with sadness, remorse, and a desire to "measure" more accurately and behave better. Bullins's drama may lead to anger instead of sorrow, a realization of the need to destroy basic structures, not improve what exists. *In the Wine Time* is thus not "just" an authentic presentation of the black experience, it is an attempt to persuade an audience to retain the love and dignity of that experience but to reject the habits, compulsions, and environments that are slowly drowning the very things that should be saved.

NOTES

1. Ed Bullins, "Introduction," *The Theme Is Blackness* (New York: Morrow, 1973), p. 12.
2. *Ibid.*, pp. 12, 13.
3. Elsie Haley, "The Black Revolutionary Theater, LeRoi Jones, Ed Bullins and Minor Playwrights" (unpublished doctoral dissertation, University of Denver, 1971), p. 154.
4. Bullins, *The Theme Is Blackness*, p. 10.
5. *Ibid.*
6. Ed Bullins, "Interview with Ed Bullins by Marvin X," in *New Plays from the Black Theatre* (New York: Bantam, 1969), p. ix. All of the quotations cited in this paragraph in reference to Bullins's self-discovery as an artist are from this interview, especially pages ix, x, and xiv.
7. Clayton Riley, "On Black Theater," in *The Black Aesthetic*, Addison Gayle, Jr., ed. (New York: Doubleday, 1972), p. 308.
8. Bullins, *The Theme is Blackness*, p. 12.
9. Bullins, "Interview with Ed Bullins by Marvin X," p. viii.
10. Ed Bullins, *In the Wine Time*, in *Black Theater*, Lindsay Patterson, ed. (New York: Dodd, Mead, 1971), p. 593. All other citations are from this source.
11. Imamu Amiri Baraka, "Symposium on We Righteous Bombers," in *Black Theater*, 4 (April 1970), 19.
12. John Lahr, "Introduction" to *In the Wine Time*, in *The Great American Life Show*, John Lahr and Jonathan Price, eds. (New York: Bantam, 1974), pp. 1–4.
13. *Ibid.*, p. 1.
14. *Ibid.*, p. 2.

15. William Faulkner, *Light in August* (New York: Random House, 1959), p. 104.
16. Robert Macbeth and Marvin X, "The Ritual Theater," in *Black Theater*, 3 (1969), 24.
17. *Ibid.*
18. These final actions, and the affirmations of love and dignity previously discussed, seem to me strong arguments against Helen Armstead Johnson's contention that Bullins's play is disappointing because it offers no direction for change or relief from despair. Bullins makes clear that it is the static and oppressive structure of the American society that must be changed, and *In the Wine Time* urges that a reassessment of our values and consciousness can bring about such change. See Helen Armstead Johnson, "Black Influences in the American Theater; Part II, 1960 and After," in *The Black American Reference Book*, Mabel M. Smythe, ed. (Englewood Cliffs, N.J.: Prentice-Hall, 1976), pp. 711, 712, 733.

8 | LOCATING THE RAINBOW: GESTURES OF DRAMA AND POLITICAL ACTS

Since the formation of the African Company in New York City in 1821, the strengths and vulnerabilities of black theater have been inseparable from its attempts to define and sustain an audience. Any drama is the servant of two masters—the playwright whose vision it makes public and the public whose way of seeing the world must be met and moved. For many kinds and periods of drama, these masters are the assumptions of the art, unquestioned not out of cowardice or conservatism but because the juxtaposed visions of the playwright and the public mark the limits that give form to the art. Black dramatists in America, however, have always had to begin with the understanding that the worlds they depict and the audiences for whom their work is performed are *problems*. They are problems not only because each is veiled by ignorance and fear, thus revealing markings that are at best ambiguous, but also because for the playwright to be master of his vision has often meant a devious servitude toward his audience.

Increasingly in the twentieth century, ambiguities of audiences and the ambivalences of the black playwrights' intentions toward spectators have been matters not only of confronting the two worlds—black and white—of American society but also of discerning communities with sufficient coherence within either of those worlds to allow the possibility of becoming a genuine audience. When, in the 1960s, playwrights like Baraka and Bullins cast aside the commercial white theater to create black theaters in the urban neighborhoods where black people lived, they knew that they would also have to "create" audiences, but they saw this task as feasible once they were relieved of the burden of pleasing whites. The initial enthusiasm with which such efforts were greeted seemed to affirm strongly the judgment of the black separatists; playwrights, actors, spectators, and sources of funds appeared in cities all over the United States, eager to work for black theater. Black writers began to articulate a distinctive black aesthetic, based on an appreciation of the educative and political purposes of art; black theaters not only became the nexus for black cultural life but were felt vividly as constituting a movement in which black people could take pride and to which white people were compelled to pay attention.

Within ten years, or by the mid-1970s, more than half of those same black theaters had vanished, and there is no longer an identifiable "movement." Explanations of the demise of these theaters have already been offered: "Outside" funding from foundations and government grants has been cut, often totally; overt political gestures, including riots in cities and legislation in Congress, which called forth a self-conscious ethnic identification in the 1960s, have been absorbed and dispersed in the hazy maze of "affirmative action;" competent black theater artists—directors, designers, technicians—are scarce; film and television have substantially increased their presentation of "black" material, and these media forms are more physically and financially accessible to black audiences.[1]

Such explanations describe events but, in fact, tell us little about the viability or importance of black drama in America. Most of these reasons have been offered, with some accuracy, in previous periods to explain the difficulties of black drama and the demise of black theaters and companies. The cyclic nature of the history of black drama is revealing; it can evoke a justifiable and bitter cynicism about the actual lack of change in American society in this century. The ways in which theater functions in a society—including where it is located and for whom it is performed—have often disclosed larger patterns of community and discourse within a society, and this is no less true of modern America than it was of ancient Greece or Elizabethan England. As sociologist and drama critic Raymond Williams argues, precisely because we can, by analyzing drama, get "through to some of the fundamental conventions which we group as society itself,"[2] our analysis must not be cut short by hurried observations or immediately recognizable understandings.

My concern, then, is that students and spectators of black drama will look at recent events and turn aside with boredom or frustration. To do so would be to mistake one kind of failure for the failure of the whole, but would also mean, I believe, that we are insisting too narrowly on one kind of question and response. We need to ask, for example, not only why black theaters in black communities have repeatedly failed to sustain themselves, but how and why they reappear in every decade. We need to consider, on more than just a commercial basis, why and how black dramatists have vacillated between the "mainstreams" of American theaters and the black community theaters, and we need to acknowledge within such consideration that although black community theaters have once again had difficulties, extraordinary black dramas have been written and successfully performed in the last five years. We need, too, to consider whether black and white remain the basic divisions of American society and American theater or whether the black consciousness and the white consciousness in America is increasingly less a matter of racial origin than a metaphor for communities of values that might be more accurately described under terms of class.

All of these questions point us back to the texts of the plays themselves. Here, too, patterns emerge; unlike the repetitions apparent in the emergence and disappearance of black theater companies, or the sudden surges apparent in box office sales and publications of black plays, the recurrent gestures of the plays are not static data but suggestive acts that when rearranged in new contexts, often yield new understandings. I am not here thinking of repeated motifs or themes, such as the manhood of black male characters or the difficulty black men and women have finding work that allows the survival of personal dignity. While the recurrence of these ideas or issues in all the plays I examined here mounts imposing evidence against the goodness of life in America, the pattern itself is neither dynamic nor dramatic. It is impotent, as its very endurance attests.

There are, however, patterns in black drama that do challenge spectators and readers, black and white, to see the world differently and to keep seeing in new ways. DuBois's models of the plays of inner life and the plays of contact of black and white work in just such a way. Initially, they serve to clarify what I have called the ambivalent intentions of the texts; they distinguish one kind of strategy, which is intended to unveil the hidden worlds of black men and women, from another kind, which is intended to protest the indecency and injustice inherent in the meetings of black and white Americans. If we understand that these are two distinct concerns with two differently conceived audiences, we may be less apt to ignore or misunderstand, more able to "measure the plays right." As with many ways of ordering the world, however, once we begin to fit specific instances to general categories, as much is learned from the misfits as from the occasional perfect examples. An important instance of such resonance appears when we examine the plays of inner life. With the possible exception of *Dutchman*, every play I have discussed attempts to some degree to penetrate the "inner life" less profoundly and convincingly than those whose focus is wholly away from the white world. But even with the two that can be most appropriately called plays of inner life—

Richardson's *The Broken Banjo* and Bullins's *In the Wine Time*—the outer life, the "big white fog," as Theodore Ward so aptly named it, cannot be dismissed. Indeed, the more thoroughly any spectator, black or white, becomes engaged by the inner life in black drama, the more forcefully he feels its context, its consanguinity with the surrounding American society. Thus, DuBois's categories begin to suggest a paradox. The plays of inner life, while limited to the worlds of black people in what they show, may provoke a stronger challenge to the spectator's way of perceiving encounters of blacks and whites than that induced by plays that display these encounters directly.

The important resemblances in black drama, then, are not those of cans of soup on a supermarket shelf (works of literature are not, as Stanley Fish urges, containers for meaning)[3] but are the affinities we discover in two handshakes, or two wounds, distinct in origin, time, and place, yet connected by the effects they have on us. Perhaps because black art has never had the distrust of purpose apparent in much Western art (it has always affirmed with W. E. B. DuBois that "all art is propaganda"), black critics have been among the first and firmest to argue an aesthetic centered on intentions toward an audience. Addison Gayle articulates this without apology in his introduction to *The Black Aesthetic:*

> A critical methodology has no relevance to the black community unless it aids men in becoming better than they are. Such an element has been sorely lacking in the critical canons handed down from the academies by the Aristotelian Critics, the Practical Critics, the Formalist Critics, and the New Critics. Each has this in common; it aims to evaluate the work of art in terms of *its* beauty and not in terms of the transformation from ugliness to beauty that the work of art demands from its audience.
>
> The question for the black critic today is not how beautiful is a melody, a play, a poem, or a novel, but how much more beautiful has the poem, melody, play or novel made the life of a single black man?[4]

Gayle's question is misunderstood if it is taken to mean that critics must now become pollsters, armed with questionnaires demanding of the theatergoer, "is your life now more or less beautiful than it was before entering the theater?" The point is not to turn us away from the play but toward it, and toward it in such a way that we ask not whether its transformations please or cohere but whether it can, in fact, transform.

There is no better evidence of the fruitfulness of this question than its ability to penetrate the enigma posed by the startling success of a black drama that played for several years on Broadway. The play, *for colored girls who have considered suicide/ when the rainbow is enuf*, by Ntozake Shange, is both historically and strategically an archetype for black drama; yet precisely because it is consistent with the most potent and unyielding energies in its "genre," it would have seemed doomed to commercial failure. The title alone seems destined to reduce the audience to but a few spectators. Not only does the title name a specific group of people for whom the play is intended, but the very words "colored girls" are discomforting reminders for blacks and whites, and especially for women, of a mode of naming that we have only recently been educated to reject. Nor is clarity or ease achieved if we move beyond the initial three words. The play's title beckons the audience to a world of despair and warns us that we will have to grapple with opaque and perplexing metaphor to locate the world of the play. The words of the title, *for colored girls who have considered suicide/ when the rainbow is enuf*, proclaim that the road toward the illusory pot of gold in the American dream is the source of such frustration that it leads to self-destruction; they also intimate, however, that a different kind of rainbow, a rainbow of self-determination, can suffice. (Thus the last lines of the play are a slight variation on the title: "& this is for colored girls who have considered suicide/ but are movin to the ends of their own rainbows" [p. 64]).

Yet *for colored girls* "enveloped" almost six thousand people a week at the Booth Theater, in the very heart of Broadway.[5] Its history before the Broadway production had little in common with the usual paths to that location. It was begun in 1975 as a series of seven poems conceived in conjunction with dance; the author, Ntozake Shange, and a dancer, Paula Moss, first performed the kernel of the play in dance studios and clubs in San Francisco. The two women next brought the show to New York, where they again performed in dance studios and bars. During this time, four other women joined the company and Oz Scott took over the direction of the play from its author. *For colored girls* was next performed as a workshop showcase at the Henry Street Theater and moved to the Public Theater in June 1976 in close to its present form. From Shange's description, the evolution and success of the play were never matters of high-visibility publicity or sudden floods of financial support; instead, she asserts, "Lines of folks and talk all over the Black & Latin community propelled us to the Public Theater in June."[6]

All this talk, eventually in the white community as well as in the black and Latin communities, was about a play that challenges the aesthetic and social values of middle-class America while incorporating all that has been exciting and commanding in black drama and experimental theater in the past fifty years. *For colored girls* fulfills the aspirations of a "poor theater" as conceived by Jerzy Grotowski in the 1960s: It focuses on the movements and sounds of actors as persons,[7] while strongly de-emphasizing the customary theatrical supports of sets, costumes, lights, and elaborate blocking. The play asserts its genealogical debt to black drama in its sharp concentration on the inner lives of black people, its unhesitant use of colloquial, metaphoric black language, and its transparent, balanced structure, which at once calls forth a folk tradition while making the performance an extraordinary occasion.

The setting for the play is a bare stage, painted black, including barely discernible ramps that project offstage. One large, red paper rose glows upstage. The setting remains the same throughout the performance, altered only by occasional subtle changes in lighting and by the words and motions of the actors. Seven black women, the entire cast, begin the play by running onto the stage and freezing in "postures of distress."[8] We never know these characters by name, although some momentarily become named characters in particular stories. In the script, each character is identified by a color: the lady in brown, the lady in yellow, the lady in purple, the lady in red, the lady in green, the lady in blue, and the lady in orange. Together, these colors form a rainbow that notably and accurately lacks both black and white. In performance, the identifying colors appear in the simple costumes, which otherwise are similar for each actress and are altered in only a few instances. The lady in brown speaks first, demanding of the other women onstage, and of the audience, that they allow a black girl to sing, that they acknowledge her song, that they "let her be born." It is a demand the spectator is not yet prepared to meet, but its candor startles us to attention.

The other "ladies" then speak, each announcing where she is: One is "outside" Chicago, another "outside" Houston, still another "outside" Manhattan. That each is from "outside" a different American city prevents the spectator from seeing this world as limited or peculiar to one situation in America, and immediately removes any expectations we might have that the familiar aspects and conventions of realism's enclosed room will ever be made evident. We are not only drawn "outside" any large American city; we are led outside to the kind of space Bullins revealed in *In the Wine Time*. It is a space where people shout and sing and curse and shove and dance; in this space, gestures must be large to be perceived; the intricate or subtle manners of living rooms have no place here.

In the remaining hour and ten minutes of the play, each woman tells a story about a moment in the life of a black girl growing up. Each story contributes to a whole or perfect vision, not necessarily of a single character or individual but of a world that could and does include each of these stories, each of these voices. The lady in yellow tells of "graduation nite" at the end of high school, and really hot dancing, and how she was the only virgin at the beginning of the night, but by daybreak she was a woman and "just cant stop grinnin" (p. 10). The lady in blue talks of her father's and her own imaginings that they were Puerto Rican, but how they "waz just reglar niggahs wit hints of spanish" (p. 11), and how that Spanish was revealed in her dancing, which in turn led to her discovery of "archie shepp and subtle blues." The lady in red then relates her devotion to a lover until she could no longer stand "not being wanted when i wanted to be wanted." Before the next story begins, the ladies in red, blue, and purple discuss rape and the variety of rapists they have encountered.

The various stories and exchanges that have thus far occurred in the play are interspersed with song and dance and told with such sharp wit and conscious irony that we can easily overlook the pain also present. We can do so, that is, until the lady in blue follows the exchange on rape with the brief and stark narrative of an abortion. There is no self-mocking grin or chuckle here onstage, nor is any smile allowed the spectator because

> this hurts
> this hurts me
>
> & nobody came
> cuz nobody knew
> once i wuz pregnant & shamed of myself.   [p. 23]

The shame of the lady in blue sets up the next story, the tale of Sechita, spoken by the lady in purple and danced by the lady in green. Sechita's shame is to have believed she could find pleasure at a cracker carnival in Natchez, Mississippi; instead, she found that "god seemed to be wipin his feet in her face" (p. 24).

The lady in brown's story, which follows that of Sechita, is also of a young girl's fantasy of finding a rainbow south of the Mississippi. The girl, all of eight years old, packs a brown paper bag and leaves home in search of Toussaint L'Ouverture, whom she initially discovered in the local library. The girl never makes it to Haiti but, instead, finds Toussaint Jones, a young black boy who, like the hero of her books, "dont take no stuff from no white folks." With this, the longest and most humorous of the stories thus far told, we are invited to laugh, but we are also being unabashedly educated. The black spectator is reminded of both grand and ordinary heroic figures in black history, and the white spectator is reprimanded for failing to acknowledge these same heroes.

Although the audience has not been forewarned, the remembered tale of the voyage to Toussaint is the last chance it is given for unhesitant, straightforward laughter. We now move into the stories of women whose lives were inseparable from men and loneliness. One woman speaks of her attempts to maintain her own space while she worked as a prostitute; another tells of the impossibility of being just a woman in Harlem; a third tells of how three women tossed friendship aside for the false love of one man, only to find genuine love with each other when each had been rejected by that man. Each of these stories reminds women, especially, of the frustrations of unfulfilled love and of the bonds they should have out of repeated and shared experience, but the voices of the speakers are not simple assaults on the men in the audience, because each speaker admits within her anger her own needs and responsibility for her despair.

Recognition of this shared responsibility is crucial at this point in the play, for it allows the spectator to acknowledge two remaining voices that might not otherwise be fully heard. The first of these is that of the lady in green, who, as if through her own experience of listening to her "sisters" on stage, has now discovered a new and fiercely assertive self. The lady in green's poem is less a narrative of events than a metaphor extended to but not beyond the edges of its possibility. The central notion of that metaphor is contained in the opening line: "somebody almost walked off wid alla my stuff." The spectators are now trapped; as witnesses to all the previous stories, we cannot help but understand just what the lady in green means by her justifiably self-righteous assertion. We are reminded to protect our own "stuff" and to be wary of usurping hers. We are also reminded, by the responses of the women onstage to the lady in green's poem, that to say "I'm sorry" for taking someone else's stuff does not suffice.

The wit and strength and slight distance from pain in the story of the woman who almost lost all of her stuff allow the spectators a moment of self-retrieval, a moment when the experience we have been engaged in takes on a clarity of recognition. What is striking about the words of this last speaker is how precisely they present a particular form of outrage, and how specifically the words onstage describe our own ordinary sentiments. Many of the stories we have been told have involved events and situations, but the care and focus in each speech have been to describe with candor and exactitude the feelings both present and remembered from each encounter. The rigor in these voices, combined with the frequent gestures of irony, prevents the display of emotion from becoming melodramatic and allows the spectators a vulnerability to their own feelings that can renew their ability to act with others in the world outside the theater. For an American audience particularly, for whom the archetypical dramatized hero is the "dandy,"[9] the stoical, self-controlled male figure who only barely reveals the slightest emotion, this is an exceptional experience. It is, after all, central to the middle-class American consciousness to believe that virtue exists in self-control, that weakness is exposed in the display and expression of feelings.

It is necessary, however, that this vulnerability be established by this point in the play for the audience to acknowledge the final story, that of Crystal, her children, and Beau Willie, the father of her children. In this, the most detailed narration in *for colored girls*, we are confronted with a woman who rejects the man she loves, the man who has fathered her children. A veteran of the Vietnam War, he repeatedly returns to this woman to demand her love, to demand that she marry him, but his only way of expressing his need is through a violence that almost kills her. Crystal and Beau Willie are connected by a tension that must either snap or yield; the spectator is caught between them, forced to recognize the depth of Beau Willie's despair and the agony of Crystal's need to protect herself and her children. As the story nears its conclusion, our helplessness as spectators is acute: Beau Willie has seduced the children away from their mother and stands holding them outside a window five stories above the ground; he threatens to drop them unless Crystal proclaims, publicly and irretrievably, that she will marry him. The narration, presented initially in nervous rushes and bursts of recollected terror, ends quietly: "i stood by beau in the window/ with naomi reachin for me/ & kwame screamin mommy mommy from the fifth story/ but i cd only whisper/ & he dropped em" (p. 60). In finishing her account, the woman who has been telling us *about* Crystal so fluidly shifts from "she" to "i" that the spectator must take a moment to comprehend how fully this human being has revealed herself. We are in the presence of a nakedness that daily life rarely allows and that theater offers only when it knows without question what it is about.

Tragedy, and all drama meant to be taken seriously, has always been intended, as the philosopher Stanley Cavell reminds us, "to make us practical, capable of acting."[10] But as Cavell goes on to say,

Now its work is not to purge us of pity and terror, but to make us capable of feeling them again, and this means showing us that there is a place to act upon them. This does not mean that tragedy now must become political. Because, first, it was always political, always about the incompatibility between a particular love and a particular social arrangement for love. Because second, and more specifically, we no longer know what is and is not a political act, what may or may not have recognizable political consequences.[11]

For colored girls who have considered suicide/ when the rainbow is enuf is, like most of the black dramas I have discussed, a vividly political act. In its closing moments, after the story of Beau Willie and Crystal, it shows us without disguise what its political consequences might look like, and what they will not look like. For the women onstage, the shared witnessing of Crystal's nakedness breaks the barriers of isolation and introspection. The women of all colors approach one another and lay their hands on one another out of necessity and desire; they are no longer able to sing or speak or dance alone. Their power comes from the acknowledgment of shared feeling, and their power is awesome. It is the power of a community.

For colored girls shows the audience a place to act and helps it to reconsider "what is and is not a political act" in drama. Few works of the American theater can make this claim. Richardson's *The Chip Woman's Fortune* makes no such attempt, and Hansberry's *A Raisin in the Sun* mistakes manipulation and affirmation of a deceptive social structure for a political act. But each of the other plays I have discussed does point to a place to act that is indeed political. By revealing to us onstage worlds and characters whose wholeness makes them especially vulnerable to actions and values we ordinarily accept without hesitation, they warn us to question the workings of those same values in our own less ordered and perfect worlds. It may no longer be the case, as Alain Locke argued in 1925, that "all classes of a people under social pressure are permeated with a common experience; they are emotionally welded as others cannot be." Not the social stresses to which Locke refers but the burdens of comfort and security and self-protection have weakened even the strongest pillars supporting common experience. The lady in blue in *for colored girls* speaks harshly of these oppressions:

> we deal wit emotion too much
> so why dont we go on ahead & be white then/
> & make everythin dry & abstract wit no rhythm & no
> reelin for sheer sensual pleasure/ yes let's go on
> & be white/ we're right in the middle of it/ no use
> holdin out/ holdin out/ holding onto ourselves/ . . .   [p. 45]

The lady's self-negation is, of course, finally in the saying an affirmation. It is an affirmation of emotion, rhythm, and sensuality, but also of the "we" as contrasted with an "I." It is no weakness but the strength of *for colored girls* that the play has no "star" and no "lead" part, no particular character or characters who especially attract our admiration or concern. Even when Trazana Beverley, an enormously charismatic stage presence, performed the story of Crystal and Beau Willie, her power surprised the audience and was quickly undercut. If, given our expectations from the conventions of most traditional theater, we examined the figures onstage in the early moments of *for colored girls* in search of the character or actress who would eventually stand apart from the others, the result would inevitably be surprise and frustration. Each time we are tempted to claim a single voice as particularly poignant or appealing, another voice or group of voices instantly overpowers or undermines such singularity. Or if our eye moves repeatedly to the prettiest or most graceful actress onstage, we will be abashed when it is the lady in red who speaks of and for Crystal and succeeds in engaging us most fully; for, with Trazana Beverley as the model, this role is deliberately played by an actress who, in her physical appearance, conscious awkwardness of movement, and uneven voice quality, repudiates all notions of the "star."

It is also no mistake that *for colored girls* does not end with Crystal's tragedy. The play's major structural problem lies in its too rapid shift of focus to the entire group of women and its hurried mood swing from the sorrow and horror evoked by Crystal's story to a song of joy sung by all the women, first to one another and then more and more to the audience. That we are not allowed a moment of transition makes the final image appear too arbitrary. But the "closed tight circle" of the "ladies" at the end of *for colored girls* is at once a theatrical and a political gesture. While it may be read by some spectators as too limited, associated not with the politics of race or class but with feminism, the limitation here would be in the perception not the intention of the image. For the single most persistent strategy of black drama has been to warn the spectators that to place their hopes in the success of the individual, to embrace the peculiar American admiration for "each man out for himself," is both aesthetically and politically suicidal. Black drama urges that theater, in allowing us to recognize those who are other, demands that we be responsible to others as well as to ourselves. And this is a political act not just for and toward whites *or* blacks *or* women but for and toward any human being.

NOTES

1. Helen Armstead Johnson, "Black Influences in the American Theater; Part II, 1960 and After," in *The Black American Reference Book*, Mabel M. Smythe, ed. (Englewood Cliffs, N.J.: Prentice-Hall, 1976). While such explanations come from a variety of conversations and articles, they are most specifically articulated by Johnson.
2. Raymond Williams, *Drama in a Dramatized Society* (Cambridge, U.K.: Cambridge University Press, 1975), p. 18.
3. Stanley Fish, *Self-consuming Artifacts* (Berkeley: University of California Press, 1972), p. 425.
4. Addison Gayle, Jr., "Introduction," in *The Black Aesthetic* (New York: Doubleday, 1972), p. xxii.
5. Ntozake Shange, *for colored girls who have considered suicide/ when the rainbow is enuf* (New York: Macmillan, 1977), p. xv. All subsequent references to the text are to this edition.
6. *Ibid.*
7. The phrase "actors-as-persons" resonates to but is not the same as Michael Goldman's term "actors-as-characters." For a discussion of the difference, see my article, "I Love You. Who Are You?: The Strategy of Drama in Recognition Scenes," *PMLA* (March 1977), and Michael Goldman, *The Actor's Freedom: Toward a Theory of Drama* (New York: Viking, 1975), especially pp. 6, 7, and 28.
8. Shange, *for colored girls who have considered suicide/ when the rainbow is enuf*, p. 3.
9. Stanley Cavell, *The World Viewed* (New York: Viking, 1971), p. 55. Cavell draws the term "dandy" from Baudelaire and applies it particularly to film, but as a description of a hero it is more generally applicable to dramatized images in America.
10. Stanely Cavell, *Must We Mean What We Say?* (New York: Scribner's, 1969), p. 347.
11. *Ibid.*

APPENDIXES

A | DRAMA AND THE STRATEGIC APPROACH

In my general comments at the beginning of this study and throughout my discussion of specific works, I have frequently referred to the *strategy* of the play. The term "strategy" and the idea of a strategic method of criticism are central to my approach to drama. Because these words are not ordinarily used in discussions of drama, I want to clarify how and why I use them.

My concept of the term "strategy" comes initially from Kenneth Burke, who has emphatically urged its usefulness in literary criticism. In Burke's essay "Literature as Equipment for Living," he argues at some length with critics who have quarreled with its use. After citing three dictionary definitions of "strategy," he explains:

> Looking at these definitions, I gain courage. For surely, the most highly alembicated and sophisticated work of art, arising in complex civilizations could be considered as designed to organize and command the army of one's thoughts and images, and to so organize them that one "imposes upon the enemy the time and place and conditions for fighting preferred by oneself." One seeks to "direct the larger movements and operations" in one's campaign of living. One "maneuvers" and the maneuvering is an "art."
>
> Are not the final results one's "strategy?" One tries, as far as possible, to develop a strategy whereby one "can't lose." One tries to change the rules of the game until they fit his own necessities. . . . One tries to fight on his own terms, developing a strategy for imposing the proper "time, place and conditions."
>
> But one must also, to develop a full strategy, be *realistic*. . . . One must *size things up* properly. One cannot accurately know how things *will be*, what is promising and what is menacing, unless he accurately knows how things *are*. So the

wise strategist will not be content with strategies of merely a self-gratifying sort. He will "keep his weather eye open." He will not too eagerly "read into" a scene an attitude that is irrelevant to it . . . He won't sit on the side of an active volcano and "see" it as a dormant plain.[1]

I have quoted Burke at length here because it is necessary to make clear a term whose connotations might well distort an understanding of my approach to black drama, and to stress that as Burke presents strategy and as I use the term, it is a matter of seeing and understanding as well as structuring materials.

Thus, to talk about plays in terms of their strategies means not so much that I am looking *for* something special or particular, but that I am looking in a particular fashion, which I am calling a strategic method.

The strategic approach to drama is one that seeks to discover in the sequential development of the script the intentions of that script at each moment and, finally, as a whole toward its audience. A strategic analysis attempts to answer questions such as: How am I, as spectator, intended to respond to this character, this event? What is the nature of the experience the script creates for an audience? Because the experience for the audience is created through a series of moments in time, I examine the script sequentially, as it would, of course, be performed. Thus, I have considered how scenes and devices are juxtaposed, and how the playwright provokes the reader or viewer to particular responses in a specific order.

Burke's own application to drama of the strategic method in his essay "Antony in Behalf of the Play" is one of the best pieces of evidence I can offer to illustrate the rich understanding this approach can yield in drama criticism. In a relatively brief article, Burke imagines a speech Antony might deliver to the theater audience to explain the strategy of the famous oration Antony gives in Shakespeare's script of *Julius Caesar*, Act III. Antony, as portrayed by Burke, becomes a "critical commentator *upon* the play, explaining its mechanism and its virtues."[2] The following excerpt, from the beginning of Antony's speech as conceived by Burke, illustrates one way in which a strategic analysis can be expressed:

Friends,   Romans,   countrymen . . . one-two-three   syllables: hence, in this progression, a magic formula. "Romans" to fit the conditions of the play, "countrymen" the better to identify the play-mob with the mob in the pit—for we are in the Renaissance, at that point when Europe's vast national integers are taking shape, and all the wisdom that comes of the body is to be obscured by our putting in the place of the body the political corpus, while we try to run this bigger hulk with the instincts for the little one— . . . Anyway, consider how much better my one-two-three arrangement is than was the opening salutation in Brutus' speech: "Romans, countrymen, lovers." He is an orator—but because you of England have thought the untrustworthy Latins eloquent, and because you don't think you are nearly so clever as you'd like to be, I shall seem closer to you if I apologize for bluntness. Yet, how much more competent my opening syllables are: how much *truer* since true to the processes of a spell, stressing a charm's *threeness*.[3]

Besides delighting the reader with the revelation of the specific intentions of Antony's seductive rhetoric, the passage suggests two fundamental aspects of strategic criticism. First, no word is irrelevant to a strategic criticism, and, in fact, it would be fruitful to consider every word. That, like Burke, I do not pay attention to every word in a script but, instead, search out larger groupings of words or particular words that make crucial differences in the whole of the play's strategy is a matter of limitations of time and space and not of critical theory. Second, although critics have aptly noted the affinities between Burke's work and structuralism,[4] neither Burke's criticism nor my own approach to the black dramas in this study is the same critical activity as that associated with such structuralists as Claude Levi-Strauss, Roman Jakobson, or (in a somewhat different direction) Roland Barthes.[5] I do not deny that in the example cited from the "Antony" speech Burke uses material and makes inferences similar to those a structuralist might use about the relationship of syllables and the formula of the words. But, unlike most structuralists, Burke does not conclude with these perceptions. Instead, he uses them to show how a given "formula" is intended to *affect an audience*.

My frequent use of various forms of the words "intention" and "effect" may raise for some readers the specters of Wimsatt and Beardsley.[6] When I speak of the "intentions" of a playwright or a play or the "effects" of that play on an audience, I am not committing what Wimsatt and Beardsley call the intentional and affective fallacies;[7] that is, I am not seeking the meaning of a work in evidence external to that work, such as an interview with the playwright or an observation of a specific audience. I am asserting that a script's meanings have to do with the interaction it evokes between the performance and the audience, not a set of ideas or conclusions. Further, I am arguing that a play works to move an audience in specific ways and that if such reaction does not occur, either the playwright has failed, the director has misinterpreted the script, or the audience is, for some reason, unable or unwilling to acknowledge the performance. Furthermore, I believe that readers *can* discover those intentions in a script with varying degrees of accuracy and profundity, depending on the complexity of the script and what knowledge and care they bring to it. I firmly believe, too, that the intentions we discover in a script will most frequently be those of the playwright, so that it is not an error to speak of the playwright's intentions. As Stanley Cavell states in his discussion of the limitations of Wimsatt and Beardsley's notions of intentionalism, "I do not wish to claim that everything we find in a work is something we have to be prepared to say the artist intended to put there. But I am claiming that our not being so prepared is not the inevitable state of affairs; rather it must be exceptional."[8]

But once I make clear that to discover intention I must look inside the work, the play, I return to the question "What is it I am looking for?" This suggests still another question: "How do I look?" The important understanding here is that I am not seeking a summarizing statement about the conflict or the conclusion of the play and thus am not attempting to draw lists of images, speeches, or actions from which I can synthesize. What I ask of the play is "What are this character, this set, these words doing to each other and to the spectator?" I call such questions matters of strategy. Furthermore, they are not concerned with the psychology of the playwright. My questions ask, "What do these words and gestures in this play do?"

The question "What does a play do?" is neither unique to my study nor drawn solely from the work of Kenneth Burke, but it is seldom posed. My emphasis on Burke is not meant to refute or belittle other examples of drama criticism that genuinely attempt to perceive a script as potential performance and as one pole in a dialogue with audiences. Burke's use of the *term* "strategy" and his detailed application of the strategic method in the "Antony" essay make his work most explicitly relevant to my approach to black drama, but the writings of J. L. Styan, Stanley Fish, and Stanley Cavell also bear mention.[9] Styan's *The Elements of Drama* overtly and consistently focuses on the relationship of script to audience. He sets out to look at the "elements of drama" as they are particular and unique in drama and as they are made such by their relationship to the audience. Styan's contention in his introduction to *The Elements of Drama*, quoted early in this study, seems to me worth repeating: "We are not judging the text, but what the text makes the actor make the audience do." This is remarkably similar to Stanley Fish's assertion that instead of asking of literature, "What does this sentence mean?" we should ask, "What does this sentence do?"[10] Fish's work is not concerned primarily with drama, but his argument that literature be approached "as an action made upon a reader rather than a container from which a reader extracts a message"[11] seems, in fact, particularly relevant to drama. We cannot conceive of theater without envisioning both actors and audience; some *inter*action between the two thus *seems* apparent. Yet traditionally we imagine the spectators, including ourselves, as passive, as removed from any action occurring on the stage.

Stanley Cavell writes especially lucidly of the spectator's perplexing activity in the theater.[12] He speaks of drama purposefully and persistently in terms of a play's presence to, and intentions toward, an audience. His assertion that "the first aesthetic fact about performances is that they have audiences"[13] may seem obvious, but it is exactly his understanding that the obvious must not be ignored that leads him to ask questions about audiences. And these questions in turn make the plays he examines remarkably accessible. What Cavell understands is that for the audience to be in a world separate from that onstage does not preclude the stage world from acting directly upon us.

I have emphasized the common concern with the relationships between script and audience that is apparent in the writings of Burke, Styan, Fish, and Cavell and that informed my own examinations of the seven black plays covered in this study. My approach, however, has also developed from my sense of the differences among these critics' methods. A full discussion of these differences would require another book, but some brief indications here may help the reader understand what I am attempting.

None of the critics mentioned has a wholly developed theory of drama, that is, a set of beliefs about what drama *is*. Fish does not even give particular mention to drama and so is not of immediate interest here. Each of the others, however, has a set of approaches, or a method, for getting at what a particular drama is doing, and often, as I have suggested, these approaches overlap. Of the critics mentioned, Kenneth Burke comes closest to offering a theory, although his theory is not restricted to drama. In an Aristotelian fashion, he sees all literature as the art of persuasion, meant to equip an audience for living. The central device he perceives in this art is identification. Thus, for Burke, the critic's task is to find the sources of identification, to be "concerned with a work's processes of appeal."[14] Burke's work, for which he openly claims the label "rhetorical criticism," is particularly appropriate to black drama because black playwrights and black aestheticians are less hesitant than most artists and theorists to think of their writing in terms of persuasion and equipment for living.[15]

J. L. Styan would probably not deny that his criticism is "concerned with a work's processes of appeal," but for Styan, the key word is "performance" not "rhetoric." Certainly performance and rhetoric can and do overlap, but "performance" suggests a fluid activity that is observed, whereas "rhetoric" connotes a set of devices that control. In the introduction to his *The Elements of Drama,* Styan says that the book rests on "a simple and empirical theory . . . that meaning is created in the theatre by putting two or more stage ingredients together for a spectator to observe."[16] I see this statement leading readers or spectators not to a theory of what drama is but to a useful method of analyzing a play. That is, we are shown by Styan how to infer from a script the various ingredients of a play, to put these together in such a way that we can imagine or judge a performance, and to see how these evoke a particular response in spectators. Styan's method might be called "performance-creating criticism."

In contrast to Styan and to a greater extent than Burke, Stanley Cavell is interested in what it means to be persuaded by a drama or to be an observer of a performance. Cavell does not attempt to extract meaning from a play, any more than Styan or Burke does or Stanley Fish would, but he is particularly concerned with what the activity of a drama *as meaning* makes possible (or impossible) for a person as he exists in the theater and outside it. Thus, while Cavell's comments on a particular line or scene might be identical with those of Burke or Styan, Cavell will go on to ask how the experience of the play reflects and alters the experiences of the world we live in. This is not remote from Burke's sense of literature as "equipment for living" or his emphasis on identification but is based on the interaction of acknowledgment rather than the manipulation of persuasion. Cavell himself calls his efforts "philosophical criticism."[17]

This study has been concerned with the sorts of understandings of self and the world made possible by each of the black dramas discussed. As Styan demonstrates acutely, such understandings are in response to the nonverbal as well as verbal ingredients of a play. My concentration on the ways each line or gesture in a play relates to what precedes and follows it, so that the spectator is led to specific responses, has been intended to reveal the plays' strategies. Once the reader has been shown a play's strategy, fully imagining or appreciating the play as a performance and asking the right questions about his responses can become natural and necessary elements of criticism.

NOTES

1. Kenneth Burke, *The Philosophy of Literary Form* (New York: Vintage, 1957), pp. 257–58. The italics in the passage are Burke's.
2. Kenneth Burke, p. 279.
3. *Ibid.*, pp. 279–80. The italics are Burke's.
4. William H. Rueckert, "Kenneth Burke and Structuralism," *Shenandoah*, 21 (Autumn 1969), 19–28.
5. Structuralist criticism has its own differences among its practitioners; two well-known but distinctly different examples are Roman Jakobson and Claude Levi-Strauss, " 'Les Chats' de Charles Baudelaire," *L'Homme*, 2 (January-April 1962), 5–21, and Roland Barthes, *Sur Racine* (New York: Hill & Wang, 1964), and *Writing Degree Zero and Elements of Semiology* (Boston: Beacon, 1970). It should be noted, however, that Barthe's more recent work has moved toward exploration of the text's relation to the audience.
6. See W. K. Wimsatt, Jr., and M. C. Beardsley, "The Intentional Fallacy," and "The Affective Fallacy," in *The Verbal Icon* (Lexington: University Press of Kentucky, 1954). Wimsatt and Beardsley, identified with the school of "new criticism," claim that there is a significant error in using biographical information, expressed intention, or impressions of emotional effects on a reader to judge the value of a work of art.
7. *Idem.*
8. Stanley Cavell, *Must We Mean What We Say?* (New York: Scribner's, 1969), p. 235. Note that Cavell's entire discussion of intentionalism is well worth reading for his understanding of the mistakes in Winsatt and Beardsley's arguments and for his own illumination of the word.
9. It is impossible to cite all of the writings on drama, not to mention conversations, that have stimulated or implemented my critical understandings, but those of Friedrich Nietzsche, Harley Granville-Barker, Elia Kazan, Tom Whitaker, and Michael Goldman, as well as those personally acknowledged previously, should surely be recalled here.
10. Stanley Fish, "Appendix," in *Self-consuming Artifacts* (Berkeley: University of California Press, 1972), p. 386; also appeared in *New Literary History*, 2 (Autumn 1970).
11. *Ibid.*
12. Although I cite particular passages and chapters from Cavell's *Must We Mean What We Say?* throughout this study, that book works better as a whole than its appearance as a collection of essays on topics from Wittgenstein to music to theater would suggest.
13. Cavell, *Must We Mean What We Say?* p. 156.
14. Burke, p. 279.
15. Helen Armstead Johnson, "Playwrights, Audiences and Critics," *Black World*, April 1970, pp. 17–24; Loften Mitchell, "I Work Here to Please You," in Addison Gayle, ed., *The Black Aesthetic* (New York: Doubleday,

1972), pp. 275–87. Mitchell has written many articles on black drama, and all deal at least tangentially with the problem of audience-script relationships.

16. Styan, p. 5.

17. Cavell, *Must We Mean What We Say?* pp. xviii, 313–14.

B | A SURVEY OF CRITICISM

THROUGHOUT THIS STUDY I have cited or referred to critics who have commented on black drama, but it was never appropriate to my discussion to survey the critical perspective on black drama. Because a summary of criticism and critics of black drama may be helpful to readers, I have appended the following comments on black-drama criticism. This appendix and the bibliography that follows it are meant to lead the reader to other understandings and information about black drama and should put my own work in some perspective.

My descriptions in the introduction to this book of the backgrounds of black drama are not a response to an abyss. Critical study of black drama is limited, but statements like one that was made by Douglas Turner Ward can be deceiving. In a *New York Times* article on the Negro Ensemble Company, Ward says, "If the history of the black theater movement is written, it would have to be written from white sources. This is a movement by blacks for blacks, but there is no black critical perspective."[1] I would guess that what Ward intends to suggest here is that the kinds of skills and knowledge necessary for such critical work have been demonstrated by white writers, at least in reference to works by white dramatists, whereas in neither scholarship nor journalism has there been much evidence of black writers committed to theater criticism. I find Ward's comment misleading, however, because it obscures the limitations and inaccuracies found in criticism of black drama by white critics (weaknesses that may well be the result of faulty scholarship and not necessarily a matter of distorted racial perspective) and because it ignores a number of pieces by black writers that, if certainly not sufficient, are indeed important.

As early as the 1920s, when white American drama was thriving and a great surge of literary activity among black men and women created the Harlem Renaissance, Alain Locke, one of the spokesmen of the period, prophesied a "dramatic renascence"[2] growing out of a

Negro "peasant folk art."[3] In 1925, Montgomery Gregory described briefly his perceptions of the beginnings of Negro drama (for him, this meant drama about or by blacks). He discussed the break with the minstrel tradition, the origin of "serious" Negro drama, and called for a national Negro theater with many small community branches.[4] Another significant contribution to black drama criticism came in 1937, when Sterling Brown completed both a bibliography of black poetry and drama and a study of black performers and black theater in *The Negro on the Stage*.[5]

I mention these early examples of commentary on black theater not to argue the existence of any substantial tradition of black drama criticism but to suggest that where and when such a tradition is assessed, it must account for a number of early and isolated pieces. The more complicated question then becomes whether or not a black critical perspective has been established in the significant quantity of writing on black drama since the late 1950s. What is clear is that after the popular success of Lorraine Hansberry's *A Raisin in the Sun* in 1959 and controversial productions five years later of Imamu Amiri Baraka's *Dutchman* and James Baldwin's *Blues for Mr. Charlie*, substantial numbers of play reviews and some more developed critiques did appear. Since 1964, at least twenty-five major productions of plays by black playwrights have gained box-office success in New York; many black dramas have received critical acclaim; numerous black community theaters have appeared or reappeared in towns and cities all over the country; more than a dozen anthologies of black drama have been compiled and published.

The greatly increased activity since the mid-1960s in black drama production and publication has elicited at least four different kinds of responses from critics. The most plentiful kind has been the play reviews, which now appear with consistency in black and white journals and newspapers. Most of the responses from white critics remain in the form of play reviews, but a few established critics—most notably, Robert Brustein, Harold Clurman, Richard Schechner, and Gerald Weales—have occasionally attempted longer and more analytical pieces. These writers focus their criticism on recognized black playwrights; Hansberry, Baraka, and Baldwin are the consistent choices. Minimal historical and comparative comments often surround plot explications intended simply to call attention to certain plays.[6] The only recent attempt by a white critic to do a thorough study of black drama has been Doris Abramson's *Negro Playwrights in the American Theatre, 1925–1959*, published in 1969. This work is comprehensive in its approach, combining historical, analytical, and evaluative discussions, but it suffers from some inaccuracies and omissions.[7]

In contrast to the emphases of white critics, black writers on black drama have been most concerned with the aesthetics and theoretical bases of an evolving black theater. Often writing from the perspective of their own experiences as black playwrights, such men as Baraka, Ed Bullins, Larry Neal, Hoyt Fuller, Ron Karenga, Addison Gayle, and Woodie King make up only a part of the growing list of black writers attempting to define and determine the evolution of black theater.[8] Although their views frequently differ and create a constant dialogue rather than a stance, they are all concerned with the discovery of appropriate forms, the political intent of black drama, and the nature of the audience *for* black drama.

Often similar in concern to the black playwrights and aestheticians of the 1960s and 1970s, but distinct in tone and approach, are the black scholars who have paid consistent attention to black drama. Loften Mitchell, Darwin T. Turner, Carlton Mollette, Clayton Riley, and Helen Armstead Johnson have made significant contributions to our knowledge of the history of black drama, and each has offered insightful if limited discussions of specific scripts.[9] Both Turner and Mitchell are particularly helpful in their suggestions of patterns in black drama: Turner's emphasis is more frequently on thematic and structural similarities and changes, whereas Mitchell focuses articulately on the social and political problems facing all those engaged in black theater.

Most striking and especially relevant to this study is the concern of these black scholar-critics with the problem of the relationship between black drama and its audience. Loften Mitchell and Helen Johnson are notably perceptive in their discussions of the manipulations of materials and problems of attitude facing black playwrights.[10] Unlike many white critics writing on white or black drama, Mitchell and Johnson emphasize the need to scrutinize the relationship of drama to audience, not just after a play is performed but in discussing the scripts as well.

NOTES

1. Mel Gussow, "Negro Ensemble Finds Hit Play Poses Problem," *New York Times*, February 7, 1973, p. 30. The quotation is taken from an interview with Ward in which he discusses the problem faced by him and the Negro Ensemble Company when a production becomes a hit. The commitment of the NEC is to the nurturing of new scripts and talents, not, Ward says, to the promotion of "success and career." But the company needs money and hits bring money, so a success creates a dilemma.

   An obscurity in the quotation is that it is unclear whether by "black theatre" Ward means all drama written by blacks or only the theater of the 1960s, Black Arts Theatre, or something else.

2. Alain Locke, "The Negro in the American Theatre," in *The Black Aesthetic*, Addison Gayle, ed. (New York: Doubleday, 1972), p. 256.

3. *Ibid.*

4. Montgomery Gregory, "The Drama of Negro Life," in *Black Expression*, Addison Gayle, ed. (New York: Weybright & Talley, 1969), pp. 128–233.

5. Sterling Brown, *Negro Poetry and Drama* (Washington, D.C.: Associates in Negro Folk Education, 1937). This is a critical as well as bibliographic study. Also *The Negro on the Stage* (1937), materials compiled for the Carnegie-Myrdal study and available on microfilm from several university libraries.

6. For further details on the criticism of black drama by white critics, see both the introduction (Chapter 1) and separate entries in my bibliography of black drama, *Bulletin of The New York Public Library* (Winter 1974–75).

7. This may be the time to assert that my work is not meant as an argument against or refutation of Abramson's book, which I see as moving in essentially different directions from my own. Omissions such as the failure to mention Willis Richardson, however, should be remarked.

8. The names of Marvin X, Clayton Riley, and Ronald Milner could easily be added to this list. I refer the reader again to my bibliography and to such journals as *Black Theatre*, *Black World*, and *Black Creation*.

9. Willis Richardson, Langston Hughes, Theodore Ward, Louis Peterson, William Branch, and Alice Childress are among the playwrights who receive some attention from black scholars and little attention elsewhere.

10. Helen Armstead Johnson, "Playwrights, Audiences and Critics," *Black World* (April 1970), 17–24. Loften Mitchell, "I Work Here to Please You," in *The Black Aesthetic*, Addison Gayle, ed. (New York: Doubleday, 1972), pp. 275–87. Mitchell has written many articles on black drama, and all deal at least tangentially with the problem of audience-script relationships.

BIBLIOGRAPHY

ANTHOLOGIES

The anthologies listed here are restricted to anthologies of black American drama; not included are anthologies of black American literature that include drama. Contents of each anthology are listed after publication information.

A Black Quartet: Four New Black Plays by Ben Caldwell, Ronald Milner, E. Bullins and LeRoi Jones. Introduction by Clayton Riley (New York: New American Library, 1970).
> Ben Caldwell, *Prayer Meeting, or, The First Militant Minister*
> Ed Bullins, *The Gentleman Caller*
> Ronald Milner, *The Warning—A Theme for Linda*
> LeRoi Jones, *Great Goodness of Life (A Coon Show)*

ADAMS, WILLIAM, et al., eds. *Afro-American Literature: Drama* (Boston: Houghton Mifflin, 1970).
> Lorraine Hansberry, *A Raisin in the Sun*
> Loften Mitchell, *A Land Beyond the River*
> Ossie Davis, *Purlie Victorious*

BRASMER, WILLIAM, and DOMINICK CONSOLO, eds. *Black Drama: An Anthology.* Introduction by Darwin T. Turner (Columbus, Ohio: Merrill, 1970).
> Langston Hughes, *Mulatto*
> Douglas Turner Ward, *Day of Absence*
> Adrienne Kennedy, *Funnyhouse of a Negro*
> Ossie Davis, *Purlie Victorious*
> Ted Shine, *Contribution*

This bibliography was first published, with an introductory essay and illustrations, in the *Bulletin of The New York Public Library* 78:iii (Spring 1975) 276–346, and is reprinted with the permission of The New York Public Library and the successor journal, *Bulletin of Research in the Humanities.*

BULLINS, ED, ed. *The New Lafayette Theatre Presents; Plays with Aesthetic Comments by 6 Black Playwrights: Ed Bullins, J. E. Gaines, Clay Goss, Oyamo, Sonia Sanchez, Richard Wesley* (Garden City, N.Y.: Anchor, 1974).

BULLINS, ED, ed. *New Plays From the Black Theatre* (New York: Bantam, 1961).

      Malcolm X, "Interview with Ed Bullins" (Introduction)
      LeRoi Jones, *The Death of Malcolm X*
      Kingsley B. Bass, Jr., *We Righteous Bombers*
      Sonia Sanchez, *Sister Son/ji*
      Marvin X, *The Black Bird*
      Herbert Stokes, *The Man Who Trusted the Devil Twice*
      Ed Bullins, *In New England Winter*
      Ben Caldwell, *The King of Soul or The Devil and Otis Redding; Family Portrait of My Son the Black Nationalist*
      Salimu, *Growin' into Blackness*
      N. R. Davidson, Jr., *El Hajj Malik*
      Charles H. Fuller, Jr., *The Rise*

CHILDRESS, ALICE, ed. *Black Scenes: Collections of Scenes from Plays Written by Black People About Black Experience* (New York: Doubleday, 1971).

COUCH, WILLIAM, JR., ed. *New Black Playwrights* (Baton Rouge: Louisiana University Press, 1968).

      Douglas Turner Ward, *Happy Ending*
      Adrienne Kennedy, *A Rat's Mass*
      Lonne Elder III, *Ceremonies in Dark Old Men*
      Ed Bullins, *Goin' a Buffalo*
      William Wellington Mackey, *Family Meeting*

HATCH, JAMES VERNON, and TED SHINE, eds. *Black Theater, U.S.A.; Forty-five plays by Black Americans 1847–1972* (New York: Free Press, 1974).

JONES, LEROI, and LARRY NEAL, eds. *Black Fire: An Anthology of Afro-American Writing* (New York: Morrow, 1968).

      Jimmy Garrett, *We Own the Night*
      Marvin E. Jackmon, *Flowers for the Trashman*
      Charles Patterson, *Black-Ice*
      Ronald Drayton, *Notes from a Savage God; Nocturne on the Rhine*
      LeRoi Jones, *Madheart*
      Ben Caldwell, *Prayer Meeting, or, The First Militant Minister*
      Ed Bullins, *How Do You Do*
      Joseph White, *The Leader*
      Carol Freeman, *The Suicide*

The exception to the rule of inclusions stated at the start of this section, because it contains so many works not published elsewhere.

KING, WOODIE, JR., and RON MILNER, eds. *Black Drama Anthology* (New York: Columbia University Press, 1971).

      LeRoi Jones, *Junkies are Full of (Shhh. . . . .); Bloodrites*
      Archie Shepp, *Junebug Graduates Tonight*
      Ed Bullins, *The Corner*

Ron Milner, *Who's Got His Own*
Lonne Elder, *Charades on East Fourth Street*
Clifford Mason, *Gabriel*
Douglas Turner Ward, *Brotherhood*
Oliver Pitcher, *The One*
Donald Greaves, *The Marriage*
Philip Hayes Dean, *The Owl Killer*
William Wellington Mackey, *Requiem for Brother X, a Homage to Malcolm X*
Joseph A. Walker, *Ododo*
Ben Caldwell, *All White Caste*
Langston Hughes, *Mother and Child*
Charles Gordon (Oyama), *The Breakout*
Ron Zuber, *Three X Love*
William Branch, *A Medal for Willie*
Peter DeAnda, *Ladies in Waiting*
Martie Charles, *Black Cycle*
Loften Mitchell, *Star of Morning*
Elaine Jackson, *Toe Jam*
LOCKE, ALAIN, and MONTGOMERY GREGORY, eds. *Plays of Negro Life: A Sourcebook of Native American Drama* (New York: Harper Bros., 1927).
Willis, Richardson, *The Flight of the Natives*
Frank H. Wilson, *Sugar Cane*
John Matheus, *Cruiter*
Eulalie Spence, *The Starter*
Jean Toomer, *Balo*
Thelma Duncan, *The Death Dance*
Georgia Douglas Johnson, *Plumes*
Also contains some plays by white American playwrights, which are not listed above.
MITCHELL, LOFTEN, ed. *Voices of the Black Theatre* (Clifton, N.J.: James T. White, 1975).
OLIVER, CLINTON F., ed. *Contemporary Black Drama from A Raisin in the Sun to No Place to Be Somebody.* Introduction by Clinton F. Oliver; Stephanie Sills, coeditor (New York: Scribner's, 1971).
Lorraine Hansberry, *A Raisin in the Sun*
Ossie Davis, *Purlie Victorious*
Adrienne Kennedy, *Funnyhouse of a Negro*
LeRoi Jones, *Dutchman*
James Baldwin, *Blues for Mr. Charlie*
Douglas Turner Ward, *Happy Ending; Day of Absence*
Ed Bullins, *The Gentleman Caller*
Charles Gordone, *No Place to Be Somebody*
PATTERSON, LINDSAY, ed. *Black Theatre: A 20th Century Collection of the Work of Its Best Playwrights* (New York: Dodd, Mead, 1971).
Arna Bontemps and Countee Cullen, *St. Louis Woman*
Louis Peterson, *Take a Giant Step*

William Branch, *In Splendid Error*
Alice Childress, *Trouble in Mind*
Langston Hughes, *Simply Heavenly*
Lorraine Hansberry, *A Raisin in the Sun*
Ossie Davis, *Purlie Victorious*
LeRoi Jones, *Dutchman*
James Baldwin, *The Amen Corner*
Ed Bullins, *In the Wine Time*
Charles Gordone, *No Place to Be Somebody*
Lonne Elder, *Ceremonies in Dark Old Men*

RICHARDSON, WILLIS, ed. *Plays and Pageants from the Life of the Negro* (Washington, D.C.: Associated, 1930).

Thelma Duncan, *Sacrifice*
John Matheus, *Ti Yette*
May Miller, *Graven Images; Riding the Goat*
Willis Richardson, *The Black Horseman; The House of Sham; The King's Dilemma*
Maude Cuney-Hare, *Antar of Araby*

Includes some pageants and plays by nonblack American playwrights, which are not listed above.

RICHARDSON, WILLIS, and MAY MILLER, eds. *Negro History in Thirteen Plays* (Washington, D.C.: Associated, 1935).

Willis Richardson, *Antonio Maceo; Attucks, the Martyr; The Elder Dumas; Near Calvary; In Menelek's Court*
Georgia Douglas Johnson, *Frederick Douglass; William and Ellen Craft*
Randolph Edmonds, *Nat Turner*
Helen Webb Harris, *Genifrede*
May Miller, *Christophe's Daughters; Harriet Tubman; Samory; Sojourner Truth*

TURNER, DARWIN T., ed. *Black Drama in America: An Anthology.* Introduction by Darwin T. Turner (New York: Fawcett, 1971).

Willis Richardson, *The Chip Woman's Fortune*
Langston Hughes, *Emperor of Haiti*
Theodore Ward, *Our Lan'*
Owen Dodson, *Bayou Legend*
Louis Peterson, *Take a Giant Step*
Randolph Edmonds, *Earth and Stars*
Ossie Davis, *Purlie Victorious*
LeRoi Jones, *The Toilet*
Kingsley B. Bass, Jr., *We Righteous Bombers*

GENERAL HISTORY AND CRITICISM

Books

ABRAMSON, DORIS E. *Negro Playwrights in the American Theatre, 1925–1959* (New York: Columbia University Press, 1969). A critical history of dramas by Afro-Americans produced in the professional theater in New York City between 1925 and 1959. Attempts to interrelate these plays and to place them in a social and political context.

ADAMS, WILLIAM, et al. *Afro-American Literature: Drama (Afro-American Literature Series)* (New York: Houghton Mifflin, 1970). This appears to be a textbook for grades 9–12.

ARATA, ESTHER S., and NICHOLAS J. RITOLI. *Black American Playwrights, 1800 to the Present: A Bibliography* (Meachen, N.J.: Scarecrow, 1976).

BIGSBY, C.W.E., ed. *The Black American Writer* (Deland, Fla.: Everett Edwards, 1970). Vol. 1—Fiction; Vol. 2—Poetry and Drama. A collection of essays and articles. Pieces relevant to drama are annotated separately under the appropriate author.

BOND, FREDERICH WELDON. *The Negro and the Drama: The Direct and Indirect Contribution Which the American Negro Has Made to Drama and the Legitimate Stage with the Underlying Conditions Responsible* (College Park, Md.: McGrath, 1969; originally published Washington, D.C.: Associated Publishers, 1940).

BONTEMPS, ARNA, and JACK CONROY. *Anyplace But Here* (New York: Hill & Wang, 1965). Chapter on Karamu, pp. 206–12.

BRADY, OWEN E., III. "The Consciousness Epic: LeRoi Jones' Use of American Myth and Ritual in *The Baptism, The Toilet, Dutchman, The Slave* and *A Recent Killing*. Ph.D. dissertation, University of Notre Dame, 1973.

BROWN, STERLING A. *The Negro in American Fiction and Negro Poetry and Drama;* two volumes in one (New York: Arno, 1964).

CARTER-HARRISON, PAUL. *The Drama of Nommo* (New York: Grove Press, 1972).

CLARKE, JOHN HENRIK. *Harlem U.S.A.* (New York: Seven Seas Books, 1964).

Conference of Negro Writers, First, New York, 1959. *The American Negro Writer and His Roots: Selected Papers.* (New York: American Society of African Culture, 1960). Collection of essays by black authors about black writers and their heritage, present situation, problems, and opportunities.

DAVIS, JOHN T. *The American Negro Reference Book* (Englewood Cliffs, N.J.: Prentice-Hall, 1966). One-volume "encyclopedia" of articles and "facts about American Negroes."

DENT, THOMAS C., RICHARD SCHECHNER, and GILBERT MOSES. *The Free*

Southern Theatre by the Free Southern Theatre: A Documentary of the South's Radical Black Theatre, with Journals, Letters, Poetry, Essays and a Play Written by Those Who Built It (New York: Bobbs-Merrill, 1969).

Dictionary Catalog of the Schomburg Collection of Negro Literature and History (Boston: G.K. Hall, 1962), plus supplements 1 and 2 (1967, 1970, 1972).

GAYLE, ADDISON, JR., ed. *The Black Aesthetic* (New York: Doubleday, 1972). Contains articles relevant to black drama annotated separately under appropriate author. Includes a variety of aesthetic perspectives with emphasis on black arts movement.

GAYLE, ADDISON, JR., ed. *Black Expression: Essays by and About Black Americans in the Creative Arts* (New York: Weybright & Talley, 1969). Contains critical, historical and theoretical articles. Those relevant to black drama have been annotated separately under the appropriate author.

GIBSON, DONALD B., ed. *Five Black Writers: Essays on Wright, Ellison, Baldwin, Hughes and LeRoi Jones.* Introduction by Donald B. Gibson (New York: New York University Press, 1970). Articles relevant to black drama include Schneck, Costello, and Heal on Jones, Davis on Hughes's *Mulatto.*

HATCH, JAMES VERNON. *Black Image on the American Stage: A Bibliography of Plays and Musicals, 1770–1970* (New York: DBS Publications, 1970).

HILL, HERBERT. *Anger and Beyond: The Negro Writer in the United States* (New York: Harper & Row, 1966). Contains essays relevant to black drama, annotated under appropriate author.

HUGHES, LANGSTON, and MILTON MELTZER. *Black Magic: A Pictorial History of the Negro in American Entertainment* (Englewood Cliffs, N.J.: Prentice-Hall, 1967). A historical account of entertainment personalities, theatrical events, companies, and theaters, with some mention of playwrights and many illustrations.

MITCHELL, LOFTEN. *Black Drama: The Story of the American Negro in the Theatre* (New York: Hawthorne, 1967). A historical account of personalities and events in Afro-American theater, with the stress on theater. Contains personal reminiscences and anecdotes.

The Negro Handbook. Compiled by the editors of *Ebony* (Chicago: Johnson, 1966). See Section 14, on creative arts, pp. 355–73.

The Negro in the United States: A List of Significant Books, 9th rev. ed. (New York: New York Public Library, 1965). A quinquennial.

O'DANIEL, THERMAN B. *Langston Hughes: Black Genius; A Critical Evaluation* (New York: Morrow, 1971). Includes Darwin T. Turner's "Langston Hughes as Playwright," listed and annotated under Hughes in the playwrights list.

PATTERSON, LINDSAY. *Anthology of the American Negro in the Theatre,* vol. 4 of *International Library of Negro Life and History.* Compiled under the auspices of The Association for the Study of Negro Life and History (New

York: Publishers Company, 1967–68). Includes critical, historical, and theoretical essays of major scholarly significance, annotated under the appropriate author.

PLOSKI, HARRY A., and ERNEST KAISER, eds. *The Negro Almanac*, 2d ed. (New York: Bellwether, 1971).

RALPH, GEORGE. *The American Theatre, the Negro, and the Movement* (Chicago: City Missionary Society, 1964). A bibliography with detailed references.

REARDON, WILLIAM, and THEODORE HATLEN. "The Black Teacher and the Drama." Pamphlet, University of California at Santa Barbara (October, 1968).

SANDLE, FLOYD L. *The Negro in the American Educational Theatre: An Organizational Development: 1911–1964* (Ann Arbor: Edwards Bros., 1964).

SELBY, JOHN. *Beyond Civil Rights* (Cleveland: World, 1966). A history of Karamu House with photographs.

TURNER, DARWIN T., ed. *Afro-American Writers*. Goldentree Bibliographies in Language and Literature (New York: Appleton-Century-Crofts, 1970). Includes primary and secondary bibliographical entries on Afro-American drama and all other areas of Afro-American literature.

WEAKES, GERALD. *The Jumping-Off Place: American Drama in the 1960's* (London: Collier-Macmillan, 1969).

WELSCH, ERWIN K. *The Negro in the United States: A Research Guide* (Bloomington: Indiana University Press, 1965).

Scholarly Theses and Dissertations

BADARES, LESLIE. "Oh, Freedom: Theoretical and Practical Problems of the Transformation of Three American Slave Narratives into Original Plays for Young People." Ph.D. dissertation, New York University, 1973.

BELCHER, FANNIN SAFFORE, JR. "The Place of the Negro in the Evaluation of the American Theatre, 1767–1940." Ph.D. dissertation, Yale University, 1945, *ca.* 1969; Ann Arbor: University Microfilms, 1969 (Microfilm-Positive), 1 reel (Publication No. 17658).

BLITZGEN, SISTER MARY JOHN CAROL. "Voices of Protest: An Analysis of the Negro Protest Plays of the 1963–64 Broadway and Off-Broadway Season." Master's thesis, University of Kansas, 1966.

BRADLEY, GERALD S., JR. "The Negro in American Theatre." Master's thesis, Carnegie Institute of Technology, 1963.

COLLE, ROYAL. "Negro Image and the Mass Media." Ph.D. dissertation, Cornell University, 1967. Discusses newspaper, magazine, film, radio, and TV images of black people.

COLLINS, JOHN D. "American Drama in Anti-Slavery Agitation." Ph.D. dissertation, State University of Iowa, 1963. Argues that abolition playwrights were generally successful in adapting drama to persuasive ends.

DAVIS, BROTHER JOSEPH MORGAN. "A Compilation and Analysis Concerning the Contributions of the Negro to the American Theatre in 1950–60." Master's thesis, Catholic University, 1962.

EIKLEBERRY, BURTON. "The Negro Actor's Participation and the Negro Image on the New York Stage, 1954–1964." Master's thesis, University of Kansas, 1965.

GOODMAN, GERALD THOMAS. "The Black Theatre Movement," Ph.D. dissertation, University of Pennsylvania, 1974.

GROSSMAN, SAMUEL LARRY. "Trends in the Avant Garde Theatre of the United States During the 1960s." Ph.D. dissertation, University of Minnesota, 1974. Includes a study of five playwrights: Sam Shepard, Adrienne Kennedy, Rosalyn Drexler, Maria I. Fornes, Ronald Tavel.

HALEY, ELSIE GALBREATH. "The Black Revolutionary Theatre: LeRoi Jones, Ed Bullins and Minor Playwrights." Ph.D. dissertation, University of Denver, 1971. An account of the evolution and aesthetics of the Black Arts Movement with particular emphasis on Black Revolutionary Theatre. Includes critical comments on plays by Jones, Bullins, and a number of minor playwrights of the late 1960s and early 1970s.

HALL, FREDERICK DOUGLASS. "The Black Theatre in New York from 1960–1969." Ed.D. dissertation, Columbia University, 1973.

HARDWICK, MARY R. "The Nature of the Negro Hero in Serious American Drama, 1910–1964." Ph.D. dissertation, Michigan State University, 1968. Examines Negro male hero in dramas written by Negroes. "Aims at lending new and positive insights into the needs, desires, dreams, direction and future of the Negro in relation not only to his society but to himself." Comments particularly on Jones's *Dutchman*, *The Toilet*, and *The Slave*, and Baldwin's *Blues for Mr. Charlie*.

HICKLIN, FANNIE E. F. "The American Negro Playwright, 1920–1964." Ph.D. dissertation, University of Wisconsin, 1965. An excellent source for information about black plays and playwrights. Attempts to place black drama in context of other genres of black literature and white American drama. Well-researched appendix listing black American plays 1920–64 is a good source for unpublished manuscripts.

HILL, EDWARD STEVEN. "A Thematic Study of Selected Plays Produced by the Negro Ensemble Company." Ph.D. dissertation, Bowling Green State University, 1975.

JEYIFONS, BIODUN. "Theatre and Drama and the Black Physical and Cultural Presence in America: Essays in Interpretation." Ph.D. dissertation, New York University, 1975.

JONES, NORMA RAMSAY. "The Image of the 'White Liberal' in Black American Fiction and Drama." Ph.D. dissertation, Bowling Green State University, 1973.

KEYSSAR-FRANKE, HELENE. "Strategies in Black Drama." Ph.D. dissertation, University of Iowa, 1974.

LAWSON, HILDA JOSEPHINE. "The Negro in American Drama." Ph.D. dissertation, University of Illinois, 1939. A bibliography of contemporary Negro drama.

OGURBIY, YEMI. "New Black Playwrights in America (1960–1975): Essays in Theatrical Criticism." Ph.D. dissertation, New York University, 1976. .

PITTS, ETHEL LOUISE. "The American Negro Theatre: 1940–1949." Ph.D. dissertation, University of Missouri, 1975.

ROBINSON, EDWARD ARLEN. "Toward a Theory of the Utilization of Afro-American Drama in Education: Perspective for Teaching." Ph.D. dissertation, University of Arizona, 1974.

SHERMAN, ALFONSO. "The Treatment of the Negro Character in American Drama Prior to 1860." Ph.D. dissertation, Indiana University, 1964. Describes historical background of Negro in America and discusses the relationship to colonial theater. "Negro characters were never truly described because there was no voice to speak for them." Does not discuss black American playwrights.

SILVER, REUBEN. "A History of the Karamu Theatre of Karamu House, 1915–1960." Ph.D. dissertation, Ohio State University, 1961.

SIMPLETON, CAROLE WATERS. "Black Theatre as Cultural Communication: An Educative Process." Ph.D. dissertation, University of Maryland, 1975.

THOMAS, MARJORIE ANN. "An Overview of Miss Anne: White Women as Seen by Black Playwrights." Ph.D. dissertation, Florida State University, 1973.

THOMPSON, SISTER FRANCESCA. "The Lafayette Players, 1915–1932: America's First Dramatic Stock Co." Ph.D. dissertation, University of Michigan, 1972.

WILLIAMS, JOHN ROOSEVELT. "Modes of Alienation of the Black Writer: Problems and Solutions in the Evolution of Black Drama and Contemporary Black Theatre." Ph.D. dissertation, McGill University, 1974.

WOODS, PORTER A. "The Negro on Broadway. Transition Years, 1920–1930." D.F.A. dissertation, Yale University, 1965.

ZIELTON, EDWARD ROBERT. "Wright to Hansberry: The Evolution of Outlook in Four Negro Writers." Ph.D. dissertation, University of Washington, 1967.

Articles and Essays

This section includes articles and essays of a general or comprehensive nature, including theory, criticism, and history. Also listed here are articles that make superficial reference to particular playwrights or include too many playwrights to be usefully cross-referenced in the listing by playwrights in the next section of this bibliography.

The following abbreviations for names of periodicals have been used. In citations of periodicals, after the abbreviated name appear the volume number, publication date, and page numbers, in that order.

A	America	L	The Liberator
AF	African Forum: A	MD	Modern Drama
	Quarterly Journal of	N	The Nation
	Contemporary	NALF	Negro American
	Affairs		Literature Forum
AR	The Antioch Review	NAR	North American Review
BT	Black Theatre	NHB	Negro History Bulletin
BW	Black World	NR	The New Republic
C	The Crisis	Nw	Newsweek
CLAJ	College Language	NYr	The New Yorker
	Association Journal	NYRB	New York Review of
Ct	Commentary		Books
Cw	Commonweal	NYTM	New York Times
Cy	Community		Magazine
E	Ebony	O	Opportunity
Es	Esquire	P	Phylon
F	Freedomways	PW	Publishers Weekly
H	Harper's Magazine	R	Ramparts Magazine
J	Jet	S	Sepia
JBS	Journal of Black Studies	SR	Saturday Review
JHR	Journal of Human	T	Time
	Relations	TDR	The Drama Review
JNE	Journal of Negro		(formerly Tulane
	Education		Drama Review)
JNH	Journal of Negro		
	History		

ABRAMSON, DORIS E. "Negro Playwrights in America," *Columbia University Forum*, 12 (Spring 1969):11–17.

ADAMS, G. R. "Black Militant Drama," *American Image* 28 (Summer 1971):107–28. Bibliographical footnote.

"Advent of the Negro Actor on the Legitimate Stage in America," *JNE* 35 (Summer 1966):237–45.

"African-American Cultural Exchange," *E* 17 (March 1962):87–94. Describes festival in Lagos, which sought comparisons by pairing African and American artists in same category. Many pictures. Includes comments from two Lagos newspapers that panned festival for poor selection of artists and weak organization.

"Annual Round-Up: Black Theater in America" (Peter Bailey, Francis and Val Gray Ward, Kalamu Ya Salaam, Jeanne-Marie A. Miller, and Richard Wesley), *BW* 21 (April 1972): 31–48, 70–74. Reviews black-theater activities of 1971 in New York City, Chicago, New Orleans, Washington, D.C. Bailey comments on great quantity of black drama in 1971, accented by "telling it like it is." Notes formation of Black Theatre Alliance and of Black Theatre Workshop in Harlem. Calls for sense of responsibility in black playwrights. Asserts invalidity of Western aesthetics for black art.

"Apollo: Mecca of Black Show Business; Excerpts from Uptown; the Story of Harlem's Apollo Theatre," *E* 26 (April 1971):114–16.

"Apollo Story," *S* 15 (January 1966):14–20.

APTHEKER, HERBERT. "Afro-American Superiority: A Neglected Theme in the Literature," *P* 31 (Winter 1970):336–43.

BAILEY, PETER. "Black Theater," *E* 24 (August 1969):126–28ff.

———. "Black Theatre in America: Metropolitan New York," *BW* 20 (April 1971):4–8. Reviews of plays by and about black people in 1970. Pans *Purlie* but remarks its popular success with black audiences. Urges more black music in black theater. Lauds Baraka's *Slaveship* as great political theater, calls *King Heroin* best play of year. Says Bullins's plays at New Lafayette are too talky and Negro Ensemble Company doesn't know where it's at. Black theater groups need to work together and offer solutions to problems.

———. "The Importance of Being Black," *Nw* 73 (February 24, 1969):102–3.

———. "Is the Negro Ensemble Company *Really* Black Theatre?" *BW* 17 (April 1968):16–19.

———. "Report on Black Theatre: New York," *BW* 18 (April 1969):20–23.

"Bar Stool in a Black Hell," *T* 93 (May 16, 1968): 85–86.

BARKSDALE, RICHARD K. "White Tragedy—Black Comedy," *P* (third quarter 1961):226–33.

BARROW, WILLIAM. "Gallery of Leading Men," *BW* 12 (October 1963): 45–48.

———. "Introducing the Concept: New Theatre in Detroit," *BW* 12 (May 1963):77–79.

———. "Man of Many Faces: Frank Silvera," *BW* 12 (September 1963): 40–43.

BIGSBY, C. W. E. "Black Drama in the Seventies," *Kansas Quarterly* 3 (Spring 1971):10–20.

"Black Drama Finds New Audience," *Race Relations Reporter* 4-6 (February 7, 1972).

"The Black Entertainer in the Performing Arts," in *The Negro Almanac* 2d ed., pp. 745–53.

"Black Playwrights Get a Break," *S* 17 (November 1968):20–23.

"Black Theater—A Bid For Cultural Identity," *Black Enterprise* 1 (September 1971):30–34, 44.

"Black Theatre: A Need for the Seventies" *Soul Illustrated* 2, No. 3 (1970):38–94.

"Black Theatre—An Evolving Force," in Rhoda L. Goldstein *Black Life & Culture in the U.S.* (New York: Crowell, 1971).

"Black Theatre in America: A Report" (by Peter Bailey, Val Ferdinand, Harry Dolan and Hoyt W. Fuller), *BW* 19 (April 1970):25–37, 42,85,98. Reviews black theater of 1969, describes continuing financial problems of black theater. Challenges white critics' praise for *No Place to Be Somebody*; says play is full of contempt for blacks. Describes failures, successes, and activities of black theater groups around the country.

"Black Theatre in the Black Colleges," *Tuesday Magazine* (August 1972):10.

"The Blacks (Off-Broadway Stage)," *E* 17 (September 1962):47–53. Comments on success of the play despite audiences being mostly white and Genet's view being harsh to whites. Says play creates feelings of guilt, indignation, even fear in white audiences.

BONTEMPS, ARNA. "Harlem in the Twenties," *C* 73:431–34, 451–56. Traces the folk origins and literary background of Harlem Renaissance. Mentions shows and entertainers of the 1920s.

———. "The Negro Contribution to American Letters," in Davis, *The American Negro Reference Book*, pp. 850–78.

BRADLEY, GERALD. "Goodbye, Mr. Bones. The Emergence of Negro Themes and Characters in American Drama," *Drama Critique* 7 (Spring 1964) 79–85. Concern is with years 1893–1917, when minstrel shows were crumbling and plays by O'Neill and others were gaining attention. Traces plays with Negro themes of the nineteenth century.

"Breaking New Ground: Ford Foundation Grant to Establish Negro Ensemble Company," *Nw* 69 (May 29, 1967):90.

BROWN, LLOYD W. "The Cultural Revolution in Black Theatre" *NALF* 8 (1974):159–64.

BROWN, MARION E. "The Negro in the Fine Arts," in Davis, *The American Negro Reference Book*, pp. 766–74.

BROWN, STERLING A. "Negro in the American Theatre," in *The Oxford Companion to the Theatre* 3d ed. (London: Oxford University Press, 1967), pp. 672–79.

BRUSTEIN, ROBERT SANFORD. "The Negro Revolution," in Robert S. Brustein, ed., *The Third Theatre* (New York: Knopf, 1969), pp. 107–51.

BULLINS, ED. "Black Theatre Groups: A Directory" *TDR* 12 (Summer 1968):172–75. A limited list of black theater groups essentially playing in black communities. Arranged geographically, includes some annotation.

———. "Black Theatre Notes," *BT* 1 (October 1968):4–7. Introductory editorial to Bullins's *Black Theatre*. Describes his tensions with established white New York theater, particularly his reasons for being unwilling to participate in O'Neill Foundation panel. Makes interesting contrast of white audience to black and pans Clifford Mason's *Sister Sadie and the Sons of S*.

CADE, TONI. "Black Theater," in Gayle, *Black Expression*, pp. 134–43. Traces the evolution and shaping of black theater in the 1960s. Comments particularly on Douglas Turner Ward and Ed Bullins.

CAMPBELL, DICK. "Is There a Conspiracy Against Black Playwrights?" *BW* 17 (April 1968):11–15.

CLARKE, SEBASTIAN. "Black Theatre," *Plays & Players* 22 (August 1975):33–4.

CLAYBORNE, JON L. "Modern Black Drama and the Gay Image," *College English* 36 (November 1974):381–84.

CLAYTON, EDWARD T. "The Tragedy of Amos and Andy," *E* 12 (October 1961):66–73.

CLURMAN, HAROLD. "Theatre," *N* 200 (January 4, 1965):16–17.

———. "Theatre," *N* 208 (May 12, 1969):612–13.

"Committee for the Employment of the Negro Performer" (CENP), *F* 2 (Spring 1962):310.

COTTON, LETTIE JO. "The Negro in the American Theatre," *NHB* 23 (May 1960):172–78.

COUCH, WILLIAM, JR. "Introduction," *New Black Playwrights*, pp. ix–xxiii. Laments lack of attention and respect for Negro playwrights in selective historical account of black drama. Comments briefly on each of the plays anthologized and applauds "renewal of strength of black playwrights."

DAVIS, OSSIE. "The English Language is My Enemy," *NHB* 30 (April 1967):18.

———. "Flight from Broadway," *BW* 15 (April 1966):14–19. Recalls value of earlier Harlem community theaters—Rose McClendon Players and American Negro Theater—and calls for recognition of Broadway's limitations and the establishment of new Harlem community theater.

———. "The Wonderful World of Law and Order," in Hill, *Anger and Beyond*, pp. 154–80. Conversational essay discusses protest content of Negro humor, particularly in Step'n Fetchit and Davis's *Purlie Victorious*.

DENT, TOM. "Beyond Rhetoric Toward a Black Southern Theatre," *BQ* 20 (April 1971):14–24. Dent describes the conflict between making Free Southern Theatre a New York-based touring company or a New Orleans, southern black troupe. He advocates the second, emphasizes prior clear existence of southern community and culture. Search for drama to satisfy black needs, natural to black people, a place of communion. Helpfully outlines goals of black theater as he sees it. Briefly reviews new theater groups in the South.

———. "The Free Southern Theatre," *BW* 16 (April 1967):40–44ff. Discusses the founding and growth of the Free Southern Theatre from February 1967 on; tells of the theater's involvement with the community and calls for more community-connected theater.

DICKSTEIN, MORRIS. "Black Aesthetic in White America," *Partisan Review* 38 (Winter 1971–72):376–95.

"Digging it: Washington's DIG*IT Troupe," *NW* 75 (April 27, 1970):64ff.

DIXON, MELVIN. "Black Theatre: The Aesthetics," *BW* 18 (July 1969):41–44.

DODSON, OWEN. "Playwrights in Dark Glasses," *BW* 17 (April 1968):31–36.

"Drama in Black Colleges: Black Faces or White Masks?" *Black Collegian* (January-February 1972, March-April 1972):29–30, 51.

DUBERMAN, MARTIN. "History and Theatre," *Columbia University Forum* 10 (Fall 1967):3.

———. "Theater 69: Black Theatre," *Partisan Review* 36 (1969):488.

DUBOIS, W. E. B. "Criteria of Negro Art," *C* (May 1922).

ELDER, LONNE. "A Negro Idea Theatre," *American Dialog* 1 (July-August 1964):30–31.

FABRE, GENEVIEVE E. "A Checklist of Original Plays, Pageants, Rituals and Musicals by Afro-American Authors Performed in the United States from 1960–1965," *BW* 23, no. 6 (April 1974):81–97.

FAUSET, JESSIE. "The Gift of Laughter," in Gayle, *Black Expression*, pp. 159–65. Sees black's gift of laughter as strength, particularly for the theater coming out of sorrow and pain. Describes Bert Williams.

FEAGANS, J. "Atlanta Theatre Segregation: A Case of Prolonged Avoidance," *JHR* 13 (Second Quarter 1965):203–18.

FERDINAND, VAL. "News" *BT* 3 (1969). Reviews black theater activity in Newark and Dashiki Project Theatre in New Orleans. Newark theater seeks audiences. Describes objectives of Dashiki including community involvement, creating forum for blacks and whites, and significant aesthetic pleasure.

————. "News from Blackartsouth," *BT* 4 (April 1970):4. Says theater has been very active, mentions particular productions, calls attention to book on Free Southern Theatre.

FORD, CLEBERT. "Towards a Black Community Theatre," *L* 4 (August 1964).

"Four Portraits; D. T. Ward of the Negro Ensemble Company," *SR* 3 (November 15, 1975):18.

FRANCE, ARTHUR. "A Raisin Revisited," *F* 5 (Summer 1965):403–10.

FULLER, HOYT W. "Black Theatre in America: An Informal Survey," *BW* 17 (April 1968):83–93.

————. "Up in Harlem: New Hope," *BW* 14 (October 1965):49–50ff, 83. Comments on writers' conference in which critic-reviewer Richard Gilman said Negros' playwrighting was in a preliminary stage. Fuller commends Jones's establishment of Harlem Repertory Theatre School as proper response to lack of understanding.

————. "World Festival of Negro Arts," *E* 21 (July 1966):96–106.

GAFFNEY, FLOYD. "Black Theatre: Commitment of Communicator," *The Black Scholar* 1 (June 1970):10–15.

GARDNER, BETTYE, and BETTYE THOMAS. "Cultural Impact of the Howard Theatre on the Black Community," *JNH* 55 (October 1970):253–65.

GAYLE, ADDISON, JR. "Cultural Strangulation: Black Literature and the White Aesthetic," *BW* 18, no. 9 (July 1969):32–39.

————. "Debate: The Black Aesthetic (Defender)," *BW* 24, no. 2 (1974): 31–43.

————. "Reclaiming the Southern Experience: The Black Aesthetic 10 Years Later," *BW* 23, no. 11 (1973):20–29.

GHENT, HENRI. "Black Creativity in Quest of an Audience," *Art in America* 58 (May 1970):35.

GIBSON, WILLIAM. "Certain Fiction . . . and Uncertain Hopes," *Liberation* 10 (October 1965):12–13.

GONCALVES, JOE. "The Mysterious Disappearance of Black Arts West," *BT* 2 (1969):23–25. Suggests that theater that gave many black playwrights and actors a start vanished into "thought." Favorably reviews productions of BANTU players in San Francisco.

————. "West Coast Drama," *BT* 4 (April 1970):27. Somewhat obscure piece suggesting drama on West Coast is "life" and political and not limited to theater.

GREAVES, WILLIAM. "First World Festival of Negro Arts," *C* 73 (June-July 1966):309–14, 332. Says festival focused on issue of "Negritude." Describes work of particular companies, both African and Afro-American, and describes festival as brilliant and theatrical.

GREENWOOD, FRANK. "Burn, Baby, Burn," *F* 7 (Summer 1967):244–47.

GREGORY, MONTGOMERY. "The Drama of Negro Life," in Gayle, *Black Ex-*

pression, pp. 128–233. Remarkably relevant to writings in black aesthetics, essay of 1920s calls for national Negro theater and small black community theaters across the country. Notes briefly black theater activity in first quarter of century.

HANAU, D. "Ghetto Theatre: Vital Drama or Social Therapy?" *Cy* 26 (April 1967):7–10.

HANSBERRY, LORRAINE. " 'Me Tink Me Hear Sounds in De Night,' " *Theatre Arts* 44 (October 1960):9–11ff. Ranges over general problems of blacks in theater, stressing difference between black playwrights and white playwrights of "Negro" drama, giving examples.

"Harlem Fine Arts School," *E* 21 (May 1966):80–86. Describes activities and success of this school for training young artists.

HARRIS, HENRIETTA. "Building a Black Theatre," *TDR* 12 (Summer 1968):157–58. Describes steady development and success of Aldridge Players/West.

HARRISON, PAUL CARTER. "Black Theater and the African Continuum," *BW* 21 (August 1972):48.

HATLEN, THEODORE, and WILLIAM REARDON. "Beautiful Black," *UCSB* [*University of California at Santa Barbara*] *Alumnus*, August 1972, pp. 22–29.

HAY, SAMUEL A. "Alain Locke and Black Drama," *BW* 21 (April 1972):8–14. Discusses Locke's concepts of reality in drama, of need for detachment, of propaganda and art, attempting to show contemporary relevancy and problems in Locke's view. Says we should be concerned not about propaganda but about whether black drama is didactic and boring.

HENDERSON, AUSTRALIS. "Black Female in Afro-American Theatre: Images Old and New," *Afriscope* 5 (1975):no. 8, 46–47, 49–50; no. 9, 44, 46–49.

HEWES, HARRY. "Black Hopes; Presentations in New York City," *SR* 53 (February 14, 1970):30.

———. "Broadway Postscript: Crossing Lines" *SR* 48 (January 7, 1965):46.

HILL, HERBERT. "Introduction" and "Biographical Notes," in *Soon One Morning: New Writing by American Negroes, 1940–62* (New York: Knopf, 1963).

———. "Stuff of Great Literature," *C* 73 (February 1966):110–14. Excerpt from introduction to *Anger and Beyond*. Stress on trends, particularly in fiction.

———. "*Uncle Tom:* An Enduring American Myth," *C* 72 (May 1965):189–95, 325. Mentions the Tom shows and Tom plays and quantities of companies performing versions of *Uncle Tom's Cabin* in late nineteenth and early twentieth centuries. Compares "myth" to history and comments on Stowe's book.

HILLIARD, ROBERT L. "The Drama and American Negro Life," *Southern Theatre* 10 (Winter 1966):12–13.

"Historical Precis: "The New Lafayette Theatre," *BT* 6 (1972):21. Lists productions, dates, and playwrights of New Lafayette Theater from October, 1967 to Fall, 1971.

"How Liberal Is Show Business?" *S* 12 (March 1963): 40–43.

HUDSON, BENJAMIN F. "Another View of *Uncle Tom*" *P* 24 (First Quarter 1963):79–87.

HUGHES, LANGSTON "The Need for an Afro-American Theatre," *Chicago Defender*, June 12, 1961. Hughes proposes creation of national Afro-American theater because the nature of Broadway prevents scripts and performances by Negroes; Negroes must create their own audience; and the black community as well as all Americans need a stage where revivals and new works by Negro dramatists can be seen and worked out.

———. "The Negro and American Entertainment," in Davis, *American Negro Reference Book*, pp. 826–49.

———. "When I worked for Dr. Woodson," *NHB* 30 (October 1967):17.

———. "Writers: Black and White," in Conference of Negro Writers, *The American Negro Writer and His Roots*, pp. 41–45. Calls for Negro writers to "get outside" themselves. Disparages *Requiem for a Nun* and *Porgy and Bess*.

HUSTON, JEAN BLACKWELL. "The Schomburg Collection," *F* 3 (Summer 1963):431–35.

"In Black America," *Nw* 69 (March 20, 1972):98–99.

JEYIFONE, ABIODUM. "Black Critics on Black Theater in America," *TDR* 18, no. 3 (September 1974):34–45.

JOHNSON, HELEN ARMSTEAD "Playwrights, Audiences and Critics," *BW* 19 (April 1970):17–24. Describes different kinds of black audiences, black playwrights' attitudes toward audiences, the complexity of these. Asserts that young black theater audience is growing. Brief emphasis on Ward's *Day of Absence* and plays of William Branch.

JONES, LEROI (IMAMU AMIRI BARAKA). "Black (Art) Drama Is the Same as Black Life," *E* 25 (February 1971):74–76ff.

———. "Black 'Revolutionary' Poets Should Also be Playwrights," *BW* 21 (April 1972):4–6. Calls for small companies of black poets-turned-playwrights in every town to inspire revolution. Condemns many poets and playwrights for individualism as opposed to revolutionary nationalism.

———. "Communications Project," *TDR* 12 (Summer 1968):53–57. Outline form lists specific ways of communicating with black communities using the arts and other media. A comprehensive list of vast communications.

———. "In Search of the Revolutionary Theatre (Black Arts Repertory)," *BW* 15 (April 1966):20–24. Urgent, passionate voice calls for theater that realizes dreams, a theater of assault, a theater that exposes and destroys "America" and creates new ways and new heroes.

———. "Philistinism and the Negro Writer," in Hill, *Anger and Beyond*, pp. 51–57. Describes problems of Negro artist's double role in and outside of American culture; lauds recent achievements of black American writers.

———. "The Revolutionary Theatre," in LeRoi Jones, *Home: Social Essays* (New York: n.p., 1966), pp. 210–15.

———. "What the Arts Need Now," *BW* 16 (April 1967):5–6. Jones calls for plays of specific finding—plays for city hall, the police department, and so on, a "post American form."

JURGES, ODA, ed. "Books and Articles Related to Black Theatre Published from 1/1960–2/1968," *TDR* 12 (Summer 1968):176–80. Lists sixteen playwrights and some articles, mostly from black periodicals or written by black writers. Helpful, but far from complete. Not annotated. Series of epigrammatic statements that assert central characteristics of black art. Summary is almost impossible, but thrust is toward emphasis on feeling, motif of revolution, need for a new language: "all art must be collective, committing and functional."

KELLER, F. R. "Harlem Literary Renaissance," *NAR* 5 (May 1968):29–34.

KEYSSAR-FRANKE, HELENE. "Afro-American Drama and Its Criticism, 1960–1972; An Annotated Check List with Appendices," *Bulletin of The New York Public Library* 3 (Spring 1975):276–346.

KGOSITSILE, K. W. "Towards Our Theatre: A Definitive Act," *VW* 16 (April 1967):14–16. Writer seeks theater as poetry that reveals future direction. Highly commends Jones's *Black Mass*.

KILLENS, JOHN OLIVER. "Broadway in Black and White," *AF* 1 (Winter 1966):66–76.

KILSON, MARTIN. "Debate: The Black Aesthetic (Opponent)," *BW* 24, no. 2 (1974):30, 44–48. See Gayle above.

KING, WOODIE, JR. "Black Theatre: Present Condition," *TDR* 12 (Summer 1968):117–24. Disavows connection between "true" black theater and traditional Western theater and labels many seemingly black companies (the Negro Ensemble Company, the New Lafayette, the Theatre of Living Arts, and so on) as nonblack, still oriented to white communities. Wants theater to respond to demands of proximate community.

———. "Black Theatre: Weapon for Change," *BW* 16 (April 1967):35–39. Says theater can and should be politically effective, for "social welfare." Describes political theater of past, calls for federally sponsored black community theater for "truth."

———. "The Dilemma of Black Theatre," *BW* 19 (April 1970):10–15, 86–87. Brief, thoughtful survey of American theater and its connections to black theater in the twentieth century. Describes audience for black theater and urges black community to support it as patrons and audience.

———. "Educational Theater and the Black Community," *BW* 21 (April 1972):25–29. Article comments on problems of audience in university theater, differences between professional and educational theater, problems of directing black drama, relative success of Ron Milner's *Who's Got His Own* and *A Black Quartet*.

———. "Evolution of a People's Theatre," introduction to King and Milner, *Black Drama Anthology*. Asserts separation of black theater from American theater physically and aesthetically. Very briefly describes contents of anthology.

———. "Problems Facing Negro Actors," *BW* 15 (April 1966):53–59. King calls attention to problems of playing Americans and Negroes simultaneously, of playing Negroes to white audiences' conception of Negro character. Describes plight of beginning black actors in white groups, of university theater, horrors of drama schools; calls for unity of playwrights and actors and for building a Negro community audience.

"King Heroin: Harlem Play on the Destructive Effects of Dope Addiction in the Black Community," *E* 26 (June 1971):56–58.

KINNEMAN, JOHN. "The Negro Renaissance," *NHB* 25 (May 1962):197–200.

KUPA, KUSHAURI. "Cassius Clay a/k/a Muhammad Ali as Big Time Buck White," *BT* 4 (April 1970):43–44. Reviewer writes about this play to focus on Clay's role, which he harshly condemns.

———. "Close-up: The New York Scene," *BT* 6 (1972):38–51. Capsulizes 1970–71 New York black theater scene; comments in detail on more than a dozen plays by black playwrights; calls attention to the great productivity of 1970–71 black theater season. Reviews are critical and descriptive, concerned with effectiveness of the plays as theater and content.

LA BRANT, LOU. "Untapped Resources of Negro Students," *NALF* 1 (Winter 1967):15–17.

LADWIG, R. V. "Black black comedy of Ben Caldwell," *Players Magazine* 51 (February 1976):88–91.

"Lafayette Theatre Reaction to 'Bombers,' " *BT* 4 (April 1970):16–25. A variety of voices, including Marvin X, Askia Muhammad Toure, Robert Macbeth, Larry Neal, Imamu Amiri Baraka, respond on tape to merits and revolutionary nature of *We Righteous Bombers*. Discussion becomes argument over nature and purpose of black theater, particularly in reference to definition of revolutionary theater.

LEAKS, SYLVESTER. "In White America," *F* 4 (Spring 1964):280–81. Review briefly stating dilemma of black playwrights' relations to *In White America* urges getting beyond these problems.

LERMAN, LEO. "Something to Talk About; Negro Ensemble Company," *Mademoiselle* 66 (June 1968):116–19.

LEWIS, CLAUDE. "Black Theatre (the New Theatre," *Tuesday Magazine* (February 1969) 6–8, 10, 23.

LEWIS, THEOPHILUS. "Trumpets of the Lord; Soulfest of Negro Spirituals" *A* 12 (May 1969):599. Reviews musical based on James Weldon Johnson's *God's Trombones*, calls it "a rewarding theatrical novelty." Suggests experience for audience is obsolete vicarious church worship.

LINDSAY, POWELL. "We Still Need Negro Theatre in America," *NHB* 27 (February 1964):112.

LITTLEJOHN, DAVID. "Negro Writers Today: the Playwrights," in Littlejohn, *Black on White: A Critical Survey of Writing by American Negroes* (New York: Viking, 1969), pp. 66–79. A 1966 article asserting only major black playwrights to be Jones, Baldwin, Davis, and Hansberry, saying only Jones is engaged in "Potential of living theatre." Condemns *Blues for Mr. Charlie* as artless bullying. Condemns *The Toilet* and *The Slave*, lauds *Purlie Victorious*, but saves most praise and discussion for *Dutchman*.

"The Living Premise (off-Broadway Spoof)," *E* 19 (November 1963):59–62. Calls this satiric series of skits about "U.S. race problem" "vigorous, irreverent and occasionally shocking." Many pictures.

LOCKE, ALAIN. "The Drama of Negro Life," in Gayle, *Black Expression*, pp. 123–28. Pivotal essay of earlier period treats context, origins, and suggested function of "race" drama.

————. "The Negro and the American Theatre, 1927," in Gayle, *The Black Aesthetic*, pp. 249–56. Variation on "The Drama of Negro Life" noted above, this essay having more clearly aesthetic, as opposed to historical, purpose.

LONG, R. E. "Black Is Box-Office," *NAR* 6 (Winter 1969):71–72.

MACBETH, ROBERT. "Macbeth Speaks," *BT* 6 (1972):14–20. Macbeth speaks about history, character, and direction of black theater. Asserts it is "the total art of the people," that it began in the last decade and must include the participation of audiences. Also calls for a new language.

MACKAY, BARBARA. "Studies in Black and White," *SR* 2 (July 12, 1975):52.

MAPP, EDWARD. "The Image Makers (Negro Stereotype)," *NHB* 26 (December 1962):127–28.

MARVIN X. "Manifesto: The Black Educational Theatre of San Francisco," *BT* 6 (1972):30–31. Strongly antiwhite statement. Stresses move away from individualism to nationalism as educational task of black theater. Asserts that black theater is *not* for entertainment; that language must and will change; that black communities must financially support black theater.

"Mecca for Blackness; Chicago's Afro-Arts Theatre," *E* 25 (May 1970):96–98ff.

MILLER, ADAM DAVID. "It's a Long Way to St. Louis: Notes on the Audience for Black Drama," *TDR* 12 (Summer 1968):147–50. Defines major problem of black dramatists as that of defining their audience, avoiding ambivalence. Says plays of Hughes, Hansberry, Baldwin, Davis, and even, in a peculiar way, Jones are really addressed to white audiences, but there are playwrights like Bullins, Marvin X, and Ahmad addressing themselves to black audiences.

————. "News from the San Francisco East Bay," *BT* 4 (April 1970):5. Cites increasing amount of theater activity, much of which holds promise. Offers assistance, guidance to others wanting to establish black theaters.

MILLIAN, BRUCE E. "Detroit Repertory Theatre," in "News," *BT* 2 (1969): 4. Sees central problem as that of audience recruitment and initiation. Calls street theater "more romantic than good."

MILNER, RONALD. "Black Magic: Black Art," *BW* 16 (April 1967):8–12ff. Talks about potential power of black art to topple white, racist America. Uses Charlie Parker as example; calls for literature to assert and state and thus be "black."

————. "Black Theatre, Go Home!" *BW* 17 (April 1968):5–10.

————. "Evolution of a People's Theatre," introduction to King and Milner, *Black Drama Anthology*, pp. vii–x.

MITCHELL, LOFTEN. "Alligators in the Swamp," *C* 72 (February 1965):84–87. Claims that blacks (and some whites like Arthur Miller) are being pushed down wrong roads and that their innovative, creative work is ignored or condemned by white producers, publishers, and critics, particularly when it is realistic and concerns contemporary problems.

————. "Black Drama," *BW* 16 (April 1967):75–87. Criticizes *The Emperor Jones* and *Shuffle Along*, both of which are seen as setting precedents for theater for many years. Describes beginning of Harlem Renaissance and theater in 1920s. Says theater became middle-class luxury because it avoided speaking to the truth of the daily lives of the people.

——. "The Black Teacher and the Dramatic Arts," mimeographed paper, University of Iowa (1969). Discussed in Appendix B, above.

——. "I Work Here to Please You," in Gayle, *The Black Aesthetic*, pp. 275–87. Discusses in semihistorical context how black drama has had to maneuver and deal with white audiences.

——. "Negro in the American Theatre," in *The Oxford Companion to the Theatre*, 3d ed., pp. 679–81.

——. "The Negro Theatre and the Harlem Community," in Gayle, *Black Expression*, pp. 148–59. Mentions Negro characters in early American drama, discusses origin of minstrel tradition, effects of movies on theater, theater activity in Harlem, movement of black playwrights to Broadway and Off-Broadway: Presents pessimistic view for Negro in theater but urges producers to recognize numerous Negro playwrights, calls for Negro producers. Also in *F* 3 (Summer 1963):384–94.

——. "The Negro Writer and His Materials," in Conference of Negro Writers, *The American Negro Writer and His Roots*, pp. 55–60. Discusses problems of Negro writers in selecting and rejecting material for their works according to what audiences want. Particularly noteworthy comments on critics' attempts to isolate Negro writers as the only "protest" writers. Brings up question of white-audience response to black characters.

——. "On the "Emerging Playwright," in C. W. E. Bigsby, *The Black American Writer*, 2:129–36. Calls attention to "emergence" of black drama in early nineteenth century and abundance and quality of black drama in recent decades.

MOLETTE, CARLTON, II. "Afro-American Ritual Drama," *BW* 22 (April 1973):4–12.

——. "The First Afro-American Theatre," *BW* 19 (April 1970): 4–9. Condemns application of Euro-American standards to evaluations and definitions of Afro-American drama. Mentions first black theater in America— the African Company of the 1820s in New York City. Says Afro-American theater derives from oral tradition and cites need for thorough non-European American history of Afro-American theater.

MOOTRY, MARIA K. "Themes and Symbols in Two Plays by LeRoi Jones," *BW* 18 (April 1969):42–47.

MORRISON, ALLAN. "Negro Women in the Arts," *E* 21 (August 1966):90–94. Mentions how few black women playwrights exist. Remarks on Angelina Grimke (*Rachel*, 1913), Alice Childress, and Lorraine Hansberry. Also surveys women in all other art fields.

——. "A New Surge in the Arts," *E* 22 (August 1967):134–38.

——. "One Hundred Years of Negro Entertainment," *E* 18 (September 1963):122–28. Careful in accuracy of details, information; traces history of Negroes in theater and entertainment world, stressing individual "stars." Is optimistic that time is near when "Negro" entertainment will be inseparable from American entertainment.

MOSES, GILBERT, DORIS DERBY, and JOHN O'NEAL. "The Need for a Southern Freedom Theatre," *F* 4 (Winter 1964):109–12.

National Black Theater (Barbara Ann Teer). "We Are Liberators Not Actors,"
   Essence 1 (March 1971):56–9.
NEAL, LARRY. "Any Day Now: Black Art and Black Liberation," *E* 24 (August
   1969):54–58.
————. "The Black Arts Movement," in Gayle, *The Black Aesthetic*, pp.
   257–74. Stresses importance of theater as most social of arts, importance
   of Jones in black theater. Calls black theater a radical alternative to
   decadent American theater. Critical discussions of works of Jones, Milner,
   Garrett, and Caldwell. Also in *TDR* 12 (Summer 1968):29–39, and in
   Bigsby, *Black American Writer*, 2.
————. "The Cultural Front," *L* 5 (June 1965):26–27.
————. "Cultural Nationalism and Black Theatre," *BT* 1 (October 1968):8–10.
   Essentially a review of Cruse's *The Crisis of the Negro Intellectual*. Calls
   it important but limited in not exploring or understanding fully differences between Western and Afro-American culture and particularities
   of the latter. In this context, briefly discusses the need for black theater
   to include all facets of an extended black community.
————. "Toward a Relevant Black Theatre" *BT* 4 (April 1970):14–15. Describes
   form of *We Righteous Bombers* as dead and European; often directly
   taken from Camus's *Les justes*, but main concern is with need for new
   forms and cooperation in all black theater.
"Negroes on Broadway," *E* 19 (April 1964):186–94. Reviews variety of Broadway plays about or including Negroes; asserts that racial picture is
   brightening in New York theater.
New York Times, October 10, 1976, II, 5:3. Article on increase in number of
   black films and theatergoers and subsequent increase in black entertainment.
"News," *BT* 2 (1969):4–6, 34–35. Series of brief articles by many reporters
   survey plays produced and running and aesthetic problems in eight
   community theaters across the nation (Chicago and Detroit annotated
   separately). Good source for names and productions of new plays.
"News," *BT* 5 (1971):2–11. Contains reports on black community theaters
   across the country, including New Haven, Washington, D.C., New Or-
   leans (Dashiki Project Theatre and New Orleans Dillard Players), New
   York City and State (Afro-American Studio, African Culture Center of
   Buffalo, Bed-Stuy Theater, Brownsville Laboratory Theatre Arts, Inc. of
   Brooklyn), Seattle, Jamaica, and Mexico.
"News," *BT* 6 (1972):2–10. Reviews black theatre activities in Harlem, East
   Harlem, Brooklyn, Philadelphia, Massachusetts, Ohio, Tennessee, New
   Orleans, Texas, San Francisco. Notable for information on evolution of
   new black theater groups.
NICHOLAS, DENISE. "View from the Free Southern Theatre," *L* 6 (July
   1966):20.
NOVICK, J. "Theatre," *N* 210 (June 15, 1970):733–34.
O'BRIEN, JOHN. "Let Us Have a New American Theatre," *BW* 13 (March
   1964):44–47. Concerned that race not be a consideration in casting, par-
   ticularly in school theaters but also in all theatres. Condemns typecasting

and notion of theater reflecting life as sources of inadequate use of Negro actors.

OLIVER, CLINTON F. "An Introductory Essay: The Negro and the American Theatre," in Oliver, *Contemporary Black Drama from A Raisin in the Sun to No Place to Be Somebody*, pp. 3–25. Succinct, careful account of history of Afro-American theater groups and dramas, culminating in discussion of "revolutionary theater." Suggests Afro-American drama has much cultural significance in any attempt to understand America.

OLIVER, EDITH. "Off Broadway: Revue by Voices, Inc.: *The Believers*," *NYr* 44 (May 1968):75. Describes production of *The Believers*, a musical revue structured around the history of black people in America. Calls show "heartfelt" and "stirring."

O'NEAL, FREDERICK. "Problems and Prospects: The Negro in Today's Theatre," *BW* 15 (April 1966):4–12. Article emphasizes problems of Negro actors in New York: few stars, few roles, insufficient training. Says situation improving because of less race-casting, more plays by Negro playwrights and civil rights support for arts. Urges Negro playwrights to recognize that prime goal of good play is to entertain.

O'NEAL, JOHN. "Motion in the Ocean: Some Political Dimensions of the Free Southern Theatre," *TDR* 12 (Summer 1968):70–77. Concerns FST and its efforts to make black theatre integral with southern black culture. Speaks of aim to create active and critical audience. Says art and politics should not be separated and that black art is weakened when it has to explain to whites.

ORMAN, ROSCOE. "The New Lafayette Theatre," *BT* 4 (April 1970):6. Stresses growth of company and annotates its recent season and future production plans.

———. "The New Lafayette Theatre," *BT* 5 (1971):12–13. Praises meaningful work of theater from "insider's" view, commenting particularly on production of Bullins's *Duplex* and on cooperative spirit and efforts of the technical company members. Admonishes both black and white critics not to bother evaluating but to pay attention to audience response.

PATTERSON, LINDSAY. "Introduction," in Patterson, *Black Theatre: A 20th Century Collection of the Work of Its Best Playwrights*, pp. vii–ix. Suggests thematic continuity in anthology revolving around idea of "loss of innocence." Considers difference between reading and producing a play. Briefly describes plays in anthology.

———. "Not By Protest Alone," *NHB* 31 (April 1968):12–14.

———. "The Waste Lands" in Patterson, *Anthology of the American Negro in the Theatre*, pp. 269–70.

PAWLEY, THOMAS D. "The First Black Playwrights," *BW* 21 (April 1972):16–24. Surveys early-nineteenth-century achievements of Mr. Brown's African company, later nineteenth-century works of Ira Aldridge, Victor Sejour, William Wells Brown. Gives plot summaries of some of the early plays and critical comments on Brown's *The Escape*.

"Play Versus Players," *T* 92 (December 27, 1968):47.

RAMBEAU, DAVID. "Concept East and the Struggle Against Racism," *BW* 16

(April 1967):22–27ff. Historical documentation of conflicts between white-arts establishment and this black community theater; specifically describes discrimination in the University of Michigan theater.

———. "Long Live Black Revolutionary Theatre," *TDR* 12 (Summer 1968):84. Photograph and statement that assert black political revolution must have black cultural revolution as its foundation. Tells of dissolution of Black Arts/West and founding of the Black House.

RASHIDD, NAIMA. "Black Theatre in Detroit," *BT* 4 (April 1970):3. Describes briefly Crescent Moon Cultural Center in Detroit and labels Detroit Repertory Theatre fraudulent in presenting itself to *Black Theatre* as black; says it is a white and Negro theater.

REAVY, CHARLES D. "Satire and Contemporary Black Drama," *Satire Newsletter* 7 (Fall 1969):40–48.

RECOD, WILSON C. "The Negro as Creative Artist" *C* 72 (March 1965):153–58, 193. Does not speak directly to drama but sees much of Negro art evolving out of the folk story, the spiritual, and jazz.

"Repertory: Negro Ensemble Company," *T* 91 (January 12, 1968):40.

RIACH, W. A. D. " 'Telling It Like It Is': An Examination of Black Theatre as Rhetoric," *The Quarterly Journal of Speech* 56 (April 1970):179–186.

RILEY, CLAYTON. "On Black Theater," in Gayle, *The Black Aesthetic*, pp. 313–30. First section speaks of task of black theater to assert "legitimacy." Second part presents laudatory critical analysis of work by Jones, Bullins, and Milner, with particularly close comment on Clay in *Dutchman*. Third part asserts black theater to be a theater of warfare and distinct from white American theater. Contains harshly negative criticism of Abramson's *Negro Playwrights in the American Theatre, 1925–1959.*

———. "Song of the Lusitania Bogey," *L* 8 (February 1968).

———. "We Thought It Was Magic," *NYTM* (November 7, 1976):36–38.

ROGERS, RAY. "The Negro Actor" *F* (Summer 1962):310–13.

"Rolling Thunder" *T* 95 (April 6, 1970):62.

ROSS, RONALD. "The Role of Blacks in the Federal Theatre, 1935–1939," *JNH* 59 (January 1974):38–50.

SCHECHNER, RICHARD. "Free Theatre for Mississippi," *H* 231 (October 1968):31–32, 34, 36, 38

———. "White on Black," *TDR* 12 (Summer 1968):25–27. Describes why he completely turned over editorship of this issue to black writers. Describes his own changes in attitudes toward black theater; says black drama speaks to blacks but can come over to whites.

"See How They Run (Tennessee A and I Players)," *J* 41 (March 10, 1960); *J* 60 (April 28, 1960).

SHEFFER, ISAIAH. "Black Theatre in America," *N* 209 (August 25, 1969):151–52.

SHERMAN, JIMMIE. "From the Ashes," *AR* 27 (Fall 1967):285–93. Tells of writing his play *A Ballad from Watts*, the search for a theater group, the founding and growth of The Theatre of Watts. Brief but detailed.

SHERR, P. C. "Change Your Luck: A Negro Satirizes White America," *P* 32 (Fall 1971):281–89.

SILVERA, FRANK. "Towards a Theatre of Understanding," *BW* 18 (April 1969):33–35.

SIMMONS, BILL. "Third World Revelationist," *BT* 4 (April 1970):39–40. Describes work of group that performs skits to increase black consciousness. Praises this theater activity for its non-Western, audience-oriented structure.

SPRINGARN, ARTHUR B. "Books by Negro Authors in 1967," *C* 75 (March 1968):81–87, 99–101. Annual bibliography in *Crisis*. Includes drama but is very selective.

SUTHERLAND, ELIZABETH. "Theatre of the Meaningful," *N* 199 (October 19, 1964):254–56.

"Symposium: The Negro in the American Theatre," *BW* 11 (July 1962):52–58.

TALBOT, WILLIAM. "Every Negro in His Place: The Scene on and off Broadway," *Drama Critique* 7 (Spring 1964):92–95.

"Talking of Black Art, Theatre, Revolution and Nationhood." Part I—First Pan African Cultural Festival; Part II—Black Theatre, "A Forum," *BT* 5 (1971):18–37. Series of interviews in Algeria, downtown Manhattan, and Harlem, in which eighteen notable black artists, critics, and political figures—including Baraka, Bullins, Caldwell, King, and Wesley—discuss the cultural and political connections between Africa and black America and the critics and audience of black theater in America. Issues include definition of theater and importance of theater and criticism in 1971.

"The Task of the Negro Writer as Artist, A Symposium," *BW* 14 (April 1965):54–83. Series of statements by black and white writers, famous and unknown, about the role of the Negro writer in a segregated society and how this role differs from that of the white writer. Includes statements by playwrights Ossie Davis, Bill Gunn, Langston Hughes, LeRoi Jones, and William Branch. Most statements stress need for honesty; some, concern for black audience.

A Taste of Honey, *E* (April 1961):53–56.

TEER, BARBARA ANN. "The Great White Way Is Not Our Way—Not Yet," *BW* 17 (April 1968):21–29.

"Tell It Like It Is," *Nw* (August 24, 1964):84–85.

THOMPSON, LARRY. "Black Writing If It Is Not Going to Disappear," *Yale Literaty Magazine* 138 (September 1969):4–6.

THOMPSON, T. "Burst of Negro Drama," *Life* 56 (May 29, 1964):62a–70.

TRENT, T. "Stratification Among Blacks by Black Authors," *NHB* 34 (December 1971):179–81.

TROTTA, G. "Black Theatre," *Harper's Bazaar* 101 (August 1968):150–53.

TURNER, DARWIN T. "The Black Playwright in the Professional Theatre of the United States of America, 1858–1959," in Bigsby, *The Black American Writer*, 2, pp. 113–28. Historical account of Afro-American playwrights that gives brief plot and theme descriptions of many plays, focusing particularly on the 1950s.

————. "The Negro Dramatist's Image of the Universe, 1920–1960," *CLAJ* 5 (December 1961):106–20. An overview of the changing patterns of content in black drama. Areas covered are the Negro dramatist's image of his hero; his attitudes toward education, superstition, and religion; his images of the North and his own society; and "future" images. Thesis is that movement goes from idealization, to self-conscious defense of vices, to objectivity. Many plays mentioned.

———. "Negro Playwrights and the Urban Negro," *CLAJ* 12 (September 1968):19–25. Reviews plays with urban settings, stressing particularly *Take a Giant Step, Raisin in the Sun, The Toilet,* and *Dutchman.* Concludes that evidence of urban settings does not significantly alter substance or form of black drama and that no conclusions can yet be drawn about future of southern settings in black drama.

———. "Past and Present in Negro Drama," *NALF* 2 (1968):26–27.

———. "Visions of Love and Manliness in a Blackening World: Dramas of Black Life from 1953–1970," *Iowa R* 6, no. 2 (1975):7–13.

TURNER, SHERRY. "An Overview of the New Black Arts," *F* 9:156–63.

"Unusual Appeals Bring Broadway Cash (Producer Oscar Brown, Jr.)" *E* 16 (June 1961):73–80.

WARD, DOUGLAS TURNER. "American Theatre: For Whites Only?" *New York Times,* August 14, 1966, in Patterson, *Anthology of the American Negro in the Theatre,* pp. 81–84.

———. "Needed: A Theatre for Black Themes" *BW* 17 (December 1967):34–39.

WARD, THEODORE. "News: The South Side Center of the Performing Arts, Inc.," *BT* 2 (1969):3–4. Briefly surveys the history of South Side Black Theatre Company and its problems with clarification of organization, finding audience, and money. Asserts that black community can and should support black theater.

"Welcome to the Great Black Way!" *T* 108 (November 1, 1976):72ff.

WHITMORE, GEORGIA, E. "Bibliography," *JNE* 33 (Fall 1964):421–35. Contains current materials in black studies, including some primary and secondary drama entries.

WILLIAMS, JIM. "The Need for a Harlem Theatre," *F* 3 (Summer 1963):395–404.

———. "Pieces on Black Theatre and the Black Theater Worker," *F* 9 (Spring 1969):146–55.

———. "Survey of Afro-American Playwrights," *F* 10 (first quarter, 1970): 26–45.

WILLIAMS, JOHN A. "The Negro in Literature Today," *E* 18 (September 1963):73–76. Williams asserts that black artists are becoming freer to do what they want. Article mentions Hansberry and Davis.

WILLIS, RICHARD A., and HILDA MCELROY. "Published Works of Black Playwrights in the United States, 1960–1970," *BW* 21 (April 1972):92–98. Fairly careful but far from complete list of black dramatists 1960–70, most helpful in providing publication data and a fairly extensive list of plays by Bullins and Jones. List of secondary materials emphasizes reference books and includes no articles.

WILLIS, ROBERT J. "Anger and the Contemporary Black Theatre," *NALF* 8 (1974):213–15.

YOUNG, M. "The Cool World," *S* 9 (May 1960):36–40.

BLACK PLAYWRIGHTS AND THEIR PLAYS

The following list of plays, biography, and criticism is arranged according to playwright. In order to organize the secondary materials, what follows is as complete a list as possible of Afro-American playwrights of the nineteenth and twentieth centuries and their plays. Where available, the production date of each play is noted after the title, except in the case of plays published either in a periodical or in book form. References follow to the producing company, theater, or city of production, particularly where there is no bibliographical reference. Although many of the lesser-known playwrights from 1960 to 1976 have received no biographical or critical notice, they have been included. Where there are biographical or critical works on the plays (by the playwrights or others), they are listed after the record of the plays. Critical articles by the playwrights not specifically related to their works appear in the preceding section of this bibliography.

Reviews that are not annotated or that have no distinctive title are listed together at the end of entries under each playwright. Works for which Fannie Hicklin's unpublished dissertation "The American Negro Playwright, 1920–1964" (see page 238) is the only source are indicated by an "(H)" at the end of the entry. If the play has been reviewed in the *New York Times*, the abbreviation "(*NYT*)" appears after production information.

There are three kinds of cross-references: (1) References that specify anthologies refer to the "Anthologies" section at the beginning of the bibliography; (2) references to listings under the names of other playwrights in this same section are introduced by the phrase "see under"; and (3) all other cross-references are to the "Books" subsection of the "General History and Criticism" section of the bibliography, which follows the "Anthologies" section.

Abbreviations of periodical titles are the same as those listed at the beginning of the immediately preceding section.

Mba Acaz
The Ambassadors, 1970–71, The Other Stage, Public Theatre, New York.

Dorothy Ahmad
Papa's Daughter, 1969, Dillard University Players, New Orleans. In *TDR* 12 (Summer 1968): 139–45.

Ira Aldridge
The Black Doctor, 1870. An adaptation of a French play by Auguste Anicet Bourgeois and Pinel Dumanior.
Titus Andronicus, 1849. An adaptation of Shakespeare's play.

Lewis Alexander
Pierrot at Sea, Fall 1929, Krigwa Players (H).

Hughes Allison
The Trial of Dr. Beck, 1937, Maxine Elliott Theatre, New York (*NYT*). WPA New Jersey Federal Theatre, Union City and Newark.

Garland Anderson
Appearances, 1925, New York *(NYT)*. The New York Public Library, Theatre
    Collection (Film Reproduction *Z17-): 1930, London.

Thomas Anderson
Crispus Attucks (New York: New Dimensions, 1970).

Walt Anderson
Bitter Bread! A Dramatic Reading (New York: Seabury Press, 1964).

Regina M. Andrews
Underground, April 1932, Harlem Experimental Theatre, New York (H).

Earl Anthony
Charlie Still Can't Win No Wars on the Ground, 1970–71, New Federal
    Theatre, New York.
(Mis)Judgment 1970–71, New Federal Theatre, New York.

William Ashby
Booker T. Washington, 1940–41, Rose McClendon Players, New York (H).

Russell Atkins
The Nail (Cleveland: Free Lance, 1971). "To be set to music." Adapted from
    the short story of the same name by Pedro Antonio de Alarcon.

James Baldwin
The Amen Corner (New York: Dial, 1967), also in Patterson anthology.
Blues for Mister Charlie (New York, Dial, 1964), also in Oliver anthology.
    BIOGRAPHY AND CRITICISM
BALDWIN, JAMES. "How Can We Get the Black People to Cool It?" *Es* 70 (July
    1968):49–53. Interview.
———. "James Baldwin on the Negro Actor," *Urbanite* (April 1961); also in
    Patterson. Asserts that most American drama is untruthful, does not re-
    create experience to allow audience to deal with it; this is extended and
    much worse for black actors and characters. Sees the "Negro in America"
    as the central problem in American life, and calls for a bloodless revolu-
    tion and "scaring" the businessman.
———. "Negroes Are Anti-Semitic Because They're Anti-White," *NYTM* (April
    9, 1967):26–27.
———. "Sidney Poitier," *Look* (July 23, 1968):50–54.
———. "Sweet Lorraine," *Es* 72 (November 1969):139–40.
———. "Theatre: The Negro In and Out," *BW* 15 (April 1966):37–44. De-
    scribes the problem in American theater as that of breaking through
    images—both black and white. Calls for "bloodless revolution" in theater
    to scare the daylights out of the tired businessman. Discusses Albee at
    length with disappointment and sympathy.
BIGSBY, C. W. E. "James Baldwin," in C. W. E. Bigsby, *Confrontation and
    Commitment: A Study of Contemporary American Drama, 1959–1966*
    (Columbia: University of Missouri Press 1968), pp. 122, 129–37, 166; also
    in *Twentieth Century Literature* 13 (1967):39–48, under title "The Com-
    mitted Writer: James Baldwin as Dramatist."

"Blues for Mr. Charlie," *E* 19 (June 1964):188–93. Discusses plot and praises the play and production. Says that the play roars with the spirit of current Negro revolt, that it is overwritten but engrossing. Comments that criticism has been mixed, but it is mostly whites who find severe fault with it.

BRUSTEIN, ROBERT. *Seasons of Discontent* (New York: Simon & Schuster, 1965), pp. 161–65. Criticism of *Blues for Mister Charlie.*

CLARKE, J. B. "Alienation of James Baldwin," *JHR* 12 (first quarter 1964):30–33.

CLURMAN, HAROLD. *The Naked Image: Observations in the Modern Theatre* (New York: Macmillan, 1966), pp. 37–39. Criticism of *Blues for Mister Charlie.*

COHEN, NATHAN. "A Flawed Talent," *National Review* 16 (September 8, 1964):780–81. Criticism of *Blues for Mister Charlie.*

DRIVER, TOM. "*Blues for Mister Charlie,*" *BW* 13 (September 1964):34–40. Thoughtful, careful appraisal, more aptly criticism than review, which asserts that other critics have panned the play because they do not like its message. Argues that the play is a summons, a Brechtian "call to action," and that such plays succeed when audiences *like* their messages. Review treats play's content and form.

FREEDMAN, MORRIS. *American Drama in Social Context* (Carbondale: Southern Illinois University Press, 1971), p. 86. More notable for its lack of discussion of black playwrights than for anything else on black drama. Contains a paragraph on the success of *A Raisin in the Sun* compared to *Blues for Mister Charlie* and *Dutchman.*

HOWE, IRVING. "James Baldwin: At Ease in Apocalypse," *H* 237 (September 1968):92ff.

ISAACS, HAROLD R. "Five Writers and Their African Ancestors," *P* 21 (Fall-Winter 1960):243–65, 317–36. On Hughes, Wright, Baldwin, Hansberry.

"James Baldwin: A Literary Assessment," *BW* 13 (January 1964):61–68.

LONG, R. E. "From Elegant to Hip," *N* 206 (June 10, 1968):769–70.

LUMLEY, FREDERICK. *New Trends in 20th Century Drama* (London: Barrie & Rockcliff, 1967), pp. 339–40. Criticism of *The Amen Corner* and *Blues for Mister Charlie.*

McWHIRTER, W. A. "Parting Shots: After Years of Futility Baldwin Explodes Again," *Life* 71 (July 30, 1971):63.

MARGOLIES, EDWARD. *Native Sons: A Critical Study of Twentieth-Century Negro American Authors* (Philadelphia: Lippincott, 1968), pp. 122, 124–26.

MARKHOLD, OTILLIE. "*Blues for Mister Charlie* Reconsidered: White Critic, Black Playwright: Water and Fire," *BW* 16 (April 1967):54–60. Compares critical praise for Martin Duberman's *In White America* with condemnation by white critics of *Blues for Mister Charlie* for "pushing hate." Demonstrates gaps and weaknesses in *In White America* and a cultural view of *Blues* that is unacceptable to whites.

MERIWETHER, L. M. "*The Amen Corner,*" *BW* (January 1965):40–47. Describes the initial success of *The Amen Corner* in terms of its universality, its way of stripping layers off characters and audience, its emotional intensity. Also describes content and exalts the experiences and performance of the play.

MESERVE, WALTER. "James Baldwin's 'Agony Way,'" in Bigsby, 2, pp. 171–86. Analyses of *The Amen Corner* and *Blues for Mister Charlie*. Attempts through thematic and structural commentary to prove that Baldwin is continually working out an autobiographical thesis that the serious answer to all human problems is "love through suffering."

"Milk Run," *T*, June 7, 1968, p. 104.

OGNIBENE, E. R. "Black Literature Revisited: Sonny's Blues," *English Journal* 60 (January 1971):36–37.

PHILLIPS, LOUIS. "The Novelist as Playwright: Baldwin, McCullers, and Bellow," in William E. Taylor, ed., *Modern American Drama* (Deland, Fla.: Everett/Edwards, 1968), 145–61.

POTTER, VILMA. "Baldwin and Odets: The High Cost of 'Crossing,'" *California English Journal* 1, no. 3 (1965):37–41. Review of *Blues for Mister Charlie*.

ROGOFF, GORDON. "Muddy Blues," *Cw* 80 (May 29, 1969):299–300. Review of *Blues for Mister Charlie*. Condemns *Blues* for lack of argument, banalities, clichés, and stereotypes. Says play is appearances without reality, that Baldwin has the talent and a workable notion that he does not make work.

ROTH, PHILIP. "Channel X: Two Plays of the Race Conflict," *NYRB* 2 (May 28, 1964):10–13. Review of *Blues for Mister Charlie*.

SIMMONS, BILL. "Some Impressions of *The Amen Corner*," *BT* 2 (1969):32–33. Praises performance but calls the plays irrelevant in 1968. Calls production by Afro-American Studio "tragic" because one can see the same thing "for real."

SONTAG, SUSAN. *Against Interpretation and Other Essays* (New York: Farrar, Straus & Giroux, 1966), pp. 51–55. Criticism of *Blues for Mister Charlie*.

STANDBY, FRED L. "James Baldwin: The Crucial Situation," *South Atlantic Quarterly* 65 (1966):371–81.

TURPIN, WATERS E. "The Contemporary American Negro Playwright," *CLAJ* 9 (September 1965):12–24. Surveys some of the steps in the evolution of Afro-American drama, beginning with Torrence's depiction of Negro life in "Three Plays for a Negro Theatre," 1917. Includes comment and plot summaries on Louis Peterson's *Take a Giant Step*, Hansberry's *A Raisin in the Sun*, Ossie Davis's *Purlie Victorious*. Condemns critics' ill appraisal of *Blues for Mister Charlie* and considers and praises LeRoi Jones's early work at some length.

TYNAN, KENNETH. *Tynan Right and Left: Plays, Films, People, Places and Events* (New York: Atheneum, 1967), pp. 144–45. Criticism of *Blues for Mister Charlie*.

WAGER, WALTER. "Playwright at Work: James Baldwin," *Playbill* 1 no. 7 (July 1964):12–14. Review of *Blues for Mister Charlie*.

WOLFF, G. "Muffled Voices," *Nw* 77 (May 24, 1971):100ff.

Imamu Amiri Baraka (LeRoi Jones)

Arm Yourself or Harm Yourself (Newark, N.J.: Jihad, 1967).

The Baptism, 1970, Afro-American Studio for Acting and Speech, New York.

The Baptism and The Toilet (New York: Grove, 1967).

A Black Mass, 1969 ("under production"), Blackarts Midwest, Minnesota.

Bloodrites, in King and Milner anthology.

Columbia, The Gem of the Ocean, 1972–73, Howard University, Washington, D.C.

The Dead Lecturer, 1965.

The Death of Malcolm X, in Bullins anthology.

Dutchman, 1964, New York *(NYT)*.

Dutchman and The Slave (New York: Morrow, 1964).

The Eighth Ditch

Four Black Revolutionary Plays (Indianapolis: Bobbs-Merrill, 1969). Contains *Experimental Death Unit #1; A Black Mass; Great Goodness of Life; Madheart.*

Great Goodness of Life (A Coon Show), 1969, New York *(NYT)*.

Home on the Range, 1968, New York *(NYT)*. In *TDR* 12 (Summer 1968):106–11.

Jello (Chicago: Third World, 1970).

Junkies are Full of (Shhh. . . .), 1970, Newark, N.J. In King and Milner anthology.

Madheart, 1970, Spirit House Players, Newark, N.J.

Police, in *TDR* 12 (Summer 1968):112–15.

A Recent Killing, 1973, New York.

The Slave, 1964, New York *(NYT)*.

Slave Ship: An Historical Pageant, 1969–70, New York *(NYT)*; (Newark, N.J.: Jihad, 1969).

The Toilet, 1964, New York *(NYT)*.

BIOGRAPHY AND CRITICISM

ALSOP, STUART. "American Sickness," *Saturday Evening Post* 241 (July 13 1968):6.

BARAKA, IMAMU AMIRI (LEROI JONES). "The Black Aesthetic," *BW* 18:5–6 (September 1969).

————. "Black (Art) Drama Is the Same as Black Life," *E* 26 (February 1971):74–82.

————. "What Is Black Theater?" (interview), *BW* 20 (April 1971):32–6.

BERRY, FAITH. "Black Artist, Black Prophet," *NR* 154 (May 28, 1966):23–25. Review of Baraka's *Home,* a collection of essays. At times snidely condescending, at times admiring. Describes Baraka's description of Black Arts Repertory Theatre and evolution of his thinking.

BIGSBY, C. W. E. "LeRoi Jones," in C. W. E. Bigsby, *Confrontation and Commitment, A Study of Contemporary American Drama, 1959–1966* (Columbia, Mo.: University of Missouri Press, 1968), pp. 138–55.

BRADY, OWEN E., III. "Cultural Conflict and Cult Ritual in LeRoi Jones' *The Toilet,*" *Educational Theatre Journal,* 28 (March 1976):69–78.

BRUSTEIN, ROBERT. "The New American Playwrights," in Philip Rahv, *Modern Occasions* (New York: n.p., 1966), pp. 134–35.

———. "Three Plays and a Protest," *NR* 152 (January 23, 1965):32–36. Criticism of *Toilet* and *Slave*.

CLURMAN, HAROLD. "Challenge of the New Theatres," *N* 198 (February 1964):122–24.

COLEMAN, MIKE. "What is Black Theater?: An Interview with Imamu Amiri Baraka," *BW* 20 (April 1971):32–36. Baraka says black theater functions to liberate black people, that critics of black drama must have the same values as those that inform the work. He says that whites have created a Negro theater structure dependent on whites; it is, therefore, not black. Drama must talk to the actual needs of the community.

COSTELLO, D. P. "Le Roi Jones: Black Man as Victim," *Cw* 88 (June 28, 1968):436–40. Pans *The Baptism* as fury without target. Gives plot descriptions at length and praises *Toilet* and *Dutchman* for their dramatic control. Contains careful, close reading of *Dutchman*. Calls *Slave* rabid and full of invective and comments on its call for ritual drama. Stresses Jones's perception of the black man as victim and recalls Jones's call for revolutionary theater. Calls Jones's art suicidal and sees his role as critic as an attempt to try to deal with aesthetics.

"Curtains for LeRoi," *T* 91 (January 12, 1968):14.

DACE, LETITIA. *LeRoi Jones: A Checklist of Works by and About Him* (London: Nether Press, 1971).

DENNISON, GEORGE. "The Demagogy of LeRoi Jones," *Ct* 39 (February 1965):67–70. Severely negative criticism of *The Toilet* and *The Slave* and Jones personally. Calls him an "upside-down liberal" who attempts nothing and resolves nothing. Condemns Jones's language and racism; bias of writer is toward integration of white and black radicals. Compares plays to Genet's *The Blacks*.

"*Dutchman* and *The Slave*: Companions in Revolution," *Black Academy Review*, Spring–Summer 1971, pp. 101ff.

FREEDMAN, MORRIS (see entry under BALDWIN).

FULLER, HOYT W. "*The Toilet* and *The Slave*," *BW* 14 (July 1965):49–50. Critical review warns audience to accept harsh language maturely, finds *Toilet* an effective artistic creation, *Slave* too wordy, too slow, not very interesting, though concerned with important message. Plot descriptions are sketchy and misleading. Fuller seems unable to decide whether to praise or condemn.

GAFFNEY, F. "Black Theatre: the Moral function of Imamu Amiri Baraka," *Players Magazine* 50 (Summer 1975):122–31.

HENDERSON, JAMES. "*The Slave* and *The Toilet*, by Leroy [*sic*] Jones," *Harlem Youth Report Newsletter* 3 (March 12, 1965):3.

HOWARD, RICHARD. "Two Against the Chaos," *N* 200 (March 15, 1965):289.

HUDSON, THEODORE R. *From LeRoi Jones to Amiri Baraka: The Literary Works* (Durham, N.C.: Duke University Press, 1973).

HUGHES, LANGSTON. "That Boy LeRoi," *Chicago Defender*, January 11, 1965.

JACKSON, KATHRYN. "LeRoi Jones and the New Black Writers of the Sixties," F 9 (1969):232–48.

KESSLER, J. "Keys to Ourselves," SR 53 (May 2, 1970):36ff.

LLORENS, D. "Ameer (LeRoi Jones) Baraka," E 24 (August 1969):75–78ff.

MARGOLIES, EDWARD. Native Sons: A Critical Study of Twentieth-Century Negro American Authors (Philadelphia: Lippincott, 1968), pp. 195–97.

MARVIN X. "Everythin's Cool: An Interview with LeRoi Jones," BT 1 (October 1968):16ff. Jones describes the origins and financial problems of Spirit House. Calls for a National Black Arts Conference to bring together all kinds of black artists to create unity and responsibility to the large black community. Condemns the Negro Ensemble Company as white-controlled, sees emergence of a national black theater out of small, scattered black theaters. Calls for new language—of black man as conqueror—for theater. Asserts that art preaches. Marvin X questions with empathy.

MARVIN X and FARUK. "Islam and Black Art: An Interview with LeRoi Jones," BW 18 (January 1969):4–10.

———. "LeRoi Jones Talks with Marvin X and Faruk," BT 2 (1969):14–19. Jones traces his deepening involvement in Islam and emphasizes its stress on unity and "high morality." Draws connections between Islam and art, saying they both are magic and suggest the presence of God. Calls for total emphasis on the eastern (oriental) in black art.

MEYER, JUNE. "June Meyer on Negro Aims," Mademoiselle 62 (April 1966):84, 86, 89. Criticism of Dutchman.

NEAL, LAWRENCE P. "Development of LeRoi Jones," L Part 1 (January 1966):4; Part 2 (February 1966):18–19.

NELSON, HUGH. "LeRoi Jones' Dutchman: A Brief Ride on a Doomed Ship," Educational Theatre Journal 20 (March 1968):53–59. Close, critical analysis of Dutchman places play in context of legend of the Flying Dutchman with particular reference to Wagner's opera. Sees Jones as significant playwright connected to great modern European dramatists. Article contains very concrete praise.

"New Script in Newark," T 91 (April 26, 1968):18–19.

PEARSON, LOUANNE. "LeRoi Jones and a Black Aesthetic," Paunch 35 (1972):33–66.

PHILLIPS, LOUIS. "LeRoi Jones and Contemporary Black Drama." In Bigsby, The Black American Writer, pp. 203–15. Remarks black dramatists' present address to black audiences. Asserts that criticism of Jones's plays is poor and attempts to rectify this with close analysis of parts of Dutchman, The Slave, and The Toilet in particular. Stress is on Jones's themes.

"Poetic Justice," Nw 71 (January 15, 1968):24.

REAVY, CHARLES D. "Myth, Magic and Manhood in LeRoi Jones' Madheart," Studies in Black Literature 1 (Summer 1970):12–20.

RESNIK, H.S. "Brave New Words," SR 50 (December 9, 1967):28–29.

RICH, CYNTHIA JO. "Where's Baraka's Jones?" BT 4 (1970):1, 6–7.

ROTH, PHILIP. "Channel X: Two Plays on the Race Conflict," NYRB 2 (May 28, 1964):10–13. Review of Dutchman.

RUSSELL, CHARLES L. "LeRoi Jones Will Get Us All in Trouble," *L* 4 (June 1964):10–11.

SACKETT, SAMUEL S. [Review of *Black Fire*], *NALF* 8 (1974):252–53.

SCHNECK, STEPHEN. "LeRoi Jones, or, Poetics and Policeman, or, Trying Heart, Bleeding Heart," *R* 6 (June 29, 1968):14–19.

"*Slave Ship*" *NYr* 45 (December 6, 1969):168. Review calls play "more a demonstration of Conditions" than a play. Says play evokes horror and anger but no pity; lauds music.

SMITH, R. H. "Jersey Justice and LeRoi Jones," *PW* 193 (January 15, 1968):66.

SONTAG, SUSAN. *Against Interpretation and Other Essays* (New York: Farrar, Straus & Giroux, 1966), pp. 152, 155–157. Criticism of *Dutchman.*

"Spasms of Fury," *T* 84 (December 15, 1964):62–63. Review of *The Toilet* and *The Slave.*

"Theatre: Underground Fury," *Nw* 63 (April 13, 1964):60.

TURPIN, WATERS E. (see entry under BALDWIN).

VELDE, P. "Pursued by the Furies," *Cw* 88 (June 28, 1968):440–41. Brief comments on Jones's *Home on the Range.* More basic discussion of his role as poet and problems of *being* in the West. Mention of Jones's arrest.

WEALES, GERALD. "The Day LeRoi Jones Spoke on the Penn Campus, What Were the Blacks Doing in the Balcony?" *NYTM* (May 4, 1969):38–40ff.
    REVIEWS
"*Dutchman*": *American Imago* 29 (Fall 1972):215–32; *Vogue* 144 (July 1964):32; *L* 7 (1967).

A Recent Killing, *N* 216 (February 12, 1973):218–19; *NYr* 48 (February 10, 1973):75; *Nw* 81 (February 19, 1973):75.

George Bass

Black Masque, April 1971, Brown University, Providence.
The Booby, March 1967, Yale School of Drama, New Haven.
The Funhouse, September 1968, Long Wharf Theatre, New Haven.
Games, August 1966, Circle in the Square, New York.
A Trio for Living, April 1968, Yale School of Drama, New Haven.

Kingsley B. Bass, Jr. (Ed Bullins)

We Righteous Bombers, 1969. In Bullins and Turner anthologies.
    BIOGRAPHY AND CRITICISM
"Lafayette Theatre Reaction to 'Bombers,' " *BT* 4 (April 1970):16–25.

Marita Bonner

Exit, an Illusion, *C* 36 (October 1929):335–36, 352.
The Pot-Maker, *O* 5 (February 1927):43–56.
The Purple Flower, *C* 35 (January 1928):9–11.

Arna Bontemps

St. Louis Woman, 1946, New York *(NYT)*. By Arna Bontemps and Countee Cullen. Adapted from Bontemps's novel *God Sends Sunday.* Lyrics by Johnny Mercer, music by Harold Arlen. In Patterson anthology.
When the Jack Hollers, 1936. By Arna Bontemps and Langston Hughes.

William Blackwell Branch

Fifty Steps Toward Freedom: A Dramatic Presentation in Observance of the Fiftieth Anniversary of the National Association for the Advancement of Colored People (New York: NAACP, 1959).

In Splendid Error, October 24, 1954, New York *(NYT)*. The New York Public Library, Schomburg Center, mimeographed. Also in Patterson anthology.

Light in the Southern Sky, TV drama.

A Medal for Willie, October 15, 1951, Club Baron, New York *(NYT)*. The New York Public Library, Schomburg Center, mimeographed. Also in King and Milner anthology.

A Wreath for Udomo, 1960(?), Cleveland. Based on Peter Abrahamson's novel.

BIOGRAPHY AND CRITICISM

BRANCH, WILLIAM BLACKWELL. "Marketing the Products of American Negro Writers," in Conference of Negro Writers, pp. 46–50. Discusses problems of selling and six points toward solutions

EVANS, DONALD T. "Playwrights of the Fifties: Bringing It All Back Home," *BW* 20 (February 1971):41–45. Evans argues the relevance and force of black drama of the 1950s, arguing against the notion that it is "honkyhead." He comments particularly on Louis Peterson's *Take a Giant Step*, Branch's *A Medal for Willie*, Loften Mitchell's *A Land Beyond the River*, and Alice Childress's *Trouble in Mind*.

MITCHELL, LOFTEN. "Three Writers and a Dream," *C* 72 (April 1965):219–23. Probes reasons why talented Afro-American playwrights like Branch and Childress are produced once or twice, then forgotten. Suggests that the content of their plays displeases white audiences. Urges black businessmen to support drama.

A Wreath for Udomo (at Karamu), *J* (March 31, 1960):60.

A Wreath for Udomo (Broadway Preparation), *J* (March 2, 1961):59.

Arrow Brown

All for the Cause, 1972, Kuumba Workshop, Chicago, *BW* (April 1972):38. Report calls this "a one-act 'play.' "

Cecil Brown

Gila Monster, March 1969, Aldridge Players/West, Merritt College Jazz Festival, Oakland.

Real Nigger, March 1969, Aldridge Players/West, Merritt College Jazz Festival, Oakland.

Rhozier T. (Roach) Brown

Xmas in Time, December 22, 1969, Inner Voices, Lorton Correctional Complex, Washington, D.C.

William Wells Brown

The Escape; or, A Leap for Freedom (Boston: Wallcut, 1858).

Experience; or, How to Give a Northern Man a Backbone, 1856.

Miralda, 1855.

Theodore Browne

The Natural Man (Based on the Legend of John Henry): A Play in Eight

Episodes, 1936. The New York Public Library, Schomburg Center, Mimeographed. Production title was *Natural Man.*

Ed Bullins

Clara's Ole Man, 1968, New York *(NYT).* In *TDR* 12 (Summer 1968):159–71.

C'mon Back to Heavenly House, 1977, Amherst, Mass.

The Corner. In King and Milner anthology.

Daddy

Death List, October 1970, Theatre Black, University of the Street, New York. In *BT* 5 (1971):38–43.

The Devil Catchers 1970, New Lafayette Theatre, New York.

The Duplex: A Black Love Fable in Four Movements, 1970, New Lafayette Theatre, New York; (New York: Morrow, 1971).

The Electronic Nigger, 1968, New York *(NYT).* In *Five Plays,* below.

The Fabulous Miss Marie, 1971, New York.

Five Plays (Indianapolis: Bobbs-Merrill, 1969). Contains *Goin'a Buffalo; In the Wine Time; A Son, Come Home; The Electronic Nigger; Clara's Ole Man.*

Four Dynamite Plays (New York: Morrow, 1972, ca. 1971). Contains *It Bees Dat Way; Death List; The Pig Pen; Night of the Beast (a Screenplay).*

The Gentleman Caller, 1969, New York *(NYT);* (Sante Fe, N.M.: Illuminations Press, 1971). Also in *A Black Quartet* and Oliver anthology.

Home Boy, 1976, New York.

How Do You Do: A Nonsense Drama, 1968, New York *(NYT);* (Mill Valley, Calif.: Illuminations Press, 1968).

The Hungered One, 1974.

I Am Lucy Terry, 1976, New York.

In New England Winter, 1970, New Federal Theatre, New York.

In the Wine Time, 1976, New York.

Jo Anne! 1976, New York.

The Pig Pen, 1970, New York *(NYT).*

Ritual, 1970, New Lafayette Theatre, New York.

A Short Play for a Small Theatre. In *BW* 20 (April 1971):39. Play. Directions state that audience must be at least two-thirds black. Action is for actor to shoot all whites in the audience. No dialogue.

A Son, Come Home, 1968, New York *(NYT).* In *BW* 17 (April 1968):54–73.

State Office Building Curse (A Scenario in Ultimate Action). In *BW* 19 (April 1970): 54–55.

Street Sounds, 1970, New York *(NYT).*

The Streetcorner (The Corner?), 1970, Black Arts/West, Seattle, Washington.

The Taking of Miss Janie," 1975, New York Shakespeare Festival *(NYT,* March 18, 29:4; May 18, II, 5:1).

You Gonna Let Me Take You Out Tonight Baby? 1970, Black Arts/West, Seattle, Washington. In Ahmed Alhamisi and Harun Kofi Wangara, *Black Arts: An Anthology of Black Creations* (Detroit: Black Arts Publications, 1969).

BIOGRAPHY AND CRITICISM

ANDERSON, JERVIS. "Profiles," *NYr* 49 (June 16, 1973):40–44. Lengthy biographical article emphasizes Bullins's role in the New Lafayette Theatre in Harlem and discusses his public image and his notions of black theater. Includes survey and some critical comments on Bullins's plays.

BAILEY, PETER. "*Electronic Nigger* and Others," *E* 23 (September 1968):97–98. Review. Describes Off-Broadway pressure to change title of plays, describes plots of *Electronic Nigger, Clara's Ole Man,* and *A Son, Come Home.* Says plays were well-received by New York critics and describes Bullins's work and position in reference to black theater as community theater for black audiences.

BULLINS, ED. "A Short Statement on Street Theatre," *TDR* 12 (Summer 1968):93. Discusses and defines street theater. Its purpose—to communicate to large masses of black people. Its method—to draw a crowd. Its types—short, sharp plays. Everyone in crowd should be confronted.

———. "The So-Called Western Avant-Garde Drama." In Addison Gayle, Jr., *Black Expression: Essays by and About Black Americans in the Creative Arts* (New York: Weybright & Talley, 1969), pp. 143–46. Asserts that black Theater is not avant-garde because there is no such thing in America, only extensions of old Western dramatic forms and themes, but technology *might* change this. Black theater is "post-American."

———. "Theatre of Reality," *BW* 15 (April 1966):60–66. Broad, disjointed survey of problems of black actors becoming "white" actors, of inadequate numbers of radical producers, of nature and discovery of audience. Calls for "theatre of reality" that can use any style or form but aims at honesty. Criticizes whites for labeling all black literature "protest" literature.

EVANS, DON "The Theater of Confrontation: Ed Bullins Up Against the Wall," *BW* 23, no. 6 (April 1974):14–18.

GUSSOW, MEL. "New Playwrights," *Nw* 71 (May 20, 1968):115.

HAY, SAMUEL A. " 'What Shape Shapes Shapelessness?' Structural Elements in Ed Bullins' Plays," *BW* 23, no. 6 (April 1974):20–26.

JEFFERS, LANCE. "Bullins, Baraka and Elder: The Dawn of Grandeur in Black Drama," *CLAJ* (September 1972):32–48.

MARVIN X. "The Black Ritual Theatre: An Interview with Robert Macbeth," *BT* 3 (1969):20–24. Describes ritual theater as denying separation between audience and actors; there *is* no audience in ritual theater. Says theater is Western form not appropriate to blacks, but does not really define this form except in terms of audience; says that rituals are very potent, therefore frightening—others may not be ready for them; says audiences will return to ritual drama repeatedly. Comments particularly on Bullins's *In the Wine Time.*

———. "Interview with Ed Bullins." Introduction to Bullins, *New Plays.* Discusses rapid development of black theater and reasons for it in the late 1960s. Bullins says black theater is literature of the people. Describes connection between two plays in this anthology. Stresses importance of Jones in his own work and in American theater.

MASON, CLIFFORD "The Electronic Nigger Meets the Gold Dust Twins."

Taped interview of Mason (WBAI, 99.1 FM, New York City) questioning Robert Macbeth and Bullins. Macbeth describes origins and community-centered nature of New Lafayette Theatre. Both Bullins and Macbeth call for original theater oriented to a specific community and cite differences in performances for white and for black audiences. Macbeth says Bullins's plays have no message, are not political, sociological, and so forth, but are about "glorification" of human lives.

NORDEL, RODERICK. "Bullins and Black Theatre," *Christian Science Monitor*, June 4, 1969.

OLIVER, EDITH. "*In New England Winter*" *NYr* 46 (February 6, 1971):72. Review notes clear differences in responses of black and white audience members: white puzzled, blacks aware. Says play focuses on people and mutual feelings. Reviewer seems to admire Bullins's poetic and stylistic truthfulness.

——. "Three Cheers: *The Electronic Nigger* and Others," *NYr* 44 (March 9, 1968):133–34. Review summarizes plots of *A Son, Come Home, The Electronic Nigger*, and *Clara's Ole Man*, giving particular high praise to the last. Says the honesty of plays sets them "apart from propaganda"

PATTERSON, LINDSAY. "New Home, New Troupe, New Play: *In the Wine Time* on Off Broadway Theatre," *NHB* 32 (April 1969):18–19.

"*The Pig Pen*," *NYr* 46 (May 30, 1970):72–73. Reviewer is admirer of Bullins. Lauds play for giving strong illusion that stage holds "actual living." Summarizes plot and suggests this world is "new" for audience but contains little critical comment.

RILEY, CLAYTON. "Introduction," in *A Black Quartet*, pp. vii–xxii. Riley suggests black dramatists' debt to "dramatists of color" but emphasizes that playwrights of *A Black Quartet* are new breed. Sees Jones as pivotal playwright starting with and evolving from *Dutchman*. Laudatory analyses of work by LeRoi Jones, Ben Caldwell, Ron Milner, and Ed Bullins. Criticism is socio-political and concerned at points with audience.

SMITHERMAN, GENEVA. "Ed Bullins/ Stage One: Everybody Wants to Know Why I Sing the Blues," *BW* 23, no. 6 (April 1974):4–13.

TENNER, R. L. "Pandora's Box: A Study of Ed Bullins's Drama," *CLAJ* 19 (June 1976):533–44.

REVIEWS

The Duplex: N 214 (March 27, 1972):412; *NYr* 48 (March 18, 1972):85; *Nw* 79 (March 20, 1972):98–99; *T* 99 (March 27, 1972):81.

The Electronic Nigger: Cue (March 23, 1968); *N* 206 (March 25, 1968):420–31; *Nw* 71 (March 18, 1968):110.

Fabulous Miss Marie: NYr 47 (March 20, 1971):94–95.

Goin' a Buffalo NYr 48 (March 4, 1972):83.

Home Boy: NYr 52 (October 11, 1976):81.

I Am Lucy Terry: NYr 52 (February 23, 1976):82.

In the Wine Time: NYr 52 (May 10, 1976):104–5; *NYT*, April 30, 1976, III 4:5.

JACKSON, KENNELL, JR. "Notes on the Works of Ed Bullins and *The Angered One*," *CLAJ* 18 (December 1974):292–99.

Jo Anne!: *NYr* 52 (October 25 1976):62ff.; *NYT*, August 20, 1976, III, 2-2.

"No Miracles: *Black Quartet*," *Nw* 74 (August 11, 1969):82.

The Pig Pen, *N* 210 (June 1, 1970):668.

RILEY, CLAYTON. "Three Short Plays by Ed Bullins," *L* 8 (May 1968):20.

STASIO, MARILYNN. "Review: *In New England Winter*, *Cue* (February 6, 1971):8.

The Taking of Miss Janie, *America* (May 31 1975):132–427; *N* 22 (April 5, 1975):414; *NR* 172 (June 7, 1975):20; *NYr* 51 (March 24, 1975):61–3; *SR* il 2 (July 12, 1975):52; *T* (May 19, 1975):80.

Irving Burgie (Lord Burgess)

Ballad for Bimshire, 1963, New York *(NYT)*. Irving Burgie and Loften Mitchell

Mary Burrill

Aftermath, a play in one act. May 8, 1928, Krigwa Players Little Negro Theatre, New York. In *The Liberator* (1919).

Andrew M. Burris

You Mus' Be Bo'n Again, 1931, Gilpin Players, Cleveland (H).

DeReath Byrd Busey

The Yellow Tree, 1922.

James W. Butcher, Jr.

Brother Cain (one of The Last Poets)

Epitaph to a Coagulated Trinity, 1970, Black Arts/West, Seattle.

The Seer. In Sterling A. Brown, Arthur P. Davis, and Ulysses Lee, *The Negro Caravan* (New York: Dryden Press, 1941).

BIOGRAPHY AND CRITICISM

SIMMONS, BILL. "The Last Poets," *BT* (1969):32–33. Reviews Cain's play in context of general praise for liberating experience of work of The Last Poets, a group of communally oriented writers.

Ben Caldwell

All White Caste (After the Separation). In King and Milner anthology.

Family Portrait; or, My Son the Black Nationalist. In Bullins anthology.

First Militant Preacher (Newark, N.J.: Jihad, 1967).

"Four Plays: *Riot Sale, or, Do-lar Psyche Fakeout; The Job; Top Secret, or, A Few Million After B.C.; Million Accomplished*." In *TDR* 12 (Summer 1968):40–52.

Hypnotism. In *Afro-Arts Anthology* (Newark, N.J.: Jihad, 1966).

The Job, 1969, Contra Costa College Fesitval, San Pablo, California. In "Four Plays," above.

The King of Soul; or, The Devil and Otis Redding. In *BT* 3 (1969):29–33. Also in Bullins anthology.

Mission Accomplished, 1969 ("under production"), Blackarts Midwest, Minnesota. In "Four Plays," above.

Prayer Meeting; or, The First Militant Minister, 1969, New York *(NYT)*. In *A Black Quartet* and Jones anthologies.

Riot Sale. In "Four Plays," above.

Runaround, 1970, The Black Magicians, Third World Discotek, Bronx, New York.

Top Secret, 1969, Performing Arts Society of Los Angeles (PASLA). In "Four Plays," above.

BIOGRAPHY AND CRITICISM

JUNKER, HOWARD. "No Miracles: *Black Quartet, Nw* 74 (August 11, 1969):82. Review.

PERRIER, PAULETTE. "Review: The Black Magicians," *BT* (1971):51–52. Gives description of Black Magicians Third World Theatre in the Bronx and summarizes plots and themes of *Runaround*, Oyamo's *The Lovers*, and Martie Charles's *Job Security*. Praises all three plays.

RILEY, CLAYTON. See under Bullins biography and criticism.

Herbert Campbell

Middle Class!Black? 1971, Bed-Stuy Theatre, Brooklyn.

BIOGRAPHY and CRITICISM

GANT, LIZ "*Middle Class! Black?* at the Bed-Stuy Theatre," *BT* 5 (1971):52. Highly favorable review and description of Campbell's first play for Brooklyn company.

Martie Charles

Black Cycle, 1970(?), Black Theatre Workshop, New York. In King and Milner anthology.

Jamimma, 1970–71 Black Playwrights' Workshop and Oneness Productions, New York.

Job Security, 1970, The Black Magicians, Third World Discotek, the Bronx, New York.

Where We At? 1971, New York.

BIOGRAPHY AND CRITICISM

PERRIER, PAULETT. See under Caldwell biography and criticism.

Alice Childress

Florence, 1966, South Side Center of the Performing Arts, Chicago.

Gold Through the Trees, 1952.

Just a Little Simple, 1950–51, Club Baron, New York.

Mojo: A Black Love Story, 1971, New York. In *BW* 20 (April 1970):54–82.

String, 1969, New York *(NYT)*.

Trouble in Mind, 1955, New York *(NYT)*. In Patterson anthology.

Wedding Band, 1972, New York.

When the Rattlesnake Sounds, A Play (New York: Coward McCann & Geoghegan, 1975).

Wine in the Wilderness, 1971, New York.

The World on a Hill. In *Plays to Remember* (New York: Macmillan, 1968).

BIOGRAPHY AND CRITICISM

CHILDRESS, ALICE. "Why Talk About That?" *BW* 16 (April 1967). Discusses her play *Wedding Band*, how and why it was written, and the lack of public performances of plays about racial controversy in America.

———. "A Woman Playwright Speaks Her Mind," *F* 6 (Winter 1966):14–19.

EVANS, DONALD T. See under Branch biography and criticism.

MITCHELL, LOFTEN. See under Branch biography and criticism.

"The Negro Woman in American Literature," *F* 6 (Winter 1966):14–19.

OLIVER, EDITH. *String, NYr* 45 (April 12, 1969):131. Likes play, particularly for comic byplay and nightmare ending. Piece essentially describes situation of play. Has reservations about Ted Shine's "contribution," although she did enjoy it.

REVIEWS

Wedding Band: N 215 (November 13, 1972):475; *NR* 167 (November 25, 1972), 22ff; *NYr* 48 (November 4, 1972):105.

Earl Chishold
Two in the Back Room, 1972.

China Clark
Clark is listed on the back cover of *BT* 6 (1972) as the author of at least óne play; however, no title is listed next to his name.

Artie Climons
My Troubled Soul, 1969–70, Aldridge Players/ West, Oakland.

Raft Coleman
The Girl from Back Home, in *Saturday Evening Quill* (April 1929).

Erostine Coles
Festus de Fus', MS only. Atlanta University Players, Atlanta (H).
Mimi La Croix, 1934, Atlanta University Summer Theatre (H).

Curtis Cooksey
Starlight, June 1942, American Negro Theatre at Boy's Club, New York (H).

Joseph Seamon Cotter, Sr.
Caleb, the Degenerate: A Play in Four Acts; a Study of the Types, Customs, and Needs of the American Negro (New York: Henry Harrison, 1940; originally published Louisville: Bradley, West, 1903).

Countee Cullen
One Way to Heaven, 1936, New York *(NYT)*.
St. Louis Woman. See under Bontemps.
The Third Fourth of July, n.d., Drama Division New School for Social Research, New York. By Countee Cullen and Owen Dodson.

Cecil Cummins
Young Blood, Young Breed, 1969, Brownsville Laboratory of Theatre Arts, Brooklyn.

Maud Cuney-Hare
Antar of Araby. In Richardson anthology.

N. R. Davidson, Jr.
El Hajj Malik, the Life and Death of Malcolm X, 1970, New York *(NYT)*. In Bullins anthology.
Falling Scarlet (a musical), 1972.
The Further Emasculation of . . . , 1970 Dashiki Project Theatre, Afro-American Festival of Arts, Dillard University, New Orleans.
Jammer, 1971, Dashiki Project Theatre, Afro-American Festival of Arts, Dillard University, New Orleans.
Short Fun, 1970, Dashiki Project Theatre, Afro-American Festival of Arts, Dillard University, New Orleans.
Window, 1971, Dashiki Project Theatre, Afro-American Festival of Arts, Dillard University, New Orleans.
BIOGRAPHY AND CRITICISM
OLIVER, EDITH. *El Hajj Malik*, NYr 47 (December 11, 1971):102. Describes the play as chronological scenes illustrating life and death of Malcolm X from his own writings. Lauds "show."
REVIEWS
El Hajj Malik, A 125 (December 18, 1971):534; N 213 (December 20, 1971):669.

Al Davis
Man, I Really Am, 1969–70, Blackartsouth Touring Ensemble, New Orleans.

Milburn Davis
Sometimes the Switchblade Helps, 1969 ("under production"), Blackarts Midwest, Minnesota; 1969–70(?), Black Theatre Workshop, New York.

Ossie Davis
Alice in Wonder, September 1952, Elks Community Theatre, New York.
The Big Deal, 1953, New York *(NYT)*.
Purlie, 1970, New York *(NYT)*. A musical version of *Purlie Victorious*.
Purlie Victorious, a Comedy in Three Acts, 1961–62, New York *(NYT)*; (New York: Samuel French, 1961). Also in Adams, Brasmer, Oliver, Patterson, and Turner anthologies.
BIOGRAPHY AND CRITICISM
BIGSBY, C. W. E. "Three Black Playwrights: Loften Mitchell, Ossie Davis, Douglas Turner Ward." In Bigsby, 2, pp. 137–55. Thorough plot analyses and some critical discussion of Mitchell's *A Land Beyond the River*, Davis's *Purlie Victorious*, and Ward's *Day of Absence* and *Happy Ending*. An attempt to draw attention to plays Bigsby feels have had too little critical attention.
DAVIS, OSSIE. "Purlie Told Me!" F 2 (Spring 1962):155–59.
LEAKS, SYLVESTER. "Purlie Emerges Victorious," F I (Fall 1961):347.
"Purlie Victorious," E 17 (March 1962):55–60. Remarks *Purlie's* success and

calls play "the cleverest spoof of Southern segregation since *Finian's Rainbow*." Mostly pictorial description.

TURPIN, WATERS E. See under Baldwin biography and criticism.

Philip Hayes Dean

Freeman, 1972, New York.

The Owl Killer. In King and Milner anthology.

Sty of the Blind Pig, 1971, New York.

BIOGRAPHY AND CRITICISM

GANT, LIZ. "A Drama Review: *The Sty of the Blind Pig*," *BW* 21 (April 1972):81–82. Lauds play as one of the best produced by Negro Ensemble Company. Describes play's theme and plot and suggests problem of Christian Church as presented is crucial one for black audiences.

REVIEWS

Sty of the Blind Pig: N 213 (December 20, 1971):668; *NYr* 47 (December 4, 1971):131; *Nw* 78 (December 6, 1971) 122; *T* 98 (december 6, 1971):81.

Peter DeAnda

Ladies in Waiting. In King and Milner anthology.

Sweetbread

Thomas C. Dent

Feathers and Stuff, 1969.

Hal DeWindt

Raisin' Hell in the Son, MS only, 1962, New York (H).

Owen Dodson

Amistad, 1939, Talladega College, Talladega, Alabama.

The Ballad of Dorie Miller (a poem-play), February 1943, Camp Robert Smalls; 1944 CBS TV, "Pearl Harbor Day 1944." A "much condensed" version appears in *Theatre Arts* 27, no. 7(July 1943):436.

Bayou Legend. In Turner anthology.

The Christmas Miracle (a libretto), n.d., Howard University.

Divine Comedy. In Sterling A. Brown, Arthur P. Davis, and Ulysses Lee, *The Negro Caravan* (New York: Dryden Press, 1941); previously published in *La Caravella* (Italy). To be published separately by Harper & Row.

Everyone Join Hands (choral drama). In *Theatre Arts* 27, no. 9 (September 1943):555–65.

Garden of Time, 1939, The American Negro Theatre, New York; 1939, Yale University, New Haven; 1945, New York (*NYT*).

New World A-Coming (a pageant), during WW II, Madison Square Garden, New York.

The Third Fourth of July. See Under Cullen.

Dennis Donoghue

Legal Murder, 1934.

Ronald Drayton

Black Chaos

The Conquest of Africa in the Memory of Antoine Artaud

Nocturne on the Rhine. In Jones and Neal anthology.
Notes from a Savage God. In Jones and Neal anthology.

Herman Dreer
The Man of God. In *Oracle Magazine* (September 1936).

W. E. B. DuBois
Haiti
The Star of Ethiopia, 1913.
     BIOGRAPHY AND CRITICISM
DUBERMAN, MARTIN. "Dubois as Prophet," *NR* 158 (March 23, 1968):36–39.

Aaron Dumas
Encounter: Three Acts in a Restaurant, 1969, New Group Theater, Seattle.
Poor Willie, 1969, New Group Theater, Seattle.

Thelma Duncan
Black Magic. In *Yearbook of Short Plays* (New York: Row, Peterson, 1931).
The Death Dance, 1923. In Locke and Gregory anthology.
Sacrifice. In Richardson anthology.

Randolph Edmonds
Bad Man. In *Six Plays . . .* , below.
Bleeding Hearts. In *Six Plays . . .* , below.
The Devil's Price. In *Shades and Shadows*, below.
*Earth and Stars: A Problem Concerning Negro and White Leadership in the
    South* (Tallahassee: Florida A & M University Press, 1961)
Everyman's Land. In *Shades and Shadows*, below.
Gangsters over Harlem. In *The Land of Cotton . . .* , below.
Hewers of Wood. In *Shades and Shadows*, below.
"The High Court of Historia." In *The Land of Cotton . . .* , below.
The Land of Cotton and Other Plays (Washington: Associated Publishers,
    1942); also contains *Gangsters over Harlem, Yellow Death, Silas Brown,
    The High Court of Historia.*
Nat Turner. In *Six Plays . . .* , below. Also in Richardson and Miller anthol-
    ogy.
The New Window. In *Six Plays . . .* , below.
Old Man Pete. In *Six Plays . . .* , below.
The Phantom Treasure. In *Shades and Shadows*, below.
Shades and Shadows. In *Shades and Shadows*, below.
Shades and Shadows (Boston: Meador, 1930). Contains *The Devil's Price, Ev-
    eryman's Land, Hewers of Wood, The Phantom Treasure, Shades and
    Shadows, The Tribal Chief.* (Reprinted, Ann Arbor: University Mic-
    rofilms, 1970.)
Silas Brown. In *The Land of Cotton . . .* , above.
Six Plays for a Negro Theatre. Foreword by Frederick H. Koch (Boston:
    Baker, 1934). Contains *Bad Man, Bleeding Hearts, Breeders, Nat
    Turner, The New Window, Old Man Pete.* (Reprinted, Ann Arbor: Uni-
    versity Microfilms, 1970.)

The Tribal Chief. In *Shades and Shadows,* above.
Yellow Death. In *The Land of Cotton . . . ,* above.

H. T. V. Edwards
Job Hunters, C 38 (December 1931):417.

Lonne Elder III
Ceremonies in Dark Old Men, 1969, New York *(NYT);* (New York: Farrar, Straus & Giroux, 1969). Also in Couch and Patterson anthologies.
Charades on East Fourth Street. In King and Milner anthology.
    BIOGRAPHY AND CRITICISM
BIGSBY, C. W. E. "Lonne Elder III: An Interview" in Bigsby, 2, 219–26. Elder condemns blacks who attempt to define roles, audiences, and tastes for other black artists. He says he writes out of black experience but not for an all-black audience; rather, for an audience not yet in existence. He says critics are often asinine, sometimes helpful and astute. Discusses work with Negro Ensemble Company.
    REVIEWS
Ceremonies in Dark Old Men, Life 66 (April 4, 1969):14; *N* 208 (February 24, 1969):254; *NYr* 44 (February 14, 1969):90 (long review praises Negro Ensemble Company, the plot, the individual scenes; calls writing controlled without "rhetoric"); *SR* 52 (February 22, 1969):29; *T* 93 (February 14, 1969):62; *Vogue* 153 (April 15, 1969):32.

Ron Everett
The Babbler, 1971, Neo-Otun-Dila-Theatre, Philadelphia.
A Cup of Time, 1971, Neo-Otun-Dila-Theatre, Philadelphia.
Wash Your Back, 1971, Neo-Otun-Dila-Theatre, Philadelphia.

Al Fann
King Heroin, 1971, Al Fann Theatrical Ensemble, Harlem.
    REVIEWS
E 26 (June 1971):8. Suggests play has problems relating to white audience.

Peter S. Feibleman
Tiger, Tiger Burning Bright: A Play, 1962, New York *(NYT);* (Cleveland: World, 1963).
    BIOGRAPHY AND CRITICISM
Unsinkable Kate, Look 32 (August 6, 1968):63–70.

Haleemon Shaik Felton
Backstage, Ms only, 1933; 1937, Xavier College, New Orleans, (H).
College Blunders, MS only, September 13, 1931, St. Peter Claver School, New Orleans (H).
The Diamond Necklace, MS only, 1931, St Peter Claver School, New Orleans (H).
Drifting Souls, MS only, 1931, St. Peter Claver Auditorium, New Orleans (H).
House of Eternal Darkness, MS only, 1941, Dillard University, New Orleans (H).

Val Ferdinand
Black Liberation Army, 1969, Blackartsouth Touring Ensemble, New Orleans.
Homecoming, 1969–70, Blackartsouth Touring Ensemble, New Orleans.
Picket, 1969–70, Blackartsouth Touring Ensemble, New Orleans.

Rudolph Fisher
The Conjur' Man Dies, 1936, Lafayette Theatre, New York *(NYT)*.

J. E. Franklin
Black Girl, 1971, New York.
Cut Out the Lights and Call the Law, 1972, New York.
First Step to Freedom, 1964, Mississippi CORE-SNCC activity.
The In Crowd, 1967, Montreal Expo.
Mau Mau Room, n.d., Negro Ensemble Company, New York.
Prodigal Daughter n.d., street-theater project at Lincoln Center and on Bronx
    street corners, New York.
Two Flowers, n.d., The New Feminists Theatre, New York (?).
    BIOGRAPHY AND CRITICISM
PARKS, CAROLE A. "Perspectives: J. E. Franklin, Playwright," *BW* 21 (April
    1972):49–50. Review praises simple poignance of *Black Girl* and gives
    some background on Franklin's work as playwright.
    REVIEWS
Black Girl: N 123 (November 1, 1971):445; *NYr* 47 (June 26, 1971):76; *Nw* 77
    (June 28, 1971):85.

Carol Freeman
The Suicide. In Jones and Neal anthology.

Charles H. Fuller, Jr.
Love Song for Robert Lee, 1968, Afro-American Thespians, Heritage House,
    Philadelphia.
The Perfect Party, 1969, New York *(NYT)*.
The Rise. In Bullins anthology.
The Sunflower Majorette, 1971, Afro-American Arts Theatre, Philadelphia.
An Untitled Play, 1971, Afro-American Arts Theatre, Philadelphia.
The Village: A Party, 1968, New York *(NYT)*.

Roger Furman
The Long Black Block, 1972, New York.

J. E. Gaines
Don't Let It Go to Your Head, 1972, Henry Street Theatre, New York.

Jimmy Garrett
And We Own the Night: A Play of Blackness, 1969, Performing Arts Society of
    Los Angeles (PASLA). In Jones and Neal anthology. Also in *TDR* 12
    (Summer 1968):62–69.

Ted Gilliam
What You Say?; or, How Christopher Columbus Discovered Ray Charles,

Summer 1970 (proposed), Dashiki Project Theatre, New Orleans. A children's play based on comedian Flip Wilson's "Columbus" story.

Charles F. Gordon
(see OYAMO)

Charles Gordone
No Place to Be Somebody: A Black Comedy in Three Acts, 1969, New York (*NYT*). Introduction by Joseph Papp (Indianapolis: Bobbs-Merrill, 1969). Also in Oliver and Patterson anthologies.

BIOGRAPHY AND CRITICISM

From the Muthuh Lode, Nw 75 (May 25, 1970):95.

GARLAND, PHYL. "The Prize Winners: C. Gordone, M. Moore and C. Little," *E* 25 (July 1970):29–32ff. Comments on Gordone's difficulties with getting play presented, his admiration for Jones, his own concern with human condition.

"A Good Place to Be: *No Place to Be Somebody*," *NYr* (May 17, 1969):112ff. Describes structure, content, and audience reaction to play. Commends both play and performance—finds both very active.

GORDONE, CHARLES. "Quiet Talk with Myself," *Es* 73 (January 1970):78–81ff.

LEWIS, THEOPHILUS. "*No Place to Be Somebody*," *A* 121 (September 6, 1969):145. Essentially describes contents of play, calls it first-rate-drama, "a reflection of contemporary race relations," but finds problems with play's "polemics."

REVIEWS

No Place to Be Somebody: N 208 (May 19, 1969):644; *NYr* 45 (January 10, 1970):64; *Nw* 73 (June 2, 1969):101; *SR* 52 (May 1969):18; *T* 93 (May 16, 1969):85–86.

Clay Goss
Being Hit, 1970, Howard University, Washington.
Homecookin', Five Plays (Washington: Howard University Press, 1974).
Ornette, 1970, Howard University, Washington, D.C.

Arthur J. Graham
The Last Shine (San Diego: Black Book Production, 1969).
The Nationals: A Black Happening in Three Acts (San Diego: Black Book Production, 1968).

Ottie Graham
Holiday, C 26 (May 1923).

Shirley Graham
Coal Dust, MS only, April 26–30, 1938, May 1–7, 1938, Gilpin Players (H).
Dust to Earth, MS only, January 1941, Yale University Theatre; 1941, Gilpin Players, Cleveland (H).
Elijah's Raven, MS only, 1942, Gilpin Players, Cleveland (H).
I Gotta Home, February 7, 1940, Gilpin Players, Cleveland, at Oberlin (H).

Donald Greaves
"*The Marriage*." In King and Milner anthology.

Angelina Grimke
Rachel: A Play in Three Acts, 1916, Neighborhood Theatre, New York (Boston: Cornhill, 1920).

Bill Gunn
Johannas, 1969, Black Alley Theater, Washington, D.C. In *TDR* 12 (Summer 1968):126–38.
Marcus in the High Grass, 1960, New York *(NYT)*.

William Hairston
Walk in Darkness, 1963, New York *(NYT)*.

Roland Hamilton
Crack of the Whip (a play in one act), April 1935, Columbus, Ohio Drama Festival; October 1935, New Theatre League Conference, Chicago (H).

Lorraine Hansberry
Les Blancs: The Collected Last Plays of Lorraine Hansberry, 1970, New York *(NYT)*; Robert Nemiroff, ed. Introduction by Julius Lester (New York: Random House, 1972).
A Raisin in the Sun, 1959, New York *(NYT)*. (New York: Random House, 1959). Also in Adams, Oliver, and Patterson anthologies.
The Sign in Sidney Brustein's Window 1964, New York *(NYT)*; (New York: Random House, 1965).
To Be Young, Gifted and Black; Lorraine Hansberry in Her Own Words, 1969, New York *(NYT)*. Adapted by Robert Nemiroff. Introduction by James Baldwin (Englewood Cliffs, N.J.: Prentice-Hall, 1969).
    BIOGRAPHY AND CRITICISM
BALDWIN, JAMES. "Sweet Lorraine," *Es* 72 (November 1969):139–40.
BIGSBY, C. W. E. "Lorraine Hansberry." In Bigsby, *Confrontation and Commitment*, pp. 156–73.
BROWN, LLOYD W. "Lorraine Hansberry as Ironist: A Reappraisal of *A Raisin in the Sun*," *JBS* 4 (1974):237–47.
CRUSE, HAROLD. "Lorraine Hansberry." In Harold Cruse, *The Crisis of the Negro Intellectual* (New York: Morrow, 1967). Detailed discussion attempts to place Hansberry's work in history in terms of social and aesthetic implications. Condemns her for imitating the white world and attempting to elevate the Jewish image while not dealing with black world, and condemns her "clichéd" leftist involvement as leading her down narrow paths.
DAVIS, OSSIE. "The Significance of Lorraine Hansberry," *F* 5 (Summer 1965):397–402.
"Elegy for Lorraine: Presentation of *To Be Young, Gifted and Black*," *T* 93 (January 10, 1969):43.
FORD, GLEBERT "Lorraine Hansberry's World," *L* 4 (1964).
FREEDMAN, MORRIS. See under Baldwin biography and criticism.
"From a Time of Racial Hope," *Life* 72 (January 14, 1972):14.
GANT, LIZ. "Reviews: *Les Blancs*," *BW* 20 (April 1971):46–47. Praises the play in general terms. Asserts that the play was killed before opening by "rumors."

GILL, GLENDA. "Techniques of Teaching Lorraine Hansberry: Liberator from Boredom," *NALF* 8 (1974):226–28.

GUTTMANN, ALLEN. "Integration and Black Nationalism in the Plays of Lorraine Hansberry." In Alfred Weber and Siegfried Neuwiller, eds., *Amerikanisches Drame und theater in 20. Jahrhundert* (Göttingen: Vandenhoeck, 1975) pp. 248–60.

HANSBERRY, LORRAINE. "American Theatre Needs Desegregating, Too," *BW* 10 (June 1961):28–33.

————. "He Who Must Live," *Encore* 6 (November–December 1959):30–35.

————. "My Name Is Lorraine Hansberry, I Am a Writer," *Es* 72 (November 1969):140–41.

ISAACS, HAROLD R. See under Baldwin biography and criticism.

KILLENS, JOHN O. "Broadway in Black and White," *AF* 1 no. 3 (Winter 1965):66–70. Surveys Afro-American achievements in theater and film from 1958 production of *Raisin in the Sun* to 1965. Praises Hansberry, Ossie Davis, Baldwin, Branch, Loften Mitchell, LeRoi Jones, Childress. Remarks previous financial problems and problems of white critics and black theater; calls for black artists to unite and create own resources. Mentions Ossie Davis's play *Alice in Wonder*, produced in Harlem.

Les Blancs, Cw 93 (January 22, 1971):397. Review simply and briefly describes play and suggests it was altered greatly by others than Hansberry.

Les Blancs, NYr 46 (November 21, 1970):104. Review that pans play for its datedness, didactic tone, and melodrama, while commending the performance of James Earl Jones.

LEWIS, THEOPHILUS. "Social Protest in *A Raisin in the Sun*," *Catholic World* 190 (October 1959):31–35.

MILLER, JORDAN Y. "Lorraine Hansberry." In Bigsby, 2, pp. 157–70. Thorough discussion of themes and structures of *A Raisin in the Sun* and *The Sign in Sidney Brustein's Window;* applauds Hansberry's work as "good old-fashioned" drama whose forms and contents set good examples.

OLIVER, EDITH. "Off Broadway: Presentation of *To Be Young, Gifted and Black*," *NYr* 44 (January 11, 1969):58.

"*Raisin in the Sun* Sets Record (Number of Performances)," *J* (March 10, 1960):58.

TURPIN, WATERS E. See entry under Baldwin.

TYNAN, KENNETH. *Curtains: Selections from the Drama Criticism and Related Writings* (New York: Atheneum, 1961), pp. 306–9. Discussion of *A Raisin in the Sun.*

WEALES, GERALD. "Losing the Playwright," *Cw* 90 (September 5, 1969): 542–43.

————. "Thoughts on *A Raisin in the Sun*," *Ct* 27 (June 1959):527–30. Calls *Raisin* A good play with a number of imperfections. Weales points to evidence that a play by a Negro will remain a "Negro play," perceives various effects of "being a Negro" on critics and audiences. Says naturalism of *Raisin* is anachronistic, that play in no way revitalizes dying American theater.

REVIEWS

Les Blancs: N 211 (November 30, 1970):573; *N* 211 (December 7, 1970):606; *Nw* 76 (November 30, 1970):98.

Clarence Harris

The Trip. In Etheridge Knight, *Black Voices from Prison* (New York: Pathfinder Press, 1970), pp. 77–83.

Helen Webb Harris

Frederick Douglass. In *NHB* (February, March, April 1972), written in 1941.
Genifrede; or, Genefred. In Richardson and Miller anthology.

Neil Harris

Cop and Blow, 1972 New York.
Players Inn, 1972, New York.
The Portrait, 1970 (?), Black Theatre Workshop, New York.
REVIEWS
Cop and Blow and *Players Inn, N* 214 (April 17, 1972):508; *NYr* 48 (April 8, 1972):98–99; *T* 99 (May 1, 1972):53.

Paul Carter Harrison

Tabernacle. In *BW* 21 (August 1972):48.

Samuel A. Hay

BW 21 (April 1972):14, mentions Hay as a playwright whose works have been produced at Cornell University and in Baltimore but cites no specific plays.

Robert Hayden

The History of Punchinello, NADSA *Encore,* 1st ed., 1948.

Alvira Hazzard

Little Heads. In *Saturday Evening Quill* (April 1929).
Mother Liked It. In *Saturday Evening Quill* (April 1928).

Donald Heywood

How Come, Lawd, 1937, Negro Theatre Guild, New York (H).
Ol' Man Satan, 1932, Forrest Theatre, New York (H).

Abram Hill

Anna Lucasta, 1944, New York *(NYT).* Adaptation of Phillip Yordan's play. By Abram Hill and Harry Wagstaff Gribble.
Liberty Deferred, 1930s. By John Silvera and Abram Hill.
On Strivers Row: A Comedy about Sophisticated Harlem, 1946, New York *(NYT).* The New York Public Library, Schomburg Center, mimeographed.
The Power of Darkness, 1948, New York *(NYT).* Adapted from Leo Tolstoy.
Walk Hard, 1944, 1946, New York *(NYT).* Based on the Len Zinberg novel *Walk Hard—Talk Loud.*

Leslie Pinckney Hill

Toussaint L'Ouverture (Boston: The Christopher Publishing House, 1928).

John Hines

The Boyhood Adventures of Frederick Douglass: A Play (New York: New Dimensions, 1968).

The Celebration: A Play (New York: New Dimensions, 1968).

The Genius of Benjamin Banneker: A Play (New York: New Dimensions, 1968).

In Memory of Jerry (New York: New Dimensions, 1970).

The Outsider (New York: New Dimensions, 1970).

Harold Holifield

Cow in the Apartment, 1950–51, New York.

J. Toth, 1950–51, New York.

Pauline Elizabeth Hopkins

One Scene from the Drama of Early Days

Slave's Escape; or, The Underground Railroad, 1897; title varies: (a) *Escaped from Slavery; or . . . , "* (b) *Peculiar Sam; or . . ."*

  BIOGRAPHY AND CRITICISM

SHOCKLEY, ANN ALLEN. "Pauline Elizabeth Hopkins: A Biographical Excursion into Obscurity," *P* 33 (Spring 1972):22–26.

Langston Hughes

Angelo Herndon Jones, May 1938, Harlem Suitcase Theater. *New Theatre Magazine*, manuscript in Yale University Library.

The Barrier, 1950, New York *(NYT)*.

Black Nativity, 1961, New York; 1969, Afro-American Studio, New York *(NYT)*.

Don't You Want to Be Free? In *One-Act Play Magazine* 2 (October 1938).

Emperor of Haiti. In Turner *Black Drama in America.*

Five Plays. Edited and introduced by Webster Smalley (Bloomington: Indiana University Press, 1963). Contains *Mulatto; Soul Gone Home; Little Ham; Simply Heavenly; Tambourines to Glory.*

Front Porch, 1938.

Gospel Glow, 1962, New York *(NYT)*.

Joy to My Soul, 1937. In *Five Plays*, above.

Little Ham

Mother and Child: (A Theater Vignette), 1966, American Place Theatre, New York. In King and Milner anthology.

Mulatto, 1935, New York; 1967, New York *(NYT)*. In *Five Plays*, above. Also in Brasmer anthology.

The Prodigal Son, 1965, New York *(NYT)*.

Scottsboro Limited: Four Poems and a Play in Verse (New York: Golden Stair, 1932).

Shakespeare in Harlem, 1960, New York *(NYT)*.

Simply Heavenly, 1957, New York *(NYT)*; (New York: Dramatists Play Service, 1957). Also in *Five Plays*, above, and Patterson anthology.

Soul Gone Home 1959, New York *(NYT)*. In *Five Plays*, above.

The Sun Do Move, 1942.

Tambourines to Glory, 1963, New York *(NYT)*. In *Five Plays*, above.

Troubled Island, 1935–36.

When the Jack Hollers, 1936. By Langston Hughes and Arna Bontemps.

BIOGRAPHY AND CRITICISM

BERRY, FAITH, ed. *Good Morning Revolution: Uncollected Social Protest Writings by Langston Hughes* (New York: Lawrence & Hill, 1973).

BROOKS, GWENDOLYN. "Obituary," *N* 205 (July 3, 1967):7.

DANDRIDGE, RITA B. "The Black Woman as a Freedom Fighter in Langston Hughes's *Simple's Uncle Sam*," *CLAJ* 18 (December 1974):273–83.

DICKENSON, DONALD C. *A Bio-Bibliography of Langston Hughes, 1902–1967*, 2d ed., rev., n.p. Preface by Arna Bontemps. (Hamden, Connecticut: Shoe String Press, 1972; Archon Books).

————. "Langston Hughes and the 'Brownie' Book," *NHB* 31 (December 1968):8–10.

GORDON, CHARLES F. (OYAMO). "Reviews: *Black Nativity*," *BT* 3 (1969):34. Brief description of play as celebration of blackness and black magic, but more clearly an attempt to distinguish between Hughes's European-derived work and the non-Western trend of Black Arts.

HUGHES, LANGSTON. "Ballad of Negro History," *NHB* 30 (October 1967):17.

————. *Big Sea, an Autobiography* (New York: Hill & Wang, 1963).

"Hughes at Columbia," *NYr* 43 (December 30, 1967):21–23.

ISAACS, HAROLD R. See under Baldwin.

KING, WOODIE, JR. "So Near to Our Hearts," *BT* 3 (1969):12–16. An anecdotal narration of King's encounters with Hughes that creates image of Hughes as beneficent guardian of black writers and black theater.

KINNEMON, KENNETH. "Man Who Created Simple" *N* 205 (December 4, 1967):599–601.

"Langston Hughes Dies at Sixty-Five," *NHB* 30 (October 1967):16.

MALOFF, S. "Death of Simple," *Nw* 69 (June 5, 1967):104.

MITCHELL, LOFTEN. "An Informal Memoir for Langston Hughes and Stella Holt," *BW* 17 (April 1968):74–77.

NICHOLS, LEWIS. "Langston Hughes Describes the Genesis of His *Tambourines to Glory*," *New York Times*, October 27, 1963, II:3.

"Obituary," *PW* 191 (June 12, 1967):37.

PRESLEY, JAMES. "The American Dream of Langston Hughes," *Southwest Review* 48 (Autumn 1963):380–86.

SPENCER, T. J., and CLARENCE J. RIVERS. "Langston Hughes: His Style and Optimism," *Drama Critique* 7 (Spring 1964):99–102. Explains reasons for Hughes's obscurity as a playwright. Suggests segregated thought patterns, difficulty in communication and says Hughes is not an innovator in dramatic technique. He has no "structural" style but does have a style in sense of controlling manner of thought. Praises Hughes for not "advocating a cause" or limiting his audience.

TURNER, DARWIN T. "Langston Hughes as Playwright," *CLAJ* 11 (June 1968):297–309. A critical survey of Hughes's dramas that suggests interconnections and perceives a development in quality culminating in the somewhat flawed but good dramas of the 1960s—*Emperor of Haiti* and *Tambourines to Glory*. Turner speaks of Hughes's stereotyping in drama, of his problems with language and sagging plots, and gives him credit for establishment of all-Negro theater companies.

WERTZ, I. J. "Langston Hughes: Profile," *NHB* (March 1964), 146–47.

REVIEWS

"*Black Nativity* Opens Off-Broadway," *J* (December 28, 1961), 56; " 'Tambourines to Glory' " (Hazel Scott in Lead), *J* (July 21, 1960), 62.

Ruby Hult

The Sage of George W. Bush. In *BW* 2 (September 1962):88–96.

Elizabeth Maddox Huntley

Legion, the Demoniac. In Herman Dreer, *American Literature by Negro Authors* (New York: Macmillan, 1950).

What Ye Sow (New York: Court, 1955).

Zora Neale Hurston

The First One, 1926. In *Ebony and Topaz* (H).

Great Day, 1932, John Golden Theatre, New York (H).

Sermon in the Valley, 1931, 1934; 1949, Gilpin Players, Cleveland (H).

Yusef Iman

Praise the Lord, but Pass the Ammunition, 1970, (proposed) Hill Arts Theatre, New Haven; (Newark: Jihad, 1967).

Marvin E. Jackmon (Nazzam Al Fitnah) See Marvin X.

Elaine Jackson

Toe Jam. In King and Milner anthology.

William Jackson

"Burning the Mortgage," February 1931, Harlem Players (H).

Gertrude Jeanette

Bolt from the Blue, 1950–51, New York.

Light in the Cellar, MS only. "Showcased" in 1960; 1963, presented to New York high schools (under option, March 1964) (H).

This Way Forward, 1950–51.

Fenton Johnson

The Cabaret Girl, 1925.

Georgia Douglas Johnson

Blue Blood. In Frank Shay, *Fifty More Contemporary One-Act Plays* (New York: Appleton, 1928).

Frederick Douglass. In Richardson and Miller anthology.

Plumes. In *O* 5 (May 1925):200–01, 217–18. Also in Locke and Gregory anthology.

William and Ellen Craft. In Richardson and Miller anthology.

Hall Johnson

Run Little Chillun! 1933, 1943, New York (*NYT*); 1939, San Francisco; The New York Public Library, Schomburg Center, typewritten.

James Weldon Johnson

God's Trombones, 1960 New York (*NYT*). Dramatization of Johnson's poem performed with Langston Hughes's *Shakespeare in Harlem*.

BIOGRAPHY AND CRITICISM

ADELMAN, LYNN "A Study of James Weldon Johnson," *JNH* 52 (April 1967):128–45.

LeRoi Jones See Imamu Amiri Baraka.

Walter Jones
The Boston Tea Party at Annie Mae's House, 1970–71, Ellen Stewart Theatre, New York.
Jazznite, 1970–71, Cornbread Players, Public Theatre, New York.
Nigger Nightmare, June 1971, Cornbread Players, Public Theatre, New York.

Adrienne Kennedy
A Best's Story, 1969, New York *(NYT)*.
Cities in Bezique, 1969, New York *(NYT)*.
Funnyhouse of a Negro, 1964, New York *(NYT)*. In Patterson, Brasmer, and Oliver anthologies.
In His Own Write, 1968, New York *(NYT)*. An adaptation of John Lennon *In His Own Write* (the original title of this play was *Scene Three Act One*).
A Lesson in Dead Language. In Edward Parone, *Collision Course* (New York: Vintage, 1968), pp. 33–40.
The Owl Answers, 1963. In William M. Hoffman, *New American Plays*, 2 (New York: Hill & Wang, 1968).
A Rat's Mass, 1969, New York *(NYT)*. In Couch anthology.
BIOGRAPHY AND CRITICISM
CLURMAN, HAROLD. "Theatre," *N* 198 (February 10, 1964):154. Review of *Funnyhouse of a Negro*.
REVIEWS
Cities in Bezique, NYr (January 25, 1969):77.

John Oliver Killens
Ballad of the Winter Soldiers, 1964. By John Oliver Killens and Loften Mitchell.
BIOGRAPHY AND CRITICISM
KILLENS, JOHN O. See under Hansberry biography and criticism.

Woodie King, Jr.
Simple's Blues 1967.
Weary Blues, October 1966, Lincoln Center, New York. An adaptation of some of Langston Hughes's poetry and prose.
BIOGRAPHY AND CRITICISM
KING, WOODIE, JR. See under Hughes biography and criticism.

Arthur Clifton Lamb
Beebee (The Drama of a Negro Lady Doctor), 1940, University of Iowa, master's thesis play.
The Faith-Cure Man, MS only, 1930, Grinnell College (H).
God's Great Acres, MS only, 1939, Prairie View State College, Texas (H). Awarded Sergel Prize in Regional Playwrighting at the State University of Iowa.

Mistake into Miracle (originally a TV production). December 1961, Morgan
State College, Baltimore (H).
Portrait of a Pioneer. In *NHB* 12 (April 1949) Radio play on Ira Aldridge.
Reachin' for the Sun, MS only, Grinnell College (H).
Roughshod Up the Mountain, 1953, State University of Iowa; 1964, Paris.

Raymond League
Mrs. Carrie B. Phillips, 1970, The Lambs Club, New York. A Musical comedy.

Maryat Lee
Dope, 1970, Bed-Stuy Theatre, Brooklyn.

C. D. Lipscomb
Frances. In *O* 3 (May 1925):148–53.

Myrtle A. Smith Livingston
For Unborn Children. In *C* 31–33 (July 1926):122. Also in Hatch and Shine,
Black Theater U.S.A.

K. Curtis Lyle
Da Minstrel Show, 1969, Black Arts/West, Seattle.
Days of Thunder, Nights of Violence, 1969, New Group Theatre, Black Arts/
West Seattle.
Guerrilla Warfare, 1969, New Group Theatre, Black Arts/West, Seattle.

Aubrey Lyles
Keep Shufflin', 1928, New York *(NYT)*. A musical comedy. Book by Flournoy
E. Miller and Aubrey Lyles; music by Jimmy Johnson, F. Waller, and
Clarence Todd; lyrics by Henry Creamer and Andy Razaf.
Runnin' Wild, 1923, New York *(NYT)*. A musical comedy. Book by Flournoy
E. Miller and Aubrey Lyles; music and lyrics by Ames Johnson and Cecil
Mack.

Robert Macbeth
A Black Ritual. In *TDR* 13 (Summer 1969):129–30, and *BT* 2 (1969):8–9.

Rose McClendon
Taxi Fare, MS only. By Rose McClendon and Richard Bruce. February 1931,
Harlem Players (H).

Milton McGriff
And Then We Heard the Thunder, 1968, Lee Cultural Center, Philadelphia.
An adaptation of the John Oliver Killens novel.
Nigger Killers, 1971 (proposed), Black Arts Spectrum Theatre, Philadelphia.

Ray McIver
God Is a (Guess What?), 1968, New York *(NYT)*.
BIOGRAPHY AND CRITICISM
LEWIS, THEOPHILUS. "*God Is a (Guess What?)*," *A* 120 (January 11, 1969):50.

Lewis finds this "minstrel show" diverting and fun, but does not attempt to deal with it on any but its surface level.

OLIVER, EDITH. "The Comic View: Performance of R. McIver's *God Is a (Guess What?)* by Negro Ensemble Company," *NYr* 44 (December 28, 1968):50–51. A somewhat chaotic description of McIver's play, which labels it protest drama. Suggests Oliver's discomfort with same but likes the play's wit and music.

REVIEWS

God Is a (Guess What?), *T* 92 (December 27 1968):47.

Edwin Charles McKenney

Mr. Big (New York: Pageant, 1954).
Virgin Islands (New York: William-Frederick, 1951).

William Wellington Mackey

Behold! Cometh the Vanderkellans, 1971, New York (New York: Azazel, 1967).
Billy Noname; or, Bill Noname, 1970, New York *(NYT)*.
Family Meeting. In Couch anthology.
Requiem for Brother X, a Homage to Malcolm X. In King and Milner anthology.

BIOGRAPHY AND CRITICISM

Behold! Cometh the Vanderkellans, review, *NYr* 47 (April 10, 1971):67–68.

Will Anthony Madden

Two and One (New York: Exposition 1961). Two stories and one drama.

Marvin X (Marvin E. Jackmon, Marvin X. Jackmon, Nazzam Al Fitnah)

The Black Bird, 1969 ("under production") Blackarts Midwest, Minnesota. In Bullins anthology.
Come Next Summer
Flowers for the Trashman, 1970, Afro-American Studio for Acting and Speech, New York. In Jones and Neal anthology.
Flowers for the Whiteman (new title for *Take Care of Business*).
The Resurrection of the Dead! A Ritual. In *BT* 3 (1969):26–27.
Take Care of Business, 1966–69, Afro-American Studio for Acting and Speech, New York (retitled *Flowers for the Whiteman*).

BIOGRAPHY AND CRITICISM

MARVIN X. See Bullins biography and criticism.
———. "Interview with Ed Bullins." Introduction to Bullins anthology (see also under Bullins biography and criticism: Marvin X. "Interview . . .").
———. "An Interview with Ed Bullins: Black Theatre," *BW* 18 (April 1969):9–16.
———. "Moon on a Rainbow Shawl," *BT* 1 (October 1968):30. Review discusses plot and commends West Indian playwright John's control of language and true revelation of condition of black people, but says play is not revolutionary because it does not go beyond present image—something black drama should do.

MARVIN X and FARUK. "Islam and Black Art: An Interview with LeRoi Jones." *BW* 18 (January 1969):4–10.
———. See under Baraka biography and criticism.

Clifford Mason
Gabriel: The Story of a Slave Rebellion. In King and Milner anthology.
Sister Sadie and the Sons of Sam, 1968, The New Dramatists' Workshop, New York.
BIOGRAPHY AND CRITICISM
MASON, CLIFFORD. See under Bullins biography and criticism.

John Matheus
Black Damp. In *Carolina Magazine* 49 (April 1929).
'Cruiter. In Locke and Gregory anthology.
Guitar
Ti Yette. In Richardson anthology.

Julian Mayfield
417, 1961, New York *(NYT).*
The Other Foot, 1950–51, New York.
A World Full of Man, 1950–51, New York.

Flournoy E. Miller
Keep Shufflin'. See under Lyles.
Runnin' Wild. See under Lyles.

May Miller
Christopher's Daughter. In Richardson and Miller anthology.
Graven Images. In Richardson anthology.
Harriet Tubman. In Richardson and Miller anthology.
Riding the Goat. In Richardson anthology.
Samory. In Richardson and Miller anthology.
Scratches. In *Carolina Magazine* 49 (April 1929).
Sojourner Truth. In Richardson and Miller anthology.

Ronald Milner
Life Agony
M (Ego) and the Green Ball of Freedom. In *BW* 20 (April 1971):40–45.
The Monster. In *TDR* 12 (Summer 1968):94–105.
The Warning—A Theme for Linda, 1969, New York *(NYT).* In *A Black Quartet* anthology.
What the Wine-Sellers Buy, a three-act play (New York: Samuel French, 1974).
Who's Got His Own, 1966, New York *(NYT).* In King and Milner anthology.
BIOGRAPHY AND CRITICISM
EVANS, DONALD. "*Who's Got His Own* at Cheyney," *BW* 19 (April 1970):43–48, 97–98. Describes the process of choosing and rehearsing

Milner's play at Cheyney State College. Out of his own experience, Evans draws the conclusions that black plays are easier to play if centered on characters rather than harangues, that clichés are dangerous in black theater, that theater calls for special language. He lauds Milner's play, but is anxious about weakness in much black drama. Stresses importance of black college theater.

JEANPIERRE, WENDELL A. "Who's Got His Own," C 74 (October 1967):423. Lauds this drama as deeply moving and well constructed.

JUNKER, HOWARD. "No Miracles: Black Quartet," review, Nw 74 (August 11, 1969):82.

MITCHELL, LOFTEN. "The Season Is Now," C 74 (January-February 1967):31–34. Praises Milner's play as "interesting" and "overpowering." Slightly ironic consideration of why critics responded poorly.

"A New Playwright," BW 15 (October 1966), 49–50. Discusses Milner, the production plans for Who's Got His Own, and the success of the new American Place Theatre, where play was to be produced.

RILEY, CLAYTON. See under Bullins biography and criticism.

Joseph S. Mitchell
The Elopement. In Saturday Evening Quill (April 1930).
Help Wanted. In Saturday Evening Quill (April 1928).

Loften Mitchell
The Afro-Philadelphial, 1970.
Ballad for Bimshire, 1963, New York (NYT). By Loften Mitchell and Irving Durgie.
Ballad of the Winter Soldiers, 1964. By Loften Mitchell and John Oliver Killens.
The Bancroft Dynasty, 1950–51, New York.
Bubbling Brown Sugar, 1976, New York (NYT), March 3, 30:1.
The Cellar, 1950–51, New York.
A Land Beyond the River, 1957, New York (NYT) (Cody: Pioneer Drama Service, 1963). Also in Adams anthology.
Star of the Morning: Scenes in the Life of Bert Williams, 1965. Music and lyrics by Louis Mitchell and Romare Bearden. In King and Milner anthology.
Tell Pharaoh, 1967.

BIOGRAPHY AND CRITICISM

BIGSBY, C. W. E. See Ossie Davis biography and criticism.
EVANS, DONALD T. See under Branch biography and criticism.
MITCHELL, LOFTEN. See under Milner biography and criticism.

Molette, Barbara, and Carlton W. Molette II
Booji Wooji, July 1971, Atlanta University Summer Theatre, Atlanta; December 1972 (revised version), Morehouse-Spelman Players, Atlanta.
Dr. B. S. Black (musical version), July 1972, Atlanta University Summer Theatre, Atlanta.
Rosalee Pritchett, May 1970, Morehouse-Spelman Players, Atlanta; 1971, New York.

BIOGRAPHY AND CRITICISM

Rosalee Pritchett review, *NYr* 26 (January 30, 1971):56–57.

Carlton W. Molette II

Dr. B. S. Black, n.d., Morehouse-Spelman Players, Atlanta; 1970, Howard University, Washington, D.C. In *Encore* (National Association of Dramatic and Speech Arts) 13 (1970).

Peter Morell

Turpentine, 1936, Federal Theatre, New York. By J. Augustus Smith and Peter Morell.

Gilbert Moses

Roots, 1970, Afro-American Studio for Acting and Speech, New York. In Dent, pp. 185–206.

F. Carlton Moss

Sacrifice, MS only, February 1931, Harlem Players.

Natalie Nelson

More Things That Happen to Us (New York: New Dimensions, 1970). For young children.

Things That Happen to Us (New York: New Dimensions, 1970). For young children.

George Norford

Joy Exceeding Glory, 1938–39, Rose McClendon Workshop Theatre, New York.

Oyamo (Charles F. Gordon)

Bignigga, 1970, Henry Street Settlement, New York.

The Breakout. In King and Milner anthology.

Chumpanzee, 1970, Henry Street Settlement, New York.

Hillbilly Liberation (A Grossly Understated Prayer of Theatrical Spectacles, Social Position and Poetry), New York, Oyamo Ujama, 1976.

The Lovers, 1970, The Black Magicians, Third World Discotek, the Bronx, New York.

Out of Site. In *BT* 4 (1969):28–31.

The Thieves, 1970, Black Arts/West, Seattle.

BIOGRAPHY AND CRITICISM

CLARKE, SEBASTIAN. "Magical Delights," *BT* 5 (1971):54–55. Review and descriptions of *Bignigga* and *Chumpanzee*. Says audiences were very responsive.

PERRIER, PAULETTE. See Caldwell biography and criticism.

Oblamola Oyedele

The Struggle Must Advance to a Higher Level. In *BT* 6 (1972):12–13.

Lynn K. Pannel

It's a Shame, May 1971, Theatre Black, Bed-Stuy Theatre, Brooklyn.

Charles Patterson

Black-Ice. In Jones and Neal anthology.

The Super

Thomas D. Pawley, Jr.
Crispus Attucks (Son of Liberty), MS only, March 1948, State University of
    Iowa (H).
FFV, MS only, November 1963, Lincoln University Stagecrafters, Missouri
    (H).
Judgement Day. In Sterling A. Brown, Arthur P. Davis, and Ulysses Lee,
    Negro Caravan (New York: Dryden, 1941).
Messiah, MS only, July 1948, State University of Iowa (H).
Smoky, MS only, April 1939, University of Iowa (H).

Eugene Perkins
The Image Makers, 1973, Chicago.

Leslie Perry
The Minstrel Show, 1970–71, San Francisco Bay area.
The Side Show, 1970–71, San Francisco Bay area.

Louis S. Peterson
Count Me for a Stranger
Entertain a Ghost, 1963, New York *(NYT)*.
Take a Giant Step, 1953, 1956, New York *(NYT)*; (New York: Samuel French,
    1954). Also in Patterson and Turner anthologies.
        BIOGRAPHY AND CRITICISM
TURPIN, WATERS E. See Baldwin biography and criticism.

Oliver Pitcher
The One. In King and Milner anthology.

Richard Powell
Aaron Asworth (New York: New Dimensions, 1970).

Doris Price
The Bright Medallion. In Kenneth T. Rowe, *University of Michigan Plays* (Ann
    Arbor: University of Michigan Press, 1932).
The Eyes of the Old. In Rowe; see preceding item.
Two Gods: A Minaret. In *O* 10.

Ira D. Reid
John Henry, MS only, Summer 1937, Atlanta University Summer Theater (H).

Stanley Richards
District of Columbia. In *O* 23 (January-March 1945):88–91. Also in Hatch and
    Shine, *Black Theater U.S.A.*

Mel Richardson
The Breach, March 1969, Aldridge Players/West, Merritt College, Oakland.

Thomas Richardson
Place: America (A Theatre Piece) (based on the history of the NAACP).
    Foreword by Sterling A. Brown (New York: NAACP, 1940).

Willis Richardson
Antonio Maceo. In Richardson and Miller, *Negro History in Thirteen Plays.*
Attucks, the Martyr. In *Negro History in Thirteen Plays.*

The Black Horseman. In Richardson, *Plays and Pageants (PPLN).*

Boot-Black Lover

The Broken Banjo: A Folk Tragedy. In Locke and Gregory, *Plays of Negro Life (PNL).*

The Chip Woman's Fortune, 1923, New York *(NYT).* In Turner, *Black Drama in America.*

Compromise. In Alain Locke, *The New Negro* (New York: Atheneum, 1970).

The Deacon's Awakening. In *C* 21 (November 1920):10–15.

The Elder Dumas. In *Negro History in Thirteen Plays.*

The Flight of the Natives. In *PNL.*

The House of Sham. In *PPLN.*

The Idle Head. In *Carolina Magazine* 49 (April 1929).

In Menelek's Court. In *Negro History in Thirteen Plays.*

The King's Dilemma and Other Plays for Children (New York: Exposition, 1956). *The King's Dilemma* also in *PPLN.*

Miss or Mrs., MS only, May 1941, Bureau Engraving Dramatic Club, Washington, D.C. (H).

Mortgaged. In Otilie Cromwell, Eve Dykes, and Lorenzo Fuller, *Readings from Negro Authors* (New York: Harcourt, 1931).

Near Calvary. In *Negro History in Thirteen Plays.*

The Peacock's Feather, January 1928, Krigwa Players of Washington, (H).

The Shell-Road Witch.

The Victim, MS only.

BIOGRAPHY AND CRITICISM

PETERSON, BERNARD L., JR. "Willis Richardson: Pioneer Playwright," *BW* 24, no. 6 (April 1975):40–48, 86–88.

Garrett Robertson

Land of Lem, 1971, Afro-Arts Cultural Center, New York.

Juan Rodriquez

Why We Lost the Series (New York: New Dimensions, 1970). For young children.

John Ross

The Purple Lily, 1947–48, Fisk University Stagecrafters, Nashville (H).

Wanga Doll, 1945–46, Fisk University Stagecrafters, Nashville (H).

Charles L. Russell

Five on the Black Hand Side, 1970, New York *(NYT);* (New York: Samuel French, 1970).

BIOGRAPHY AND CRITICISM

LEWIS, THEOPHILUS. *"Five on the Black Hand Side,"* A 122 (February 7, 1970):142. Lauds play as a robust comedy that suggests "wealth of invisible knowledge of Negro life."

RUSSELL, CHARLES L. See under Baraka biography and criticism.

Kalamu Ya Salaam

The Destruction of the American Stage (A Set for Non-believers). In *BW* 21 (April 1972):55–69.

Salimu

Growin' into Blackness, 1970, (proposed) Hill Arts Theatre, New Haven. In *BT* 2 (1969):20–22. Also in Bullins anthology.

Sonia Sanchez

The Bronx Is Next, October 1970, Theatre Black, University of the Street, New York. In *TDR* 12 (Summer 1968):78–83.
Malcolm/Man Don't Live Here No Mo. In *BT* 6 (1972):24–27.
Sister Son/ji, 1969/70(?), Sudan Arts/Southwest, Houston; 1972, New York. In Bullins anthology.
    REVIEWS
Sister Son/ji, N 214 (April 17, 1972):508; *NYr* (April 8, 1972):97–98; *T* 99 (May 1, 1972):53.

Jimmy Scott

Money, 1969, North Richmond Theatre Workshop, University of California at Berkeley.

John Scott

Ride a Black Horse, 1971, Negro Ensemble Company, New York.
    BIOGRAPHY AND CRITICISM
Ride a Black Horse, *NYr* (June 5, 1971):100.

Charles Sebree

Mrs. Patterson, 1954, 1957, New York *(NYT)*. By Charles Sebree and Greer Johnson.

Charles Self

The Smokers, February 1968, Free Southern Theatre, Afro-American Festival, Dillard University, New Orleans.

Ntazake Shange

for colored girls who have considered suicide/ when the rainbow is enuf (New York: Macmillan, 1975).

Ruth A. Gaines Shelton

The Church Fight. In *C* 31–32 (May 1926):17ff. Also in Hatch and Shine, *Black Theater U.S.A.*

Archie Shepp

Junebug Graduates Tonight, 1967. In King and Milner anthology.
Revolution, 1969.

Ted Shine

Cold Day in August
Contribution, 1969–70, New York *(NYT)*. In Brasmer and Consolo anthology.
Epitaph for a Bluebird, 1958, Master's thesis play, University of Iowa.
Idabell's Fortune, July 1973, Atlanta University Summer Theatre, Atlanta.
Morning, Noon and Night, December 1962, Howard University (H).
Plantation, 1969–70 *(NYT)*
Sho Is Hot in the Cotton Patch
Shoes, 1960–70, New York *(NYT)*.

BIOGRAPHY AND CRITICISM

OLIVER, EDITH. *NYr* 45 (April 12, 1969):131. Oliver has reservations about
Contribution, although she did enjoy it.

————. See under Childress, biography and criticism.

John Silvera

Liberty Deferred, 1930s. By John Silvera and Abram Hill.

Paul Sinclair

Color-Blind. In *The Stylus* (June 1934).

Donald Smith

Harriet Tubman (New York: New Dimensions, 1970).

J. Augustus Smith

Louisiana, 1933, New York *(NYT)*.
Turpentine. See under Morell.

Jean Smith

O.C.'s Heart. Excerpts appear in *BW* 19 (April 1970):56–76.

Eulalie Spence

La Divina Pastora (a Spanish miracle play), 1931, New York *(NYT)*.
Episode. In *The Archive* (April 1928).
The Fool's Errand (New York: Samuel French, 1927).
Foreign Mail (a play in one act), October 1926, Krigwa Players; January 1927,
New York (H).
Her (a play in one act), MS only, January 7, 19, 24, 1927, Krigwa Players'
Little Negro Theatre, New York, at the 135th Street Library Theatre
(H).
The Hunch. In *The Carolina Magazine* (May 1927).
The Starter. In Locke and Gregory anthology.
Undertow. In *Carolina Magazine* 49 (April 1929).
The Whipping (based on the novel by Roy Flannagan), sold to Paramount Pic-
tures, 1934 (H).

Ron Steward

Sambo, 1969, New York *(NYT)*. A musical. By Ron Steward and Neal Tate.

Sharon Stockard

Boson's Box Truth
Proper and Fine, 1969, Blackartsouth Touring Ensemble, New Orleans.

Herbert Stokes (Damu)

The Man Who Trusted the Devil Twice. In Bullins anthology.
The Uncle Toms, 1968, Spirit House Movers, Newark; (Newark: Jihad, 1967).
Also in *TDR* 12 (Summer 1968):58–60.

George Streator

New Courage. In *C* (January 1934):9ff.
A Sign (a play in one act). In *C* (January 1934):

Neal Tate
Sambo. See under Steward.

Eloise Bibb Thompson
Africannus (a play in one act), MS only, 1922, Los Angeles (H).
Caught, MS only, 1925, Ethiopian Folk Players, Chicago.
Cooped Up, MS only, 1924, Lafayette Players, New York.

Wallace Thurman
Harlem, 1929, New York *(NYT).* By Wallace Thurman and William Jourdan
    Rapp.

Jean Toomer
Balo: A Sketch of Negro Life. In Locke and Gregory anthology.
A Drama of the Southwest
Kabnis. In Jean Toomer *Cane* (New York: Harper & Row, 1966).
Natalie Mann
The Sacred Factory
            BIOGRAPHY AND CRITICISM
FULLINWIDER, S. P. "Jean Toomer: Lost Generation or Negro Renaissance?" *P*
    27 (1966):369–403.
TURNER, DARWIN T. "The Failure of a Playwright," *CLAJ* 10 (June
    1967):308–18. Places Toomer in the context of modern American and
    European drama and attempts to clarify Toomer's particular style and
    effect by analysis of *Natalie Mann, Balo, Kabnis,* and *The Sacred Fac-
    tory.*

Joseph Dolan Tuotti
Big Time Buck White, 1968, New York *(NYT).*
            BIOGRAPHY AND CRITICISM
LEWIS, THEOPHILUS. *"Big Time Buck White,"* A 120 (January 11, 1969):50.
    Lewis calls this an interesting discussion but not a play—an article of
    commerce to "sell" black power. Review is descriptive, with mocking
    undertone.
            REVIEWS
" 'Big Time Buck White,' " *N* 208 (January 13, 1969):60–61; *NYr* 44 (December
    21, 1968):65.

Waters Turpin
Let the Day Perish, MS only. Written for, and produced by, the Ira Aldridge
    Players, Baltimore, during the 1950s (H).
St. Michael's Dawn, MS only. Written for, and produced by, the Ira Aldridge
    Players, Baltimore, during the 1950s (H).

Nathan Uwen
Martin Luther King, Jr. (New York: New Dimensions, 1970).

Melvin Van Peebles
Ain't Supposed to Die a Natural Death, 1970, New York.
            BIOGRAPHY AND CRITICISM
ALPERT, H. "Van Peebles Story," *SR* 51 (August 3, 1968):35.
COLLIER, EUGENIA. "A Drama Review: *Ain't Supposed to Die a Natural*

Death," *BW* 21 (April 1972):79–81. Asserts that black playwrights cannot afford simply to entertain and that Van Peebles's play is an unaffordable luxury. Condemns play for lack of significant theme, lack of character development, and lack of "wise" and compassionate vision of mankind. Says play is unnecessarily "filthy" and somtimes demeaning to black heritage.

Glory Van Scott
Miss Truth, 1971, Afro-American Studio for Acting and Speech, New York. A poetic suite based on the life of Sojourner Truth.

Ferdinand Voteur
A Right Angle Triangle, 1939, Rose McClendon Players (H).
The Unfinished Symphony (Boston: Bruce Humphries, n.d.).

Evan K. Walker
East of Jordan, 1969, Freedom Theatre, New York; 1969, Free Southern Theatre Touring Ensemble, New Orleans.
The Message, 1969, Performing Arts Society of Los Angeles (PASLA).

Joseph A. Walker
The Believers, 1968, New York *(NYT).*
The Harangues, 1970 *(NYT).*
Ododo, 1970, New York *(NYT).* A musical. In King and Milner anthology.
The River Niger, 1972, New York.
BIOGRAPHY AND CRITICISM
HEWES, H. " 'Harangues,' " *SR* 53 (February 14, 1970):30.
JOHNSON, HELEN ARMSTEAD. "Reviews: 'Ododo,' " *BW* 20 (April 1971):47–48. Says playwright has no clarity of purpose or vision; play contains distortion and contradiction. Questions direction of Negro Ensemble Company.
OLIVER, EDITH. *Harangues, NYr* 45 (January 24, 1970):58. Discusses content and form—two one-act plays, a prologue, and an interlude—of *The Harangues,* then suggests connection between Jones and Walker. Commends some entertaining moments but condemns diatribes and condescending paragraphs as "deplorable tradition" in black drama.
REVIEWS
Harangues, N 210 (February 2, 1970):124–25.

Douglas Turner Ward
Brotherhood, 1970, New York *(NYT).* In King and Milner anthology.
Day of Absence, 1965, 1970, New York *(NYT).* In Brasmer and Consolo and Oliver anthologies; and *Two Plays,* below.
Happy Ending, 1965, New York *(NYT).* In Couch and Oliver anthologies; and *Two Plays,* below.
The Reckoning, 1969, New York *(NYT).*
Two Plays: Happy Ending and Day of Absence (New York: Dramatists Play Service, 1966).
BIOGRAPHY AND CRITICISM
BIGSBY, C. W. E. See Ossie Davis biography and criticism.

DOWNER, ALAN S. "Total Theatre and Partial Drama: Notes on the New York Theatre, 1965–1966," *Quarterly Journal of Speech* 52 (October 1966):234–35.

KUPA, KUSHAURI. "A Review of 'The Reckoning,' " *BT* 4 (April 1970):42. Condemns play for doing and saying nothing and boring audience with overlong soliloquies, but does add that audience was entertained at many points at which Kupa was not.

LEWIS, THEOPHILUS. " 'The Reckoning,' " *A* 121 (September 17, 1969):144–45. Commends realistic characterization and poetic language but criticizes play as a whole, condeming its lack of moral satisfaction. However, labels it social drama and calls it engrossing.

OLIVER, EDITH. " 'The Reckoning,' " *NYr* 45 (September 13, 1969):105. Unclear tone of this review calls play a "black daydream," in which Ward's passion is alive but audience experience is deliberately "hateful." Sees play as faulty but vital.

REVIEWS
"Brotherhood and Day of Absence," *NYr* 46 (March 28, 1970):84.

Francis Ward and Val Gray Ward
The Life of Harriet Tubman, 1972, Kuumba Workshop, Chicago. A dramatic re-enactment of Harriet Tubman's life.
Trumbull Park (based on the novel by Frank London Brown), 1967, Chicago.

Theodore Ward
Big White Fog, 1930s, Federal Theatre, Chicago; 1940, New York *(NYT)*. Excerpt in Brown, Davis, and Lee, *Negro Caravan*, in Hatch anthology.
Candle in the Wind, 1967.
John Brown, 1950, New York *(NYT)*.
Our Lan', 1947, New York *(NYT)*. In Turner anthology.
Whole Hog or Nothing, 1966, South Side Center of the Performing Arts, Chicago.

Helen Webb See Helen Webb Harris.

Richard Wesley
Black Terror, 1971, Howard University, Washington; 1971, Public Theatre, New York.
Gettin' It Together, May 1971, Theatre Black Bed-Stuy Theatre, Brooklyn; 1972, New York.
Knock, Knock—Who Dat? October 1970, Theatre Black, University of the Street, New York.

BIOGRAPHY AND CRITICISM
COLEMAN, LARRY. "Reviews: *Black Terror*," *BT* 6 (1972) 36–37. Describes play in detail. Says it is dangerously powerful because it deals with "the reality of now." Calls for it to be reproduced soon.

REVIEWS
Black Terror: *A* 125 (December 18, 1971):534; *N* 213 (November 29, 1971):572–73; *NYr* 47 (November 29, 1971):119–20; *Nw* 78 (November 29, 1971):110; *SR* 55 (January 8, 1972):38.

Gettin' It Together: N 214 (April 17, 1972):508; *NYr* 48 (April 8, 1972):99; *T* 99 (May 1, 1972):53.

Joseph White

The Hustle, 1970, Kuumba House Theatre of Newark, Operation Wecare, Rutgers University, Newark.

The Leader, 1970, Kuumba House Theatre of Newark, Operation Wecare, Rutgers University, Newark; 1971, Kuumba Workshop, Chicago. In Jones and Neal anthology.

Old Judge Mose Is Dead, 1969, New York *(NYT).* In *TDR* 12 (Summer 1968):151–56, under title *Old Judge Moses Is Dead.*

    BIOGRAPHY AND CRITICISM

KUPA, KUSHAURI. "Black Art at the Kuumba House, Newark," *BT* 5 (1971):52–53. Review of Black Arts Festival on Rutgers, Newark, campus includes praise and descriptions for *Leader* and *Hustle.*

Ellwoodson Williams

Voice of the Gene

Frank Wilson

Brother Mose, 1934, New York (revival of *Meek Mose*).

Colored Americans, 1914–24.

Confidence, 1914–24.

Meek Mose, 1928, New York *(NYT).*

Race Pride, 1914–24.

Sugar Cane. In *O* 4 (June 1926):181–84, 201–3. Also in Locke and Gregory anthology.

Walk Together Chillun, 1936, New York *(NYT).*

Elton Wolfe

Men Wear Moustaches, August 1968, Aldridge Players/West, San Francisco.

Richard Wright

Daddy Goodness, 1968, New York *(NYT).* Adapted by Richard Wright from Louis Sapin.

Native Son: A Biography of a Young American, 1941–42, New York *(NYT);* (New York: Harper, 1941). An adaptation by Richard Wright and Paul Green of Wright's novel *Native Son.*

    BIOGRAPHY AND CRITICISM

BAILEY, PETER. " 'Daddy Goodness,' " *BT* 1 (October 1968):31. Pans play as mediocre drama, containing no new insights. Also briefly mentions discrepancy in Negro Ensemble Company between good actors and increasingly poor plays.

HIMMELSTEIN, MORGAN Y. *Drama Was a Weapon: The Left-Wing Theatre in New York, 1929–1941* (New Brunswick: Rutgers University Press, 1963), pp. 120–22.

ISAACS, HAROLD R. See under Baldwin biography and criticism.

LEWIS, THEOPHILUS. " 'Daddy Goodness,' " *A* 118 (June 22, 1968):800. Ambivalent review that stresses performance while admitting confusion as to meaning of play—does not make clear whether problem of clarity is his or playwright's.

SIEVERS, W. DAVID. *Freud on Broadway* (New York: Hermitage House, 1955), pp. 319–21. Criticism of *Native Son*.

YOUNG, STARK. *Immortal Shadows* (New York: Scribner's, 1948), pp. 223–26. Criticism of *Native Son*.
REVIEWS
Daddy Goodness: NYr 44 (June 15, 1968):65; L 8 (July 1968):21.

Clarence Young III

Perry's Mission, 1969, African Culture Center of Buffalo; 1970, Howard University, Washington, D.C.; 1971, New York.
REVIEWS
Perry's Mission, NYr 46 (January 30, 1971):56.

John Zellars

Tribute to Otis Redding, 1971, Theatre of the Living Soul, Community Center 13 Inc., Temple University, Philadelphia. Zellars is co-author.

Ron Zuber

Three X Love. In King and Milner anthology.

WORKS NOT EXPLICITLY RELATED TO BLACK DRAMA

AUSTIN, J. L. *Philosophical Papers*, J. O. URMSON and G. J. WARNOCK, eds. (Oxford: Clarendon, 1961).

BARTHES, ROLAND. *Sur Racine* (New York: Hill & Wang, 1964); *Writing Degree Zero and Elements of Seminology* (Boston: Beacon, 1970).

BRADLEY, A. C. *Shakespearean Tragedy* (London: Macmillan, 1904).

BURKE, KENNETH. *Philosophy of Literary Forms* (New York: Vintage, 1957).

CAVELL, STANLEY. *Must We Mean What We Say?* (New York: Scribner's, 1969).

CRUSE, HAROLD. *The Crisis of the Negro Intellectual* (New York: Harcourt, Brace & World, 1930).

ELLISON, RALPH. *Invisible Man* (New York: New American Library, 1947).

FAULKNER, WILLIAM. *Light in August* (New York: Modern Library, 1932).

FISH, STANLEY. *Self-consuming Artifacts* (Berkeley: University of California Press, 1972).

HUGHES, LANGSTON. *The Best of Simple* (New York: Hill & Wang, 1961).

———. *Simple Speaks His Mind* (New York: Simon & Schuster, 1950).

———. *Simple Stakes a Claim* (New York: Rinehart, 1957).

———. *Simple Takes a Wife* (New York: Simon & Schuster, 1953).

———. *Simple's Uncle Sam* (New York: Hill & Wang, 1965).

———. *Simply Heavenly* (New York: Dramatists Play Service, 1959).

HURSTON, ZORA NEALE. *Mules and Men* (Philadelphia: Lippincott, 1935).

JACOBSON, ROMAN, and CLAUDE LEVI-STRAUSS. " 'Les Chats' de Charles Baudelaire," *L'Homme*, 2 (January–April 1962):5–21.

LAHR, JOHN. *The Great American Life Show* (New York: Bantam, 1974).

MEIER, AUGUST, and ELLIOTT M. RUDWICK. *From Plantation to Ghetto: An Interpretive History of American Negroes* (New York: Hill & Wang, 1966).

MILLER, ARTHUR. "Tragedy and the Common Man," in *Aspects of Drama*, Sylvan Barnet, Morton Berman, and William Burto, eds. (Boston: Little, Brown, 1962).

RUECKERT, WILLIAM H. "Kenneth Burke and Structuralism," *Shenandoah* 21 (Autumn, 1969):19–28.

SONTAG, SUSAN. *Against Interpretation* (New York: Dell, 1969).

STYAN, J. L. *The Elements of Drama* (Cambridge, U.K.: Cambridge University Press, 1960, reprinted 1969).

INDEX

Abramson, Doris, 8, 9, 51, 78, 114, 116, 228; quoted, 80

Acknowledgment, 15, 16, 31, 38, 40, 47, 68, 70, 71, 74, 100, 114, 151, 167, 172, 174, 214–17, 222, 224

Affective and intentional fallacies, 221–22

African Company, 6, 207

African identity, 56, 58, 67, 72, 83, 86, 87, 89, 92, 98, 117, 128–31, 136, 147, 188

Albee, Edward, 1, 4, 148, 152

All God's Chillun Got Wings (O'Neill), 20

Ambivalent intentions, 3, 5, 6, 10, 13, 14, 23, 47, 57, 72, 73, 150, 207, 209

Amen Corner, The, 13

American drama, 1–5, 11, 13, 46, 146, 178, 209, 216

American dream, 4, 110, 111, 115–17, 125, 132, 133, 151, 165, 167, 170, 211

American Dream, The (Albee), 152

American Negro Company, 8

Amy Spingarn prize, 19, 20

Anderson, Garland, 7, 20

Anti-Semitism, 98, 101

"Antony in Behalf of the Play" (Burke), 220, 221

Appearances (Anderson), 20

Audience, 2–16, 24, 25, 32, 79; relationship of script to, 13, 14, 23, 28–34, 36–47, 54, 55, 57, 59–74, 80, 83–85, 87–112, 120–44, 153–75, 182–205, 211, 220–24, 229

Balance of attention, 45, 46, 55, 65

Baldwin, James, 11, 13, 228

Baptism, The (Baraka), 148

Baraka, Imamu Amiri, 6, 9, 11, 13, 14, 21, 147–75, 180, 228, 229; quoted, 182 (*see also* Jones, LeRoi)

Barthes, Roland, 221

Beardsley, M. C., 221, 222

Beckett, Samuel, 1

Bellamy, Edward, 87

Big White Fog (Ward), 6, 78–111, 117, 166, 180, 184, 194

Black aesthetic, 13, 14, 148, 182, 205, 208–10, 217, 223, 229

Black Arts Theater, 13, 14, 32, 77, 79, 147, 148

Black community theaters, 7, 8, 20, 25, 47, 148, 178, 207–9, 228

Black drama, 1–16, 19–22, 48, 50, 77, 108, 113, 144, 148, 149, 200, 207–12, 216, 217, 220, 223, 228, 229; defined, x

Black House, 178

"Black revolutionary commercial," 179

Black Revolutionary Theater, 13, 14, 21, 79, 148; drama of, 14, 149, 150

Black separatism, 14, 207

Black Theater 175, 177

Blues, 21, 132, 170, 171, 185, 195

Blues for Mr. Charlie (Baldwin), 11, 228

Blues People (Baraka), 21

Brecht, Bertolt, 1, 179

Broadway, 3, 5, 8, 12, 19, 20, 32, 33, 51, 79, 108, 114, 211

Broken Banjo, The (Richardson), 6, 20–33, 36, 42, 44–47, 109, 181, 194, 204, 205, 210, 216

Brown, Sterling, 228

Brown, Theodore, 79

Brustein, Robert, 228

Bullins, Ed, 6, 13, 14, 32, 177–205, 210, 212, 229

Burke, Kenneth, 14, 222–25; quoted, 219–21

Cavell, Stanley, 15, 222, 223; quoted, 215, 216

Childress, Alice, 11, 13

Chip Woman's Fortune, The (Richardson), 6, 19, 22, 32–47

Chorus, 164

Christianity, 42, 60, 86, 109, 126–28, 162, 165, 168, 190, 191

Clara's Ole Man (Bullins), 179
Class, 4, 9, 16, 61, 74, 81, 117, 144, 145n, 149, 170, 209, 216, 217 (*see also* Middle class; Working class); consciousness, 4, 117, 209, 215
Cleaver, Eldridge, 178
Clurman, Harold, 228
C'mon Back to Heavenly House (Bullins), 179
Cobb, Jonathan, 170
Comedy, 45, 58, 66, 118 (*see also* Humor)
Commercialism, 3, 5, 9, 32, 33, 79, 207
Communism, 101, 103, 107, 110, 161, 164
Community, 4, 8, 12, 16, 32, 47, 54, 69, 77, 79, 99, 110, 134, 148, 164, 166, 175, 197, 207–10, 216, 217
Connelly, Marc, 20
"Contact of black and white," plays of, 6, 19, 50, 51, 57, 73, 74, 77, 114, 117, 209
Corbin, John, 34; quoted, 33
Corner, The (Bullins), 179
Costumes, 59, 61, 66, 98, 129, 130, 154, 160, 212
Crime, 31, 42, 69
Crisis, The (DuBois), 5, 7, 19
Cruse, Harold, 9, 114, 142; quoted, 141

Dance, 67, 72, 130, 168, 196, 211–13, 216
Davis, Ossie, 11, 144
Deacon's Awakening, The (Richardson), 20
Death of a Salesman (Miller), 4, 68
Dessalines, Jean Jacques, 52–74, 76n
Dialectical strategy, 84–110
Didacticism, 39, 40, 41, 100, 123, 138, 149
"Discrepant awareness," 45, 55
Dodson, Owen, 79
Don't You Want to Be Free? (Hughes), 51
Dramatic irony, 65, 92, 134
Drums of Haiti (Hughes) (*see Emperor of Haiti*)
Drunkenness, 31, 32, 47, 85, 125, 130–33, 181, 186, 188, 190, 195, 199, 201
DuBois, W. E. B., 5, 6, 16, 19–22, 46, 50, 51, 209, 210; quoted, 47
Duplex, The (Bullins), 179
Dutchman (Baraka), 6, 9, 13, 148, 150–75, 178, 180, 209, 228

Edmunds, Randolph, 7
Education, 53, 58–61, 63, 72, 80, 84, 85, 90, 93, 96, 117, 133, 151, 188, 194, 208, 214
Eighth Ditch, The (Baraka), 148
Elder, Lonne, 13, 144
Elements of Drama (Styan), 14, 222, 224
Ellison, Ralph, 89, 153
Empathy, 100, 121, 128, 135, 180, 195
Emperor Jones, The (O'Neill), 20
Emperor of Haiti (Hughes), 6, 50–74, 79, 80, 87, 110, 180, 184

Ethiopian Players, 7, 20
Exoticism, 33, 39, 58–60, 163
Expressionism, 21, 191, 194, 196

Family, 22, 24, 31, 33–36, 41, 80–111, 117–44, 180, 184, 198, 203
Faulkner, William, quoted, 198
Federal Theater Project, 7, 8, 77, 78; and "Negro units," 7, 77, 78
Fish, Stanley, 210; quoted, 222–24
Folk drama, 21, 25, 31, 47, 181, 204, 212, 228
for colored girls who have considered suicide/when the rainbow is enuf (Shange), 211–17
Franklin, John Hope, 50
Front Porch (Hughes), 51
Fuller, Hoyt, 229

Garvey movement, 83, 86–94, 97–99, 104, 112n
Gayle, Addison, 229; quoted, 210
Gilpin Players, 7, 51
Glass Menagerie, The (Williams), 183
Goin' a Buffalo (Bullins), 179
Gold Piece, The (Hughes), 51
Gordone, Charles, 11, 13
Great Goodness of Life (A Coon Show) (Baraka), 149, 150, 168
Greek tragedy, 28, 49n
Green, Paul, 20
Green Pastures, The (Connelly), 20
Gregory, Montgomery, 228
Grotowski, Jerzy, 212
Guilt, 29, 31, 100, 149, 150, 187

Haiti, 51–53, 73, 75n 76, 213
Hansberry, Lorraine, 6, 11, 113–44, 151, 180, 216, 228
Harlem (Thurman), 20
Harlem Renaissance, 19, 50, 78, 227
Harlem Suitcase Theatre, 51
Henry IV (Pirandello), 23
Hicklin, Fannie, 10, 51; quoted, 44
Hidden Injuries of Class (Sennett and Cobb), 170
Historical contexts, 2–16, 19–22, 31, 52, 75–80, 84, 85, 88, 90, 98, 112n, 113–15, 120, 124, 170, 175
History plays, 51, 73, 78–80, 111
Hooks, Robert, 144
Howard Players, 19, 20
Hughes, Langston, 6, 7, 50–74, 78, 79, 110, 113; poem by, quoted in full, 115; quoted, 109
Humor, 36, 37, 45, 58, 66, 85, 98, 118, 120, 125, 129, 133, 135, 141, 192, 202, 204, 213, 214

Ibsen, Henrik, 28, 83
Identification, 15, 31, 45, 46, 49n, 60, 156,
    223, 224
In Abraham's Bosom (Green), 20
In New England Winter (Bullins), 179
In the Wine Time (Bullins), 6, 32, 179–205,
    210, 212
"Inner Life," plays of, 6, 19, 32, 46, 47, 50,
    51, 73, 74, 78, 109, 179, 209, 210, 212
Instruction, 3; use of, in drama, 12, 21, 22,
    31, 40, 41, 47, 48, 80, 100, 149, 214
Integration, 9–12, 63, 113, 114, 117
Integrationist drama, 9–14, 113–14, 117,
    118, 123, 142
Intentional and affective fallacies, 221–22
Invisible Man (Ellison), 89, 153
Irony dramatic, 65, 92, 134

Jakobson, Roman, 221
Johnson, Georgia Douglas, 7, 21
Johnson, Hall, 8
Johnson, Helen Armstead, 229
Jones, LeRoi, 158 (*see also* Baraka, Imamu
    Amiri)
Joy to My Soul (Hughes), 51

Karenga, Ron, 229
King, Woodie, 144, 229
King Lear (Shakespeare), 58, 64, 173
Krigwa Little Negro Theater, 7, 20, 22
Ku Klux Klan, 21

Lafayette Theatre, 7, 20
Lahr, John, quoted, 182, 191
Language, 12, 13, 55, 56, 72–74, 79, 86–88,
    103, 109, 110, 117, 119, 120, 122, 131,
    134, 155, 156, 158–60, 163, 164, 166, 168,
    169, 171, 174, 181, 184, 185, 187, 188,
    191, 192, 195, 199–202, 212–16; and black
    dialect, 12, 56, 60, 73, 119, 120, 197, 200,
    211
Les Blancs (Hansberry and Nemeroff), 113
Levi-Strauss, Claude, 221
Light in August (Faulkner), 198
Lincoln Theater, 7
Lindsay, Powell, 79
Little Ham (Hughes), 51
"Little theater movement," 7
Locke, Alain, 21; quoted, 216, 227
Looking Backward (Bellamy), 87
L'Ouverture, Toussaint, 75n, 213, 214
Lukács, Georg, 146n

Macbeth, Robert, 177, 178, 200
Macbeth (Shakespeare), 8
Marvin X, 13, 178, 200
Matheus, John, 7, 21
Melodrama, 40, 44, 56, 215
Men, roles of, 123, 129, 138, 139, 166, 180,

184, 189, 193, 194, 196, 209, 215
Middle class, 1, 4, 6, 8, 9, 11–13, 25, 31, 32,
    45, 46, 61, 110, 117, 126, 141–43, 149,
    150, 151, 159, 160, 161, 164, 168–71, 174,
    178, 179, 181, 195, 211, 215
Miller, Arthur, 1, 4, 68, 101, 118; quoted,
    53, 54
Milner, Ron, 13, 144
Mitchell, Loften, 8, 229
Modern drama, 28, 53
Mollette, Carlton, 229
Mortgaged (Richardson), 19
Moss, Paula, 211
Mulatto (Hughes), 51
Mulattoes, 53–59, 63, 66, 69, 72, 73, 80, 83,
    99
Music, 2, 23, 24, 26, 37, 56, 59, 66, 67, 126,
    153, 171, 185, 195, 212–13, 216
Myth, 1, 150, 152–54, 157, 158, 163, 164,
    167, 178

Native Son (Wright), 116
Naturalism, 20, 34, 48n, 178, 191, 197
Neal, Larry, 153, 229
Negro Art Theatre, 50
Negro Ensemble Company, 227
Negro History in Thirteen Plays (Richard-
    son, ed.), 19
Negro on the Stage, The (Brown), 228
Negro Playwrights Company, 8, 78
Negro Renaissance, 19, 227
Nemeroff, Robert, 113, 115
New Lafayette Theatre, 177, 178, 200
No Place to Be Somebody (Gordone), 11, 13
Norford, George, 78

Odets, Clifford, 77
Oedipus Rex (Sophocles), 68, 101
O'Neill, Eugene, 1, 20, 48n, 118
Opportunity, 7, 19
Our Lan' (Ward), 10, 79, 80, 111
Outlaws, 24, 31, 40–42, 179

Peterson, Louis, 11, 114
"Philosophical criticism," 224
Pinter, Harold, 1
Pirandello, Luigi, 23
"Poor theater," 212
Poverty, 23, 24, 34, 37, 39, 61, 78, 80, 81,
    93, 94, 95, 106, 119, 127
Propaganda, 47, 210, 223, 224
Protest plays, 11, 109, 171
Psychic traps, 27, 28, 30, 54, 123, 184, 214
Purlie Victorious (Davis), 11, 144

Racism, 2, 6, 10, 11, 13, 24, 37, 72, 74, 79,
    80, 82, 84, 85, 89, 100, 106, 108, 109,
    117, 134, 151, 168, 217, 227; and race
    riots, 21, 85

Raisin in the Sun, A (Hansberry), 6, 11, 113–44, 151, 166, 180, 194, 216, 228
Realism, 1, 4, 5, 9, 21, 31, 80, 81, 98, 110, 118, 119, 178, 212
Recognition scenes, 70, 74, 100, 101, 151, 169, 214, 215
Richardson, Willis, 6, 7, 19–48, 51, 72, 73, 109, 181, 194, 204, 205, 210, 216
Rider of Dreams, The (Torrence), 20
Riley, Clayton, 157, 171, 229; quoted, 154, 156, 170, 173
Ritual, 66, 67, 83, 87, 178, 196
Run Little Children (Johnson), 8

Salomé (Wilde), 19
Sanchez, Sonia, 178
Schechner, Richard, 228
Scheff, Thomas, 46, 49n; quoted, 45
Schomberg Center, 80
Segregation, 10, 11, 22, 88, 114, 135
Self-consciousness, 45, 200, 208
Semple, Jesse B., 58
Sennett, Richard, 170
Sentimentality, 40, 44, 56, 66, 69, 71, 85, 102, 125, 141, 189, 190
Separatism, black, 14, 207
Settings, 1, 4, 13, 23, 34, 55, 61, 68, 81, 93, 101, 119, 153, 154, 164, 179, 180, 182, 189, 212
Sex roles, 87, 124, 126, 129, 136, 158, 200, 214
Sexism, 123, 124, 200, 217
Sexuality, 34, 36, 40, 41, 74, 121–23, 131, 151, 154–57, 160, 162–65, 168, 181, 187, 188, 192, 195–97, 200, 201, 213, 214
Shakespeare, William, 8, 50, 58, 64, 74, 76n, 172, 173, 220, 221
Shange, Ntozake, 211–17
Shine, Ted, 2
Sign in Sidney Brustein's Window, The (Hansberry), 113
Skyloft Players, 50
Slavery, 54–61, 66, 71, 138, 160, 168
Smith, Bessie, 170, 171
Socialism, 87, 88, 97, 112n
Sontag, Susan, quoted, 108
Sophocles, 23, 68, 101
Spirit House, 147, 148
Stereotypes, 12, 25, 31, 34, 36, 83, 87, 98, 101, 109, 124, 126, 139, 156, 157, 186, 199, 203, 204
Strategy, 5, 11, 12, 15, 22, 23, 25, 28, 29,

31, 34, 38, 40, 43–45, 53–55, 57, 59, 62–64, 71–74, 84–110, 114, 117, 118, 120, 126, 128, 130, 131, 133, 136–39, 141, 142, 150, 152, 156, 157, 169, 170, 173, 174, 178, 181, 182, 184, 187, 191, 193, 200, 203, 204, 209, 217, 219–24; defined, 14
Structuralism, 221
Styan, J. L., quoted, 14, 222–24
Suitcase Theatre, 50

Take a Giant Step (Peterson), 11, 114
Tambourines to Glory (Hughes), 51
Theater of black experience, 21, 205
Theme Is Blackness, The (Bullins), 177–79
Thurman, Wallace, 7, 20
To Be Young, Gifted and Black (Hansberry and Nemeroff), 113, 115
Toilet, The (Baraka), 11, 178
Toomer, Jean, 7, 21
Torrence, Ridgely, 20
Tragedy, 23, 45, 53, 54, 92, 139, 140, 204, 215
Trouble in Mind (Childress), 11, 13
Troubled Island (Hughes) (*see Emperor of Haiti*)
Turner, Darwin T., 34, 51, 229; quoted, 33

"Uncle Tom," 155, 168
Uncle Tom's Cabin (Stowe), 7

Violence, 27, 29, 31, 55, 69, 79, 104, 107, 108, 151, 156, 169, 172, 187, 192, 193, 200–203, 215
Virtue, 38–40, 42–44, 93, 109, 172, 181, 186, 188, 204, 214
Voodoo, 59, 60, 67

Ward, Douglas Turner, 144; quoted, 227
Ward, Theodore, 6, 8, 10, 77–112, 117, 180, 194
Weales, Gerald, 228
Who's Afraid of Virginia Woolf? (Albee), 4
Wilde, Oscar, 19
Williams, Raymond, quoted, 208
Williams, Tennessee, 2, 118, 183, 198
Wimsatt, W. K., 221, 222
Women, roles of, 36, 88, 96, 121–24, 129, 132, 136, 138, 158, 197, 211, 214
Work, 37, 38, 44, 53, 54, 63, 93, 96, 116, 117, 136, 142, 194, 195, 209
Working class, 31, 32, 37, 110, 116, 117, 170
Wright, Richard, 116, 153